The Civilization of the American Indian Series

AMERICAN INDIAN HOLOCAUST AND SURVIVAL

American Indian Holocaust and Survival

A Population History Since 1492

by Russell Thornton

University of Oklahoma Press : Norman and London

BY RUSSELL THORNTON

Sociology of American Indians: A Critical Bibliography (With Mary K. Grasmick)
(Bloomington, Ind., 1980)
The Urbanization of American Indians: A Critical Bibliography (with Gary D.
Sandefur and Harold G. Grasmick) (Bloomington, Ind., 1982)
*We Shall Live Again: The 1870 and 1890 Ghost Dance Movements as Demographic
Revitalization* (New York, 1986)
American Indian Holocaust and Survival: A Population History Since 1492 (Norman,
1987)

Library of Congress Cataloging-in-Publication Data

Thornton, Russell, 1942–
American Indian holocaust and survival.

(The Civilization of the American Indian series;
v. 186)
Bibliography: p.
Includes index.
1. Indians—Population. 2. America—Population.
I. Title. II. Series.
E59.P75T48   1987   304.6′08997073   87-40216
ISBN 0-8061-2074-6 (alk. paper)

American Indian Holocaust and Survival: A Population History Since 1492 is Volume
186 in The Civilization of the American Indian Series.

The paper in this book meets the guidelines for permanence and durability of the
Committee on Production Guidelines for Book Longevity of the Council on Library
Resources, Inc.

To my parents, Faye Garrett Thornton and Walter Gilbert "Gip" Thornton

For all those Indian lives unlived

Where today are the Pequot? Where are the Narragansett, the Mohican, the Pokanoket, and many other once powerful tribes of our people? They have vanished before the avarice and the oppression of the White Man, as snow before a summer sun. —TECUMSEH (SHAWNEE)

CONTENTS

ILLUSTRATIONS

FIGURES

MAPS

PREFACE

EACH OF THE WORLD'S PEOPLES has had many histories over decades, centuries, and millenniums. None is so fundamental as their history as a physical population. Yet as basic as this history is, it is often ignored, frequently unrecognized, and more frequently unwritten. This is particularly true of the North American Indians. We know much about North American Indian social and cultural history subsequent to contacts with Europeans, but little has been written about their demographic history. This book is an attempt to redress that imbalance. It is a demographic history of the populations of American Indians north of present-day Mexico, particularly those in the conterminous United States of America.

Some 500 years ago Christopher Columbus arrived in the Western Hemisphere. Columbus did not, however, *discover* the "New World." It was already old when he came to it. Furthermore, Columbus was not even the first to arrive from Europe. The Vikings had preceded him by 500 years. Others traveling across the oceans may have preceded him both before and after the Vikings. The first human beings to arrive—the ancestors of the American Indians, Eskimos, and Aleuts living on the continent when Columbus arrived—had preceded him by thousands and thousands of years.

The demographic effects of Columbus's "discovery" were nevertheless important in many ways. There was a marked shift in the world's populations as Europeans and others migrated to the Western Hemisphere, where they experienced remarkable population growth. Great countries developed in a very short span of human history. Euro-American people have much cause to celebrate Columbus's arrival in his New World.

Another demographic history exists, however. It is the history of the people Columbus met here: the descendants of the first humans to arrive on the land, the first to populate it, the first to prosper on it. For them 1492 also marked a turning point in population history. The date, however, is not one to be celebrated. Far from it! In the centuries after Columbus these "Indians" suffered a demographic collapse. Numbers declined sharply; entire tribes, often quickly, were "wiped from the face of the earth."

This is certainly true of the American Indians on the land that was to become the United States of America. For them the arrival of the Europeans marked the beginning of a long holocaust, although it came not in ovens, as it did for the Jews. The fires that consumed North American Indians were the fevers brought on by newly encountered diseases, the flashes of settlers' and soldiers' guns, the ravages of "firewater," the flames of villages and fields burned by the scorched-earth policy of vengeful Euro-Americans. The effects of this holocaust of North American Indians, like that of the Jews, was millions of deaths. In fact, the holocaust of the North American tribes was, in a way, even more destructive than that of the Jews, since many American Indian peoples became extinct.

It is truly remarkable that during these 500 years somehow—reasons range from chance to adaptation to determination—most North American Indian tribes survived the horrendous history. Even more remarkable, numerous tribes have shown recent population gains. Their stories are tributes to human survival instincts, perseverance, and hope.

In this book I trace the history of North American Indians as a physical population, considering both their numerical decline after about 1492 and their recent resurgence. I occasionally compare the American Indian population history with that of the non-Indians who later created the United States of America. The 500-year population curves of the two groups are very different, as shown in figures P-1 and P-2.

In Chapter 1, I describe the arrivals of the people who would become American Indians and other Native Americans. I also briefly discuss the far more recent arrivals of the Europeans in the Western Hemisphere. In Chapter 2, I turn attention to American Indians as a population on the eve of their destruction. How the European arrival affected North American Indian populations during the next four centuries is the subject of Chapters 3 through 6. The effect was disastrous: a demographic collapse. In Chapter 3, I examine the long-term pattern and the general causes of this collapse: disease, including alcoholism; warfare and genocide; geographical removal and relocation; and destruction of ways of life.

I generally organize discussion in Chapters 4 and 5 around these four major causes of the population decline. Chapter 4 considers depopulation events during the 300 years of the sixteenth, seventeenth, and eighteenth centuries. Particular attention is devoted to the effects of the early European colonization on the East Coast of North America, which seriously impacted the native populations there. In Chapter 5, I detail how the four general causes of depopulation affected American Indian populations in the nineteenth century and how the causes interacted with one another.

This is a disproportionate amount of attention given to the nineteenth century, but that was when the American Indian population reached nadir. More significantly, we simply know more about American Indian populations since 1800 than before 1800, particularly their demography. It does not mean that fewer important events, demographic and otherwise, occurred in the first three centuries after the European arrival. Many did, and perhaps they were the most important ones. The difficulty is that today we are either unaware or little aware of them.

In Chapter 6, I discuss American Indian reactions to population collapse, particularly the Ghost Dance religions of 1870 and 1890. This topic may seem inappropriate in a work on population history, but the Ghost Dances were brought about more or less directly by the depopulation of the Indians. More important, they were deliberate efforts to confront, even reverse, the demographic collapse that the Indians had experienced by the late nineteenth century.

After about 400 years, North American Indians reversed the depopulation

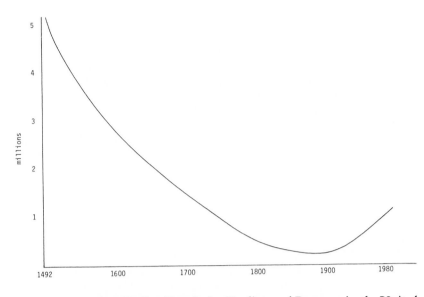

Fig. P-1. American Indian Population Decline and Recovery in the United States Area, 1492–1980

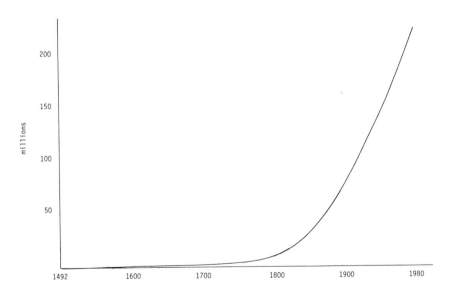

Fig. P-2. Non-Indian Population Growth in the United States Area, 1492–1980

trend. In Chapters 7 and 8, I describe the contemporary American Indian population in the United States, discussing demographic and nondemographic factors involved in the remarkable recovery.

Chapter 9 describes the recent movement of American Indians into urban areas of the United States. Included is a discussion of the implications for the demographic future of American Indians. They are dangerous, I conclude, perhaps even as dangerous as those almost 500 years past when three tiny European vessels reached a small island in the Caribbean.

One appendix is provided. It is an outline of the population histories of Native Americans north of the conterminous United States area in Alaska, Canada, and Greenland. Native populations of these areas are neglected in the book, because of the distinctiveness of these populations as well as a consideration of book length. And many of the data I draw upon simply do not include Alaska, Canada, or Greenland.

Much, though by no means all, of my information is drawn from the work of colleagues in history, cultural and physical anthropology, archaeology, sociology, and demography. I am grateful for their research, demographic and otherwise, on the original inhabitants of this continent. Without their important scholarly contributions, this book could not have been written.

Some of the information here may be considered controversial. The population history of the Indians is lost to us. Nor do we know all there is to know about fundamental demographic processes among the tribes or of any one group. Scholars have drawn diverse conclusions about what happened to American Indians and why. Nevertheless, the population history of American Indians can be approximated on the basis of what we do know. That is what I do in this book.

Scholars are a cautious group, typically reluctant to go beyond what can be known for certain. The availability of complete, orderly, and certain information often determines which topics they choose to study and the ways they approach selected topics. As a result, many important issues are unstudied or studied from limited perspectives. For example, this is true of a topic to which I devote much attention: the history of epidemic disease. William H. McNeill both explains and elaborates this basic point: "We all want human experience to make sense, and historians cater to this universal demand by emphasizing elements in the past that are calculable, definable, and, often, controllable as well. Epidemic disease . . . ran counter to the effort to make the past intelligible. Historians consequently played such episodes down" (McNeill, 1976:4).

In writing this book about American Indian population history, I use what information I can, in what way I can. Moreover, I attempt to write from the perspective of the American Indians themselves. The result is sometimes neither definable, complete, nor orderly; but my justification is simple: The story is important; it should be told as best it can.

Minneapolis, Minnesota   RUSSELL THORNTON

ACKNOWLEDGMENTS

OVER THE PAST SEVERAL YEARS I have taught a college course that was variously titled but always on the history of the American Indian population. Much of this book is taken from the course. I thank my students at the University of Minnesota and the University of California, Los Angeles, for questions, comments, insights. I hope they learned from me; I learned from them.

I have published and presented orally numerous scholarly articles, papers, and books on American Indian demography during the same time period. Much of this book is taken from those works. I thank colleagues for their responses to my efforts over the years.

My research and writing from 1979 to 1984 were under the auspices of a Research Scientist Career Development Award from the National Institute of Mental Health (no. 5-K01-00256) through the University of Minnesota Family Study Center. During the final writing of this book in 1985 and 1986, I was on sabbatical and had received a Bush Supplemental Sabbatical Fellowship from the University of Minnesota, a Smithsonian Institution Fellowship, and a Distinguished Lectureship from the University of California, Berkeley. I was Visiting Research Associate in the D'Arcy McNickle Center for the History of the American Indian of the Newberry Library, Chicago, in 1981; Visiting Professor in the Population Research Laboratory of the University of Southern California in 1980 and 1982; Visiting Professor in the Department of Sociology, University of California, Los Angeles in 1984; a Fellow of the National Museum of Natural History of the Smithsonian Institution, Washington, D.C., in 1985 and 1986; and a Chancellor's Distinguished Visiting Lecturer in the Graduate Group in Demography, University of California, Berkeley, in 1986. My debt for this support is gratefully acknowledged. I particularly want to thank Fred Lukermann, Robert Leik, the late Reuben Hill, and Mary Ann Beneke at the University of Minnesota; Fred Hoxie and David Miller at the Newberry Library; Kingsley Davis, Maurice Van Arsdale, and David Heer at the University of Southern California; Adrienne Kaeppler, Bill Merrill, and Douglas Ubelaker at the Smithsonian Institution; and Gene Hammel, Ron Lee, Ken Wachter, and Sheila Johansson at the University of California, Berkeley. Special thanks are extended to Fred Lukermann, who has been supportive of me and my scholarly projects over the years; to Kingsley Davis, who encouraged me a few years ago to undertake this project when I was contemplating it; and to Douglas Ubelaker, who gave freely of his expertise on American Indian populations.

Matthew Snipp, at the University of Maryland; Gary Sandefur, at the University of Wisconsin; Douglas Ubelaker, at the Smithsonian Institution; John Moore, at the University of Oklahoma; and anonymous reviewers read drafts of the entire manuscript. William Swagerty, at the University of Idaho, read a draft of selected chapters; and Tim Dunnigan, at the University of Minnesota, Karl Taeuber, at the University of Wisconsin, and Richard Potts, at the Smithsonian Institution, read parts of a draft of Chapter 1. Sheila Johansson, at the University of California, Berkeley, read a draft of Chapter 2. All provided useful comments, insights, and suggestions. I thank them.

Velma Salabiye, librarian of the American Indian Studies Center Library, University of California, Los Angeles, has freely offered invaluable expertise and the library's resources during my many visits over the past several years; as did Mary Kay Davies, librarian of the Anthropology Department Library in the National Museum of Natural History, during my stay there. I thank both.

Bill Merrill, in the Department of Anthropology of the National Museum of Natural History, provided invaluable help in securing many of the illustrations. I thank him. Rebecca Thornton helped in the final selection of illustrations to be included. Thank you, Rebecca.

Russell Garrett Thornton provided excellent bibliographic assistance and spent time and energy searching the libraries of the University of Minnesota, often for obscure publications. Thank you, Russell.

Gloria DeWolfe of the Sociology Department in the University of Minnesota spent hours and hours and hours inputting and revising the manuscript on the word processor, attempting to read horrendous handwriting, deciphering confusing directions, occasionally correcting improper grammar, and always offering encouragement. My debt to her extends well beyond our formal relationship. Thank you, Gloria.

My wife, Joan, was constantly supportive while I wrote the manuscript and helped me overcome periods of what I was convinced was terminal writer's block. Had it not been for her I doubt if the book would have been written. Thank you, Joan.

Finally, my editors at the University of Oklahoma Press, John N. Drayton and Sarah I. Morrison, contributed in many valuable ways to the manuscript that became this book. Thank you, John and Sarah.

R.T.

AMERICAN INDIAN HOLOCAUST AND SURVIVAL

1. ARRIVALS IN THE WESTERN HEMISPHERE

Loneliness is an aspect of the land. All things in the plain are isolate; there is no confusion of objects in the eye, but *one* hill or *one* tree or *one* man. To look upon that landscape in the early morning, with the sun at your back, is to lose the sense of proportion. Your imagination comes to life, and this, you think, is where Creation was begun.
—N. SCOTT MOMADAY (KIOWA), *The Way to Rainy Mountain*

The White man does not understand the Indian for the reason that he does not understand America. He is too far removed from its formative process.
—LUTHER STANDING BEAR (SIOUX)

To the edge of the earth, to the edge of the earth, to the edge of the earth.
Snap all the people! Snap all the people!
To the edge of the earth, to the edge of the earth.
—WINTU SHAMAN'S SONG

THE DIFFERENT PEOPLES OF THE WORLD have different explanations of how they came into being. Origin stories may tell of beginnings as physical human beings or as a social group, tribe, or society. Some origin stories depict both, with one description intertwined with another. The stories serve to answer the very fundamental question, Who are we? They are often part of the religious expression of a society.

Origin explanations are critically important to a people and tend to be revered and accepted at face value. Individuals typically do not like to discuss whether the stories are literally true; to do so is often considered heresy. There is some cognitive incongruity, however, for more than one explanation may be present in a society. Western societies today have systems of belief blending traditional, religious, and scientific knowledge, and each system may have its own unique explanation of a people's origin. They all relate to the arrival of American Indians in the Western Hemisphere.

According to the *biblical explanation*, American Indians and all other peoples descend from a divinely created original couple: "So God created man in his own image, in the image of God he created him; male and female he created them" (*The Holy Bible: Revised Standard Version*, 1953 : 1). Other organized religions not using the Bible explain human creation or origin in somewhat different ways. Many American Indians today accept the biblical explanation, though some adhere to the views of other, non-Indian religions.

Most *creation traditions* are unique to tribes. They generally emphasize the natural and supernatural worlds—nature and spirit. They often encompass both human and social origins. The traditions have developed and endured over a long span of history. Many, however, have been modified and changed by American Indians during the past several hundred years in response to Christianity so that they are now somewhat similar to biblical stories of origin and Old Testament history. Various examples illustrate these points.

The Zuni Indians in New Mexico say that they were created within the four wombs of the earth by the Great Spirit, then later emerged to the surface (Cushing, 1883:13–14; Bunzel, 1932:545–609). The Pima of the Southwest believe the earth was created by Earth Doctor from dust on his chest: "Next he formed images of clay, which he commanded to become animate human beings, and they obeyed him" (Russell, 1906:208). The Pomo of California say they were created by a coyote (Kroeber, 1925:270).

The Creek Indians say they were created in the West and journeyed later to the East:

> At a certain time the Earth opened in the West, where its mouth is. The Earth opened and the Cussitaws came out of its mouth, and settled near by. But the Earth became angry and ate up their children; therefore, they moved further West. A part of them, however, turned back, and came again to the same place where they had been, and settled there. The greater number remained behind, because they thought it best to do so. Their children, nevertheless, were eaten by the Earth, so that, full of dissatisfaction, they journeyed toward the sunrise. (Quoted in Swanton, 1928:34)

The noted Kiowa author N. Scott Momaday told the story of his people's physical origin and why the Kiowa are but a small tribe:

> You know, everything had to begin, and this is how it was: the Kiowas came one by one into the world through a hollow log. They were many more than now, but not all of them got out. There was a woman whose body was swollen up with child, and she got stuck in the log. After that, no one could get through, and that is why the Kiowas are a small tribe in number. They looked all around and saw the world. It made them glad to see so many things. They called themselves *Kwuda*, "coming out." (Momaday, 1969:16)

The Kiowa story continues with a description of the tribal origin. After their physical creation the Kiowas made a long journey from the headwaters of the Yellowstone River east to near the Black Hills of present-day South Dakota and south to the Wichita Mountains of present-day Oklahoma. The migration took place because the Kiowa did not prosper on the lands of the North after they were created there. Says Momaday (1969:3): "The young Plains culture of the Kiowas withered and died like grass that is burned in the prairie wind. . . . When the wild herds were destroyed, so too was the will of the Kiowa people; there was nothing to sustain them in spirit." But then the Kiowa had a vision: they should go "forth into the heart of the continent" (Momaday, 1969:4). So "the journey began one day long ago on the edge of the northern Plains. It was carried on over a course of many generations and many hundreds of miles. In the end there were many things to remember, to dwell upon and talk about" (Momaday, 1969:3). It was during this long journey that "they acquired horses, the religion of the Plains, a love and possession of the open land. Their nomadic soul was set free. . . . In the course of that long migration they had come of age as a people. They had conceived a good idea of themselves; they had dared to imagine and determine who they were" (Momaday, 1969:4).

Biblical and tribal creation stories constitute a nonscientific paradigm of the creation of the world and human beings and their existence. They do not necessarily compete with science, rather they are apart from it. To compare them with science, and science with them, is simply to confuse both and give neither its due.

The contemporary *scientific evolutionary explanation* of American Indian origins is that all humans evolved over millions and millions of years from antecedent forms of animal life. The evolution from prehuman origins took place on the African continent, and humanlike populations gradually spread from there over the earth's surface. The first populations of the modern type of *Homo sapiens* evolved well over 30,000 years ago. We do not know when this occurred, nor do we know where. Possibly it was in Asia (Stewart, 1973:2; also Trinkaus, 1984; Wolpoff, Zhi, and Thorne, 1984); possibly in Africa (Rightmire, 1984; Brauer, 1984); but probably it was not in Europe. Scholars have concluded that it surely was not in the Western Hemisphere: The preceding "Neanderthal" type of human "has never been found on the American continent, which means that *Homo* in America is clearly not as old as on some of the other continents" (Ericson, Taylor, and Berger, 1982:12). It is also unclear how many subspecific types have evolved, and when and where in the world they did (see, for example, Wolpoff, Zhi, and Thorne, 1984). At some point, however, populations of essentially modern *Homo sapiens* came to the Western Hemisphere, eventually becoming American Indians.

FIRST ARRIVALS IN THE WESTERN HEMISPHERE

Seemingly, men and women first came to the Americas from Asia: "Most scholars agree that American Indians have an ultimate Asiatic origin and are generally related to Asian Mongoloids" (Ubelaker and Jantz, 1986:9). Scholars differ widely on when they first arrived, but have some consensus on how they came.

Most of the evidence and logic indicate that human beings migrated from Asia across Beringia, a land that then existed where now the Bering Strait separates Alaska and Russian Siberia. Migration need not have been by land; it could also have been by water, or ice in winter, across the strait, which is part of the Bering-Chukchi geological platform extending about 500 miles on either side of it. Over time the strait has been flooded or not, depending on the formation and dissolution of large glaciers. When heavy glaciation on land periodically shrank the shallow ocean waters, it created Beringia, a vast expanse of flat, low tundra and grassland, sometimes 1,000 miles wide. To do this, the sea level would have to be only 150 feet lower than it is today. Conversely, glacier melting periodically covered Beringia with water, recreating the strait (see map 1-1).

Beringia is thought to have existed three or four times during the last approximately 70,000 years: once, sometime from about 70,000 to 30,000 years

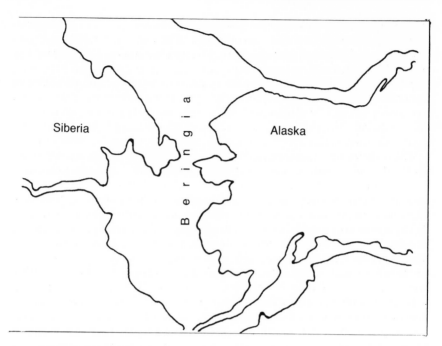

1-1. Location of Beringia

ago; again, continuously from about 25,000 to 15,000 years ago; and then a third and possibly a fourth time, about 14,000 to 10,000 years ago (Hopkins, 1967; Hopkins et al., 1982). Some contend that humans occupied Beringia during the earliest period, but that is only a contention, not a certainty. Human beings may not even have reached Northeast Asia until about 50,000 to 40,000 years ago (Jennings, 1983:27).

Movement into North America

It is not enough to establish that human beings occupied Beringia, as we are concerned with peopling the whole continent. Scholars contend that human passage into the interior was often blocked by glaciers that covered parts of present-day Canada from about the United States border to eastern Alaska. Thus human beings could have been in the Alaskan part of Beringia and still unable to migrate farther into North America. It is generally thought that just as the giant glaciers partially melted—as they did at times, producing the Bering Strait—they also receded leaving ice-free corridors across present-day Canada. One was along the West Coast and the other, the interior corridor, was bordered on the west by the Cordilleran ice sheet, and on the east by the Laurentide ice sheet (Hopkins, 1967, 1979; Bryan, 1969; Fladmark, 1986).

When the interior corridor was open, movement to the interior of the continent was possible along the eastern ridge of the Canadian Rocky Mountains, passing close to present-day Edmonton, Alberta (see Leechman, 1946). We are sure that the interior corridor existed in very early times, probably more or less coinciding with the Bering Strait's formation. We know it was present more recently, around 25,000 years ago. It is thought to have been closed sometime thereafter, until about 14,000 to 10,000 years ago, although James B. Griffin (1979:49) argues that it was closed only from about 19,000 to 15,000 years ago. It seems that land passage along this route into the interior of North America was possible before 25,000 years ago, from about 25,000 to 20,000 years ago, and since around 15,000 to 10,000 years ago.

When the Bering Strait existed, there was a mobility of marine life from north to south, south to north, as occurs today. Conversely, when Beringia existed, a mobility of animal and plant life occurred from west to east and east to west. It was nowhere near an equal mobility. During the past 75 million years almost twice as many animal forms have moved from the Eastern Hemisphere to the Western Hemisphere (from west to east) as in the opposite direction. This was especially true of the large mammals during more recent periods. From the Eastern Hemisphere came bison and mammoths, although an important early migrant in the other direction was the ancestor of the horse.

Beringia probably attracted these and some other animals because of its climate and geography. There was little forest growth. The low precipitation and cool temperatures oftentimes produced tundra and grassland that appealed to large herbivorous mammals, which in turn attracted carnivorous animals preying on them. Once there, it is said, both the herbivores and the carnivores would naturally follow the corridor farther into the interior.

Beringia and the corridor may have acted as a one-way valve restricting flow from the Western Hemisphere but allowing virtually unlimited flow from the Eastern Hemisphere. Animals from the Eastern Hemisphere would have moved into Beringia, adapted to it, then moved along the corridor when it opened. In contrast, few tundra-adapted animals evolved in North America at pertinent times to be attracted by Beringia. Moreover, "such new tundra mammals as may have appeared in central North America could only have reached Alaska about the time the land bridge was drowned by rising sea level" (Hopkins, 1967:477).

It is assumed by some that human beings followed the large mammals into Beringia from present-day Siberia, preying on them. If so, probably not many were involved. Since Beringia was undoubtedly cold and inhospitable, only sparse numbers may have moved from what is now Siberia northward to colder climates where there were fewer resources (Laughlin and Wolf, 1979: 1–2). The first human beings in Beringia were perhaps small hunting parties who settled there. The settlements would have spread as their populations grew, and as large mammals were followed into the interior of Beringia. Eventually, humans would have reached the corridor and followed the herbivores into the interior hemisphere.

The other possible passage, the corridor along the North Pacific coast, existed during various periods, and human beings may have traveled along it. Even when it did not exist as such, they could have traveled along the coast at virtually any time. They would have had to undergo a "coastal maritime adaptation" as they moved south, perhaps by boat, along the coast to the unglaciated shores of present-day Oregon and California. In fact, Knut R. Fladmark (1979, 1986) has suggested this was the more likely route, in part because the interior corridor sometimes surely resembled a "canal" of interconnected glacial lakes, free of fish, that would have seriously impeded human and animal movement. Fladmark has also suggested that at times the corridor had only modest populations of large-species animals (Fladmark, 1986:14). Earlier scholars (for example, Leechman, 1948; Bryan, 1969) argued against the coastal route, contending that it would have been difficult without better canoes than migrants might have had at the time. Also, they say "it is a notoriously perilous coast. Dangerous tide rips, sudden and violent storms, thick fogs, and a dense vegetation which makes travel almost impossible, all combine to discourage movement along the shore" (Leechman, 1946:385).

When did humans arrive, whatever the route? Anthropologists, archaeologists, and other scholars argue for three possible time periods coinciding more or less with the dates discussed above: (1) 40,000 to 30,000 years ago, (2) around 25,000 years ago, and (3) only about 12,000 to 10,000 years ago.

Early skeletal findings in the Western Hemisphere are few and confusing. Not many skeletal materials clearly older than about 12,000 years have been found, although possibly there may have been some (see, for example, Stewart, 1981; Bada and Masters, 1982; also, Smith, 1976). The oldest possible dates for skeletal findings from the conterminous United States may be three findings from southern California: a Laguna Beach human fossil dated about 17,150 years ago; a fossil from Los Angeles dated 23,600+ years ago; and the Del Mar skeleton from near La Jolla, initially dated at 48,000 years ago but recently redated at only 11,000 years (Stewart, 1981:465–66; also Bishoff and Rosenbauer, 1981).

Based on human tool-making and related traditions, arrival times from about 40,000 to about 12,000 years ago have been established (see, for example, Jennings, 1978, 1983; Dumond, 1980; Müller-Beck, 1982; Morlan and Cinq-Mars, 1982; Haynes, 1982; Martin, 1982; Snow, 1984; Yi and Clark, 1985). Some scholars have argued for earlier dates based on this lithic evidence.

Some studies of current American Indian physical characteristics, including blood types,[1] favor a middle date approximately 25,000 years ago. Physical anthropologist T. Dale Stewart (1973:55) observed that "the Indian physical type seems . . . uniform and readily recognizable and more variation, even of the facial features, would be expected if the forerunners of the present Indians had been in the hemisphere for a longer period than 20–30,000 years." There is nonetheless considerable variation, physically and genetically, among American Indians today.

Taking into account evidence of human antiquity and the chronology of

1. Douglas H. Ubelaker and Richard L. Jantz (1986:57) noted: "Native North Americans may be characterized as high in O with A[1] variable, the latter ranging from high values in the Arctic, Subarctic and Northern Plains, to values approaching zero in many populations of the Southern U.S."

Beringia and Canadian glaciers, it seems that human beings probably arrived in North America about 25,000 years ago (see, for example, Snow, 1979). They could have first arrived somewhat earlier, and possibly did; however, they also could have first arrived much later, around 12,000 years ago, as Roger C. Owens (1984) argues.

There were other early arrivals via Beringia and, possibly, other routes. These peoples, who were to be distinct from the first American Indians we know, were to become Eskimos and Aleutian Islanders, and perhaps other Native American groups. For example, a recent study of human blood G allotypes (immunoglobulins) indicated three human migrations from southeast Asia: (1) 40,000 to 16,000 years ago; (2) about 12,000 years ago; (3) about 9,000 years ago (Williams et al., 1985). Moreover, the researchers argue, each migration produced a distinct Native American population here: Paleo-Indians, Na-Dene, or Eskimo-Aleut. The Eskimos and Aleuts may have separated only about 3,000 years ago, though they perhaps had been diverging from each other for about 9,000 years and from American Indians for about 18,000 years (Stewart, 1973:133; Laughlin, Jørgensøn, and Frølich, 1979:102). The Eskimos eventually moved to the northern interior, while the Aleuts settled on the Aleutian Islands. The eastern and western Eskimos then separated more recently.[2] Eskimos, Aleuts and American Indians remain biologically distinct from one another, although there is considerable scholarly debate and discussion about their prehistories (see, for example, Ubelaker and Jantz, 1986; Szathmary and Ossenberg, 1978; Ferrell et al., 1981; Szathmary, 1979). All are considered to be *Native Americans*, nevertheless.

There is considerable agreement about the Asiatic origin of these American Indian groups, who today are seen as biologically close to some Pacific Ocean populations. Although research on their relationships to other world populations is ongoing (see, for example, Matson et al., 1967; Howells, 1973; Ubelaker and Jantz, 1986), it nevertheless suggests separate migrations from Asia into the Western Hemisphere at different times, though the migrants shared a common original Asian gene pool with others of the Pacific area (Ubelaker and Jantz, 1986:65; also Howells and Schwidetzky, 1981). There may have been continued contact among peoples in both hemispheres of the North Pacific, which Soviet scholars have maintained for some time, but which American scholars have been reluctant to accept until recently (Ubelaker and Jantz, 1986:65; also Black, 1983). Scholars have also suggested possible pre-Columbian transoceanic contacts at other parts of the hemisphere (see, for example, Riley et al., 1971; Jett, 1983b).

2. Some of the evidence for a more recent separation of the Eskimos is based on the analysis of language differences: "Comparison of Yukon and Greenland vocabularies by a complicated statistical technique, known as 'glottochronology,' yielded a figure of a thousand years as the time of separation of the eastern and western branches of Eskimos proper. In the same way the separation between Eskimoan and Aleut was set at three thousand years ago. All of which strengthens the long-held opinion that the Eskimos and Aleuts reached North America in relatively recent times" (Stewart, 1973:133).

Movement Throughout the Western Hemisphere

Descendants of the migrants spread throughout North, Central and South America. It has been asserted that they did so from Canada to the tip of South America in only 1,000 years (Martin, 1973:72, 73), but others contend it took much longer. The future Native Americans may have spread fairly quickly through present-day United States once they had arrived from the Canada area, perhaps reaching the Gulf of Mexico in only 350 years. They likely moved generally southward, perhaps following and preying on large game animals (Martin, 1973:72, 73).

From archaeological excavations we know that human beings arrived and settled in different regions of the United States area by certain approximate dates, although they may have come earlier in some instances: they were in the Northeast about 16,000 to 10,000 years ago (Funk, 1983:362); in the Midlands perhaps about 19,000 years ago (Griffin, 1983:243), but perhaps only about 10,000 years ago (Griffin, 1983:245); in the Southwest about 12,000+ years ago (Muller, 1983:374); on the plains about 12,000 years ago (Wedel, 1983:208); on the far Northwest Coast about 12,000 to 10,000 years ago (Dumond, 1983:94–95); in the Southwest about 11,500 to 11,000 years ago (Lipe, 1983:430); in the Great Basin about 11,500+ to 9,000 years ago, but perhaps considerably earlier (Aikens, 1983:165); in the Plateau region about 10,500 years ago (Aikens, 1983:184); and in the California area about 10,000+ years ago (Aikens, 1983:151).

Archaeological evidence in Mesoamerica (which extends approximately from present-day central Mexico into northern Central America) places human beings there by at least 15,000 to 9,000 years ago (Culbert, 1983:502–503). The narrow isthmus of Central America probably impeded southward movement, as it is mountainous jungle and only 31 miles wide at its narrowest in present-day Panama, through both of its coasts are passable.

We also do not know when human beings first arrived in South America. Some say they were active in present-day Peru 20,000 to 15,000 years ago, and in present-day Argentina 12,500 years ago. We also have archaeological evidence that human beings reached Patagonia and Tierra del Fuego before about 10,000 years ago (Griffin, 1979:47). It is generally concluded that human beings were widely spread through South America before 11,000 to 10,000 years ago. This, of course, implies that the first arrived earlier (Griffin, 1979:47).

If the above dates are more or less correct for the first arrivals in North America and Mesoamerica, it would seem either that human beings came more recently to the hemisphere than many now think, or it took them a fairly long time to come south across Canada, via the interior or the coast, after first arriving in the hemisphere. Similarly, if they did cross Canada, and if the dates of settlement in South America prove earlier than those for Mesoamerica and North America, then dates for the latter are undoubtedly not the dates of the earliest human arrival there. Earlier populations may have been in Mesoamerica and North America but left little trace for us to discover today,

at least as yet. Of course, trans-Atlantic ocean crossings could have populated this area prior to a populating of the area to the north.

As human beings moved throughout the Western Hemisphere and became settled there, the first human populations grew in size. The American Indians eventually numbered in the tens of millions, the Eskimos and Aleuts in the tens of thousands. During this period of, say, 25,000 years, they also developed the social, cultural, and physical differences that have distinguished the great Indian peoples of North, Central, and South America.

THE EUROPEAN ARRIVALS

While Native American populations were growing and developing, human populations remaining in the Eastern Hemisphere grew to number hundreds of millions, developing into the separate peoples of Europe, Africa, Asia, and Australia. One group of these peoples, the Scandinavian Norsemen, came to the Western Hemisphere shortly before A.D. 1000 (see, for example, Sauer, 1968; Morison, 1971; Quinn, 1971, 1977). Five hundred years later, Christopher Columbus arrived in the Caribbean Sea. Some scholars, especially the historian David Beers Quinn (1974:47–87), have suggested an arrival by Englishmen shortly before Columbus, perhaps in 1481, searching for North Atlantic fishing grounds and land areas.

The Scandinavian Arrival

From the ninth to the twelfth centuries peoples of the Scandinavian region were the leading European-area sea powers. As one might expect, Scandinavians gradually extended their sea explorations westward during that period, and they were quite successful. By about 870 they had sailed to what they appropriately named Iceland. In about 985 the Norwegian-born explorer Eric (Eirik) the Red, with, it is said, 25 shiploads of followers, sailed farther west from Iceland. He and 14 of the ships arrived at what they inappropriately named Greenland (I. Kleivan, 1984:549). Two settlements eventually were established on Greenland: Brattahlid, on the east, and Godthaab, on the west (Quinn, 1977:26). The settlements grew to number several thousand people. According to Quinn (1977:34), the total population eventually was perhaps 4,000, give or take 1,000 or 2,000.

In 1001, Eric's second son, Leif ("the Lucky") Ericsson (or Eiriksson), extended Norse colonization farther west when he arrived at what he called Vinland. Leif's discovery was named after the Scandinavian word for wineberry, *vinber*, much to the confusion of subsequent scholars, who for many years sought an area on the Northeast Coast with grapevines to ascertain the exact land Leif Ericsson found. This issue has seemingly been settled: the land seems to have been what is now called Newfoundland; grapes do not grow there, but other "wine" berries do. Leif Ericsson established a small, short-lived colony on the northern part of the island, at the now excavated L'Anse aux Meadows. His colonization consisted only of spending the winter there.

The year is given as 1005 when a second group of Norse colonists reportedly encountered nine Native Americans off the coast of Vinland (New-foundland), although it seems they could have met them during earlier years as well. The colonists called the natives *skraelings* (*skrellings*), which is trans-lated as "barbarians," "weaklings," or even "pygmies." They were perhaps Eskimos, but we do not know.[3]

Like a future warning, the Norsemen, as they recorded, promptly killed all of the natives but one, who escaped. Responding appropriately, friends of the murdered Indians later arrived and attacked the killers. This counterattack was surely to little avail, but they did manage to kill the Norse leader, Thor-vald, who was Leif's brother (Quinn, 1977:28).

What transpired between Native Americans and Scandinavians during the next several years is largely unknown. Another Scandinavian colony was es-tablished on Vinland in about 1009. Following it, there was both some trad-ing and some fighting between the two groups. It is known that five Native Americans were killed a couple of years later by the Norsemen. It is also re-corded that the Norse captured two native boys the following year, who were taken east when the Vinland colony, led by a man named Karlsefni (Karlsevni), sailed home.

The Scandinavians made another attempt to colonize Vinland in 1014, but this colony also was short-lived, and the Scandinavians deserted Vinland the following spring. There was little, if any, Scandinavian presence on New-foundland during the following several centuries. Scandinavians lasted longer in Greenland, where they were until around 1400, when they were perhaps, in part, wiped out by epidemic disease and the Eskimos (Quinn, 1977:35; I. Kleivan, 1984:555).[4]

Just as we are certain of these Native American–Scandinavian contacts, we are almost as certain that they did not make any difference to history. Neither Native Americans nor Scandinavians seem to have been significantly affected. Not until the late 1400s did a significant history begin between people from the two hemispheres. One might ask about a relationship between the Scan-dinavian colonizations and explorations in the northern oceans and Colum-bus's 1492 voyage. It seems reasonable that some knowledge of the North At-lantic and its lands spread to England and other countries, and to Columbus himself, from contacts with Iceland and from hearing the Norse sagas of Vin-land (Quinn, 1974:47–87). It is also notable that "Columbus as a young man voyaged on a Portuguese ship to the north of Iceland" (Morison, 1971:61–62; also Quinn, 1974:71).

Later Western European Arrivals

On October 12, 1492, a group of American Indians, whom we may call Ara-wak for simplification, saw three strange-looking ships—the *Niña*, the *Pinta*, and the *Santa María*—off the coast of their island, Guanahani, in the Carib-

---

3. In more recent times Newfoundland was occupied by Beothuk Indians, who are said to have become extinct in the early 1800s. A discussion of the Beothuk may be found in Rowe (1977).

4. Some scholars contend that Scandinavians may have landed on the northeast coast of con-tinental North America at some point in their voyages.

bean Greater Antilles. It is said that the Arawak promptly, and perhaps wisely, "fled to the hills." If so, they returned shortly and met some men who were undoubtedly as strange-looking as their ships. The leader, of course, was Christopher Columbus. He had landed on the Arawak island around noontime, probably after arriving offshore in the early hours of the morning and sighting the island's white cliffs and native campfires (Morison, 1974:62–66).

It is unlikely that members of either group immediately realized the importance of the event to subsequent history. The thought of the Arawak in this regard went unrecorded. Less than 20 years later, however, Hatuay, a leader of a group of Indians on the Spanish-named island of Hispaniola (today the Dominican Republic and Haiti), exclaimed: "I will go no place where I may meet with one of that accursed race" (Rosenstiel, 1983:14).

Columbus observed of the Arawak: "They invite you to share anything they possess, and show as much love as if their hearts went with it" (Morison, 1974:66); and, "How easy it would be to convert these people—and to make them work for us" (Morison, 1975:67). His observations were prophetic: the Island Arawak Indians were destroyed within 100 years, though Mainland Arawak survive today. Their destruction was a result of subjugation by the Spaniards, diseases introduced from the Eastern Hemisphere, and conflicts with their enemy, the Carib Indians (Olsen, 1974:3; also Allaire, 1980).

Reflecting, perhaps, an interest in converting the Arawak to Christianity, Columbus named their island San Salvador.[5] He named the Arawak and the other native peoples he encountered "los indios" (meaning then, people of a darker race). From this came the name American Indians. Only recently have some amends been made by use of the term *Native American* to refer to American Indians, Eskimos, and Aleuts.

In June, 1497, John Cabot landed in the Western Hemisphere. He was a former Genoese, like Columbus, but had sailed out of England. His landfall was only a few miles from where Leif Ericsson had wintered in Newfoundland (Morison, 1971:174). Cabot apparently had no contact with Newfoundland natives, though he reportedly found their fishing nets (Brasser, 1978:79). Some contend that he made it to mainland North America, (Sauer, 1971:6), perhaps reaching New England and more distant areas and coming in contact with, or at least seeing, the Micmac and other American Indians. In any event, he was lost at sea the following year.

Probably the first Europeans on either the North or the South American continent arrived in 1498 when Columbus's men landed on the coast of what would become Venezuela. Columbus made a total of four voyages between 1492 and 1506, during which he explored the West Indies, particularly the Greater Antilles, and the central and northern South American coasts. In 1494 he founded the oldest Spanish settlement in the hemisphere, Isabella, on Hispaniola.

5. The exact island Columbus landed upon is today a topic of scholarly debate. The historian Samuel Eliot Morison contended that it was the island known as Watling's Island from about 1700 to 1926, when it was renamed San Salvador. More recent research has indicated it was the island Samana Cay, some 65 miles south of present-day San Salvador.

In 1497, Amerigo Vespucci, sailing from Spain, skirted the coasts of Central America and southern North America, before returning in 1498. Perhaps he went ashore in North America; perhaps he did not. In any event, he wrote up the journey and received credit for the discovery of this land, and as we know, America is named for him (Sauer, 1971:15–23). In 1500 and 1501, Gaspar Corte-Real (and his brother Miguel on the second voyage) sailed from Portugal to the northern waters of the Western Hemisphere and along parts of mainland Canada (Sauer, 1971:13–15). On his second trip Corte-Real reportedly captured some Newfoundland Indians and took 57 of them with him, eventually sending them back to Portugal with his brother. They "were found to possess a broken sword and a pair of silver earrings, apparently left in Newfoundland by John Cabot's crew" (Brasser, 1978:79). In 1508 or 1509, Sebastian Cabot (John's son) sailed from England past Greenland, probably reaching Hudson Bay. Others came as well in the early 1500s. They were fishermen from Europe reaping the harvests of the Newfoundland Grand Banks. Possibly some made it to mainland North America, but they left no definite records.

We know conclusively that Western Europeans and mainland North American Indians met one another a little later in the sixteenth century. The meeting took place on April 3, 1513, when the Spaniard Juan Ponce de León went ashore on what he called *la Florida* about where present-day Daytona Beach is situated. Hostilities soon developed between him and the Florida Indians. He left safely, but the Indians killed him when he returned in 1521. It was, after all, on their land that he had trespassed; and he had wanted to enslave them and take them to plantations in the Caribbean.

Following Ponce de León were ever-increasing numbers of Spanish and other European invaders of North America. The American Indian demographic tragedy had commenced.

2. AMERICAN INDIAN POPULATION IN 1492

When you first came we were very many and you were few.

—RED CLOUD (SIOUX)

Lively, lively, we are lots of people.

—MAIDU SONG

TO ASCERTAIN THE DECLINE of the American Indian population following the European arrival, it is necessary to establish the size of the population before the first European contacts. There is no question that the Native American population was decimated afterwards; the issue is the magnitude of the destruction.

The size of the American Indian population in 1492 is also important because, as Henry F. Dobyns commented, "The idea that social scientists hold of the size of the aboriginal population of the Americas directly affects their interpretations of New World civilizations and cultures" (Dobyns, 1966: 395). Generally, a large aboriginal American Indian population indicates a more complex, more highly developed native society (see, for example, Carneiro, 1967). Also, the anthropologist Edward H. Spicer (1962: 99) attributed different American Indian reactions to Hispanic culture to differences in American Indian population density. Density, of course, is related to absolute numbers.

The pre-European-contact population that I establish here is for the year 1492 rather than any other time mentioned in Chapter 1. I use 1492 for three reasons: (1) it has been recognized as the year of the first important discovery of the Western Hemisphere by non-Indians; (2) no evidence exists that the earlier Scandinavian or other possible European–Native American contacts significantly impacted either hemisphere; and (3) there were important demographic effects for American Indians, and possibly also for European and African populations, almost immediately after 1492.

Of course, we do not know exactly how many American Indians were in the Western Hemisphere, or even parts of it, when Columbus came. The Indians themselves left no record of their total numbers, no European took a census in 1492, and even if one had, it would surely not have been accurate. It is possible, however, to arrive at a reasonable estimate of the American Indian population at that time.

Although the North American Indian population is of primary interest, particularly that of the conterminous United States, it is important to consider aboriginal populations elsewhere in the Western Hemisphere for several reasons. First, they place the North American Indian population estimates in perspective. Second, many of the estimates of aboriginal North America are parts of hemispherewide estimates; that is, the hemisphere totals have been deduced from estimates of separate areas, or vice versa. Third, the earliest American Indian population estimates by Europeans were for areas and groups south of the United States area, where the first extensive contacts began. It is helpful to examine such estimates to comprehend fully the later ones for North America.

EARLY AMERICAN INDIAN POPULATION ESTIMATES

Explorers, colonists, and others often made written reports and comments on native populations that they encountered. Sometimes they reported dense populations; sometimes they speculated about numbers. As might be expected, because knowledge was based on speculation, debates arose between those estimating large numbers of New World natives and those estimating smaller numbers.

The initial extensive European contacts were with natives of the Caribbean and the Mesoamerican mainland, and population size debates consequently centered on those areas. There was, for example, an early debate about the population of Hispaniola. A noted Spanish historian of the time, Bartolomé de Las Casas, calculated that island's 1492 population between 3 and 4 million, while others argued for a figure around 2 million (see Rosenblat, 1976). The contemporary Venezuelan historian Ángel Rosenblat estimated Hispaniola's population was probably only 100,000, or at the very most, 120,000, when Columbus arrived (Rosenblat, 1967, 1976), but that figure seems incredibly low, as Sherburne F. Cook and Woodrow Borah (1971–79, 1:376–410) have recently estimated Hispaniola's population as high as 7 to 8 million.

Similar debates took place during the sixteenth and seventeenth centuries, but not until the eighteenth century did the aboriginal-population debate emerge on a really wide scale (Borah, 1976:14). Then the Mexican Jesuit Francisco Javier Clavijero estimated the population of preconquest Mexico at fully 10 million people. This was considered a gross exaggeration by many, particularly the Scottish writer William Robertson, who asserted "the Spanish had found sparse settlements of barbarians which, in their surprise at seeing even modest structures, they turned into populous civilized realms with great stone temples and palaces" (quoted in Borah, 1976:14). More debates took place during the eighteenth and nineteenth centuries, with little resulting consensus (see Borah, 1976:14).

Population estimates for pre-Columbian Canada, Greenland, and Alaska are often included with those for the conterminous United States area. This is because of historic political boundaries, and because geographical areas and tribal cultures north of the Rio Grande are considered somewhat similar and somewhat distinct from those more or less south of the river.

Among the first North American estimates was that by the well-known artist George Catlin, who in the 1830s traveled among American Indian tribes recording their changing, ultimately all but vanishing, ways of life. In his diary he speculated, "The Indians of North America . . . were sixteen millions in numbers, and sent that number of daily prayers to the Almighty, and thanks for his goodness and protection" (Catlin, 1844, 1:6).

Four decades later Colonel Garrick Mallery (1877a:365) of the Smithsonian Institution reported to the American Association for Advancement of Science, "the native population of the territory occupied by the United States at its discovery has been widely over-estimated." He further noted:

> Any present attempt to ascertain by means of the literature on the subject, the Indian numbers in pre-Columbian or even early historic times, within the present area of the United States, must be through a maze of contradiction and confusion. Although the examination should be confined to authorities who did not twaddle about imaginary millions and at least pretended to furnish statistics, even those are only valuable for comparison, and when corroborated by the tests of probability and possibility applied of late years by science to all historiographers. (Mallery, 1877a:341)

Similarly, an 1894 U.S. Census report on American Indians noted:

> During the early settlement of the Atlantic coast and of the South Pacific coast the Europeans were led to believe by the natives that the interior of the present United States teemed with an aggressive, enterprising, and ingenious aboriginal population. Based upon these stories estimates of Indian population were made and names of tribes given which had only imagination for authority. Many early European writers chronicled these legends as facts. Investigation shows that the aboriginal population within the present United States at the beginning of the Columbian period could not have exceeded much over 500,000, that portions of families or stocks of Indians were given as original tribes, and that many small bands of the same tribe were given as separate tribes. (U.S. Bureau of the Census, 1894a:28)

Thus in the nineteenth century a considerable range was established for the size of the aboriginal population—from 500,000 for the United States to 16 million for North America.

TWENTIETH-CENTURY POPULATION ESTIMATES

Many twentieth-century scholars have estimated the aboriginal American Indian populations, and although some have used sophisticated methodologies and techniques, the debate has not diminished. It has perhaps even intensified, since these scholars have arrived at an exceedingly wide range of estimates. Thus the methodology of twentieth-century population estimates deserves our attention. The twentieth-century methodology for estimating population encompasses: (1) the scope of the estimates; (2) the data on which the estimates are based; (3) the techniques of data evaluation; and (4) the techniques applied to the data to derive estimates.[1]

---

1. Others have summarized this methodology differently. According to Henry Dobyns (1966:398–414), there are five principal methods for estimating population: (1) *projection* extends figures from a small area to a larger one, or extends population trends over time; (2) *dead-reckoning* establishes individual tribal or subarea estimates that are added together to form a total estimate; (3) *ethnohistorical methods* are used to examine documented sources (including cross-check-

Geographic Scope

An estimate may cover the population of the entire hemisphere or only its subregions or specific tribes. For example, many of the various Western Hemisphere estimates are composed of separate estimates for hemisphere regions (Kroeber, 1939; Dobyns, 1966; Denevan, 1976). Others are for the total hemisphere (Spinden, 1928; Borah, 1964). Similarly, some of the estimates for North America and the United States area are components of larger hemisphere estimates (Kroeber, 1939; Dobyns, 1966; Denevan, 1976); others are not (Mooney, 1910a, 1928; Thornton and Marsh-Thornton, 1981; Dobyns, 1983). In estimates provided by anthropologists James Mooney and Alfred L. Kroeber, North America is divided further into regions and tribal areas.

Occasionally, scholars are not concerned with a large area or large number of tribes and will provide population estimates for only specific subareas, such as California (Powers, 1877; Merriam, 1905; Ascher, 1959; Glassow, 1967; Cook, 1978), or specific tribes or groups (Mooney, 1889, 1907; Mook, 1944; Thompson, 1966; Turner, 1973; Feest, 1973, 1975; Miller, 1976; Snow, 1980).

Population Data

Scholars have been creative in utilizing diverse sources of data to estimate American Indian populations.

The numerous *ethnohistorical sources* include figures or estimates reported by Europeans, often explorers, who had early contact with native peoples. There are figures for total populations or for subdivisions such as villages, houses, slaves, adults, men, warriors, and deaths (Krzywicki, 1934; Cook, 1976c). Church records show converts, fiscal affairs, tribute payments, and baptisms (Borah, 1964; Cook and Borah, 1971–79; Cook, 1976b). There are as well church, government and other censuses of American Indian people

---

ing of one source or authority with another; bichronic ratio determination, or comparisons of populations at two points in time; additive methods of reconstructing specific demographic events to arrive at an earlier population size; reconstruction of aboriginal social structure to ascertain population on the basis of the complexity of the society; resource-potential estimation to ascertain how many people an ecological area could have supported; and direct observation); (4) ascertaining *disease depopulation* among native peoples—that is, the extent and rapidity of epidemics and other illnesses establishes a predisease population size based upon their mortality; and (5) *depopulation ratios* establish the population nadir (low point) and then project back in time to an earlier population size by multiplying the nadir population by a ratio of depopulation.

Douglas Ubelaker (1974:1–7) listed (1) *ethnohistorical methods*, encompassing tribe by tribe inventories, death rates, population projections, sociopolitical reconstruction, and depopulation rates; (2) *archaeological approaches*, encompassing analysis of site surface area, house and mound frequency, settlement patterns, and ecological resource potential; and (3) *physical anthropological approaches*, for which Ubelaker discussed both the "application in Old World" and the "application in New World."

William Denevan (1976:8–12) discussed: (1) *direct techniques*, including analysis of reports by Europeans about probable numbers of native peoples, reports and records pertaining to population segments, and related information such as numbers of settlements, number of warriors, slave exports, church records, and native estimates; (2) *projection methods*, including projections from an area well known to one not known and depopulation ratios, as well as more elaborate statistical techniques; and (3) *corroborative evidence*, including findings from archaeology such as skeletal counts, village size, and assumptions about the carrying capacity of the environment.

(Dobyns, 1966; Thornton and Marsh-Thornton, 1981). The main problem with such sources is accuracy. Also the proportion of the total population that they represent is often open to debate.

Archaeological data include information from the excavations of sites or mounds (Spinden, 1928; Snow, 1980; also Glassow, 1967) and middens (Ascher, 1959; Thompson, 1966; also Glassow, 1967). Also significant is evidence of settlement patterns (Heizer and Baumhoff, 1956) and extensive agriculture, for example, irrigation canals, relic fields, terraces, and other land modifications (Boserup, 1966; Denevan, 1970). These information sources are open to important questions of interpretation, sampling, and dating.

Typical *physical anthropological data* are the skeletal remains excavated from burial grounds (Hooton, 1930; Ubelaker, 1974). Since there are usually sampling and other problems associated with the remains, it is necessary to know additional information if estimates based on these data are to approach accuracy, for example, "[1] a knowledge of the completeness of the sample; [2] information about the archaeological associations of the skeletons; [3] a determination of the length of time the sample represents; [4] an adequate assessment of sex and age at death" (Ubelaker, 1974:5).

Some of the more important estimates of American Indian populations have used *ecological evidence* (Sapper, 1924; Kroeber, 1939; Dobyns, 1983). These are primarily estimates of how many people could have been supported in a given area at the level of technology used, sometimes referred to as the "carrying capacity" of the environment. As the geographer William H. Denevan (1976:12) noted, "this is an imprecise index, however, since both the environment and the technology are readily subject to change." Also, just because a population could have been supported by the environment and the technology, it does not mean that the actual population was that large (Thornton, 1984c).

Some *demographic data* have been used to estimate American Indian populations. Mortality rates, particularly in epidemics, have been a source of evidence (Cook, 1981; Dobyns, 1983). These have been derived from documents and from the application of known mortality rates of such diseases as smallpox, given knowledge that the disease was present in a population. Age-sex pyramids also have been used in estimates (Smith, 1970). Here again, the accuracy of the data is a problem. Also mortality rates from disease are influenced by such variables as general health, age and sex structure, environmental conditions, and health practices. Information on these is often not known.

The *social structure* of Indian societies has also been used as an indication of population size, for example, the political organization of the society and its degree of cultural "evolution" (Means, 1931; Smith, 1970). Such estimates must be speculative, given the inaccuracy of reports of both social structure and how it relates to population size.

Data Evaluation

Scholars typically do not accept data at face value. Several different ways to establish accuracy have been used which have developed into some general techniques of data evaluation.

In *cross-checking* one source of information merely is compared with another. Any type of data described above may be cross-checked with any other type. For example, historical documents may be compared with archaeological evidence, or with the carrying capacity of the environment (Snow, 1980). It is also beneficial to compare examples of the same type of information; for example, one set of documents with another (Mooney, 1910a, 1928).

In *temporal checking* data about two or more points in time are compared to see if they make sense. If, for example, the evidence indicates 10,000 people at one point in time and twice that number only a few years later, both figures are probably not correct. I have shown this in my work on George Catlin's and James Mooney's estimates (Thornton, 1978).

Event checking relates information about population to known historical events (Dobyns, 1983). Although some evidence indicates a particular population figure, one may know it is too low if one knows disease was present in the population earlier; or it may be too high if, for example, the population was subjugated earlier by a much smaller number of American Indians. Many scholars have not considered historic events in examining evidence and reports prepared by others. One should always be aware of such events.

Credibility checking involves either the direct credibility of the evidence or the credibility of the means whereby it was obtained. This is similar to cross-checking, but in credibility checking, one compares additional information of the same type about the population rather than other types of information. For example, many of the Europeans who had early contacts with native peoples of the Western Hemisphere widely exaggerated, often intentionally, often not, the number of Indians present, or sometimes they grossly underreported them (Rosenblat, 1976). These Europeans' reports are not credible when checked against one another. Credibility is not always dependent upon intent; one must also look at the methodological assumptions, sources, and procedures employed to obtain data.

Demography checking is, of course, desirable also. In the scientific study of human populations demographers have produced abundant knowledge about populations and techniques to obtain such knowledge. Both should be used to scrutinize information about American Indian populations (see Smith, 1970). We know many characteristics of population structure and variables of population change, and we have mathematical and statistical equations to ascertain structure and change, given incomplete data. We also know about influences on population structure and on variables of change. During any given year, for example, the young and the old are more likely to die than are adolescents or young adults, more males than females will be born, females live longer than males in some types of societies, but have shorter lives in other types of societies (because of death during childbirth and/or female infanticide), young adults are typically more likely to migrate, only women have children (typically between the ages of 15 and 44 years), there are limits on any population's fertility, and all populations are subfecund to an extent, that is, not as many children are born as is possible. We also know the typical mortality rates of diseases, the possible effects of disease on fertility and migration, and the fertility and mortality of various kinds of societies (agricultural as opposed to hunting and gathering, and so on). And we know about issues and problems involved in the collection of information on a population, particularly censuses; for example, reasons for incompleteness, bias, error, and so on.

Population-Estimation Methods

Given data and a check for accuracy, the simplest, most straightforward method of estimating population is merely to use an existing population figure, or perhaps one of many existing, if that is the case. One may simply use one's own judgment to make an evaluation of a figure's accuracy. I term this the *ethnohistorical method*, as one is generally relying on ethnohistorical information.

Typically, one does not use existing estimates for all tribes or areas that are of interest. One wishes instead to establish an estimate from other data, or if using complete tribal or areal figures, one desires to establish a figure for another point in time or modify the figures in some way, taking into account other factors. Several techniques and assumptions may be used, all involving projective techniques, as figures from an area, population, population segment, or one point in time are projected to a unit of another size or to another point in time.

In *subpopulation projections* information about a subpopulation of a larger population of interest is simply multiplied out to the larger unit (Krzywicki, 1934; Cook, 1976c). One might, for example, have figures for the number of men, women, warriors, or families of a tribe and want to establish a total population size. One may do so by first establishing the ratio of the total population that the subpopulation figure represents and then multiplying by this ratio. Obviously, the problem here lies in determining the accuracy of the ratio.

Subareal projections may be used when one has a population figure for a subarea, or even a different area entirely, and one wants to ascertain the population of the larger or other area (Kroeber, 1939; Snow, 1980). This may be done by multiplying a ratio figure derived from the smaller or other area. Here again the assumption is the use of the correct ratio.

Ecological projection is based not on American Indian subpopulations or populations of subareas, as above, but upon more indirect information (Krzywicki, 1934; Cook, 1976c; Snow, 1980). In these situations one might know the number of villages or houses in a village and want to use that number to establish a total population figure. This may be done by calculating average village or house size, then calculating the number of villages in the area or houses in a village—as above in subpopulation and subareal projections. Or an ecological assumption about the pattern of villages or houses might be made. One might assume several smaller villages or houses for every single larger village or house, and then formulate a pattern. Here again one has to assume that the ratio is correct.

Carrying-capacity projection is often used to estimate aboriginal or historic American Indian populations (Ascher, 1959; Thompson, 1966; Dobyns, 1983). Given certain environments and a certain level of technology, it is possible to establish how many people could have been supported in an ecological area. Typically a population density is developed based on this knowledge, and then the number of persons per square mile is multiplied by the total size of the area.

Despite this technique's popularity, it is problematic because of the information required and the assumptions made in arriving at the density figure. One must know, for example, what the area was like at a point in historical time, including, particularly, the levels of plant and animal foods, soil conditions, and weather, and if the people practiced agriculture, what technologies were used to exploit the environment. Such facts may be difficult to establish. Even with adequate information one must assume the percentage of resources exploited and the percentage of its possible size to which the population actually expanded. Human populations do not necessarily expand to environmental limits (Locay, 1983), though sometimes they do. Other times they even exceed limits and exhaust natural resources.

In *depopulation projections* known rates of American Indian depopulation over a period are used to work backward to other points in time and establish earlier population sizes. (Perhaps *retro*jection is a better term to use than is *pro*jection.)

One type of depopulation projection involves depopulation ratios (Dobyns, 1966). Depopulation rates are established over a period, then multiplied by a more recent, known population size to establish an estimate for the earlier time.

Another type of depopulation projection involves epidemiological projections. Depopulation rates are established from knowledge of epidemics and their mortality, then the rates are used to reconstruct earlier population sizes by applying them to a known, more recent population size (Cook, 1981; Dobyns, 1983). The cause need not be epidemiological; any cause of depopulation may be used, such as warfare, genocide, natural catastrophe.

Finally, there are depopulation projections based on mathematical and statistical formulas. Lines or curves are fitted to a known population line or curve, then projected back in time, using formulas for lines or curves, to ascertain earlier population size (Cook and Borah, 1971–79; Thornton and Marsh-Thornton, 1981).

Crucial assumptions are present in all depopulation projections. Depopulation ratios are never known for the population estimated; in using epidemiological projections, the ratio may be known, but typically, certain events after depopulation must be assumed, such as the extent of population recovery. In mathematical and statistical projections it is assumed the unknown population followed the line or curve, although this is never certain.

Western Hemisphere Total Estimates

As shown in table 2-1, Western Hemisphere aboriginal population estimates by twentieth-century scholars range from only 8.4 million, offered by anthropologist Alfred Kroeber in 1939, to a possible high of 112.5 million, estimated in 1966 by Henry Dobyns, also an anthropologist. Both Kroeber and Dobyns

TABLE 2-1: **Twentieth-Century Estimates of Western Hemisphere Total Aboriginal Population**

Estimate (000)	Scholar (Date)
40,000–50,000	Rivet (1924)
40,000–50,000	Sapper (1924)
50,000–75,000[a]	Spinden (1928)
13,101	Wilcox (1931)
8,400	Kroeber (1939)
13,385	Rosenblat (1945)
13,170	Steward (1945)
31,000	Sapper (1948)
15,491	Steward (1949)
15,500	Rivet (1952)
100,000	Borah (1964)
90,043–112,554	Dobyns (1966)
33,300	Mörner (1967)
30,000	Driver (1969)
57,300 (43,000–72,000)	Denevan (1976)

[a] Circa A.D. 1200.

arrived at hemispherewide estimates inductively by estimating the populations of hemisphere subareas, then totaling them for the overall figures shown in tables 2-2 and 2-3. However, their initial subarea populations were established through very different methodologies.

In his classic "Cultural and Natural Areas of Native North America," Kroeber examined estimates by earlier scholars for tribes and regions of Central and, particularly, North America. He also established population sizes that could have been supported in geographic subareas using certain agricultural and related technologies, again particularly for North America. From this information, Kroeber arrived at population givens or estimates; they were admittedly only such, not definitive figures.

Dobyns, in contrast, examined population histories of American Indian peoples following European contact, particularly in Central and North America. He concluded that, on the average, aboriginal populations declined to depopulation ratios about 1/20 or 1/25 of their original size before reaching nadir, that is, the low point from which they started to increase in size. Dobyns then reasoned that aboriginal population sizes can be ascertained by multiplying known nadir populations by 20 or 25.

Some American Indian populations did not recover, but became extinct; therefore, depopulation ratios were of no use. Dobyns asserted, however: "It may be possible to use a ratio to approximate the aboriginal magnitude of such extinct groups based on the number of survivors about 130 years after initial contact. There is some evidence that this was frequently the time native American populations required to reach nadir and begin to recover—at least it was so among the Central Mexicans and California Indians" (Dobyns,

TABLE 2-2: **Kroeber's Population Estimates for the Western Hemisphere in**
1500

Area	Population (000)
North of the Rio Grande River	900
Northwest Mexico	100
Northeast Mexico	100
Central and southern Mexico, Guatemala, El Salvador	3,000
Honduras, Nicaragua	100
Native North America	4,200
Inca Empire	3,000
Rest of South America	1,000
West Indies	200
Native South America	4,200
Western Hemisphere	8,400

SOURCE: Kroeber (1939:166).

TABLE 2-3: **Dobyns's Population Estimates for the Western Hemisphere in 1492**

Area	Population (000)
North America	9,800–12,250
Mexican Civilization	30,000–37,500
Central America	10,800–13,500
Caribbean Islands	443–554
Andean Civilization	30,000–37,500
Marginal South America	9,000–11,250
Western Hemisphere	90,043–112,554

SOURCE: Dobyns (1966:415).

1966:414). He also asserted depopulation by "a ratio of 50 to 1 over a century marks the approximate outer limits of human survival and population recovery" (Dobyns, 1966:414).

Based on this reasoning, Dobyns established nadir populations for sub-areas of the Western Hemisphere, multiplied them by 20 and 25, and obtained ranges of aboriginal populations.

A recent, moderate estimate of the total hemispheric aboriginal population is that of the geographer William Denevan, shown in table 2-4. Denevan's total of 57.3 million was based on the estimates of several other scholars, including Kroeber and Dobyns, as well as Denevan's own impressions, particularly of North America. Denevan asserted a possible error of 25 percent, one way or the other. Therefore his estimate is actually a range of about 43 to 72 million (Denevan, 1976:291).

Denevan's estimate seems more reasonable than Kroeber's or Dobyns's or most of those in table 2-1. A compromise to be sure, and partly an impression,

TABLE 2-4: **Denevan's Population Estimates for the Western Hemisphere in 1492**

Area	Population (000)
North America	4,400
Mexico	21,400
Central America	5,650
Caribbean	5,850
Andes	11,500
Lowland South America	8,500
Western Hemisphere	57,300

SOURCE: Denevan (1976:291).

it only more or less represents the midpoint of the extremes of others. My own view is that it is somewhat low. I consider the upper point of the range to approach the actual population. I assert that the aboriginal population of the Western Hemisphere circa 1492 numbered at least 72 million and probably slightly more. My upward revision to, say, 72+ million is based on somewhat greater totals for most of the areas that Denevan lists, particularly, as I shall discuss, for North America, but also for the Mexican area (Cook and Borah, 1971–79; Dobyns, 1983), the Caribbean (Cook and Borah, 1971–79:1), and the Andes (Cook, 1981). My estimate for 1492 is therefore close to the upper limit of H. J. Spinden's range of from 50 to 75 million for A.D. 1200, reported in table 2-1.

North America Estimates

Shown in table 2-5 are twentieth-century estimates for all of aboriginal North America and, where available, only the conterminous United States. The lowest and highest estimates are, not surprisingly, by Kroeber and Dobyns, who made the lowest and highest total hemisphere estimates. Their North America estimates are but components of their totals for the hemisphere. Kroeber estimated the aboriginal population more or less north of the Rio Grande at only 900,000; Dobyns originally estimated it as high as 12.25 million, but recently has asserted it may have been 18 million for the area north of Mesoamerica.

The conterminous United States accounted for most of Kroeber's and Dobyns's totals. Kroeber estimated that population at 720,000 or 80 percent of the Western Hemisphere aboriginal population. Dobyns did not provide a separate United States estimate, but an estimate derived from his initial work is as high as 8.31 million, or about 68 percent (see table 2-8; and Thornton and Marsh-Thornton, 1981), and an estimate derived from his later work would be *perhaps* 12 to 15 million, or about 67 to 84 percent of the total Western Hemisphere aboriginal population.

Estimates by other twentieth-century scholars fall at various points between those extremes, as indicated in table 2-5. However, most are around 1 million for the total aboriginal population of North America. This 1 million figure is undoubtedly a result of the influence of the noted Smithsonian In-

TABLE 2-5: **Twentieth-Century Estimates of the Population of Aboriginal North America**

North America (000)	Conterminous United States (000)	Scholar (Date)
1,148	846	Mooney (1910a)
1,148	. . .	Rivet (1924)
2,000–3,500	. . .	Sapper (1924)
1,153	849	Mooney (1928)
1,002	. . .	Wilcox (1931)
900	720	Kroeber (1939)
1,000	. . .	Rosenblat (1945)
1,000	. . .	Steward (1945)
2,000–2,500	. . .	Ashburn (1947)
1,001	. . .	Steward (1949)
2,240	. . .	Aschmann (1959)
1,000–2,000	. . .	Driver (1961)
9,800–12,250	. . .	Dobyns (1966)
3,500	2,500	Driver (1969)
2,171	. . .	Ubelaker (1976a)
4,400	. . .	Denevan (1976)
. . .	1,845	Thornton and Marsh-Thornton (1981)
18,000[a]	. . .	Dobyns (1983)

[a] North of Mesoamerica.

stitution anthropologist James Mooney, who in 1910 provided the first really scholarly aboriginal population estimate: 1.148 million (Mooney, 1910a). He later revised it slightly upward to 1.153 million (Mooney, 1928). His estimate quickly became the figure accepted by most scholars, despite continuing controversies over the total aboriginal-population size for the Western Hemisphere and other subareas of it.

To obtain his North America estimate, Mooney first arrived at estimates for all of the American Indian tribes north of the Mexico area. His primary sources were published reports and the notes of European explorers reporting figures—which in turn were really estimates. He also used secondary sources and even accepted estimates made by colleagues (Ubelaker, 1976b:286).[2] From such diverse sources Mooney established individual tribal population sizes. He then established regional population figures for the period that he felt marked the initial extensive European contacts with particular regions.

2. Douglas Ubelaker commented on Mooney: "For most tribal areas, he evaluated original census data from many primary ethnohistorical sources. For others, he relied upon secondary sources that he considered to be reliable (Ruttenber, Schoolcraft, etc.), and for tribes in the Southern Plains and California he relied upon estimates made by his colleagues (Bolton and Merriam) whose expertise he respected" (Ubelaker, 1976b:286).

TABLE 2-6: **Mooney's Population Estimates for Aboriginal North America**

Area	Contact Date	Population
North Atlantic States	1600	55,600
South Atlantic States	1600	52,200
Gulf States	1650	114,400
Central States	1650	75,300
Northern Plains	1780	100,800
Southern Plains	1690	41,000
Columbia Region	1780	88,800
California	1769	260,000
Central Mountain Region	1845	19,300
New Mexico and Arizona	1680	72,000
Greenland	1721	10,000
Eastern Canada	1600	54,200
Central Canada	1670	50,950
British Columbia	1780	85,800
Alaska	1740	72,600
North America		1,152,950

SOURCE: Mooney (1928:4–33).

Dates of such contact ranged from 1600 to 1845, depending on the regions. A summary yields Mooney's total estimate, as reported in table 2-6.

For half this century scholars seem basically to have accepted Mooney's figures. Consequently, most asserted that there were about 1 million aboriginal North American Indians (see table 2-5, again). Only in the last generation have Mooney's figures come under sharp criticism. It is now realized that far greater numbers of American Indians were here than was previously thought. Yet much of the criticism probably should not be directed toward Mooney or his figures, but to their subsequent use.

Mooney never indicated that his figures were for aboriginal population sizes; he indicated that they were for the periods of initial extensive European contact. He also suggested that they were only tentative figures (Mooney, 1928:1–2). In 1976, Douglas H. Ubelaker evaluated the sources and methodology of Mooney's work. He concluded:

Since Mooney utilized ethnohistorical sources, he limited his estimates to the beginning of the ethnohistorical period, or the earliest point at which he could obtain reliable European estimates of aboriginal numbers. Of course, in most areas the aboriginal population could have been reduced considerably by the time of the earliest estimates. Accordingly, in some groups Mooney appeared to adjust his calculations when the date of the earliest ethnohistorical estimate differed from the date he utilized as the beginning of decline for that tribal area. Frequently he would offer his estimate, commenting that the "original" number must have been much higher. Thus, his estimates actually were designed to serve as a beginning point from which to trace the population effects of European contact, not as a definitive estimate of maximum population numbers prior to European contact. (Ubelaker, 1976b:287–88)

Scholars have used Mooney's figures to represent American Indian populations for circa 1492, not for the periods Mooney indicated. They have also ignored the tentativeness of his figures and Mooney's stated objective of establishing *minimal* population sizes.

Mooney was at fault in assuming little important American Indian–European contact prior to his dates of extensive European contact. This was an important mistake, for in virtually every region there were significant earlier contacts between Native Americans and Europeans or Americans. The first contacts typically resulted in important population losses for American Indians, and as shown in Chapter 3, the contacts did not need to be direct to have serious demographic impacts. American Indians suffered epidemics of European disease resulting from incidental contact, or even without direct contact, as disease spread from one American Indian tribe to another.

Regarding the New Mexico and Arizona area, for example, Mooney asserted:

> The first invasion of this section, by Coronado in 1540–1, resulted in the destruction of perhaps a thousand Indians, chiefly of the Tigua tribe, but as it was not followed up by permanent occupation on a large scale until nearly a century later, we may assume that the Indians recovered from the blow and continued to increase, without special loss through mission establishment, until the general upheaval of the great Pueblo revolt and reconquest, 1680–1692. (Mooney, 1928:21)

Ignored by Mooney were likely epidemics of smallpox, measles, and the plague among American Indians of New Mexico and Arizona prior to 1680 (see, for example, Dobyns, 1983:15–20; also Kessell, 1979; Upham, 1986). Mooney also ignored other depopulating effects of Spanish conquest there that I discuss in Chapter 4.

The Smithsonian Institution *Handbook of North American Indians* is being published in 20 volumes (Sturtevant, 1978–). Authors of chapters on individual American Indian tribes were requested to give special attention to aboriginal population sizes and arrive at a reasonable tribal estimate, revised from existing sources if necessary. In 1976, Smithsonian physical anthropologist Douglas Ubelaker (1976a) compiled these population estimates, and they totaled 2,171,125 for North America. Ubelaker then compared them by region with the figures developed by Mooney, as shown in table 2-7, which illustrates how recent thinking, even if fairly conservative, revises upward Mooney's figures. Some revisions are even startling: the North Atlantic region is considered to have had three times as many American Indians as previously thought, the Gulf states four times as many, the southern plains over six times as many.

Not all of the Smithsonian *Handbook* scholars' revisions involved increases. The one for central Canada even included a decrease. Also, there were some discrepancies. I recently examined tribal estimates by the scholars of the *Handbook* for the California area and arrived at a possible total of only 275,000 in contrast to Ubelaker's 310,000 for California (Thornton, 1980). My compilation was from estimates provided by chapter authors, while Ubelaker's apparently was from a summary estimate by Sherburne Cook in the introduction

TABLE 2-7: Ubelaker's Compilation of Revised Population Estimates for Aboriginal North America

Area	Mooney's Population	Revised Estimate
North Atlantic States	55,600	157,348
South Atlantic States	52,200	92,916
Gulf States	114,400	473,616
Central States	75,300	167,919
Northern Plains	100,800	140,112
Southern Plains	41,000	264,040
Columbia Region	88,800	111,000
California	260,000	310,000
Central Mountain Region	19,300	19,300
New Mexico and Arizona	72,000	113,760
Conterminous United States	879,400	1,850,011
Greenland	10,000	10,000
Eastern Canada	54,200	81,842
Central Canada	50,950	36,684
British Columbia	85,800	119,262
Alaska	72,600	73,326
Other Areas	273,550	321,114
North America	1,152,950	2,171,125

SOURCE: Ubelaker (1976a:664).

to the *California* volume of the *Handbook*. However, that both my and Ubelaker's revised figures are so low is surprising, as present-day California is generally considered to have had a dense aboriginal population, probably one of the most dense of any area of North America.

I also have estimated the aboriginal American Indian population of the conterminous United States by ascertaining the pattern of population decline during the 1800s—the first century of reasonably accurate population estimates for American Indians—and then extending the pattern backward in time to 1492. I find the pattern of nineteenth-century decline to be a straight line, and if the earlier decline in the United States area was also a straight line, there would have been 1,845,183 American Indians here in 1492. If one deducts from Ubelaker's total his estimates of aboriginal Canada, my and Ubelaker's estimates for the conterminous United States are remarkably close (Thornton and Marsh-Thornton, 1981).

Yet, as shown below in Chapter 4, the pattern of large North American Indian population declines in the first three centuries after Columbus, circa 1492 to 1800, was undoubtedly not a straight line but a more severe downward curve (see figure P-1 in the Preface, again). Therefore it seems the aboriginal population of the United States was substantially larger than both Ubelaker's and my estimates. How much larger? Let me attempt an answer.

Henry Dobyns's estimates for North America are, as indicated, from figures for the total Western Hemisphere. They were derived from multiplying nadir populations by depopulation ratios of 20 and 25. There is, however, a serious problem with Dobyns's figure for the Indians of North America: he apparently used nadir sizes based on the 1930 United States American Indian population of 332,397, as enumerated by the U.S. Census Bureau, and enumerated Canadian and Alaskan Native American populations of 127,374 and 29,983, respectively, for that same year. He seemingly then totaled these to 490,000, multiplied by 20 and 25, and attained an estimated population of 9.8 to 12.25 million for North America.

Anthropologist Harold E. Driver (1968) and I (Thornton and Marsh-Thornton, 1981) have shown that the American Indian nadir population for the United States used by Dobyns was far too large. (Driver also considered Dobyns's depopulation ratios to be excessive.) A more correct nadir population, based on U.S. Census enumerations and information from the U.S. commissioner of Indian affairs, is about 250,000 for the decade 1890 to 1900 (U.S. Bureau of the Census, 1915:10; also Driver, 1968; Thornton and Marsh-Thornton, 1981). Multiplying this figure by Dobyns's depopulation ratios of 20 and 25 yields a smaller estimated range for the conterminous United States population, as well as the total population of North America, as shown in table 2-8. The midpoint of the more correct range yields the reduced estimate of 5.65 million American Indians for the United States area in 1492.

A lower nadir population is also in order for Native Americans in Canada. Frederick Webb Hodge's *Handbook of Indians of Canada* lists the 1911 American Indian population of Canada at 108,261 (Mooney, 1913:340), but Mooney (1928:33) asserted that the nadir population of Canada was 101,000 in 1906 (along with 266,000 Indians in the United States, 28,000 in Alaska, and 11,000 in Greenland). If he was correct the nadir population in Canada was more than 26,000 lower than the nadir population that Dobyns used, 127,374. Using Mooney's new nadir reduces Dobyns's aboriginal population estimate about 600,000 on the average, as indicated in table 2-8: 2.27 million compared to 2.87 million.

In 1983, Henry Dobyns published a new estimate of the American Indian population in 1492 north of Mesoamerica, based in part on the work of Thomas R. Malthus (1798), who argued that populations tend to increase to and beyond the limits of the food available to them at any particular level of technology. Dobyns analyzed the food-resource potential of North American Indian technologies and argued—somewhat circularly—that large American Indian populations were present because resources were available to feed them. According to this and other reasoning and the data that Dobyns used, particularly his insightful epidemiological approach,[3] there could have been 18 million American Indians north of Mesoamerica in 1492.

The problem with Dobyns's analysis is that human populations do not nec-

---

3. Henry Dobyns used other data and methods as well, in part as a cross-check. These included American Indian settlement patterns, population reports of early explorers, and population projections from American Indian warrior counts.

TABLE 2-8: **North America Population Estimates Derived from Dobyns's Depopulation Ratios and Different Population Nadirs**

Nadir	Nadir × 20 (000)	Nadir × 25 (000)	Mean (000)
Conterminous United States			
332,397 (1930)	6,648	8,310	7,479
250,000 (1890–1900)	5,000	6,250	5,625
Canada			
127,374 (1930)	2,547	3,184	2,866
101,000 (1906)	2,020	2,525	2,273

SOURCES: U.S. Bureau of the Census (1915:10), Mooney (1928:33), Dobyns (1966:415), Driver (1968), Thornton and Marsh-Thornton (1981:50).

essarily expand to the numerical limits that their technologies and natural resources allow. In fact, Malthus argued that only "plants and irrational animals . . . are . . . impelled by a powerful instinct to the increase of their species; and this instinct is interrupted by no doubts about providing for their offspring . . . and the superabundant effects are repressed afterwards by want of room and nourishment" (Malthus, 1798:6). In contrast, human beings in societies develop "preventive" checks regulating population increase, such as customs relating to marriage and child-spacing, which operate, along with what Malthus called the three "positive" checks on population growth, that is, disease, war, and famine, to limit human population size.

It may be assumed American Indians existed in somewhat less than the maximum possible numbers before the European arrival. It seems reasonable that, as American Indians developed methods of exploiting natural environments, they also developed social regulations on population size. Malthus (1798:26–43) himself argued that "preventive" checks on population growth were present among Indians, although he felt that the "positive" ones were more important in limiting size. Recent research indicates no relationship between population size and carrying capacity of their environments for aboriginal American Indian populations (Locay, 1983; also, however, Casteel, 1980). Other scholars have shown how American Indians actively limited population growth. One method was breast-feeding, which decreases fertility while the child is on the breast. Jean Louis Berlandier (1969:33) reported that Indians of Texas breast-fed children to the end of the fourth year. Conrad Heidenrich (1971:168) noted that the Huron also practiced sexual abstinence during the period of nursing. Additional American Indian birth control practices included other sexual restrictions, infanticide, and abortion.[4]

What, then, is a reasonable estimate for aboriginal North America? Mooney's estimate of 1 million is far too low, since it does not take into ac-

---

4. See also Grinde (1984) for a discussion of birth-control practices among the Yamasee, Cook (1945) for a similar discussion regarding California Indians, and Ewers (1970) for "contraceptive charms" used by Plains Indians.

count early population reductions after the European arrival. Dobyns's original estimate of 9.8 to 12.25 million is too large, since it was based on a nadir population that is too high, and his later estimate of 18 million also seems excessive.

I think the most reasonable estimate based on all current knowledge is to be derived from table 2-8, using Dobyns's depopulation ratios on a more correct 250,000 nadir population. The aboriginal population of the conterminous United States area was probably 5+ million when Columbus arrived in the Western Hemisphere in 1492. Dobyns's methodology applied to the Canadian area yields a population estimate of 2+ million. When smaller aboriginal populations for present-day Alaska and Greenland are added to these, we have a conservative total of 7+ million for the area north of Mexico.

Subarea and Tribal Populations

As there have been population estimates for the Western Hemisphere, North America, and the United States, there have been estimates for subareas and specific American Indian tribes. Some of the subtotals for the conterminous United States are particularly relevant to American Indian depopulation and population recovery.

Henry Dobyns's recent work (1983) focused on the native populations of eastern North America, particularly those of modern-day Florida. He asserted that the aboriginal Timucuan population was perhaps 722,000 in 1517, or even larger. This is over 30 times Mooney's (1928:8) estimate of 24,000 for the entire state of Florida.

Considerable work has been done on aboriginal populations of the mid-Atlantic states, in part because of the relatively intense European settlement there, and because that area and the Southeast generally contained large American Indian populations in 1492. For example, using Mooney's figures, Maurice A. Mook derived aboriginal populations of 54,600 for tidewater Virginia and 41,900 for the "South Atlantic slope," 8,000 for the Delaware Indians, and 4,700 for the Algonquin of Delaware and Maryland (Mook, 1944:206). Similarly, Christian F. Feest (1973:74; 1975) arrived at a range from 14,300 to 22,300 for the total Virginia Algonquin population. Mooney (1907:129; 1889) estimated the Powhatan Confederacy of Virginia at "more than 8,000, or about one-fifth of the whole, being the eastern tidewater section together with the two counties on the Eastern shore"; Randolph Turner (1973:60) revised that estimate upward to 10,435. And Ubelaker (1974:69) revised Mooney's estimate of 2,000 Conoy upward to between 7,000 and 8,400.

Research has been done on aboriginal populations of the New England area as well. Sherburne Cook, in a monograph on this area only (1976c), estimated that the 10 major tribal groups there totaled 71,900 in the seventeenth century (Cook, 1976c:84). Neal Salisbury (1982:30) arrived at a range of 126,000 to 144,000 for the same approximate area. Dean R. Snow (1980:35) arrived at an estimate of 105,200 for close to the same area and a range of 158,000 to 187,300 for a somewhat larger area for the year 1600 (Snow, 1980:33). Some of Cook's estimates are revised in the *Northeast* volume of the Smithsonian *Handbook of North American Indians* (Trigger, 1978). More recently, the early Mohawk population was estimated at from 13,700 to 17,000 (Snow, 1980:41; also Starna, 1980), a figure far larger than earlier estimates; and Snow (1980:36–38) estimated a population of 11,900 for the Eastern Abnaki in 1605.

Additional work has been done on the aboriginal populations of the plains and of the West Coast. Preston Holder (1970:30) estimated the aboriginal population of the Arikara as at least 30,000 and that of the Pawnee as at least 100,000. Sherburne Cook (1978) estimated the population of the California area, minus the eastern desert strip, to have been at least 310,000. Stephen Powers (1877) estimated the California population to have been as high as 705,000. Nevertheless, individual tribal figures from the *California* volume of the *Handbook* total only 186,248 to 274,552 (Thornton, 1980:703). Other related works on aboriginal California are by Robert Ascher (1959), Martin A. Baumhoff (1963), and Michael A. Glassow (1967). North of California, the lower Northwest Coast American Indian population in 1780 was estimated at 72,300 by Herbert C. Taylor, Jr. (1963:163), a size considerably larger than Mooney's estimate of 57,600. Both the Northwest Coast and the Great Lakes have been relatively neglected in recent aboriginal and historic population estimates, although both were undoubtedly highly populated.

Generally, recent estimates of pre-European specific-area and tribal populations have revised upward estimates made earlier, just as recent total estimates for North America revised upward the previous total estimates. Yet there exists today no complete set of aboriginal tribal population estimates reflecting current thinking about the numbers of American Indians in 1492. Mooney's extremely conservative estimates are all that now exist. Douglas Ubelaker (n.d.) is currently preparing such a set, largely from data obtained for existing and future volumes in the Smithsonian Institution's *Handbook of North American Indians* (Sturtevant, 1978–). The figures are scheduled for publication in *Handbook* volume 3, *Environment, Origins, and Populations.*

Suggestions for the Future

It is William Petersen's view of aboriginal and historical American Indian demography that "most of those who write on prehistoric demography show little or no acquaintance with the writings of professional demographers" (Petersen, 1975:227). Consequently, Petersen (1975:227) suggested that "the way to proceed . . . may be to make fuller use of some of the techniques that demographers have used to analyze populations in other contexts. He observes that the quality and lack of data on American Indian populations is not necessarily the problem: Demographers typically work with less than ideal data, and "the demographic data of most of the world . . . are full of holes and often quite unreliable" (Petersen, 1975:227). I agree with him (Thornton, 1979:73) and refer readers to Dobyns (1976b, 1984) and Johansson (1982) for overviews of American Indian historical demography and Nam (1979) for a discussion of demography as a scientific discipline.

In efforts to establish sizes of aboriginal and historic American Indian populations, certain paths are more fruitful to follow than others. It is probably the case that the more limited the estimate, the more accurate it is, as one typically has access to more complete and better information with which to work on a smaller scale. Also, one may consider the interplay of a larger number of variables in arriving at an estimate of a limited group. This is particularly important, since "the degrees and rates of depopulation are variable not only from region to region but within the same region" (Denevan, 1976:289). Also one may study intraregional and inter- and intratribal causes of depopulation and the different responses to it, including not only repopulation behavior and other demographic responses but also nondemographic responses. Predepopulation demographic behavior and initial population stability should also be considered.

The credibility of any subarea, regional, subhemisphere, or hemisphere-wide estimate rests ultimately on the estimate making sense at the tribal level. It does no good to postulate millions and millions of pre-European American Indians, for example, if everything we know about individual tribes indicates their populations could not possibly have totaled the estimated figure. This is not to say that large-area estimates are unimportant. Certainly Dobyns's 1966 estimate, greatly revising upward the possible numbers of pre-European Indians, shook our thinking and caused us to reexamine overly conservative estimates for individual tribes and areas. Yet sizes of individual American Indian tribes cannot be arrived at deductively, only inductively, and I hope more individual tribal estimates will be done in years to come.

A second path to follow is, as William Denevan suggested, "an application of more rigorous statistical techniques" (Denevan, 1976:289). This echoes both Petersen's and my suggestions of more use of basic demographic techniques of analysis. Related to this approach will be more extensive use of population projections back in time and for missing time periods in order to establish population sizes. Such an approach presupposes the availability of data. I also agree with Denevan that there should be "a continued effort to obtain populations from later dates in order to better establish curves of change" (Denevan, 1976:289). A third and final suggestion is that we look beyond mortality and take more into consideration the other two components of basic population change, migration and, particularly, fertility. The assumption is often made that historic American Indian populations maximized their fertility, either before European contact or following episodes of depopulation, as, for example, Henry Dobyns assumed in *Their Number Become Thinned* (1983). This was simply not always true.

Some Nonmethodological Considerations

Referring to estimates of pre-European American Indian populations, Henry Dobyns has commented, "The range of previous estimation is so great as to indicate that some methods or data must have been faulty" (Dobyns, 1966:414). This may be so, but other reasons are needed to explain the wide divergence of estimates seen in tables 2-1 and 2-5.

Overall, there seems little relationship between the types of data and methodologies used in estimating American Indian population sizes and the resulting estimates. Competent scholars have used the same basic data and the same basic techniques to yield very high or very low estimated populations.

For example, both the lowest and the highest estimates for aboriginal North American populations, those made by Kroeber (1939) and Dobyns (1983), relied in part on the same technique, ecological projection. To explain how this may be, one needs to look beyond data and methodology at the psychologies of the scholars themselves.

Two kinds of assumptions by scholars determine population estimates, according to historian Woodrow Borah (1976). The first is the nature of the pre-European Indian society. Just as population size reflected the nature and complexity of pre-European American Indian societies, so does a scholar's population estimate reflect the idea we have of the society estimated. Scholars holding the idea of elaborate and extensive societies will, other things being equal, generally hold the idea also of large numbers of people. A second determining assumption, according to Borah, is the idea we have of history. If we consider history to have been especially destructive to aboriginal people of the Western Hemisphere, then we assume larger aboriginal numbers than if we consider subsequent history to have been "kinder." Those with "kinder" views of history will, other things being equal, assert smaller aboriginal numbers than those considering history "darker." Dobyns has stated in this regard that "the central question in attempting to estimate how many Indians inhabited the Western Hemisphere prior to European discovery would seem to resolve itself into determining whether . . . severe depopulation was the rule or the exception" (Dobyns, 1966 : 410).

To Borah's two determining factors may be added a third: "political bias." Douglas Ubelaker has observed of population estimates for aboriginal North America that, "Historically, estimates have shifted from conservative in 1910 to liberal in the '20's, back to conservative in the '30's and '40's and then liberal again in the '60's" (Ubelaker, 1976a : 661). These trends may be seen in table 2-5. Similarly, another scholar has observed:

> The most important thing to remember in evaluating competing estimates is that, with few exceptions, most are overtly or covertly influenced by . . . political . . . biases. Generally, the first estimates of the total number of inhabitants of the New World at the time of contact were contributed by "pro-Europeans." . . . Hence, Europeans were regarded as colonizing a vast land with fewer than 1,000,000 people, and the subsequent demise or decline of the sparse native population was not seen as a tragedy of great magnitude. . . . Ultimately, population estimates by "pro-nativists," which exceeded 15,000,000 for North America, created in and of itself the problem of explaining how so many people could seemingly disappear so fast. (Johansson, 1982 : 137)

Probably nothing may be done to resolve these issues completely. Scholars will always have to assume certain characteristics of pre-European American Indian societies and certain events of history; scholars will also likely always be open to bias. However, the ill effects may be minimized by simply getting away from the idea that bigger is better, smaller is worse. Larger numbers of pre-European American Indians do not necessarily indicate a better life here at that time nor a "darker" subsequent history; small numbers do not necessarily indicate the converse. What scholars need to do is concentrate on trying to establish what was, not what should have been.

Population Apogee?

There is no reason to assume that the total American Indian population of the Western Hemisphere in 1492 necessarily represented the largest number of aboriginal American Indians ever present. In fact, the aboriginal population apogee may have occurred earlier than 1492: for example, H. J. Spinden's (1928 : 660) estimate of as many as 75 million aboriginal people in the Western Hemisphere is really for about A.D. 1200, not 1492.[5]

The same may be said for North America: civilizations had risen and fallen here before the European conquest. As archaeologists have shown, there were elaborate civilizations and relatively large populations centered before European contact in the Ohio and Mississippi river valleys, such as the Adena-Hopewell and related cultures from about 800 B.C. to A.D. 300+ and later; and following the Hopewell, the Mississippian cultures, which lasted perhaps until A.D. 1700, though they are thought to have reached their peak around the time of Columbus (Fitting, 1978; Brose and Greber, 1979; Griffin, 1983). The Anasazi were in the Southwest for many centuries before Columbus (Plog, 1979; Cordell, 1979), as were the Hohokam (Gumerman and Haury, 1979), Mogollon (Martin, 1979), and other cultures (Di Peso, 1979; Schroeder, 1979; Lipe, 1983). These groups populated that area relatively densely. For example, Harold S. Colton (1936 : 341) calculated that the American Indian population of northern Arizona was 3,000 in A.D. 600; 10,000 in A.D. 800; 23,000 in A.D. 1,000; 19,000 in A.D. 1150; and 7,400 in A.D. 1400.

It is possible American Indians had achieved their largest total numbers in 1492, but it is also possible that they had declined by then from a larger population. Similarly, their total population in 1492 could have been growing, declining, or stable. We do not know.

World Population, Circa 1492–1500

My figures of 72+ million aboriginal American Indians in the Western Hemisphere and 7+ million north of the Rio Grande may be compared with non-Indian populations circa 1492 to 1500. From table 2-9 we see that the population of the rest of the world circa 1500 may have totaled around 500 million. If so, there were perhaps seven times as many non-Indians as American Indians in the world. Not shown in table 2-9 are the particularly relevant European populations at the end of the fifteenth century, those having early contact with the Western Hemisphere: the population of Italy was approximately 10 million; of Portugal, 1.25 million; of Spain, 6.5 to 10 million; of the British Isles, 5 million; of France, 15 million; and the Netherlands, somewhat less than 1 million (Clark, 1977 : 82–92; McEvedy and Jones, 1978 : 49, 57, 65, 101, 103, 107).

5. According to Woodrow Borah (1964 : 380), H. J. Spinden's figure would indicate 40 to 50 million American Indians circa 1492. This is the same as Paul Rivet's and Karl Sapper's 1924 estimates.

TABLE 2-9: **Eastern Hemisphere Population Estimates for 1500**

Area	Population (000)
China	100,000–150,000
India-Pakistan-Bangladesh	75,000–150,000
Southwestern Asia	20,000–30,000
Japan	15,000–20,000
Remainder of Asia except USSR	15,000–30,000
Europe except USSR	60,000–70,000
USSR	10,000–18,000
Northern Africa	6,000–12,000
Remainder of Africa	30,000–60,000
Oceania	1,000–2,000
Total	332,000–542,000

SOURCE: Durand (1977:259).

Two Other Demographic Characteristics

Although it is important to establish the populations of American Indian groups in 1492, since these numbers will be used to examine subsequent population history, the numbers do not reveal all that we would like to know about American Indian demographic life before the arrival of Europeans. Although we often assume that a given population size indicates demographic well-being, this is not necessarily the case. Numbers do not reflect quality, demographic or otherwise; other basic demographic characteristics of American Indian populations before the European arrival may provide considerable insight into the quality of their lives. Although large amounts of data do not exist, we do have information on life expectancy and diseases present, which both are good indicators of what demographic life was like.

Life Expectancy. The important demographic characteristic of life expectancy (average number of years of life expected at birth) reflects a complex set of factors that include a population's health and general well-being.

The little information we have on aboriginal life expectancy is derived from skeletal remains of American Indians who died before, around the time of, or shortly after first European contacts. American Indian remains have been obtained from excavated graveyards and from ossuaries (see figure 2-1). From these remains it has been possible to estimate roughly the life expectancy of selected American Indian groups at points in time, some of which were after the arrival of Europeans, when the life expectancy of some American Indian populations was probably shortened by epidemic disease.

Estimates of the life expectancy of selected American Indian populations are reported in table 2-10 along with life expectancy estimates for some non-Indian populations. Considerable variation is present in North American Indian populations; estimates of life expectancy vary from *perhaps* 18.6 years for the Indian Knoll Indians to *perhaps* almost 43.0 years for Indians of the

Fig. 2-1. Excavated American Indian Ossuary at Nanjemoy Creek, Maryland.
Courtesy of Douglas H. Ubelaker and Smithsonian Institution

Southwest's Pecos Pueblo.[6] Some of the variation is undoubtedly due to methodological errors in working with the skeletal populations and a violation of methodological assumptions, as life tables, from which life expectancies are derived, assume no migration or change in the rate of population growth or decline.[7] However, some of the variation also is due to real differences, epidemiological or otherwise, in the demographic situations of American Indians. The same may be said for differences between American Indian and non-Indian populations, and among the non-Indian populations listed in table 2-10. Despite the complexity of the data, one may still conclude that, in terms of these data on life expectancy at least, American Indians around the time of first extensive European contacts were as well off as those who discovered them, if not considerably better off.

Disease-Free America. The diseases present in a population and their extensiveness and morbidity depend on a complex set of factors including the population's epidemiological and other history, health-care practices, diet and

6. Christopher B. Ruff (1981:150) has indicated mean age at death at Pecos Pueblo may have been only 25 years. Charles M. Mobley (1980:521) has calculated the life expectancy at Pecos Pueblo at 27.4 years. Mean age at death and life expectancy are slightly different measures.

7. The reader is referred to Ward and Weiss (1976), Weiss and Smouse (1976), Swedlund and Armelagos (1976), Buikstra and Konigsberg (1985), and Johansson and Horowitz (1986) for discussions of the methodology of ascertaining life expectancy and mean age at death of skeletal populations.

TABLE 2-10: **Life Expectancy of Selected American Indian and Non-Indian Populations**

Population (Date)	Life Expectancy
American Indian	
Indian Knoll, Kentucky (3000 B.C.)	18.6–19.02?
Texas Indians (A.D. 850–1700)	30.5
Pecos Pueblo (A.D. 800–1700)	25.0–27.4–42.9?
Tidewater Potomac, I (A.D. 1500–1600)	20.9
Mississipian (A.D. 1050–1200)	33.0
Mississippian (A.D. 1200–1300)	24.3
Tidewater Potomac, II (A.D. 1500–1600)	22.9
Non-Indian	
Egypt (A.D. 1050–1600)	19.2
Ancient Greece (670 B.C.–A.D. 600)	23.0
England (11th century)	35.3
European ruling families (A.D. 1480–1579)	33.7

SOURCES: Goldstein (1953:4), Ubelaker (1974:64), Lallo and Rose (1979:332), Ruff (1981:150), Storey (1985:530).

nutrition, and general well-being. The information we have on diseases among American Indians before European contact is typically not as direct as that for life expectancy, although some information has been obtained from skeletal remains. However, the information is more extensive.

There are overwhelming indications that the peoples of North America and the entire Western Hemisphere were remarkably free of serious diseases before the Europeans and Africans arrived. Early New England colonists even observed of the native inhabitants:

> the *Indians* be of lusty and healthfull bodies, not experimentally knowing the Catalogue of those health-wasting diseases which are incident to other Countries, as Feavers, Pleurisies, Callentures, Agues, Obstructions, Consumptions, Subsumigations, Convulsions, Apoplexies, Dropsies, Gouts, Stones, Tooth-aches, Pox, Measels, or the like, but spinne out the threed of their days to a faire length, numbering three-score, four-score, some a hundred yeares, before the worlds universall summoner cite them to the craving Grave. (Wood, 1634:92–93)

There is some controversy among scientists whether syphilis, tuberculosis, malaria, and yellow fever were present before the Europeans and Africans, as I discuss in Chapter 3. Other really deadly diseases undisputedly came only after 1492, such as smallpox, cholera, measles, diphtheria, some influenzas, typhoid fever, and the plague. These were definitely brought from Europe and Africa.

Yet the Americas were not a completely disease-free demographic paradise before the arrival of Columbus and those who followed him. Marshall T. Newman (1976:669) noted the following diseases already present: bacillary and amoebic dysentery; viral influenza and pneumonia; arthritides; rickett-

sial (microorganismic) fevers; viral fevers; American leishmaniasis (proto-
zoan); American trypanosomiasis (parasitic protozoans); roundworms and
other endoparasites; nonvenereal syphilis and pinta (a skin disease caused by a
treponema and related to syphilis); various nutritional deficiency diseases,
such as pellagra, caused by a diet of maize (American Indians often avoided
the resulting niacin deficiency by soaking corn in a lime solution to make
hominy); various more or less minor bacterial pathogens; and salmonella and
other kinds of food poisoning. Marshall Newman (1977:669) indicated that
the list might also include typhus, but only in a mild form.

Two Questions. It is quite clear, however, that American Indians were in far, far
better shape with regard to disease than those who discovered them in 1492.
One might well ask why this was so, given the serious diseases in the Eastern
Hemisphere; and why the life expectancies of North American Indians, reported in table 2-10, were not greater than they were?

The first question has been linked to the initial migrations of *Homo sapiens*
across Beringia, where, it has been suggested, the inhospitably cold, harsh
climate was a germ filter whereby infectious diseases present among human
migrants were screened out and prevented from entering the Western Hemisphere. It is argued that as small populations of men and women drifted
slowly into the Western Hemisphere, only the fittest survived the northern
climate; also, most diseases were gradually left behind, retarded by extremely
cold temperatures. Newman has explained:

> Clearly there is validity to this "cold screen" theory, especially in those dis-
> eases caused by pathogens having part of their life cycles outside of hosts'
> bodies, as in hookworm where neither eggs nor larvae survive in soils with
> temperatures below about 59° F. In addition, insect vectors for other patho-
> genic diseases would also be eliminated by cold, unless these vectors con-
> tinuously lived in the warm microclimates of hosts' bodies. Moreover, . . .
> Old World "crowd-type" diseases such as measles require a human reser-
> voir of several million for maintenance, whereas there is no evidence for
> trans-Bering migrants numbering more than in the hundreds. (Newman,
> 1976:668)

Even in contemporary times, it has been observed, cold, sparsely populated
Alaska has been a remarkably healthy place for humans to live, with epidemics
of measles, polio, whooping cough, mumps, meningitis, dysentery, influenza,
and rubella traceable only to newcomers from other regions, particularly after
1942–43 and the opening of the Alcan Highway (McNeill, 1976:181, 1979:96).
It is likely that most American Indian groups, in North America at least, had
become neither exceedingly large nor dense in the thousands of years after
their ancestors arrived in the Western Hemisphere (although, in fact, some
American Indian populations, in present-day Mexico and Peru, were very
large and dense). Being spread out thus may have prevented human-to-
human disease chains from developing and spreading within and from population concentrations (see McNeill, 1979).

A counterargument was offered by William C. Sturtevant (1985) of the
Smithsonian Institution, who pointed out that other aboriginal populations
who did not move through a germ filter also were free of European diseases and

suffered accordingly after contact with Europeans. For example, Europeans introduced venereal syphilis, gonorrhea, measles, whooping cough, influenza, and the deadly smallpox to Australia. The results were, as in the Western Hemisphere, a drastic depopulation of Australian aborigines (Butlin, 1983).

Another explanation of why the Americas were comparatively disease-free may be the relative lack of domesticated animals in the Western Hemisphere. Such animals have been particularly important in the history of infectious diseases among humans: "Measles, for example, is probably related to rinderpest and/or canine distemper; smallpox is certainly connected closely with cowpox and with a cluster of other animal infections; influenza is shared by humans and hogs" (McNeill, 1976:45).

North American Indians, Eskimos, and Aleuts had only dogs and turkeys (although some perhaps had semidomesticated deer and beaver), while some South American tribes had llamas, alpacas, and guinea pigs. Thus there were comparatively few opportunities in this hemisphere for horizontal transfer of infections from animal reservoirs of disease to human beings. Such transfers are more probable "if the human exposure is intense and of long duration, and if the animal host for the disease has a higher population density than man" (Newman, 1976:668). Such was clearly not the case in the Western Hemisphere, while the opposite situation prevailed in the so-called Old World, where human beings had had many kinds of domesticated animals for a long time.

Why, given the absence in the Western Hemisphere of most serious diseases known today, did the North American Indians have reported life expectancies only comparable to Europeans and not ones considerably longer? In interpreting the data at face value, perhaps a main reason for the American Indian life expectancies shown in table 2-10 is that some of the populations represented died after the European arrival in the hemisphere; for example, some of the Texas tribes and the Pecos Pueblo, and perhaps some of the tidewater Potomac Indians. Their life expectancies may very well have been reduced, perhaps greatly so, by epidemics of European diseases (see, for example, Kessell, 1979).[8]

Other reasons may be found in warfare and human-sacrifice practices and high rates of accidents and injury among some American Indian peoples. There also may have been higher rates of infant and female mortality in childbirth among American Indians than among Europeans, a situation reflecting health practices and medical care rather than disease per se. Famine and starvation also occurred among American Indian peoples, probably more often among those of the Canada and Alaska areas, as shown in articles on individual tribes in Canada, Alaska, and Greenland in works edited by June Helm (1981) and David Damas (1984). Lack of food may very well have reduced American Indian life expectancy, with infants suffering particularly. Finally, the parasitic and other diseases present were killers of American Indians (for example, dysentery and pneumonia), although they were not nearly so important as the diseases that Europeans brought from their Old World.

8. The reader may wish to examine data provided in Goldstein (1953:7–8) showing mean age at death differences between pre- and post-European Texas American Indian populations. They seem to indicate no clear differences in mean age at death between the two groups.

3. OVERVIEW OF DECLINE:
1492 TO 1890–1900

Their numbers were small, they found friends, and not enemies; they told us they had fled from their own country for fear of wicked men and come here to enjoy their religion. The white people had now found our country, and more came among us. . . . At length their numbers had greatly increased; . . . and many of our people were destroyed.
— RED JACKET (SENECA)

Perhaps when the wild animals are gone, the Indians will be gone too.
— BLACK ELK (SIOUX)

ONE OF THE MORE IMPORTANT demographic events in the history of the world may be Columbus's landing on Guanahani. Subsequently, as a direct result, the native peoples of the Western Hemisphere underwent centuries of demographic collapse and geographic concentration. Their total numbers were reduced to but a few million before a population recovery began. They still are far fewer today than in 1492. Also, many tribes were placed on reservations, small remnants of the lands that they formerly occupied, while other tribes were simply left without lands—homeless. That American Indians exist today and have shown recent population increases is a testament to perseverance over a dark period of history.

In marked contrast, the Europeans, Africans, and others who came to the American Indian world subsequently had unprecedented population growth and geographical redistribution. They populated virtually the entire Western Hemisphere while maintaining themselves in the Eastern Hemisphere also. During the four centuries after Columbus their total numbers in both hemispheres expanded from perhaps about 500 million circa 1492 to 1.5 billion. They further expanded to perhaps 5 billion in less than another century, the approximate population of the world today.

I estimated in Chapter 2 a total population of 72+ million American Indians in the Western Hemisphere in 1492. This 72+ million declined in a few centuries to perhaps only about 4 to 4.5 million (Dobyns, 1966:415; Thornton and Marsh-Thornton, 1981:48). This was a population about 6 percent its former size. It represents a tremendous population decline over the centuries.

I estimated in Chapter 2 that there were as many as 2+ million American Indians north of the conterminous United States in 1492. They had declined to only about 125,000, at the most 150,000, by the beginning of the twentieth century (U.S. Bureau of the Census, 1894a:675, 1915:10; Mooney, 1913:390, 1928:32–33). This was a population about 7 percent its former size, indicating a decline of approximately 500,000 per century.

The 5+ million American Indians in the conterminous United States area, estimated in Chapter 2, had declined to but 600,000 by 1800, the first date for which we have any reasonably good population data on American Indians of the United States. They had declined further to about 250,000 by the last decade of the nineteenth century (U.S. Bureau of the Census, 1915:10; Driver, 1968; Thornton and Marsh-Thornton, 1981:48). This was a population some 4 to 5 percent of its former size, representing a population decline of approximately 1.25 million per century. It was then, between 1890 and 1900, that the American Indian population of North America reached its nadir. It began to increase thereafter, an increase which continues today, as we shall see in Chapters 7, 8, and 9. The magnitude and pattern of decline to nadir is shown in figure P-1 in the Preface.

It is fundamental in the scientific study of human populations that a constantly defined population increases or decreases because of changes in only three variables: its births, deaths, and migrations. If more individuals are born or migrate into the defined population than die or migrate out of it, that population increases. And if fewer individuals are born or migrate into the population than die or migrate out of it, the population decreases. This may be expressed in the simple equation

$$P_{T_2} = P_{T_1} + (B - D) + (I - E)$$

where: P_{T_2} is population size at time two, P_{T_1} is population size at time one, B is births, D is deaths, I is immigrants, and E is emigrants.

Often, changes in population size are the result of changes in the rates only of births and deaths within it; migrations are not a factor, or only a very insignificant one. Changes in population size resulting from changing birth or death rates alone are called *natural increases or decreases.*

The American Indian population in the United States area decreased from 5+ million in 1492 to about 250,000 in the decade from 1890 to 1900 because there were more American Indian deaths than births between 1492 and the end of the nineteenth century. Such a population decline implies not only that some 5 million American Indians died during the 400 years but also that, in fact, many times the approximate figure of 5 million died, as new but ever numerically smaller generations of American Indians were born, lived, and died. American Indian migrations into and out of the United States area were almost insignificant to population change, although a few happened, as shall be shown.

A population decline such as that of the American Indians between 1492 and 1890–1900 may result from either higher death rates or lower birth rates, or some combination of changes in both. The American Indian decline was due to both increases in death rates and decreases in birth rates, but it is clear that the increased death rates were of primary importance.

The various reasons for the increased American Indian death rates were interrelated, and some also caused lower birth rates and even migrations. All of the reasons stemmed from European contact and colonization: introduced disease, including alcoholism; warfare and genocide; geographical removal and relocation; and destruction of ways of life. Although it is possible to assert the overall relative importance of these reasons for American Indian population decline, some reasons were more important for the decline of some American Indian tribes than for others. In 1910, James Mooney summed up the causes and their relative importance as follows:

> The chief causes of decrease, in order of importance, may be classed as smallpox and other epidemics; tuberculosis; sexual diseases; whiskey and attendant dissipation; removals, starvation and subjection to unaccustomed conditions; low vitality due to mental depression under misfortune; wars. In the category of destroyers, all but wars and tuberculosis may be considered to have come from the white man, and the increasing destructiveness of tuberculosis itself is due largely to conditions consequent upon his advent. (Mooney, 1910a:286)

I have no particular quarrel with Mooney's ranking of the causes of American Indian depopulation. I will show in detail, however, that genocide must be added to his list. It would probably fall somewhere in the middle to lower part of the ranking. It has been suggested that some depopulation was also due to diseases that American Indians shared with wild animals such as the beaver and the caribou (Martin, 1976). I doubt that such zoonoses were very important in the overall decline of the American Indian population. Also, Mooney possibly may have been mistaken about tuberculosis not coming "from the white man," though he is surely correct about the conditions of its "increasing destructiveness." And it should be pointed out that warfare between American Indians and non-Indians occurred only after the European arrival, though I agree with Mooney that war per se was of less importance than most other causes of the population decline.

MORTALITY INCREASES

Without doubt, the single most important factor in American Indian population decline was an increased death rate due to diseases introduced from the Eastern Hemisphere. Other factors were important as well, however, in mortality increases.

Disease

Europeans brought smallpox, measles, the bubonic plague, cholera, typhoid, pleurisy, scarlet fever, diphtheria, mumps, whooping cough, colds, the venereal diseases gonorrhea and chancroid, pneumonia and some unusual influenza and respiratory diseases, quite probably typhus and venereal syphilis, and only remotely possibly, tuberculosis. From Africa came the anthropod-borne diseases malaria and yellow fever and, some say, probably dysentery and syphilis, among other, less important diseases (see Ashburn, 1947:198–99; Jarcho, 1964; Wood, 1975; McNeill, 1976; Marks and Beatty, 1976; Joralemon, 1982). To those lists may be added alcoholism.

Of the diseases introduced from the Eastern Hemisphere the greatest early killers of American Indians were probably smallpox, strong strains of typhus, and measles; and smallpox was without doubt the leader of the three. Tuberculosis, though probably not first brought here from the Eastern Hemisphere, likely heads the list of more recent killers of American Indians. The destructiveness of alcoholism is surely not far behind, and it has been linked to the current high mortality rates of American Indians from suicide, accidents, diabetes, and, of course, cirrhosis.

The diseases did not merely spread among American Indians, kill them, and then disappear. On the contrary, they came, spread, and killed again and again and again. It has recently been calculated that there may have been as many as 93 serious epidemics and pandemics of Old World pathogens among North American Indians from the early sixteenth century to the beginning of the twentieth century (Dobyns, 1983:15–23). In other words, a "serious contagious disease causing significant mortality invaded Native American peoples at intervals of four years and two and a half months, on the average, from 1520 to 1900" (Dobyns, 1983:24). The year 1520 is when the first probable epidemic of Old World disease invaded North America. It was smallpox.

There has been controversy about the pre-Columbian presence of venereal syphilis, tuberculosis, and malaria and yellow fever in the Western Hemisphere. For example, some say venereal syphilis was present in the Western Hemisphere before Columbus and that it appeared in the Eastern Hemisphere only about 1493 in Barcelona, Spain, with the first epidemic occurring in Italy in the mid-1490s. This variety of syphilis was supposedly carried across the Atlantic by Columbus and his men, which is probably not correct. What seems more likely is that venereal syphilis first occurred in the world only in the early 1490s, after having developed, through mutation or adaptation to a new climate and new human hosts, as a manifestation of existing treponema, that is, as a genus of spirochetes infecting human beings and other warm-blooded animals. Treponemas were likely present in the Western Hemisphere as well as the Eastern Hemisphere at that time. The treponemal species causing venereal syphilis (*Treponema pallidum*) probably developed first in the Old World soon after Columbus returned from his New World, where it arrived later (see Wilcox, 1960; Cockburn, 1961; Hackett, 1963; Hudson, 1965a, 1965b).[1] Although it is possible that the treponema that became venereal syphilis came from the Western Hemisphere, it may also have come to Europe from other regions of the Eastern Hemisphere where the peoples of Europe were having extensive contacts through war and trade.

Unlike venereal syphilis, tuberculosis had a long history in the Eastern Hemisphere, and for a long period it was assumed to have been present in the Western Hemisphere before Columbus. Then some scholars (for example, Morse, 1961) offered dissenting arguments, and now others (for example, Allison, Mendoza, and Pezzie, 1973; Buikstra, 1981) argue again for a definite pre-Columbian presence. One group of scholars identified acid-fast bacilla, which are characteristic of the tubercle bacillus, and terminal miliary tuber-

---

1. Other discussions of the origin of treponemas and venereal syphillis, and the related diseases of endemic (nonvenereal) syphilis, yaws, and pinta, may be found in Jarcho (1964:11–15), Crosby (1972:122–61), Stewart (1973:40–42, 1979:258–59, 271), and Etling and Starna (1984).

culosis in a South American child mummified circa A.D. 700 (Allison, Mendoza, and Pezzie, 1973; also Allison, 1979). The issue may not yet be settled, but it is very likely that tuberculosis was present well before Columbus.

A similar but less intense controversy is associated with both malaria and yellow fever. It seems probable, however, that neither was present in the Western Hemisphere before 1492 (see Jarcho, 1964:5–11; Neel, 1971; Stewart, 1973:38–40; Wood, 1975; McNeill, 1976:187–89).

Not all Old World diseases appeared initially in North America during the European-conquest period; many came later, some even much later. For example, Dobyns (1983:15–23) has asserted that the first North American epidemics of smallpox probably occurred from 1520 to 1524; of measles, 1531 to 1533; of influenza, 1559; of bubonic plague, 1545 to 1548; of diphtheria, 1601 to 1602; of typhus, 1586; of cholera, 1832 to 1834; of scarlet fever, 1637; of typhoid, 1528; and of malaria, 1830 to 1833 (the malaria dates may not be correct; the first epidemic was perhaps earlier, though Dobyns [1983:23] indicated that the disease was not endemic here until at least the seventeenth century).

When the first American astronauts entered outer space there was concern they might return carrying new diseases that would wipe out millions of earthlings because of no previous exposure. The National Aeronautics and Space Administration (NASA) even quarantined returning astronauts for a period of time, and though I do not recall hearing about it, I assume the Soviet Union did likewise, or at least considered doing so. Fortunately, the fears were ungrounded, at least to this date.

The invading, eventually colonizing, Spaniards and other Europeans were not quarantined in 1492 or thereafter, which proved extremely unfortunate to native populations here. Diseases that Europeans brought from their continent—along with those brought from Africa when they journeyed from there to this hemisphere—created a demographic havoc among American Indians for several reasons. The foremost reason was that the introduced diseases found among American Indians a virgin territory to grow, spread, and kill. They produced virgin soil epidemics, "those in which populations at risk have had no previous contact with the diseases that strike them and are therefore immunologically almost defenseless" (Crosby, 1976:289). Such epidemics are particularly destructive to a population because, without any immunity whatsoever, nearly all of the afflicted population are infected by the disease at the same time. It is thought that initial epidemics of Old World pathogens destroyed exceedingly large numbers of American Indians because of this (see Cook and Borah 1948, 1971–79, particularly).

There are other reasons why the diseases were such deadly killers of American Indians. American Indians typically experienced epidemics of a single disease not once but in a long temporal sequence whereby populations that recovered from one epidemic were devastated by subsequent epidemics of the same disease. For example, "considerable lapses of time between . . . smallpox epidemics meant that whole new generations of susceptibles were subject to infection upon the return of the disease and that the repeated ordeals must have had much of the deadliness of virgin soil epidemics" (Crosby, 1976:295). Another reason why the epidemics were so deadly pertains to American Indian medical practices. Newman (1977) has argued that while American Indian medical care was sophisticated enough to handle diseases present before Europeans, it was not able to deal effectively with "crowd-type" diseases, that is, diseases developed in large, dense human populations such as those brought from Europe.[2] Medical care was, in fact, grossly inadequate. Also, certain American Indian disease treatments, such as sweathouses and plunging into cold water for smallpox, often only increased mortality rates. There is also a "genetic-weakness hypothesis" that American Indians are genetically more susceptible to various diseases than are non-Indians. Most scholars discount this.

Because of early massive American Indian depopulation, America, it has been said, was not so much a virgin territory to be conquered by Europeans as a land widowed by early epidemics: "Europeans did not find a wilderness here; rather, however involuntarily, they made one . . . The so-called settlement of America was a *re*settlement, a reoccupation of a land made waste by the diseases and demoralization introduced by the newcomers" (Jennings, 1975 : 30).[3]

The European conquest of the American Indians was initially a medical conquest, one that paved the way for the more well-known and glorified military conquests and colonizations. The colonial historian Francis Jennings (1975 : 105) has noted, "Europeans used a great variety of means to attain mastery, of which armed combat was only one." The most important other means was disease, which, in the final analysis, was more important than armed combat in the European invasion. The conquest of America was "the most striking example of the influence of disease upon history, of which we can speak with any certainty, unless the Justinian plague be an exception. It was medical history writ large" (Ashburn, 1947 : 5).

Warfare and Genocide

While warfare and genocide were not very significant overall in the American Indian population decline, they were important causes of decline for particular tribes. Some American Indian peoples were even brought to extinction or the brink of extinction by warfare and genocide or, perhaps it is more accurate to say, by genocide in the name of war.

Francis Jennings has suggested that war was only incidental in North America before European contact; that North American tribes had few motives for war, few casualties from it. With European contact the situation changed, as four types of often intense warfare occurred: "European versus European, Indian versus Indian, intermixed versus other allies and, rarely, European versus Indian" (Jennings, 1975 : 168).

I do not, as does Jennings, dismiss American Indian warfare before the European arrival. It certainly occurred and had important effects on population,

---

2. The reader is referred to Virgil Vogel's *American Indian Medicine* (1970) for a discussion of herbal drugs used by American Indians.

3. Sherburne Cook and Woodrow Borah (1948, 1971–79) have examined the effects of epidemic disease in other parts of the hemisphere.

for example, among the conquest chiefdoms of the Mississippian groups, to say nothing of the Aztecs in Mesoamerica. I do agree with Jennings that after European contact Indian-Indian wars may very well have become more prevalent and serious. Of course, alliances between American Indians and Europeans against Europeans and/or Indians added whole new dimensions to such conflicts, as Frank G. Secoy (1953) and Neal Salisbury (1982) have described. In the first three centuries of Euro-American contact there were numerous American Indian and American Indian–Euro-American wars on the East Coast from New England to Florida, dating perhaps from Ponce de León's 1513 meeting with Florida Indians through the Seminole Wars around 1840. It has been suggested in this regard that "among the wars most destructive to the Indians may be noted those in Virginia and southern New England, the raids upon the Florida missions by the Carolina settlers and their savage allies, the wars of the Natchez and Foxes with the French, the Creek War, and the war waged by the Iroquois for a period of thirty years upon all the surrounding tribes" (Mooney, 1910a:287). Starting with the arrival in 1540–41 of Francisco Vásquez de Coronado, wars of varying degrees of seriousness involving American Indians raged in the Southwest and then across the Middle West and on the plains, the West Coast, and the Northwest Coast, until the final subjugation of the Sioux by the U.S. government around 1890.

American Indians were not isolated from the Europeans' wars among themselves, as Jennings noted, and these conflicts proved costly to the Indians. For example, the Mohawk "King Hendrich" observed in 1754: "The governor of Virginia and the governor of Canada are quarreling about lands which belong to us, and their quarrel may end in our destruction" (Rosenstiel, 1983:88).

The United States Civil War in the 1860s also proved destructive to many tribes from the eastern half of the United States, particularly the Cherokee in Indian Territory.

Although the American Indian population reduction due to warfare after the European arrival is difficult to assess, it seems certain that American Indian losses were substantial and far greater than non-Indian losses when American Indians and Europeans or Americans fought one another. The U.S. Bureau of the Census asserted in 1894:

> It has been estimated that since 1775 more than 5,000 white men, women, and children have been killed in individual affairs with Indians, and more than 8,500 Indians. History, in general, notes but few of these combats.
>
> The Indian wars under the government of the United States have been more than 40 in number. They have cost the lives of about 19,000 white men, women, and children, including those killed in individual combats, and the lives of about 30,000 Indians.
>
> The actual number of killed and wounded Indians must be very much greater than the number given, as they conceal, where possible, their actual loss in battle, and carry their killed and wounded off and secrete them. The number given above is of those found by the whites. Fifty per cent additional would be a safe estimate to add to the numbers given. (U.S. Bureau of the Census; 1894a:637–38)

Assuming these figures are correct and, for purposes of illustration, adding 50 percent American Indian dead to the 30,000 estimate yields 45,000 American Indians killed in wars with Europeans and Americans between 1775 and 1890. To this might be added the above reported 8,500 American Indians killed in individual conflicts during the period, to arrive at a total of 53,500 killed, by the U.S. government's own admission. The Indians killed in wars and individual affairs before 1775 might easily double the figure. American Indians were also killed by other Indians in intertribal wars resulting from European involvement in tribal relations. As these deaths are added, the mortality figures become considerably more substantial: 150,000? 250,000? 500,000? We do not know. Suffice it to say, American Indians suffered substantial population loss due to warfare stemming from the European arrival and colonization.

We can only guess numbers of American Indians killed by genocide. And it is undoubtedly more problematic to guess the losses from genocide because genocide was neither as well recorded nor as well publicized as warfare.

We do know that in Texas and California, particularly northern California, there was blatant genocide of American Indians by non-Indians during certain historic periods. In Texas, "the facts of history are plain: Most Texas Indians were exterminated or brought to the brink of oblivion by Spaniards, Mexicans, Texans, and Americans who often had no more regard for the life of an Indian than they had for that of a dog, sometimes less" (Newcomb, 1961:334; see also chapters on individual Texas tribes in Ortiz, 1983). Mooney (1910a:286) stated with reference to the extensive nineteenth-century California Indian depopulation: "In California, the enormous decrease from about a quarter of a million to less than 20,000 is due chiefly to the cruelties and wholesale massacres perpetrated by the miners and early settlers."

The distinction between war and genocide often is not well defined: atrocities of American Indian genocide have been called war by non-Indians. For example, the so-called battle at Wounded Knee Creek in South Dakota, where several hundred old men, women, and children were massacred, was not a battle; it was genocide, as was the Sand Creek Massacre of some 150 Cheyenne (and what is happening today to American Indians in some of the countries of Central and South America). Another example is the eighteenth-century destruction of a Nootka Indian village, allegedly for plotting to plunder an American ship in Clayoquot Sound on the Northwest Coast. It has been recorded by the man responsible:

> I am sorry to be under the necessity of remarking that this day, March 27, 1792, I was sent with three boats all well manned and armed to destroy the village of Opitsatah. It was a command I was no ways tenacious of, and am grieved to think that Capt. Gray should let his passions go so far. This village was about half a mile in diameter, and contained upwards of 200 houses, generally well built for Indians; every door that you'd enter was in resemblance to a human and beasts head, the passage being through the mouth, besides which there was much more rude carved work about the dwellings, some of which by no means inelegant. This fine village, the work of ages was in short time totally destroyed. (Quoted in Gunter, 1972:74)

Removal and Relocation

Occasionally linked to events of war and genocide, occasionally not, were the removal and relocation of American Indians from one geographic area to another. Both the concentration of American Indians in small geographic areas and the dispersal of them from their homelands caused increased mortality in Indian populations, typically because of associated military actions, disease, starvation, extremely harsh conditions during the moves, and the resulting destruction of ways of life. Even today the high suicide rate of American Indians has been linked to the desolate life on the created reservations, and the mortality rate of American Indians on reservations is significantly higher than that of nonreservation American Indians (Kenen and Hammerslough, 1985).

Many if not most American Indian tribes were removed, relocated, dispersed, concentrated, or forced to migrate at least once after contact with Europeans or Americans. I have already mentioned the Scandinavian captures of *skraelings* and Corte-Real's capture of Native Americans in 1501. On mainland North America, such captures were made early in *la Florida* by the Spanish there, and in the north in 1534 by the Frenchman Jacques Cartier, in 1576 and 1577 by the Englishman Martin Frobisher, and between 1607 and 1609 by the Dutchman Henry Hudson.[4] Removals occurred in New England soon after European colonization with the establishment of so-called "praying towns" for Christian Indians, the development of various state reservations, and encouragement of American Indians to migrate west. The better known and probably more demographically important relocations involved the southeastern Indians, the Huron Indians around the Great Lakes, the tribes of the Old Northwest (present-day Ohio, Indiana, Illinois, Michigan, Wisconsin, and eastern Minnesota), the Cheyenne on the plains, the Navajo in the Southwest, the Nez Perce and other tribes of the Pacific Northwest, and many small groups in California.

Indian removals and relocations became massive during the 1800s, following passage of the Indian Removal Act of 1830. Most of the Indians removed under the act, however, were from the southern and southeastern United States, from which it is asserted that over 100,000 American Indians were removed west of the Mississippi River during the first half of the nineteenth century (Blue, 1974:iii; Doran, 1975–76:496–97). The most notable of the removals involved the Southeast's so-called Five Civilized Tribes in the early 1800s. (Whites called them civilized because they had accepted some non-Indian, that is European or American, lifeways.) The most infamous was the Cherokee removal of the late 1830s: as a result of it the Cherokee may have lost almost one-half of their population of about 20,000, mostly because of high death rates in transit or thereafter (Thornton, 1984b). Other tribes may have suffered equally.

Linked to removal and relocation was the development of elaborate state

---

4. See Sauer (1971) and Quinn (1971, 1977) for more detail on American Indians removed from North America by early explorers.

and federal reservation systems and the subsequent concentration of American Indians into small geographical areas. Oklahoma Territory and Indian Territory were used specifically for this purpose before they were joined together in 1906 to form the state of Oklahoma in 1907. Many American Indian tribes were resettled there from all over the United States, particularly the eastern half; and they remain there today. The eastern one-third of present-day Kansas was also set aside for American Indians, and many tribes from the Old Northwest were relocated there (Unrau, 1979: vii–viii, 1–3). In California small reservations and rancherias reflecting the Spanish influence were created during the nineteenth century for California Indians who were victims of American treatment. They were supposedly for the Indians' protection (see Fay, 1970). Such lands reserved for Indians in the central and western United States now represent but small fractions of former tribal lands.

The final outcome of removal, relocation, and the development of state and federal reservation systems was a massive redistribution and concentration of American Indians. As a result few tribes are now to be found east of the Mississippi River. Although many of the Indians remaining in the East reside on small state and federal reservations, most of the federal reservations are in the West and Southwest, where the non-Indian population is sparsest, and where the land was more difficult to farm by traditional European and American methods. Relocations often split tribes into two or more groups on different reservations in different regions of the country. For example, the Seminole are in both Florida and Oklahoma, the Cheyenne are in both Montana and Oklahoma, and the Sioux are on many reservations in the Dakotas, Minnesota, and Nebraska. Reservation systems sometimes placed more than one American tribe on the same reservation. For example, the Wind River Reservation in Wyoming contains both Shoshoni and Arapaho, and the Fort Berthold Reservation in North Dakota has Mandan, Gros Ventre, and Arikara.

Destruction of Ways of Life

The removals and relocations, as well as other events, destroyed American Indian ways of life, which in turn caused mortality increases. The specific numbers are hard to ascertain, but they were substantial.

Among the concerted efforts to destroy Indian ways of life were the Spanish missions in California, Florida, and Texas; the U.S. government's attempts to make Plains Indians into cattle ranchers and southern Indians into American farmers; and efforts by churches and governments to undermine Indian religious, governmental, and kinship systems. Most dramatic and perhaps most important, however, were the often deliberate destructions of flora and fauna that American Indians used for food and other purposes. Such destructions were "the strategy universally adopted by European troop commanders, who warred against Indians . . . destroying their crops, knowing that they thus destroyed the tribes' basic food supply" (Jennings, 1975: 19). The most glaring example of animal reduction—probably the one most destructive to American Indians—was the near extinction of the buffalo, which culminated during the last half of the nineteenth century. The buffalo's destruction re-

TABLE 3-1: **North American Buffalo Population History, Aboriginal Times to 1983**

Date	Population
Aboriginal times	60,000,000
1800	40,000,000
1850	20,000,000
1865	15,000,000
1870	14,000,000
1875	1,000,000
1880	395,000
1885	20,000
1889	1,091
1895	Less than 1,000
1902	1,940
1983	50,000

SOURCES: U.S. Department of the Interior (1902:3), Seton (1909:300, 1929:655–57, 670), Walker (1983:1255).

sulted in widescale starvation and the social and cultural collapse of many Plains tribes, particularly the Sioux.

Buffalo once lived in most of the United States and a large portion of Canada. They even extended south into Mexico. Two subspecies were present when Europeans first landed: *Bison bison bison*, the plains buffalo; and the larger, woolier *Bison bison athabascae*, the wood buffalo. The story is told that Hernando Cortes was the first non-Indian to see the Western Hemisphere buffalo; he did so—if the story is correct—in the zoo of Montezuma, at what is now Mexico City, in 1519. The first recorded sighting, however, was by Álvar Núñez Cabeza de Vaca in 1533. The first printed description was by Gonzalo Fernandez de Oviedo y Valdes, published between 1535 and 1537, and the first known printed likeness was in a book by Francisco Lopez de Gomara published in the 1550s (McHugh, 1972:40–42).

During the first three centuries after European contact the pre-European populations of buffalo were reduced from what Frank Gilbert Roe (1970:520) called "almost inconceivable numbers in the heyday of the living herds," probably about 60 million. They were destroyed gradually by a more or less desultory extermination process (Hornaday, 1889:484–86).

At the beginning of the nineteenth century there were still an estimated 40 million buffalo, but between 1830 and 1888 there was a rapid, systematic extermination culminating in the sudden slaughter of the only two remaining plains herds. The southern herd was destroyed between 1870 and 1874; the northern herd, between 1876 and 1883 (Hornaday, 1889:486–513).

The slaughter occurred because of the economic value of buffalo hides to Americans, and because the animals were in the way of the rapidly westward-expanding American population. One individual noteworthy for killing buffalo was the famous William F. ("Buffalo Bill") Cody. There was even a song about him:

> Buffalo Bill, Buffalo Bill,
> Never missed and never will;
> Always aims and shoots to kill
> And the company pays his buffalo bill.
>   (MCHUGH, 1972:268)

By around 1895, the formerly vast buffalo populations were virtually extinct due to the efforts of Buffalo Bill and others. Table 3-1 shows that the date of the buffalo population nadir, circa 1895, was virtually the same as the date of the American Indian population low between 1890 and 1900. Also, as shown in the table, the buffalo population has been replenished somewhat since the turn of the century: there were an estimated 50,000 buffalo in the United States and Canada in 1983. Until 1957, however, it was thought the wood buffalo was probably extinct; then a small herd of more or less "pure" wood buffalo was found in Canada.

FERTILITY DECLINES

The other determinant of natural population change, besides mortality, is fertility, that is, the number of births. Events caused American Indian birth rates to decline after 1492 until 1890 to 1900 just as they caused mortality rates to increase, and for many of the same reasons.

In assessing American Indian mortality, some direct indications of mortality or mortality rates may be obtained; but Indian fertility and fertility rates typically were not observed, and there are few reports of American Indians born or not born, or of rates of birth. As a preface, basic definitions are required: *fertility* is actual childbearing, *infertility* is a diminished ability to bring about conception, and *sterility* is total inability to conceive. In contrast, *fecundity* is the ability to reproduce, *subfecundity* a diminished ability to reproduce, and *infecundity* both a current and future total inability to reproduce. Both sub- and infecundity result not only from sterility and infertility but also from inability to engage in intercourse (*coital inability*) and from a woman not carrying a conceived child to a birth (*pregnancy loss*).

Generally, the maximum possible fecundity of human populations is around 15 children for each woman: "In other words, a population of women who engage in regular sexual intercourse from menarche to menopause without using any form of birth control would, under the most favorable reproductive circumstances, average about 15 children per woman" (McFalls, and McFalls, 1984:3). Such situations do not occur, however; the fertility of human populations is lower, ranging from about one to eight children per woman. The worldwide average fertility in 1982 was four children per woman (McFalls and McFalls, 1984:5). The lower actual fertility may be caused not only by population subfecundity but also by both individual practice of birth control and irregular sexual intercourse (see Davis and Blake, 1956).

European contacts resulted in both diminished fecundity and decreased fertility among American Indians. We do not know all the reasons nor all the particulars of any reason, but we do know, for example, that many of the new diseases brought from Europe affect fertility and, as we shall see, migration, as well as mortality. Diseases present in a population affect fertility by delaying marriage, lowering sexual desire, and producing coital inability, conceptive failure, and pregnancy loss (McFalls and McFalls, 1984:52–55). They also cause people to die before they have the opportunity to reproduce fully or reproduce at all.

European and African diseases had all of these effects on American Indians: "Evidence from around the world suggests that such epidemics of a number of diseases with reputations as Indian killers—smallpox, measles, influenza, tuberculosis, and others—carry off disproportionately large percentages of people aged about fifteen to forty—men and women of the prime years of life who are largely responsible for the vital functions of food procurement, defense, and procreation" (Crosby, 1976:293–94). Smallpox, the deadliest killer of American Indians, is known to have direct detrimental effects on fertility. For example, it causes male conceptive failure and female pregnancy loss: "Indeed it is rare for pregnancy to continue in the wake of maternal smallpox, especially in severe cases" (McFalls and McFalls, 1984:533).

Among the other diseases affecting the fertility of North American tribes was tuberculosis, which was apparently more severe among American Indians after the European arrival. The disease causes coital inability, conceptive failure, and pregnancy loss by producing painful coitus and by interfering with the passage of gametes through genital tracts and the passage of the fertilized ovum through fallopian tubes, preventing the implantation of the ovum in the uterus and producing spontaneous abortion. Moreover, tuberculosis may produce lesions in the genital area resulting in infecundity. Malaria may also affect fecundity by reducing potency, lowering coital frequency, and causing premature birth.[5] Sexually transmitted diseases brought by Europeans also affected American Indian fertility. Gonorrhea, for example, inflames the pelvic area, reducing frequency of coitus; and venereal syphilis reduces fecundity by causing pregnancy loss.[6] Alcoholism also operated to lower American Indian fertility rates. We do not know by how much birth rates were lowered by alcoholism, but we do know that they were, as they were by warfare and genocide, removals and relocations, and destructions of ways of life. This has been shown, for example, in work by Sherburne Cook (1945) and myself (Thornton, 1979, 1984a).

MIGRATIONS

Migrations of American Indians after European contact were also important in American Indian population change. Migrations generally disrupt societies and the families of those involved, and remove people capable of reproducing from a population. Also, people typically migrate away from disease-ridden areas, as did the Arikara of the northern plains after a late eighteenth-century

5. Joseph S. McFalls and Marguerite Harvey McFalls (1984:75–243, 527–34) have discussed the effects of tuberculosis, malaria, and other diseases on fecundity.

6. McFalls and McFalls (1984:247–383) have also discussed the effects of these and other sexually transmitted diseases on fecundity.

smallpox epidemic (Wedel, 1955:79; Lehmer and Jones, 1968:91–92). Such movements often spread the disease to other populations (see McNeill, 1979). For example, the war march of the Omaha after stricken with smallpox in the early nineteenth century, discussed in Chapter 5, surely spread the disease to other tribes and disrupted Omaha society, as did the dispersal of the Plains tribes during the 1836–1840 smallpox pandemic also discussed in Chapter 5.

However, such dispersal may often be deliberately intended to lessen the effects of the disease on the exposed population, as the anthropologist John H. Moore has argued for the Cheyenne in a very insightful paper. Moore (n.d.:1) stated that, "when properly organized, the dispersion tactic can remove the population from proximity to disease vectors, and can mathematically decrease the effects of the secondary attack rate." Nevertheless, American Indian societies and families and reproductive patterns were greatly disrupted by migrations, forced and otherwise, and American Indian migrations away from disease areas also contributed to the spread of the epidemics suffered by American Indians after 1492.

AMERICAN INDIAN PHYSICAL AND GENETIC CHANGE

In addition to changes in population size, American Indians have undergone physical and genetic change since European arrival: a "microevolution" has taken place. In part this resulted from a gene flow (exchange of genes between different populations) produced by an increased mixture between distinct American Indian tribes, as Richard L. Jantz (1972, 1973) has shown regarding historic Arikara populations of the northern plains, who mixed with the Mandan. In part also this resulted from gene flow produced by an increased mixture between American Indians and non-Indians, as I discuss in Chapter 7 especially, but also in Chapters 8 and 9. In many if not most instances, mixing with nontribal or non-Indian populations was a result of the depopulation of American Indians, whereby the number of potential mates had been severely restricted.

However, a certain amount of such change following the arrival of Europeans was a result of genetic drift (genetic changes in a population originating within that population, typically through isolation), which was sometimes caused by the drastic and rapid depopulations often due to epidemics (Ubelaker and Jantz, 1986:63). It sometimes happened that American Indian groups were depopulated but then partly recovered. As a result of the "population bottlenecks" represented by such depopulations and following growth, certain physical and genetic changes occurred in the population because those who survived the epidemics, or other causes of depopulation, were not a random representation of the population at the earlier time. Certain individuals with certain genetic traits of resistance to disease, say, those with certain serological characteristics, would be the more likely survivors of an epidemic. Moreover, these traits might follow family lines; or other family characteristics, such as location, might be involved in succumbing to an epidemic. Thus families and their physical and genetic characteristics were sometimes disproportionately represented in future populations. For example, the explorer

Jean Baptiste Trudeau (Truteau) wrote regarding the Arikara after severe smallpox epidemics: "In ancient times the Ricara nation was very large; it counted thirty-two populous villages, now depopulated and almost entirely destroyed by the smallpox which broke out among them at three different times. A few families only, from each of the villages, escaped; these united and formed . . . two villages . . . situated about a half a mile apart upon the same land occupied by their ancestors" (Nasatir, 1952, 1:299). These few families who escaped the smallpox and formed the future Arikara population were not, of course, an exact representation of the presmallpox Arikara population.[7]

NON-INDIAN POPULATION GROWTH, 1492–1900

While American Indian numbers were declining drastically after 1492, European and other non-Indian populations were growing in both hemispheres and becoming redistributed throughout the world. Table 3-2 shows Eastern Hemisphere population growth from 1500 to 1900. It indicates, for example, that the population in Europe grew from 70–88 million to 425–435 million during the period. This increase of about 444 percent was in marked contrast to what was happening to the original populations of the Western Hemisphere. Within Europe the rate of population increase was not uniform before 1900, but varied from country to country. Nevertheless, "it was everywhere strikingly high. Even in Spain where there had been remarkable loss of population in the seventeenth century, the population grew from 6,100,000 in 1725 to 10,400,000 in 1787 and 12,300,000 in 1833" (Langer, 1963:2).

Important in the European population explosion was the development of innoculation and, later, vaccination against a dreaded European disease of that time: smallpox. Important in feeding this European population explosion was a common food source obtained from South America, the potato, which probably originated in present-day Peru. Although Europeans reacted negatively to it at first, the potato proved an exceptional food, as it is high in nutritional value, easy to cultivate, and, grown underground, was generally safe from the ravages of war. Perhaps the best example of the potato's relationship to European population explosion may be found in the history of Ireland. Introduced in the early 1600s, perhaps from England where it supposedly had been brought by Sir Walter Raleigh in 1588 (Braudel, 1979:169), the potato was widely adopted by Irish peasants during the next 100 years, after which they were eating little else (Langer, 1963:12; Braudel, 1979:169–70). Ireland was still an impoverished country at this time, and one would typically not expect much subsequent population increase: "Yet the population did increase from 3,200,000 in 1754 to 8,175,000 in 1846, not counting some 1,750,000 who emigrated before the great potato famine of 1845–1847" (Langer, 1963:12).

Elsewhere, as well, the potato was important in feeding expanding European populations: "By 1800 . . . the common people in the Netherlands as in the British Isles, Germany, and Scandinavia were eating potatoes twice a day, and even the French peasantry (passionately devoted to white wheat bread) was rapidly capitulating. . . . This, be it noted, was a period when the French

7. Richard Jantz (1972:31–33) has made a fuller discussion of this point vis-à-vis the Arikara.

TABLE 3-2: **Eastern Hemisphere Population Growth, 1500–1900**

	1500 (000,000)	1750 (000,000)	Percent Increase	1900 (000,000)	Percent Increase
Europe	70–88	150–175	106	425–435	444
Asia	225–380	439–545	63	879–960	204
Africa	36–72	60–95	44	143–175	194
Oceania	1–2	2	33	6	300
Total	332–542	641–817	67	1,453–1,576	247

SOURCE: Durand (1977:259).

population was still increasing" (Langer, 1963:15). Moreover, it was precisely those areas most dependent upon the potato for food that showed the most population increase: Ireland, as mentioned, and also the Scottish Highlands, Lancashire in England, and the western and southwestern provinces of Germany (Langer, 1963:17).

Another important food source was introduced from the Western Hemisphere to the Eastern Hemisphere: maize, or today's corn (it probably originated in present-day Paraguay, Peru, or Guatemala, or possibly Mexico). Corn was "introduced" when Columbus himself returned from his voyage in 1493 with some grains of maize; it spread very slowly, however, and did not become widespread until the eighteenth century (Braudel, 1979:164). As with the potato, it was the peasant who first became dependent upon maize as a food; he ate his maize and sold his wheat at a higher price (Braudel, 1979:166). Although of lesser importance at the time than the potato in feeding expanding populations in Europe, maize undoubtedly did foster some population growth there.

European population growth produced emigration from Europe to the United States, which had dire implications for American Indian populations. As a consequence, Western Hemisphere non-Indian population growth was also rapid during the 400-year period. In 1492, of course, the non-Indian population of the Western Hemisphere was zero. By 1750 it had increased substantially, though not remarkably, as it took several centuries for populations from Europe and Africa to transplant themselves. The non-Indian population of the entire Western Hemisphere was probably only 10 to 16 million in the middle of the eighteenth century.[8]

It is difficult to estimate the non-Indian population of the Western Hemisphere in the late 1800s. By that time many American Indians were counted, although not distinguished as a group, in the populations of Mexico and Central and South American countries. There was more mixing of Indians and non-Indians there than in the United States—so much that by 1900 it was not appropriate to distinguish between the two populations. The total population

8. The figure of 10 to 16 million non-Indians in the Western Hemisphere in 1750 was obtained by subtracting from John Durand's (1977:259) 15-to-21-million total population Dobyns's (1966:415) estimates for the approximate time period of native populations in Mexico and Central and South America and an estimated 1+ million American Indians in North America.

of Mexico, Central America, and South America in 1900 was 71 to 78 million people (Durand, 1977: 259); they were almost all descendants of Europeans, Africans, and/or American Indians. Speculations offered by H. J. Spinden (1928: 643) and others suggest that 15 to 20 percent of this number might be considered American Indian.

It is far easier to ascertain non-Indian population growth in North America because American Indians have always constituted a distinct population segment in the United States and Canada, one that has been distinguished in these countries' more recent census enumerations (since 1860 in the United States), though they were left out of the earlier ones (see Chapter 8). By 1750 the non-Indians in North America had increased from zero to perhaps around 2 million,[9] and by 1900 they had increased to between 82 and 83 million (Durand, 1977: 259).[10]

The non-Indian population of the original 13 colonies had grown from zero in 1492 to around 1.25 million by 1750 (Greene and Harrington, 1932: 5; also Wells, 1975). The first United States census enumerated the total population at 3.9 million in 1790 (U.S. Bureau of the Census, 1982–83: 6). By 1890 the non-Indian population of the United States had grown to 62.7 million; by 1900 it was well over 75 million (U.S. Bureau of the Census, 1982–83: 6).

An important reason why non-Indian population growth was relatively slow in the United States area until about 1750 was that numbers of voluntary immigrants from Europe were relatively small before 1800. The ocean voyage to the New World was still a risky one for life and property, and there were few incentives for individuals to make the journey. After 1800 voluntary immigration from the Eastern Hemisphere accelerated considerably mainly because of rapid population growth and severe economic problems in Europe.

Until around 1890 most of the European emigrants to the Western Hemisphere were from Great Britain. For example, of 17 million European emigrants between 1846 and 1890, over 8 million were from the British Isles (1.6 million of those emigrated in just eight years from Ireland after the 1845–47 potato famine). Germany supplied 3.5 million emigrants to the Western Hemisphere between 1846 and 1890. About 75 percent of the British emigrants came to North America; almost all the emigrants from central and northern Europe came here (Borrie, 1970: 87–88).

Table 3-3 shows that the immigrants just to the United States from Great Britain and Ireland totaled over 4.75 million between 1819 and 1880. Germany contributed over 3 million. Other countries such as Italy, Russia, and the Scandinavian nations contributed much smaller numbers of immigrants. In all, over 10 million people from the Eastern Hemisphere migrated to the United States during this period.[11]

9. This figure was obtained by subtracting from John Durand's (1977: 259) range of 2 to 3 million total population of North America an estimated 1+ million American Indians.

10. It is not necessary to adjust Durand's (1977: 259) estimate, as the number of American Indians was considerably less than 500,000.

11. Paul A. F. Walter (1952: 252–53) has made a distinction between "old immigrants" and "new immigrants" to the United States: the former came from northern Europe; the latter came from the Mediterranean area, primarily during the nineteenth and twentieth centuries.

TABLE 3-3: **Immigrants to the United States from Selected Countries in the Eastern Hemisphere, 1819–1880**

Area	Millions
Germany	3.05
Ireland	2.83
Great Britain	1.95
Scandinavia	0.41
Austria-Hungary	0.08
Italy	0.08
Russia	0.42
Other	1.74
Total	10.19

SOURCE: Borrie (1970:89).

Not all of the immigration was from Eurasia; nor was it all voluntary. Millions of slaves were brought to North America, primarily from West Africa, into the mid-1800s. There was perhaps a total of 50,000 separate voyages of slave ships to the Americas from the sixteenth century into the nineteenth century; they transported some 15 million slaves, mostly male, until the trade was abolished in the mid-1800s (Mörner, 1967:16–19; Borrie, 1970:86; Wagley, 1971:24). Borrie (1970:86) has shown that almost half of the slaves came during the eighteenth century, when 7 million were transported to the Western Hemisphere. In the sixteenth century 0.9 million had come, and in the seventeenth century, 2.8 million. Before the slave trade was abolished in the nineteenth century, another 4.0 million were brought over.[12] Most of the slaves were brought by the British and Portuguese (4.5 million each), followed by the French (2 million), Dutch (1.8 million), Spanish (1 million), and Americans (1 million) (Borrie, 1970:86).

THE RESULT

Thus the first four centuries of contact between North American Indians and Europeans and Africans—later Americans—developed into two very different demographic histories, one of unprecedented decline, the other of unprecedented growth. In Chapters 4, 5, and 6, I discuss in more detail the demographic decline of the North American Indians highlighted in this chapter.

12. This was not always a permanent move; many slaves returned to former homelands: "In some of the Caribbean Islands hundreds of thousands of Negroes, faced with a situation of overpopulation about a century after the trade was finally banished, migrated back to one of the countries in which the slave traders had once descended upon their African forebears" (Borrie, 1970:86).

4. THREE HUNDRED YEARS OF DECLINE: 1500 TO 1800

What do you expect to gain by destroying us who provide you with food?
—WAHUNSONACOCK, OR POWHATAN (POWHATAN)

. . . since these Englishmen have seized our country, they have cut down the grass with scythes, and the trees with axes. Their cows and horses eat up the grass, and their hogs spoil our bed of clams; and finally we shall all starve to death. . . .
—MIANTONOMO (NARRAGANSETT)

. . . Colonel Cresap, in cold blood and unprovoked, murdered all the relations of Logan, not even sparing my women and children.
—LOGAN (MINGO)

At the time of death,
When I found there was to be death,
I was very much surprised.
All was failing.
My home, I was sad to leave it.

I have been looking far,
Sending my spirit north, south, east and west.
Trying to escape death,
But could find nothing,
No way of escape.

—LUISENO SONG

SOON AFTER THE EUROPEAN ARRIVAL, the 5+ million American Indians in what would become the United States began to decline in number. They continued to do so for four centuries as the immigrants from the Eastern Hemisphere increased in numbers and had more and more contact with the native population. In this chapter I examine this American Indian population decline during the sixteenth, seventeenth, and eighteenth centuries.

EARLY CONTACTS AND 200 YEARS OF DESTRUCTION

Most of the early Europeans in North America were Spanish explorers led by the *adelantados* ("advancers") who had been sent to the Southwest and, particularly, to what the Spanish named Florida, which at the end of the sixteenth century extended from Mexico to present-day Newfoundland (Wright, 1971:7). It is said that as many as 100,000 Spaniards came to the Western Hemisphere during the first half of the sixteenth century (Mörner,

1967:15). Juan Ponce de León, reportedly the first Spaniard in the area of the United States, explored what was called *la isla Florida* more than once, beginning in 1513. He reported that he was searching for the "fountain of youth," but really he was looking for Indian slaves, it has been said. Ponce de León finally was killed by Florida Indians in 1521. In 1517, Hernández de Córdoba also fought briefly with the Florida Indians, eventually dying from his wounds. In 1519, Álonzo Álvarez de Pineda journeyed to Florida, taking "possession" of 300 leagues of it for his king. In 1528, Pánfilo de Narváez landed on Florida's west coast to explore the land and conquer the Indians there. Hernando de Soto and Luis de Moscoso de Alvarado invaded Florida and explored westward between 1539 and 1543. Others followed them, such as Tristan de Luna y Arellano in 1559. Before long, exploration for exploration's sake and blundered attempts at colonization had ended: Saint Augustine, the first permanent settlement that the Spaniards established in the future United States, was founded in 1565 to attack the French. With its founding, formal, long-standing European colonization of North America had begun.[1]

Spaniards also were involved to some degree in explorations of the more northern East Coast. For example, Lucas Vázquez de Ayllón was a partner in a voyage that captured Indian slaves in South Carolina in 1521; the Portuguese Esteban Gómez, sailing under the Spanish flag, reported captured 58 New England Indians in 1525 during his explorations, then transported them to Spain (Sauer, 1971:69; Brasser, 1978:80); the Spaniards led by Lucas Vázquez de Ayllón established a short-lived colony south of Cape Fear in present-day South Carolina in 1526 (Sauer, 1971:72–76; Brasser, 1978:80); and Captain Juan Pardo and Sergeant Hernando Boyano explored the interior of present-day South Carolina in 1566. Mostly, however, the Spaniards limited their concern to the extreme southeastern and southern coasts (as well as to the Southwest, southern plains, and southern West Coast).

Numerous other Europeans—English, French, Italian, Dutch, and Portuguese—also journeyed to North America in the early years after the European discovery of the continent. As mentioned, John Cabot skirted the Atlantic Coast during the 1490s; he may have actually landed on the North American shore. In the early 1520s, Giovanni da Verrazzano, under the French flag, sailed to New York Bay, Narragansett Bay, and present-day Maine. Verrazzano stopped by the Chesapeake Bay on the way north, kidnapped an unwary Indian, and became the first European to describe in writing the natives of the Atlantic coast of mainland North America (Sauer, 1971:58; Wright, 1981:28). He later encountered the Indians of what would become Rhode Island, and either the Abnaki or Penobscot Indians of Maine (Sauer, 1971:61; Brasser, 1978:80). He called them *mal gente* ("bad people").

Some of the early non–Spanish explorations of the Northeast Coast involved brief colonial efforts, but they did not amount to very much. Serious ones would come later. Other Europeans besides the Spaniards arrived on the

---

1. By 1565 the Spaniards had founded Isabela (1494) and Santo Domingo (1496) on Hispaniola, New Seville (1509) in Jamaica, San Juan (1511) in Puerto Rico, and Santiago (1511) in Chile, as well as Saint Augustine, Florida.

southern coast during the sixteenth century, but they were not nearly as numerous there as the Spaniards were, and it would take them a while to drive
the Spaniards out. Meanwhile, they stayed mostly in the north. Including the
Spaniards in the Southwest and on the West Coast, Europeans managed to
become fairly numerous in North America during the sixteenth century. It
has been speculated that in sixteenth-century Florida alone the number of colonists, Spanish and otherwise, may have numbered 10,000 (Wright, 1981:42):
"This, of course, does not include the many mariners who of their own voli-
tion put in at Florida ports for repairs and supplies" (Wright, 1981:42). To
that number may be added, it has been said, more than 10,000 shipwreck survivors (Wright, 1981:42). If that is so, the total European (and African) population on the East Coast was substantial: 20,000 to 25,000 or more.

As we have seen, American Indians were remarkably free of serious disease
before meeting Europeans and the Africans who accompanied them. Not
long after explorers arrived, the situation changed drastically. American Indians became much less healthy because of Old World pathogens, and untold
numbers died early in the sixteenth century as a result. This had implications
for the real colonists who would arrive afterward. By eliminating earlier populations of American Indians, the Old World diseases prepared the way for European military conquest and full colonization.

Disease did not kill only Indians; early settlements of Europeans were often
decimated also. It has been asserted that "disease killed more white men than
the Indians did" (Ashburn, 1947; xviii). Furthermore, the European contact
with the African continent and the importation of large numbers of slaves
from there to this hemisphere brought new diseases to the Europeans in
North America, which killed them as well as American Indians.[2] Diseases
from the Eastern Hemisphere slowed the conquest of North America as European populations here struggled with their health (Ashburn, 1947:29).
Nevertheless, Old World diseases killed a far greater proportion of American
Indians than of Europeans and Africans.

The Sixteenth- and Seventeenth-Century Destruction

We lack direct evidence of a large sixteenth-century American Indian population decline in North America, but we do have evidence of such a decline in
the Caribbean and Mesoamerica. Our lack of knowledge is due largely to differences between the Spanish and the British and French who became the primary colonizers in the north. The Spanish governmental and Catholic Church
bureaucracies kept detailed records of their contacts with natives—tribute
payments, conversions to Catholicism, slave counts, even censuses. Based on
analysis of these records, we know American Indians under their influence
declined sharply during the early period of contact (see, for example, Cook
and Borah, 1948, 1971–79). The British and the French did not keep such detailed records, and they kept few records at all until the seventeenth century,

---

2. Darrett B. Rutman and Anita H. Rutman (1976) have discussed the effects of malaria on
non-Indians in early Virginia, and John Duffy (1953) has discussed the effects of several diseases
on the non-Indians.

partly because they did not establish permanent North American settlements until then.

The historian Alfred Crosby (1976:290) noted that, since the British, in particular, drove Indians away from their colonies, what transpired among Indians was not known, and therefore impossible to record. This was in contrast to the Spanish, who tended to enslave the Indians, or at least subjugate them as peons.

Another reason for our lack of knowledge of native North America, which is also somewhat important for the study of the Caribbean and Mesoamerica, was stated by Francis Jennings (1975:23): "Permanent colonies are not a prerequisite for disease transmission; mere transient contact will do, and large numbers of contacts have been recorded for the sixteenth century." Not even transient contact with Europeans was needed, however, as American Indians spread disease among themselves through contacts with one another (see Palkovich, 1981). If American Indian populations were concentrated along trails and waterways, as has been maintained (Dodge, 1967; see also Broek, 1967), then movement along them would have spread the diseases to population concentrations. The American Indian population may have thus been overlaid by a "network" or "web" of disease.

Recorded or not, it has been emphatically stated that, "the most spectacular period of mortality among the American Indians occurred during the first hundred years of contact with the Europeans and Africans" (Crosby, 1972: 37). Although we will likely never know the exact nature or extent of this depopulation of North America, we can conclude that it did occur and was extensive, based on evidence from Mesoamerica and the Caribbean and on our general knowledge of disease in virgin populations.

Old World pathogens seemingly did not appear immediately with European arrival, but they did very soon afterward. Smallpox, the first known Old World disease here, probably arrived in North America, for example, between 1520 and 1524, seven years after Ponce de León; and it may have arrived earlier, as epidemiological theory suggests earlier unreported epidemics of the disease.[3] The first recorded New World epidemic began on Hispaniola in 1507. If smallpox was much delayed, it was probably because of the lengthy ocean voyage from Europe: those carrying the virus aboard ship would have died before arrival in this hemisphere. When smallpox inevitably did arrive, it could have for any number of reasons: "An especially fast passage from Spain to the New World; the presence of a vessel of several nonimmune persons who could transmit the disease from one to the other until arrival in the Indies; the presence of smallpox scabs, in which the virus can live for weeks, accidentally packed into a bale of textiles—by any of these means smallpox could have been brought to Spanish America" (Crosby, 1972:46). And once it had ar-

3. Henry Dobyns (1983:254) asserted there may have been an earlier epidemic of smallpox: "The first epidemic of Old World disease may have swept through the native peoples of Florida in 1513–1514." It should be noted, however, that Hopkins (1983:234) stated that smallpox did not arrive in North America until the early seventeenth century. To me, this seems very late, particularly given its much earlier arrival on Hispaniola in 1507 (Hopkins, 1983:204). I agree with Dobyns regarding an early sixteenth-century arrival.

rived, however it came, smallpox quickly became the leading killer of American Indians; it continued as a leader virtually until the twentieth century.

It is impossible to ascertain how intense smallpox was initially among the virgin American Indian population. Henry Dobyns (1983:14) indicated that American Indians involved in the first smallpox epidemic suffered almost 75 percent mortality. No one knows if this percentage is correct, but the initial outbreak on Hispaniola in 1507 was said to have exterminated whole tribes (Hopkins, 1983:204). It is also known that smallpox produced very high mortality among North American Indians, and it killed far more of them than Europeans when it occurred in the settlements of both.[4] For example, the mortality rates of smallpox epidemics among the colonists of New England were only about 10 to 15 percent: "However, among the Indians, even in the nineteenth century when some immunity had already been acquired by this race, we find a case fatality among some tribes during certain of the epidemics as high as from 55% to over 90%" (Stearn and Stearn, 1945:14–15).

In addition to the 1520–24 smallpox epidemic, there were possibly one additional epidemic of smallpox and nine epidemics of other diseases among North American Indians during the sixteenth century (Dobyns, 1983:15–23). Not included among those epidemics were venereal syphilis and certain other European diseases likely to be present among American Indians at that time. Surely they had drastic effects as well. For example, according to Dobyns (1983:293), Florida's aboriginal Timucuan population of as many as 772,000 had been reduced by disease to 361,000 by 1524, further reduced to only 150,000 by 1559, and further reduced to a mere 36,450 by the early 1600s. Dobyns's aboriginal Timucuan population estimate of possibly 772,000 does, however, seem considerably high.

These diseases were not necessarily brought by ship directly from Europe. Historian David Beers Quinn has described the virulence of certain Old World diseases in tropical climates: "Plague might well be picked up in temperate latitudes; typhus was a commonplace of nautical life; in tropical waters malaria more deadly than that endemic in the Thames basin, or even yellow fever, might be had from mosquitoes. Dysentery, often associated with infected food, might in tropical varieties prove mortal, so that the 'bloody flux' was especially feared at sea" (Quinn, 1974:205).

Meanwhile, wars, battles and genocide also contributed to the decline of the American Indian population. All increased early in the sixteenth century, virtually from the first American Indian contacts with European explorers, Jesuit priests, and Spanish slave hunters. By the early seventeenth century, when real colonization began, it is certain many American Indians were hos-

---

4. The death rate from smallpox varies depending on the health care received, the virulence of the virus, and the type of smallpox, *Variola major*, *Variola minor*, or *Variola intermedius*. *V. major* was the only known species until *V. minor* was recognized late in the nineteenth century; however, *V. minor* was not distinguished in the laboratory until the 1950s. *V. intermedius* was distinguished in 1963 (Hopkins, 1983:5–6). No one knows when smallpox first affected human beings. It "probably evolved and adapted to man gradually, from one of the relatively harmless pox viruses of domesticated animals" (Hopkins, 1983:13).

tile to Europeans: "The Jamestown colonists landed among a people who already knew and hated the whites" (Mooney, 1907:129).

Effects of Colonies Established

During the late sixteenth century and the early decades of the seventeenth century, northern Europeans founded colonies at Roanoke, Virginia (1585); Sable Island, Nova Scotia (1598); Tadoussac, Quebec (1601); Port Royal, Nova Scotia (1605); Jamestown, Virginia (1607); Plymouth, Massachusetts (1620); and Massachusetts Bay (1628). Subsequently there were settlements at Albemarle (in the 1650s) in North Carolina, and Charleston (1670) in South Carolina, as well as trading posts at Quebec (1608), Fort Orange, New York (1624), and New Amsterdam (1626).

Much seventeenth-century North American Indian depopulation stemmed directly from the effects of these early colonies, particularly as colonists brought more diseases to more American Indians. Dobyns (1983:15–23), for example, has noted 12 seventeenth-century North American Indian epidemics of smallpox, four of measles, three of influenza, two of diphtheria, one of typhus, one of bubonic plague, and one of scarlet fever. Colonies also caused further conflicts between Europeans and American Indians, which resulted in warfare and genocide, famine, starvation, and destruction of American Indian ways of life, and pushed Indian tribes away from their lands into more and more restricted areas.

To be included among the depopulating effects of colonies was the introduction of alcohol to American Indians, although it seemingly took them a while to succumb to it. It was probably not until late in the seventeenth century that drunkenness became a major Indian problem (Sheehan, 1980:179). It became so, it is asserted by James Axtell, as a result of trade between Europeans and American Indians:

> Alcohol was introduced to the Indians as a gift, a companionable toast before trading or politicking began in earnest. But it quickly became a staple of the trade itself when the Europeans saw that many natives—though by no means all—acquired a large thirst for it, despite its initially unpleasant taste and their total lack of experience with fermented beverages. Despite its relative weight, "neither capacity or knowledge of the Indians, or their language [was] necessary for the sale of it" and the profits to be made were "considerable," especially when it had been watered. (Axtell, 1981:257)

American Indians at that time seemingly never learned to drink moderately: "Most drinking Indians imbibed only to become thoroughly drunk. 'Social' drinking for taste or mildly pleasant sensations was rare" (Axtell, 1981:257).[5]

Traders soon realized that a drunk Indian was far easier to exploit than a sober Indian: "Rum was in fact one of the main reasons for the traders' success with the Indians" (Jacobs, 1972:33). It would sometimes work this way:

---

5. James Axtell (1981:257–58) has given three reasons why American Indians sought to become inebriated: (1) to boost self-esteem, (2) as an excuse for evil acts, and (3) to achieve a state of "religious possession."

"Since negotiations for the sale of furs were often made in the heart of the forests (a practice the famous Hudson's Bay Company tried to avoid by having the tribesmen bring their furs to certain trading posts or forts), the trader could easily induce his warriors to have a free 'dram' of rum before the business of barter began. This was the fatal step for the Indian. One dram called for another, and before long the tribesmen were thoroughly drunk. The trader could then literally steal the skins and furs, slipping off into the night with his prizes" (Jacobs, 1972:33).

It was not long before American Indian leaders recognized what was happening and pleaded with colonial leaders to curb the spread of alcohol: "The arguments they used were two: their people were dying in excessive numbers from drinking-related murders (and, we know also, from exposure and increased susceptibility to colds, pneumonia, and other diseases), and the temperance issue" (Axtell, 1981:259). In the end, though, many native societies were virtually destroyed by the quest for alcohol: "The desire for rum impelled Indian hunters to kill more game than was necessary to purchase only dry goods, thus hastening the serious ecological imbalance in their territories. . . . Alcohol also loosened the Indian's hold on his land. More than one treaty was signed 'under the influence,' an abuse that fueled Indian-white conflict throughout the colonial period and beyond" (Axtell, 1981:259).

Roanoke. Two ships under the authority of the Englishman Sir Walter Raleigh journeyed to the mid-Atlantic coast of North America in 1584; their crews met the Indians of the area, stayed briefly, then left. However, a larger fleet, also under the authority of Raleigh and under the command of his cousin Sir Richard Grenville, returned in the following spring, 1585, to find and hold "heathen and barbarian" lands under an inherited charter from Raleigh's half-brother, Sir Humphrey Gilbert. In order to accomplish Raleigh's mandate, they eventually founded a colony on Roanoke Island on the North Carolina coast, which was then in Virginia. They had first visited the Caribbean and then had burned the Indian village of Aquascock south of Cape Hatteras, it is said. Grenville soon left the colony, but he left 108 colonists on Roanoke, and he took some plants and perhaps some Indians back to England with him. The remaining colonists stayed the winter, but they too left the following year, 1586, when Sir Francis Drake arrived with slaves, both black and Indian, to help them with their work; the colonists were in such bad shape that Drake had to rescue them from the rigors of the New World and its inhabitants.[6] Drake took the colonists back to England, ending the first English colony on North American soil (see Quinn, 1955, 1974, 1977; Hume, 1963). The Indians and blacks were supposedly left behind, perhaps along with a few colonists.

Among the Roanoke colonists during 1585 and 1586 was the surveyor Thomas Hariot, who wrote an account of the experience, *A Briefe and True Report of the New Found Land of Virginia* (1588), in which he described a large-scale epidemic of an unknown disease among natives around the colony: "The people

---

6. One is referred to Quinn (1955) for a detailed discussion of these and other events of the Roanoke voyages.

began to die very fast, and many in short space; in some townes about twentie, in some fourtie, in some sixtie, & in one sixe score, which in trueth was very manie in respect of their numbers. . . . The disease also so strange, that they neither knew what it was, nor how to cure it; the like by report of the oldest men in the countrey never happened before, time out of minde. A thing specially observed by us as also by the naturall inhabitants themselves" (Hariot, 1588:F). None of the English colonizers, Hariot observed, were known to die or even be especially sick from the epidemic. It seems probable the disease was typhus: Dobyns (1983:19–21) has asserted a 1586 typhus epidemic among American Indians from Florida all the way up the Gulf Coast to New England. Typhus or not, the epidemic killed substantial numbers of American Indians and, according to Hariot, few colonists.

Not only European diseases killed Roanoke Indians during the first year that the colony existed: the colonists also killed them. Hariot reported that "Some of our companie towards the ende of the yeare, shewed themselves too fierce, in slaying some of the people, in some towns, upon causes that on our part, might easily enough have been borne withall" (Hariot, 1588:F2).

All was not settled regarding the Roanoke colony after the first colonists left in 1586. Not by any means. Grenville soon returned to the mid-Atlantic coast, discovered the colonists gone, and left a few new ones with some provisions. To further develop Roanoke, Raleigh in 1587 sent out a fresh colony consisting of somewhat more than 100 men, women, and children, in three ships under the command of John White, who was to rule the colony as governor. When on arrival they discovered the earlier colonists were gone, they then formed another colony. White and some others left the colony a short time later, hoping to return soon with fresh supplies. War with Spain and perhaps other events delayed a quick return, and it was not until 1590 that White returned to search for the 85 men, 17 women, and 11 children left behind.

On arriving, White found the Roanoke colony deserted. Among the ruins was the word CROATOAN carved on a tree. Croatoan was the local Indian name for an island about 100 miles southwest of Roanoke where Cape Hatteras is located. The agreed-upon sign of distress, a Maltese cross, was not carved on the trees. Severe weather seems to have prevented a search for the lost colonists, and the inquirers did not investigate but returned in their ships to England (see Quinn, 1955, 1974, 1977, 1985; Morison, 1965).

Probably not until the early 1600s was a real attempt made to search Croatoan Island for the Roanoke colonists. They were not found. Why did it take so long? Perhaps Sir Walter Raleigh was afraid of not finding them and losing his patent of 1584, which had required him to establish an English colony within seven years (Quinn, 1974:442, 1977:430). We have no definite answer, but the Virginian Robert Beverley wrote of his "countrymen":

In all the latter Voyages, they never so much as endeavor'd to come near the Place where the first Settlement was attempted at Cape *Hattoras;* neither had they any Pity on those poor Hundred and Fifteen Souls settled there in 1587 of whom there had never since been any Account, no Relief sent to them, nor so much as an Enquiry made after them, whether they were dead or alive, till about Three Years after this, when *Chesapeak* Bay in *Virginia* was settled, which hitherto had never been seen by any *English* Man. So strong was the Desire of Riches, and so eager the Pursuit of a rich Trade, that all Concern for the Lives of their fellow Christians, Kindred, Neighbours and Country-men, weigh'd nothing in the Comparison; tho' an Enquiry might have been easily made, when they were so near them. (Beverley, 1705:24−25)

We today still do not know whatever happened to the "Lost Colony" of Roanoke. Quinn (1974:432−81, 1977:438, 1985:341−78) asserted that they lived with the local Indians, perhaps marrying with them, perhaps eventually being massacred, along with the local Indians, by members of the Powhatan tribe. Today the Lumbee Indians of North Carolina, some of the descendents of the Croatan Indians, believe that the colonists' blood "runs in their veins," as indicated in recent writings by Dean Chavers (1971−72), himself a Lumbee Indian, and Karen I. Blu (1980:36−65, esp. 44).

Jamestown. The English also founded Jamestown colony, in 1607, in what is now Virginia. It was in the midst of the great Powhatan Confederacy, which, then encompassed about 30 tribes, including the Pamunkey and the Chickahominy as well as the Powhatan. The confederacy was led by the chief Wahunsonacock, known to the English as Powhatan, who was also the leader of the Powhatan tribe. Scholars have estimated that there were 9,000 to 14,000 Indians in the coastal area where Jamestown was founded, and that there were perhaps almost as many elsewhere in modern-day Virginia. This adds up to a total population of 20,000 to 25,000 (Mooney, 1907:142), of which perhaps half, or about 12,000, were in the Powhatan Confederacy.

The Indians of the Powhatan Confederacy were not unaware of Europeans when Jamestown was founded in their territory. Quite the contrary! Members of the confederacy had surely encountered the explorers Verrazzano, in the 1520s, and Gómez, in 1525, and had subsequent contact with Spanish slave hunters and Jesuit priests. The Powhatan at the time of Jamestown were even said by colonists to have a strong hatred for the Spanish: Powhatan's father had allegedly been driven from the West Indies to the North American continent by them (Hamor, 1615:13).

After establishing Jamestown, the colonists themselves had a difficult time in their New World; they suffered especially from a bad diet, starvation, and an epidemic, apparently of typhoid. Life was so hard in 1609 and 1610 that the period was called "starving time." Much of the suffering, however, was apparently their own fault. Robert Beverley (1705:34) wrote 100 years afterward that this was so for "wasting their old Provisions, and neglecting to gather others." Beverley further noted of the colonists: "They continued in these scanty Circumstances till they were at last reduced to such Extremity, as to eat the very Hides of their Horses, and the Bodies of the *Indians* they had killed; and sometimes also upon a Pinch they wou'd not disdain to dig them up again to make a homely Meal of after they had been buried" (Beverley, 1705:35). Given these and other harsh circumstances, mortality rates among the Jamestowners from 1607 to early 1625 were so high that that period was designated "the great mortality." About half of the initial colony of over 100 are said to have died during the first summer alone. Supplemented by additional immigrants, the colony lost about 500 people during its first three years, and it is said that 6,040 died out of the total of 7,289 immigrants who had come to Virginia by February, 1625, or around 83 percent (Hume, 1963: 44–45; also Marks and Beatty, 1976: 164; Quinn, 1977: 449).

Nevertheless, with the help of the Powhatan Indians—probably in part because of the marriage of Powhatan's daughter, Pocahontas, to a Jamestown man, John Rolfe, and the Indians' fear of English weapons—the colonists somehow survived their first years. They even began to extend some dominance over the Powhatan.

By 1622, however, Powhatan had died and been succeeded by his brother, Opechancanough. Having had enough of the European intruders and their foreign ways, Opechancanough attacked and killed 500 of the colonists, about one-fourth of their total numbers (Wright, 1981: 85; also Hume, 1982). His undoubted satisfaction was short-lived, however, as in retaliation the English colonists began what was called "the first Indian war," in which they undertook the deliberate and systematic destruction of the Powhatan Confederacy. The colonists were instructed to root the Indians "out for being longer a people upon the face of the Earth" (quoted in Vaughn, 1978: 78). This is pretty much what they did, both to the Powhatan Confederacy and other Virginia tribes. One recorded incident is an example of the colonists' warfare: "The English in 1623 negotiated a treaty with rebellious tribes in the Potomac River area. After a toast was drunk symbolizing eternal friendship, the Chiskiack chief and his sons, advisers, and followers, totaling two hundred, abruptly dropped dead from poisoned sack, and soldiers put the remainder out of their misery" (Wright 1981: 78).

Opechancanough managed to stay alive for the following 20 years, and in 1644 he attacked again, "although now so old and feeble that he was no longer able to walk or even to open his eyes without help" (Mooney, 1907: 139). During the ensuing war another 500 colonists died—but by this time that was only about one out of 16 colonists, as their population had grown. The colonists eventually captured Opechancanough, took him to their Jamestown, and shot him while in prison.

Minor warfare continued between Virginia Indians and the colonists after Opechancanough's death, but smallpox and other epidemics are thought to have been more important in subsequent Indian depopulations in the area, although epidemics had also occurred earlier. One Virginia Indian smallpox epidemic began in 1667 as a result of an infected sailor going ashore in present-day Northampton County and transmitting the disease to surrounding Indians: "The usual fatal results transpired, and it was reported that 'they died by the hundred . . . in this way practically every tribe fell into the hands of the grim reaper and disappeared'" (Duffy, 1951: 330). Eventually, "a feeling of irresistible malaise overcame the tidewater Indians in the latter half of the seventeenth century as they suffered the effects of alcohol, disease, social breakdown, and a decline in population" (Sheehan, 1980: 180).

The net result of wars, epidemics, and a changing way of life was the decimation of the Powhatan Indians by the end of the seventeenth century. From an estimated 20,000 to 25,000 American Indians in Virginia in 1607—of which 12,000 were Powhatan—there was a decline to about 2,000 by 1700, of which less than 1,000 were Powhatan (Mooney, 1907 : 142; Sheehan, 1980 : 180). By 1700 the Indians of Virginia were reported to be all wasted by disease so that they could not raise 500 fighting men among them. By then the non-Indian population, primarily white but also black, had grown to perhaps 100,000 (Mooney, 1907 : 142).

Other Southern and Mid-Atlantic Colonies. The Roanoke and other Virginia Indians were far from being the only southern Indians depopulated during the sixteenth and seventeenth centuries as a result of colonization. The English colonies at Albemarle in North Carolina and at Charleston, South Carolina, had predictable effects on adjacent American Indian populations. There were smallpox epidemics, for example. An especially severe one happened in 1696 around Albemarle. In 1699 in South Carolina smallpox "swept away a whole . . . nation, all to 5 or 6 which ran away and left their dead unburied, lying upon the ground for the vultures to devour" (quoted in Duffy, 1951 : 332). And the so-called Westo War of 1680 greatly reduced and disbursed the Westo Indians.[7]

Farther south there were large-scale reductions of American Indians in the future Gulf States, by disease and by war, as European colonists followed the explorer De Soto and other early Spanish adventurers. The slave trade also had serious implications for southern Indians. During both the sixteenth and seventeenth centuries, tens and tens of thousands of Indians were enslaved, although, as one authority has noted, "it is too risky to estimate how many tens of thousands" (Wright, 1981 : 148). The Indians themselves, armed by the English, sometimes participated in securing slaves from other tribes. In 1702 the Chickasaw said, by way of example, that "in 12 years they had killed or captured for slave traders 2,300 Choctaw at a cost to themselves of over 800 men" (Mooney, 1928 : 7).

North of Virginia, diseases, particularly smallpox, created havoc among Indian populations of Maryland and Delaware between 1500 and 1700. Similarly, the large tribes of New Jersey and Pennsylvania, the Delaware and the Munsee and the Conestoga, also suffered great population losses. The Indians there maintained that they had lost 90 percent of their population because of smallpox epidemics by the middle of the seventeenth century (Mooney, 1911 : 333).

New England and New York Colonies. In the New England and New York areas a similar pattern occurred; American Indians there fared no better. Here again, warfare and disease created the most population destruction, mostly after permanent colonies were founded, especially Plymouth in 1620, and Massachusetts Bay in 1628.

It is hard to ascertain to what extent the Indians of New England and New York had been depopulated before colonies were founded. It is anyone's

---

7. John T. Juricek (1969) has provided a general discussion of the Westo Indians.

guess,[8] but we do know considerable population reduction had occurred before Plymouth was founded in 1620. To give an example, "the first great Indian plague of North America on record for the seventeenth century nearly
exterminated the Massachusetts tribe of the Algonquin nation" (Stearn and
Stearn, 1945:21). This epidemic in 1616 and 1617 was said to be especially intense around Boston Bay. It reportedly even "swept the islands in the harbor
clear of inhabitants" (Stearn and Stearn, 1945:21). Others (for example, Williams, 1909) recorded that the epidemic lasted from 1616 to 1620, not just from
1616 to 1617. The nature of the epidemic has also been debated. According to
different scholars, it was perhaps the bubonic plague or even yellow fever; it
may have been smallpox. Donald R. Hopkins (1983:234) stated that smallpox
from 1617 to 1619 "wiped out nine-tenths of the Indian population along the
Massachusetts coast." The tribes likely affected were the Abnaki, the Wampanoag, the Massachusetts, and the Pawtucket (Williams, 1909:347). Dobyns
(1983:15, 20) did not list this smallpox epidemic among those before 1700, but
he did list a bubonic plague epidemic between 1612 and 1619. Whatever and
whenever it was, the New England Indians were said to have "died on heaps."
   The English pilgrims landed the *Mayflower* at Cape Cod in 1620. Then, not
finding that area to their liking, they left and sailed to Plymouth. As a result of
the epidemic that had preceded them, "Miles Standish and his companions
found only 'a few straggling inhabitants, burial places, empty wigwams, and
some skeletons' when they arrived at Plymouth" (Hopkins, 1983:235). This
was not to their disappointment: the pilgrims noted, "Thus farre hath the
good hand of God favored our beginnings. . . . In sweeping away great mul-
titudes of the natives . . ., a little more before we went thither, that he might
make room for us there" (quoted in Williams, 1909:348).
   The picture regarding the area's American Indians becomes much clearer—
and even, much bleaker—after the founding of Plymouth and subsequent
other permanent colonies in New England and New York. Colonists preserved written records of the diseases and warfare that they brought to surrounding Indians. From New England colonists particularly, there are records
of the effects on native populations. In fact, it has been said that most of the
seventeenth-century evidence we have of smallpox among American Indians
relates to the tribes of the northeastern United States (Duffy, 1951:330).
   Following closely in time to the south and west of New England were the
Dutch West Indian Company trading posts at Fort Orange (present-day Al-
bany, New York) in 1624 and New Amsterdam (present-day New York City) in
1626. Both the trading posts and the cities that eventually grew from them had
lasting effects on Indian tribes in the New York area. There was, to give an
example, an area smallpox epidemic in 1633. According to Sherburne Cook
(1973b:485), it, along with the Boston Bay area epidemic in the 1610s, "caused
up to 100 percent mortality in local areas and killed close to 7,000 Indians in
the aggregate," and this was probably an underestimation on Cook's part.

---

8. David Quinn (1971, 1974) has discussed possible early English voyages to the New England
area.

Cook (1973b:493) reported further that, "after the decade 1630–1640, small pox was never absent among the populations of eastern North America." The disease was not always epidemic, but as Cook (1973b:493) has said, "at intervals it flared into epidemic proportions as it reached new Indian tribes, or attacked the non-immune younger generations in older territory." It became virtually endemic among surviving Indians in New England and on occasion reached epidemic proportions there.

In addition to smallpox and other European diseases, probably especially the plague, New England Indians suffered from chronic diseases such as tuberculosis and dysentery. These were also effective in reducing their numbers steadily between 1600 and 1700. Cook (1973b:501) estimated that in the seventeenth century alone four-fifths of the New England Indians died of various disease epidemics.

War and its related activities also took their toll of American Indians in New England and the future state of New York. There were five years of war between the Dutch and Indians beginning in 1640, known as the Governor Kieft War after the Dutch governor. During the war's middle years, between 1643 and 1644, almost 1,000 Indians were killed (Grumet, 1983:7). Cook (1973a:1) concluded that one-fourth of the total number of Indians in the New England area died between 1620 and 1720 due to war with Europeans.

The so-called Pequot War was fought between the Pequot Indians and European settlers in the Connecticut Valley in 1637. King Philip's War in 1675–76, between the English and the Wampanoag and the Narragansett, was named after the Wampanoag Indian Metacom whom the English called King Philip. The war involved, according to Samuel Eliot Morison (1965:110), "the toughest battle, not excepting Bunker Hill, ever fought on New England soil," in which approximately 2,000 Narragansett were either killed or burned to death on a swampy battlefield on the site of South Kingstown, Rhode Island. Balanced against the 2,000 Indian dead were English losses of 80 men, which Morison called "severe" but "worth the cost": "The Great Swamp Fight broke the power of the Narragansett" (Morison, 1965:110). Metacom was thereafter shot.

The Demise of Huronia

Although originally from the Canadian area, some of the Huron Indians eventually migrated to the United States, where they still exist today. Their story is long, complicated, and sad.

In 1608 the French established a trading post at Quebec and became closely involved with both the Huron and the Iroquois tribes. The Huron were first described by French Jesuits arriving in the Saint Lawrence Valley early in the seventeenth century. United against powerful Iroquois neighbors on the south, they were a confederacy composed of five Algonquin bands—the Attignawantan, Attigneenongnahac, Arendaronon, Tahontaenrat, and Ataronchronon—plus neighboring Petun (Khiononteteronon).

The Huron called themselves Quendat or Wendat, meaning "the one language," "the one land apart," or "the one island" (Heidenreich, 1978:368; 1971:21). There are two explanations for the name Huron: "[it] was first used

TABLE 4-1: **Huron Population History, Early 1600s to 1980**

Date	Population
Huron of Huronia	
Early 1600s	20,000–35,000
1640	10,000
Wyandot	
Mid-1660s	500
1880	251
1890	288
1900	339
1910	353
1980	1,091
Huron of Lorette	
1966	979

SOURCES: U.S. Bureau of the Census (1915:85, 1981), Heidenreich (1978:369–70), Morissonneau (1978:392), Tooker (1978:403–404).

by some French soldiers or sailors as a nickname for a group of Indians whose haircut reminded them of the ridge of erect bristles on the head of a boar (*hure* 'boar's head, bristly head'). A second explanation is that the name may be from an Old French word meaning 'ruffian, knave, lout' or simply 'unkempt person'" (Heidenreich, 1978:387).

The Huron land, Huronia, was on the northeastern tip of Lake Huron, north of present-day Toronto, where it roughly coincided with present-day Simcoe County, Ontario. It covered approximately 340 square miles, within which were barrens of pine and oak; forests of birch, maple, basswood, pine, and oak along the lakeshores; mixed forests and meadows; and large swampy areas. The Huron lived principally by growing corn, but they also grew beans, pumpkin, and squash and gathered some fruits and other vegetables. They occasionally hunted deer, and fish and shellfish were also important foods.

Estimates of the Huron population at the time of early French contacts vary widely. It may only be said that they numbered between 20,000 and 35,000 (see table 4-1). They were settled in 28 villages, whose populations ranged in size from a few hundred to the large village of Teanaustaye which had approximately 2,400 people (Heidenreich, 1971:102). Villages were relocated every 10 to 20 years, probably as surrounding soil and firewood became exhausted; and some 139 historic village sites are known to scholars (Heidenreich, 1978:375). The villages consisted of as many as 100 longhouses and perhaps more, each about 25 feet wide and 100 feet long and composed of posts covered with sheets of elm, cedar, or ash bark. The longhouses were occupied by extended Huron families. Often log palisades—in single, double, triple, or more rows—surrounded the villages.

When first contacted by the French, the Huron were at war with the powerful Iroquois Confederacy, particularly its Seneca tribe (Heidenreich, 1978:385). To promote their economically profitable fur trade, the French established friendly relations with the Huron, and they built missions to convert the Huron to Christianity, including the central one, Sainte Marie, in 1639.

About that time the unfortunate demise of Huronia and the Huron Indians commenced. The demise was caused mainly by European diseases, although it was sealed by the war with the Iroquois. From 1634 to 1640 the Huron suffered a series of depopulating epidemics, particularly of smallpox. During one epidemic in 1636, it is said: "Terror was universal. The contagion increased as autumn advanced; and when winter came, its ravages were appalling. The season of the Huron festivity was turned to a season of mourning; and such was the despondency and dismay, that suicides became frequent. . . . Everywhere was heard the wail of the sick and dying children; and on or under the platforms at the sides of the house crouched squalid men and women, in all stages of distemper" (Parkman, 1867:87).

The Huron soon lost one-half to two-thirds their population as a result of the epidemics; they numbered only about 10,000 by 1640. The sudden, severe population losses resulted in the vacating of traditional tribal leadership roles held by older men and women. Despite this leadership vacuum, there was no legitimate means whereby younger Huron might acceptably gain power within the tribe. Political factions consequently developed; and political confusion resulted, particularly regarding the impending Iroquois threat.

The decade following the epidemics, 1640 to 1650, was one of continued suffering as battle after battle with the Iroquois was fought and, unfortunately for the Huron, lost. The battles culminated in the Iroquois Campaign of 1649. Called "one of the most important battles ever fought on the North American continent" (Otterbein, 1979:141), the campaign took place in March of 1649, near Georgian Bay in present-day Ontario. The Huron were soundly defeated in the battle; some have asserted that at this time "the Hurons as a tribe had ceased to exist" (Heagerty, 1928:26). Huron survivors abandoned Huronia, their traditional land: "Some eventually found refuge at Lorette near Quebec; others fled to the Petun and ultimately to the Neutral and Erie. Some Huron dispersed to, and intermarried with, the Ottawa. A large part of the Huron were adopted by the Iroquois" (Heidenreich, 1978:387).[9]

Today only two remnants of the once huge and populous Huron Confederacy may be identified. One remnant is descended from refugees who journeyed in 1650 to Quebec with Jesuit missionaries. After some wandering around the area, the remnant settled on the Saint James River northwest of Quebec, where they remain today at Village-des-Hurons. They are often called the Huron of Lorette after the neighboring village of Jeune-Lorette. In 1966 they numbered close to 1,000 (Morissonneau, 1978:392).

The second Huron group, called today the Wyandot, had an even more troubled wandering. They fled to neighboring allies, the Petun, and even-

9. Eventually the Iroquois were depopulated by seventeenth-century smallpox epidemics. It was said of one epidemic in the early 1660s, "[it] has wrought sad havoc in their villages and has carried off many men, besides great numbers of women and children; and as a result their villages are nearly deserted, and their fields are only half-tilled" (quoted in Duffy, 1951:329). During another epidemic in 1679 the Iroquois were said to spend their time "bewailing the dead, of whom there is already an immense number" (quoted in Duffy, 1951:331).

tually moved west to Lake Michigan and Lake Superior and present-day Wisconsin late in the seventeenth century. Then they relocated south and east again to Lake Erie during the first years of the eighteenth century. The latter move was in response to continued attacks, first by the Iroquois and then by the Sioux (who have been called the Iroquois of the West), and in efforts to maintain their former fur trade with the French (Tooker, 1978:398–99). For a while the Wyandots occupied settlements in what are now the states of Ohio and Michigan and the province of Ontario, but in the 1830s and 1840s they were removed to the future Kansas Territory. At what was to become Kansas City, they obtained lands from the Delaware, who had migrated there earlier.

In the 1850s those Kansas Territory Wyandot lands were allotted to individual Huron tribal members, and some Huron moved south to northeastern Indian Territory. There they settled on the Seneca reservation, at the invitation of former enemies. A few decades later, most of the Huron remaining in Kansas moved to these lands. Between 1888 and 1890 this land, too, was allotted. Today descendants of these Huron continue to live in Oklahoma (Tooker, 1978:404).

European Reactions

Given the tremendous destruction of eastern American Indians during the sixteenth and seventeenth centuries, one might suppose that the colonists viewed it with some alarm or guilt. After all, they were the ones reponsible, directly or indirectly, intentionally or unintentionally. On the contrary, the 200-year America Indian depopulation was often considered a blessed event by colonists. The maxim that "the only good Indian was a dead one characterized relations between the whites and Indians in British North America from the beginning of colonial times" (Duffy, 1951:326). They even thought it the work of their God. For example, New England colonist Increase Mather wrote: "About this time [1631] the Indians began to be quarrelsome touching the Bounds of the Land which they had sold to the English, but God ended the Controversy by sending the Smallpox amongst the Indians of Saugust, who were before that time exceeding numerous" (quoted in Ashburn, 1947: 22). Mather noted that entire towns of New England Indians were destroyed by smallpox, with not so much as a single survivor.

This prevailing attitude of English colonists toward American Indian depopulation differed from that of many of their Spanish and French counterparts. Percy M. Ashburn (1947:19) wrote regarding the depopulation that, "in general it may be stated that the better and especially the religious elements of the Spanish and French deplored it and worried about it, while the English, religious or otherwise, seemed to look upon it as an evidence of God's favor to them, His chosen people."

Population Decline Elsewhere

American Indians in the central United States area, the Southwest, and the West declined in numbers also during the sixteenth and seventeenth centuries, particularly from smallpox epidemics. Depopulation, however, was probably not as great as in the East, where Europeans were more numerous.

Smallpox and Other Disease. The probable first smallpox epidemic in North America, from 1520 to 1524, seemingly affected Southwest tribes as well as Atlantic Coast Indians (Upham, 1986). It likely spread to the Southwest from the northern Mexico area in 1520. Following it north, the Spaniards gradually extended their contacts into the modern-day American Southwest and Texas regions. This began when Álvar Núñez Cabeza de Vaca was shipwrecked on the Texas coast in 1528; when Francisco Vásquez de Coronado journeyed to the Pueblo Indians and beyond, beginning in 1540; and when Hernando de Soto journeyed north and west along the Mississippi River during the early 1540s. These Spaniards' diseases were transmitted directly to the Indians, with the usual serious results. Thus, "almost from the moment of Cabeza de Vaca's arrival on the Texas coast in 1528, natives began dying from disease introduced by Europeans" (Aten, 1983:55): perhaps half the Indians he encountered on the coast died from cholera (Aten, 1983:59). And, following Coronado, the bubonic plague occurred among the Southwest's Pueblo Indians from 1545 to 1548.

In the seventeenth century explorers such as Louis Jolliet and René–Robert Cavelier de La Salle extended French contacts in North America southward along the Mississippi and eastern Texas rivers, where there were smallpox epidemics. For example, a 1675 expedition through western Texas "encountered three tribes that were being affected by smallpox" (Aten, 1983: 59). Smallpox appeared again in 1691, causing "death, blindness and disfigurement to the Illinois Indians living near the mouth of the Illinois River" (Stearn and Stearn, 1945:33). A few years later, in 1698–99, smallpox also appeared on the Arkansas and Mississippi rivers, decimating the Quapaw, the Tunica, and Indians farther south around Biloxi Bay in present-day Mississippi. In fact, "the whole lower Mississippi River may have been covered by the epidemic" (Stearn and Stearn, 1945:33).

Warfare. Few real European–Indian wars were fought west of the Mississippi River during the sixteenth and seventeenth centuries compared to what was happening along the East Coast, but there were numerous battles and lesser conflicts between local Indians and the Europeans who arrived. For example, the Indians of Zuni Pueblo fought a large battle with Francisco Vásquez de Coronado in 1540 (Woodbury, 1979:470), the Apaches fought the Spanish in the seventeenth century (Opler, 1983:420), and the Karankawas, in what is now Texas, fought the French late in the seventeenth century (Newcomb, 1983:361). One major war that did occur, however, was the Pueblo Revolt of 1680, which has been called "the most successful revolt by natives of the New World" (Sando, 1979:196).

Pueblo Revolt of 1680. The Eastern Pueblo Indians still make their home today in the state of New Mexico. In 1540, when Coronado contacted them they were living in 60 to 70 autonomous villages, or *pueblos,* that ranged in population from a few hundred up to perhaps 2,000. The villages were comprised of many compact homes, often rising several stories high: the total Eastern Pueblo Indian population is estimated to have been around 40,000 (Spicer, 1962:153–55).

During the decades after 1540, the Spaniards successfully subjugated the Pueblo Indians, but in 1680, 140 years after Coronado arrived, the Pueblo revolted against their Spanish oppressors. By that time all of the pueblos had been reduced significantly in population, and probably the Indians numbered 25,000 to 30,000, as opposed to the previous 40,000. There were 2,350 Spaniards on their land, most living in the town of Santa Fe (Spicer, 1962:162). The revolt was led by Popé of San Juan Pueblo and Francisco El Ollita of San Ildefonso Pueblo. It began when "a force of Tanos besieged Santa Fe, while Indians in all villages except Isleta and the Piro missions killed their resident missionaries and any other Spaniards whom they could lay their hands on" (Spicer, 1962:162–63). Soon the Spanish missions were destroyed, with 21 of 33 missionaries killed in the process, along with 375 to 400 of the 2,350 colonists (Spicer, 1962:163; Sando, 1979:196).

The Spaniards, and some Pueblo Indians friendly to them who had not joined in the revolt, retreated as far as El Paso, where they remained for 12 years. The Indians established a new pueblo south of that city, Isleta del Sur (which still exists today, although the city has grown around it).

In 1692 the Spaniards launched an extensive campaign under General Diego de Vargas to reconquer the Pueblo Indians. Some pueblos (for example, Zia, Santa Ana, and San Felipe) offered little resistance. The Cochiti fought but were defeated. The Santo Domingo deserted their village and fled west to Jemez Pueblo (Spicer, 1962:164). The Tanos pueblos also fought, joining with San Ildefonso, the most resistant pueblo. However, "eventually all except some Tanos surrendered and again submitted to Spanish rule" (Spicer, 1962:164).

The ensuing years were filled with further Pueblo-Spanish conflict, as well as conflicts among the Pueblo Indians themselves. The demographic result was disastrous, particularly as Spanish population increased. The anthropologist Edward Spicer stated that by the early 1700s, "The Tano population had been almost entirely removed from the Rio Grande either by war, by absorption into the Spanish population, or by migration westward. Pecos declined to a handful of people, Taos declined from 700 in 1707 to 505 in 1765. Zia, from a village of two or three thousand inhabitants, decreased to 508 by 1765. San Ildefonso in 1765 had a population of 484, less than half the number of a century before. Similarly San Juan, Santo Domingo, and Cochiti lost population. Only Santa Ana and the new village of Laguna increased at all" (Spicer, 1962:165). Following this decline even more Pueblo Indian depopulation occurred, but then it was due largely to two smallpox epidemics, in 1780–81 and 1788–89, in which the mortality rate was as high as half. Meanwhile, the Spanish population on Pueblo lands grew during the 1700s from 5,000 to 20,000 (Spicer, 1962:166).

DESTRUCTION FROM THE EAST TO CALIFORNIA, 1700–1800

European advances throughout North America greatly intensified during the eighteenth century. No United States region was unaffected. At the beginning of the century intensive settlements had been confined mainly to a strip of colonies along the Atlantic Coast extending from New England through North and South Carolina to Florida. In those areas there were approximately 300,000 colonists. To that figure should be added various other non-Indian settlements and population concentrations along the southern Gulf of Mexico and California coast, throughout the Southwest, and in the North American interior. These populations expanded considerably during the eighteenth century, as did the number of Africans through further, larger importations of slaves by Europeans.

Old world diseases remained the primary killers of eighteenth-century American Indians, and smallpox was still the most deadly one. One smallpox epidemic after another has been recorded in the literature of the last half of the century (Stearn and Stearn, 1943:43), and Dobyns (1983:15) noted 14 eighteenth-century smallpox epidemics among North American Indians. This is an average of one every seven plus years.

Wars continued as well: Indian-Indian wars, European-Indian wars, and American-European wars, including the American Revolution, which seriously impacted American Indians. Destruction of American Indian ways of life progressed in the century, and removals and relocations occurred, though on a relatively small scale compared with what would transpire in the nineteenth century.

Smallpox

In the northern United States area the Iroquois suffered particularly from smallpox during the eighteenth century. They had been depopulated earlier by mid-seventeenth-century smallpox epidemics, but had partially recovered and were even regaining population at the beginning of the eighteenth century. Mooney (1928:3) went so far as to assert that the Iroquois had doubled their post-smallpox population size by conquering and sometimes adopting other tribes such as the Huron, the Neutral, the Erie, and the Conestoga, as well as by intermarrying with non-Indians. But smallpox struck the Iroquois again. In 1717 a large Iroquois war expedition was "forced to return because smallpox broke out among them" (Stearn and Stearn, 1945:37). In 1731–32 another epidemic of smallpox caused them to flee in terror "in great numbers across the frontier and spread along the borders of Massachusetts and New Hampshire" (Stearn and Stearn, 1945:38). By this Iroquois dispersal smallpox was spread among other America Indian tribes, and it "attacked one tribe after another until, by 1733, it had caused great mortality among all of the Six Nations" (Stearn and Stearn, 1945:38). Smallpox also infected the Indians of New England as a result.

It is also during the eighteenth century that we find written reports of American Indians being intentionally exposed to smallpox by Europeans. In 1763 in Pennsylvania,

> Sir Jeffrey Amherst, commander-in-chief of the British forces . . . wrote in the postscript of a letter to Bouquet the suggestion that smallpox be sent among the disaffected tribes. Bouquet replied, also in a postscript, "I will try to innoculate the[m] . . . with some blankets that may fall into their hands, and

take care not to get the disease myself.". . . To Bouquet's postscript Amherst replied, "You will do well to try to innoculate the Indians by means of blankets as well as to try every other method that can serve to extirpate this exorable race." On June 24, Captain Ecuyer, of the Royal Americans, noted in his journal: "Out of our regard for them (i.e., two Indian chiefs) we gave them two blankets and a handkerchief out of the smallpox hospital. I hope it will have the desired effect." (Stearn and Stearn, 1945:44–45)

Shortly thereafter smallpox spread through tribes along the Ohio River, causing many deaths, for example, among the Mingo, the Delaware, and the Shawnee (Stearn and Stearn, 1945:45).

Smallpox also took a heavy toll in the South, where there were four epidemics in the Carolinas in 1711–12, 1738, 1759, and the late 1700s. The 1738 epidemic was said to have killed one-half of the Cherokee, with other tribes of the area suffering equally. The Cherokee, along with certain other tribes of the Southeast, also lost substantial numbers in the mid-1700s epidemic. On December 15, 1759, the *South Carolina Gazette* reported, for example: "It is pretty certain that the Smallpox has lately raged with great Violence among the Catawba Indians, and that it has carried off near one-half of that nation, *by throwing themselves into the River,* as soon as they found themselves ill— This Distemper has since appeared amongst the Inhabitants of the *Charraws* and *Waterees,* where Many Families are down; so that unless special care is taken, it must soon [spread] thro' the whole country" (quoted in Duffy, 1951:338). The *Pennsylvania Gazette* reported the following on August 13, 1760: "We learn from Cherokee country, that the People of the Lower Towns have carried smallpox into the Middle Settlement and Valley, where the disease rages with great violence, and that the People of the Upper towns are in such Dread of the Infection, that they will not allow a single Person from the above named places to come amongst them" (quoted in Duffy, 1951:338). When in 1783 smallpox struck the Cherokee again, it supposedly "broke their last resistance" (Stearn and Stearn, 1945:49) against the Americans.

In the Southwest local smallpox epidemics occurred in the New Mexico area in 1719, 1733, 1738, 1747, and 1749 (Hopkins, 1983:246). Another 1780s smallpox epidemic there is said to have killed large numbers of both American Indians and non-Indians. As was typical of such epidemics, Indians lost more than the others. Marc Simmons (1966:322) concluded: "In spite of the misery in the Spanish towns, the real brunt of the sickness fell on the Indian pueblos. At Sandia, north of Albuquerque, the priest ticked off the names of the dead as they were carried to their graves, and in the margin of his parish book he recorded the cause of death in each case: *De B—(De Viruelas)*." Simmons asserted that over 5,000 Pueblo Indians died during the epidemic.

In Texas there were American Indian smallpox epidemics from 1739 to 1778. The one in 1739 depopulated the five San Antonio missions, one around 1746 affected the Tonkawan and Atakapa tribes, one in 1750 afflicted the San Xavier Mission and the Tonkawan and Atakapa tribes, another in 1759 hit the Indian tribes of the eastern Texas area, still another occurred in 1763 at the San Lorenzo de la Santa Cruz Mission and affected the Lipan Apache in the western Texas area, yet another occurred in 1766 among the Karankawan Indian

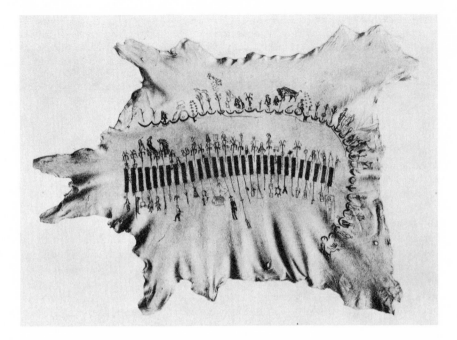

Fig. 4-1. Kiowa Winter, Summer, and Monthly Counts. Courtesy of Smithsonian Institution, National Anthropological Archives

tribes, and finally, the one in 1778 was an areawide epidemic (Ewers, 1973:
107–108).

Smallpox was present in the initial decades of the eighteenth century on the
West Coast as well. A severe 1709–10 smallpox epidemic broke out among the
Indians of southern California, "sweeping away most of the children and
many of the adults in all the missions. . . . This was followed by another epidemic in 1729–32, bringing with it horror and affliction" (Stearn and Stearn,
1943:37). The first epidemic alone reportedly killed at least 2,000 of 8,000
California Indians (Stearn and Stearn, 1945:37). In 1763 there was yet another
smallpox epidemic in California, killing more than 100 American Indians. It
started, probably unintentionally, from "a piece of cloth which a Spaniard,
just recovered from smallpox, gave to a California aborigine" (Stearn and
Stearn, 1945:44).

In 1734–35 there may have been a smallpox epidemic among the Sioux on
the plains (Mallery, 1893:300), and in 1779–80 smallpox definitely struck the
Sioux: the latter year is known as "Smallpox Used Them up Winter" (Mallery, 1893:308; also Mallery, 1886:131) in one of their winter counts. A winter
count is a pictograph recording the most significant events of a year (see Mallery, 1877b, 1886, 1893; Mooney, 1898; Praus, 1962); they were used by some
Plains tribes, particularly the Kiowa and many groups of Sioux, to record

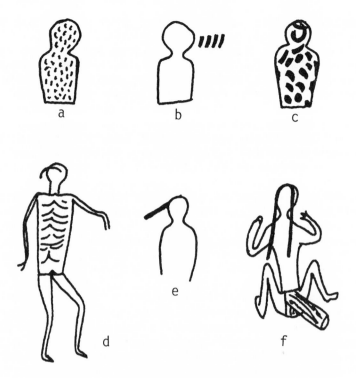

Fig. 4-2. Sioux Pictographs from Winter Counts: (a) Measles, (b) Whooping Cough, (c) Smallpox, (d) Starvation, (e) Dropsy, (f) Cholera.

tribal history (see figures 4-1 and 4-2). In the following year, smallpox struck the Sioux again, and 1780–81 is known as "Smallpox Used Them up Again Winter" (Mallery, 1893:308; also Mallery, 1886:131).

At this time smallpox also swept the Great Lakes region; the Arikara, the Mandan, and the Hidatsa; and the Columbia River in the Northwest. The pox reportedly killed about 2,000 of the Ojibwe in the Great Lakes region. The Arikara are said to have lost well over 75 percent of their people (Lehmer and Jones, 1968:91). The disease then crossed the Rocky Mountains to California again, so that the Columbia River peoples experienced similar late eighteenth-century smallpox epidemics. When a 1782–83 epidemic swept the Columbia region, reportedly after arriving from the Great Lakes after decimating the Indians there, "from all accounts it destroyed from one-third to one-half of the Indians within its area. Lewis and Clark in 1807 noted its effects at the Willamette mouth and on the coast, and it is apparent from their statements that the tribes were still far from having recovered their losses" (Mooney, 1928:13–14).

Smallpox Vaccination

In the early 1700s a slave man, Onesimus, taught Europeans in America about smallpox innoculation, or variolation, which was widely practiced in Africa. The procedure involved transferring pus from smallpox pustules of an infected patient to a noninfected individual by making incisions on the body. It was first done in the United States by Dr. Zabdiel Boylston during an epidemic in Boston and the surrounding area which, in 1721 and the early months of 1722, infected almost 6,000 people, killing, some have indicated, only between 800 and 900 of them (Stearn and Stearn, 1945: 39, 53).

Despite its apparent usefulness, innoculation was highly controversial: "Physicians, ministers, and citizens were outraged and horrified that Boylston had deliberately infected someone with smallpox" (Hopkins, 1983: 249). Innoculation continued to be somewhat controversial until 1798, when it was gradually replaced by the far more effective vaccination (Stearn and Stearn, 1945: 53; also Stearn and Stearn, 1943). Vaccination had developed in England in the late 1790s when Edward Jenner had discovered "that cowpox, naturally or artificially transmitted to man, is in itself harmless and protects the individual from smallpox" (Stearn and Stearn, 1945: 56). It quickly became widely used in England, and in 1800 the Bostonian Benjamin Waterhouse received the first vaccine from England and began to vaccinate Americans (Hopkins, 1983: 263–64). Waterhouse soon drew the attention of President Jefferson, and vaccination became widely used during the nineteenth century. Not until the last half of that century were American Indians vaccinated on a large scale, however.

Other Diseases

In addition to smallpox, there were as many as six eighteenth-century epidemics among North American Indians of measles, three of influenza, one of plague, one of typhoid, two of typhus, two of diphtheria, and two of scarlet fever (Dobyns, 1983: 15–23). Tuberculosis, syphilis, and other sexually transmitted diseases were present among them as well, as were other, less important diseases. They all devastated American Indian populations.

In New England, to give but one example, tuberculosis sometimes killed over half the American Indian children of a township or area (Cook, 1973b: 494). A 1763–64 tuberculosis epidemic on Nantucket Island struck an Indian population that had already declined due to various diseases from a seventeenth-century population of 3,000 (Cook, 1973b: 500). According to Cook (1973b: 500) the tuberculosis epidemic lasted a full six months and killed 222 out of 256 Indians infected in a total Indian population of 358 on the island. Unfortunately, Nantucket Indians declined further in the next three decades; by 1792 there were only 20 Indians left there. Similar events happened on Martha's Vineyard, where an early seventeenth-century America Indian population of about 3,000 had been reduced by diseases to only about 300 "racially-mixed" Indians by the middle of the eighteenth century (Cook, 1973b: 501–103). (See table 4-2).

Epidemics of measles, either malaria or dysentery, and either cholera or the

TABLE 4-2: **American Indian Population Decline on Martha's Vineyard and Nantucket Islands, 1642–1792**

Dates	Population	
	From	To
Martha's Vineyard		
1642–1674	3,000	1,500
1674–1698	1,500	1,000
1698–1720	1,000	800
1720–1764	800	313
Nantucket		
1659–1674	3,000	1,500
1674–1698	1,500	1,000
1698–1763	1,000	348
1763–1792	348	20

SOURCE: Cook (1973b:502–503).

bubonic plague swept Texas Indians during the eighteenth century, almost always with high mortality rates (Ewers, 1973:108). In the Pacific Northwest sexually transmitted diseases were introduced by sailors and traders in the 1780s, when ships regularly began sailing to the mouth of the Columbia River. According to Mooney (1928:14), the diseases "soon poisoned the blood of practically all the Indians west of the Cascades, resulting in a constant and rapid decay even without the agency of epidemics or wars." The Indians along the Pacific Coast and the Columbia River were also destroyed by the large quantities of liquor introduced by Russian traders. This was despite, as Mooney (1928:14) says, "the efforts of the Hudson Bay Company officers to prevent it." Meanwhile, among California Indians there were epidemics of spotted fever, syphilis, malaria, and measles (Cook, 1935:433).

The Mission Indians of California

Both the Spaniards and the French established missions among American Indians to convert them to Catholicism: the French in northeastern Canada, the Spaniards in Florida, Texas, the Southwest, and California.[10] Aside from converting many American Indians to the Catholic Church, these missions caused large reductions in Indian populations, in large part because of the diseases that they introduced and destruction of Indian ways of life.

The most elaborate and successful from the non-Indian point of view—and quite probably the most destructive—mission system was along the California coast from present-day San Diego north to just beyond present-day San Francisco. The system established by the Spanish and Mexican priests in all comprised 21 separate missions. The impact of the missions on the natives of

10. The Catholics were not the only ones to establish missions among American Indians; there were also Anglican, Episcopalian, Baptist, Methodist, Moravian, Mormon, Presbyterian, and Quaker missions among them at various times (Ronda and Axtell, 1978:9–29).

southern California was so profound that many American Indian tribes there became known as Mission Indians and are so known today.

Possibly, but only possibly, direct European contact with Indians of Alta California began as early as 1540 with the explorations of the Spaniards Hernando de Alarcón and Melchor Díaz. It is generally acknowledged, however, that the Spaniard Juan Rodríguez Cabrillo was the first non-Indian to arrive in what would become California. He did so in 1542 when he visited the southern coast (Castillo, 1978:99). But it was not until over two centuries later that much interest was shown in the area by the Spaniards or any other non-Indians.

Then, in 1769, the visitor-general of New Spain, José Galvez, organized a "sacred expedition" to establish a presidio as well as a mission at San Diego. The outpost was to be used as a way station between Baja California and a soon-to-be-established colony at Monterey. California Indian scholar Edward D. Castillo noted: "Contingents arrived in San Diego between April and July, 1769. On July 16, 1769, they founded the first of 21 California missions, and the occupation of Alta California by imperial forces of Spain became a reality" (Castillo, 1978:100).[11]

This first mission at San Diego was named San Diego de Alcalá. A second, San Carlos Borromeo, was established the following year at Carmel. Two more missions followed in 1771 and in 1772; two in 1776; and one in each of the years 1777, 1782, 1786, and 1787; two in 1791; one in 1796; three in 1797; and one each in 1798, 1804, and 1817. The final Spanish Catholic mission, San Francisco Solano, was established at Sonoma in 1823. Eleven years later, however, the entire mission system had collapsed.

California Indians were brought into mission confines sometimes forcibly, sometimes voluntarily; but once there, they were typically prevented from leaving and punished for attempted escapes. At any one time, the Indian population of single missions averaged perhaps 500 to 600, but it sometimes became as large as 1,000 to 2,000 (Cook, 1976a:86). It has been estimated that the 21 missions drew 54,000 California Indians into their confines during their existences, but that the total number of American Indian baptisms perhaps reached 81,000 (see Cook, 1976a:58–59). The Indians brought into mission confines were not only baptized and converted to Catholicism, but also tended fields of wheat, barley, beans, peas, and corn; herded cattle, sheep, and horses; worked in shops making saddles, bricks, tiles, and clothes; and performed tasks of carpentry, spinning, and blacksmithing (Phillips, 1974:294).

A main reason for the sharp population decline among Mission Indians was the high mortality rates of the new diseases to which they were exposed (see Cook, 1935). They also had a low birth rate, but that is thought to have been not so important as the increased death rates; and the low birth rate was caused in large part by high female death rates (Cook, 1940:48). Indians who

---

11. An earlier mission system had begun in Baja California by the Jesuits with the founding of Loreto in 1697. The Jesuits were replaced by Franciscans in 1768; the Dominicans arrived in 1773, founding Rosario in 1774 (Meigs, 1935:1–22). The effects on the Indians of Baja California were the same as in the north; they declined in population due to smallpox and other diseases, particularly syphilis (Meigs, 1935:155).

escaped from the missions usually returned to their lands to find only remnants of their people. Escapees were perhaps one in 24 of those subjugated (see Cook, 1976a:59).

The 65-year demographic effects of missions on California Indians have been summarized by Edward Castillo:

> The mission housing aggregated many people in a relatively small area with bad sanitation and minimal ventilation and heat, providing a favorable environment for the spread of contagious diseases. Christianization meant for many inland tribes relocating from warm interior weather to the cool damp coastal region. . . . Hispanos first infected the neophytes with venereal disease, which quickly spread to nonmission tribes as early as 1800 and thereafter increased steadily. Although it has not been proved conclusively that venereal disease decreases fertility, it certainly weakened individuals and made them more susceptible to all diseases. Three major epidemics occurred during the Spanish occupation. The first was reported at Mission Santa Clara in 1777 and was said to have been respiratory in nature. In 1802 a pneumonia and diphtheria epidemic, almost entirely confined to the young, ravaged the natives from Mission San Carlos to San Luis Obispo. The most devastating malady of this era occurred in 1806 when a measles epidemic decimated native peoples from San Francisco to Santa Barbara. In this catastrophe at least 1,600 natives died and in some missions it was reported that children under 10 years of age were almost completely wiped out. In all, modern research has determined that about 45 percent of the population decline during Spanish occupation was the direct results of introduced diseases and sickness.
>
> In addition to disease the rapid decline of Indian population under mission influence can be attributed to changes in diet and inadequate nutrition. It is doubtful that food provided in the missions was adequate. Accustomed to a rich and varied aboriginal diet of acorn, wild seeds, small game, and fish, the neophytes' diet was confined to a daily ration of a highly starchy cereal soup called atole, sometimes with a little meat. The monotonous diet had the overall effect of lowering resistance to other diseases, causing deficiency conditions such as avitaminosis, and finally causing partial or complete starvation.
>
> . . . widespread . . . was the practice of abortion to prevent births in missions. In addition, infanticide was practiced upon children born out of the forced concubinage of Indian women by priests and soldiers. A contemporary at mission San Gabriel wrote "that they necessarily became accustomed to these things, but their disgust and abhorrence never left them till many years after. In fact every white child born among them for a long period was secretly strangled and buried." (Castillo, 1978:102–104)

Little wonder that there were only 15,000 to 30,000 Indians present in the Spanish missions by 1834. They had declined even further, to only 5,000, by 1843 (Phillips, 1974:300).

Warfare

Warfare involving North American Indians was often intense in the eighteenth century. As in earlier centuries, populations of non-Indians increased on Indian lands, and the English, the French, and, later in the century, the

Americans fought for their "right" to claim ownership of parts of North America. Most of the battles and wars were in the East and South during the century. There was the Tuscarora War of 1711–12, the Yamasee War of 1715–16, and the final defeat of the Natchez in 1731. Similar wars between Indians and non-Indians took place in Florida, notably in 1703, when north-coast Apalachee towns were destroyed: many Apalachee were killed, and many more were sold as slaves.

The French and Indian War from 1755 to 1763 against the British directly reduced the populations of the Northeast tribes through casualties. It also served to spread smallpox, particularly to Canada and New York, but to New England as well. The American Revolution beginning in 1776 further reduced American Indian populations. For example, one aspect of it, the American-Cherokee War of 1776, broke the military power of the Cherokee, making them ineffectual allies with the British. Afterward, it was said of the Cherokee, "Their towns is all burned Their Corn cut down and Themselves drove into the Woods to perish and a great many of them killed" (quoted in O'Donnell, 1973:52). Indians elsewhere met similar fates as the Americans and British fought with one another.

Indians fought other Indians, too, but in large part that was because of non-Indian influences upon them, particularly among the tribes in the Southeast. In this regard, Mooney (1928:7) noted: "The populous tribes of Florida seem to have dwindled rapidly under Spanish rule, and their destruction was completed in the eighteenth century by irruptions of the Creeks, who were armed with guns by the English of Carolina, while the Spanish government refused firearms to its own Indian dependents."

Interestingly, Mooney asserted that the effects of war on Plains Indians were minimal during the 1700s, "as the hostility of the warlike tribes saved them from the demoralizing influences of intimate contact with whites" (Mooney, 1928:12). They would get theirs later. Meanwhile, in the central United States area the Fox Indians were all but destroyed by wars against the French from 1712 to 1740. Others here were also depleted by war—for example, the Shawnee, the Wea, the Miami, and the Piankashaw—and by war in conjunction with other causes of American Indian depopulation, as in the case of the Illinois.

Destruction of the Illinois Indians

Perhaps as much as for any American Indian tribe, the depopulation of the Illinois Indians during the eighteenth century resulted from the interaction of disease, war, and changed ways of life, and it has been argued that "some of the most interesting and most ambitious attempts to reconstruct the demographic history of North America have involved Illinois populations" (Johansson, 1982:136) prior to this period. In a detailed population history of the Illinois, Emily J. Blasingham summarized:

> After the arrival of European explorers and colonists in the Mississippi-Illinois drainage area, the Illinois Indians were subjected to a variety of factors which led to their eventual depopulation and virtual extinction as an

effective Indian group by the end of the 18th century. Chief among such factors were:

1) Raids on Illinois villages by other Indian groups, and as a corollary, use of the Illinois by Europeans in non-Indian inspired and non-Indian led war parties against other Indian groups
2) Diseases
3) Introduction of Christianity and monogamy
4) Excessive consumption of liquor
5) The formation of small splinter groups of Illinois Indians who were dissatisfied either with the European power sovereign over the area, or with their own native leaders. (Blasingham, 1956:373)

The Illinois were an aggregate of many American Indian groups—Kaskaskia, Maroa, Cahokia, Tamaroa, Peoria, Tapouaro, Coiracoentanon, Moingwena, Espeminkia, Chinkoa, Michigamea, and Chepoussa—forming somewhat of a confederacy (Blasingham, 1956:373; Bauxer, 1978:594; Callender, 1978:673). The area that they occupied was more or less contiguous with the boundaries of the state of Illinois, though their lands extended across the Mississippi on the west and farther south along that river, and not as far east as the border with Indiana. In aggregate, they were one of the largest American Indian groups in the central United States area at the time of the first European contacts. Probably surpassed in size there only by the more northern Ojibwe, the Illinois are estimated to have numbered over 10,500 in 1670, although by 1800 they numbered only 500 (see table 4-3).

From the first recorded European information about the Illinois until the close of the eighteenth century, they had almost innumerable small localized wars and battles with other American Indian tribes. Perhaps the most important of the earliest of these were the Iroquois, who made periodic raids into Illinois territory. The first recorded raid was in 1656, causing about 300 Illinois casualties. Subsequent conflicts occurred between 1670 and 1672, in 1680 (at which time about 700 Illinois women and children were either killed or captured, representing about 7 percent of the total Illinois population), in 1683, and 1684. Not until 30 years later did the Iroquois return, however. They apparently conducted their final raid in 1714 (Blasingham, 1956:373–75).

Meanwhile, the Iroquois were not the only Indians whom the Illinois had to fight. The Sioux had been traditional enemies, and the Illinois continued to fight with them, albeit intermittently, during the 1600s and 1700s. During this period, the Illinois also fought at one time or another the Miami, the Missouri, the Pawnee, the Osage, the Chickasaw, the Cherokee, the Shawnee, the Kaskinampo, the Fox, the Kickapoo, the Mascouten, the Sac, the Potawatomi, the Winnebago, the Menominee, and the Ojibwe. Some of these battles occurred in opposition to the French who were settling Illinois territory, some occurred with the explicit support of the French, some were even joint Illinois-French endeavors, allied fights against American Indian enemies (Blasingham, 1956:374–82).

In addition to warfare, smallpox and malaria ravaged the Illinois population during the seventeenth and eighteenth centuries. Probably, gonorrhea, measles, and other diseases were also found among them. From the late 1600s

TABLE 4-3: **Illinois Indian Population History, 1670–1980**

Date	Population
1670–80	10,500+
1700	6,000
1736	2,500
1763	1,950
1800	500
1840	200
1910	130
1956	439
1980	645

SOURCES: U.S. Bureau of the Census (1915:75, 1981), Blasingham (1956:372), Callender (1978:697).

there is evidence of a disease infecting the Illinois that could possibly have been measles. At either the end of the seventeenth century or the beginning of the eighteenth century there was the first evidence of smallpox among the Illinois. A few years later, in 1714, an unspecified epidemic killed 200 to 300 members of the tribe. Other smallpox epidemics probably followed before long, as there is documented evidence of smallpox in adjacent American Indian groups in 1732–33, 1751–52, 1756, and 1762. There was also possibly a malaria epidemic among the Illinois between 1766 and 1768, and it is not definite but quite probable that gonorrhea spread to the Illinois from the French during those years. Introduction of alcohol to the Illinois probably also reduced their population to a degree, as drunkenness apparently became a serious problem for them around 1750 and continued so until the early 1800s (Blasingham, 1956:388–90).

The Illinois had practiced polygyny quite extensively before Europeans came. Not holding to such practices, French Catholics were determined to convert the Illinois to the practice of monogamy, which, according to Blasingham, probably contributed to the depopulation of the Illinois by lowering their overall birth rate. Although monogamy often increases total fertility, Blasingham explained its effect among the Illinois as follows:

After the Illinois were converted to Catholicism the number of permissible potential mothers was probably sharply reduced. As part of their native culture, an Illinois female did not have intercourse with her husband as long as she nursed her child. This period of nursing could last as long as four years, the minimal period being at least two years, since a child would not be able to subsist entirely on meat, corn and squash much before that date. Also, even if the prohibition against intercourse was not observed, it is doubtful if a female would conceive during the lactation period. As a consequence, while the number of births per married female probably did not appreciably decrease or increase during the two generations after the inception of intensive White contact and conversion to Catholicism, the total number of births for the Illinois as a whole probably decreased by 1720, due to the reduction in number of females who were bearing full-blood Illinois children. (Blasingham, 1956:387).

Having converted the Illinois to monogamy and Catholicism, the French could more or less respectably intermarry with the Indians. Consequently, marriages between Frenchmen and Illinois women increased. This further depopulated the Illinois through racially mixed offspring, some of whom were perhaps not considered as Illinois, though children of such unions tended to be raised as Indians, not Frenchmen or French-Americans.

A final factor contributing to Illinois depopulation was what might be called "social splintering," that is, the formation of groups departing from the main Illinois tribal body, which before much European contact, had been fairly cohesive. After the mid-1700s, under French, English, Spanish, and United States influences, serious tribal splits developed as one Illinois group or another would become aligned with one or another non-Indian group. The first serious split was between the pro-British and pro-American Kaskaskia and the pro-French and pro-Spanish Peoria. A second split developed when some of the formerly pro-Spanish Peoria joined with the pro-British Piankashaw Indians. Later some of the Peoria joined the Caddo Indians on the Ouachita River and became closer to them and other tribes on the south in present-day Missouri and Arkansas than to their former Illinois confederates.

Given such complex happenings over so long a period of time, all resulting in Illinois depopulation to a greater or lesser extent, it is a wonder that any Illinois Indians exist today. Yet some do. They live under the name Peoria in northeastern Oklahoma, having settled on a reservation in Indian Territory in 1867. A total of 439 Peoria were identified in 1956; 645 Peoria and related Indians were reported in the 1980 census (see table 4-3, again).

SEEDS OF MASSIVE REMOVAL

It was during the seventeenth and eighteenth centuries, particularly the eighteenth, that the seeds of the massive removals of American Indians to reservation lands by the United States government were sown. In the seventeenth century this took the form of colonial governments restricting many eastern American Indians to particular areas. The governments established, for example, both "praying towns" for Christianized Indians in New England and various state reservations such as the Mashpee Reservation on Cape Cod (1660), the Poosepatuck Reservation on Long Island (1666), the Pequot Reservation in Connecticut (1683), the Fall River Reservation in Massachusetts (1709), and the Gay Head Reservation on Martha's Vineyard (1711). These were localized relocations of American Indians, but other tribes were persuaded to leave former tribal lands for new ones farther west; for example, the Stockbridge, who had moved to New York from Massachusetts by 1789 and then moved to present-day Wisconsin in the early 1800s.

These movements were precedents for the massive removals and relocations of American Indian tribes in the nineteenth century, which were accomplished by the U.S. War Department, established in 1789. Indian affairs were a function of that department, as was the acquisition of Indian land, supposedly only with the Indians' consent. Eventually the creation of a federal reservation system followed from article 3 of the act creating the War Department which stated: "The utmost good faith shall always be observed towards the Indians; their land and their property, rights and liberty shall never be invaded or disturbed, unless in just and lawful wars authorized by Congress, but laws founded in justice and humanity shall from time to time be made, for preventing wrongs being done to them, and for preserving peace and friendship with them" (Prucha, 1975:12). As we shall see in Chapter 5, neither the acquisition of Indian land nor the relocation of Indians on new lands happened exactly in that way. To the contrary!

THE NET EFFECT

In sum the European expansion throughout North America during the sixteenth, seventeenth, and eighteenth centuries produced a demographic collapse of American Indians, primarily because of disease, warfare, and destruction of Indian ways of life. The removal and relocation of Indians also contributed to the collapse, but probably in only a small way. The collapse was so severe that by 1800 the total United States American Indian population had been reduced to 600,000 from 5+ million in three centuries. Meanwhile, the non-Indian population of the United States had increased to over 5 million (U.S. Bureau of the Census, 1982–83:6).

5. DECLINE TO NADIR: 1800 TO 1900

Many have died of diseases we have no name for.
—LITTLE WOLF (CHEYENNE)

The Apaches were once a great nation; they are now but few, and because of this they want to die and so carry their lives on their fingernails.
—COCHISE (APACHE)

Wherever we went the soldiers came to kill us, and it was all our own country.
—BLACK ELK (SIOUX)

THE NINETEENTH CENTURY was the last century of total American Indian population decline. The total Indian population reached nadir around the end of the century, and thereafter it started to increase, though the decrease of some tribes continued into the twentieth century, while others had started to increase earlier (some increases were followed by further declines [see, for example, Meister, 1976; Paredes and Plante, 1982]). More abundant and complete information exists on nineteenth-century American Indian populations than on the populations of earlier centuries. It is therefore possible to provide more detail on the nineteenth-century population reductions produced by the four causes outlined in Chapter 3: disease, warfare and genocide, removal and relocations, and destruction of ways of life.

SMALLPOX AND OTHER DISEASES

Dobyns (1983:15–23) noted 27 nineteenth-century epidemics of Old World pathogens among North American Indians: 13 of smallpox, five of measles, three of cholera, two of influenza, and one each of diphtheria (in Canada), scarlet fever (in Canada), tularemia, and malaria. According to Dobyns, more epidemics occurred between 1800 and 1900 than during any of the three previous centuries (although this may indicate only greater information about American Indians of the nineteenth century). Other diseases, such as syphilis and tuberculosis, also devastated American Indians during the century.

The 13 major smallpox epidemics noted by Dobyns are also the most major smallpox epidemics known to have taken place during any century. They include two especially devastating pandemics: one in 1801–1802 and another between 1836 and 1840.

1801–1802 Smallpox Pandemic

The 1801–1802 smallpox pandemic occurred among tribes of the central and northwestern regions of the United States. During it the Omaha were all but destroyed, as were their neighbors the Ponca, the Oto, and the Iowa. The pandemic spread north along the Missouri River, devastating the Arikara, the Gros Ventre, the Mandan, the Crow, and the Sioux. Smallpox was transmitted to the Pacific Northwest when the Crow carried it to what was to become Washington Territory and to the Flathead Indians. In the Northwest it also infected the Semte'use, the Pend d'Oreille, the Kalispel, the Colville, the Spokane, and the Salish tribes along the Columbia River, where it eventually subsided. It is said that in the Northwest, "the Spokane suffered the worst, though all were seriously affected" (Stearn and Stearn, 1945:76).

The pandemic even raged down the Mississippi River to the Louisiana gulf, where it did not stop but spread into Texas, the rest of the Southwest, and the southern plains. It was brought to the Kiowa in northeastern Texas by a Pawnee war party returning from present-day New Mexico. From the Kiowa, the smallpox spread to adjacent Indian peoples: "The prairie tribes are said to have lost more than half their population at this time, while the Wichita, Caddo, and others in the south suffered almost as severely" (Mooney, 1898:168).

The Omaha Odyssey. One very strange reaction to the smallpox pandemic of 1801–1802 was that of the Omaha in present-day Nebraska. The tribe was originally from the Appalachian Mountains and possibly from as far east as the Atlantic Coast. They and other Siouan language peoples had made an extended migration west to the Mississippi River, the Missouri River, and beyond. The Omaha are related to, among others, the Ponca, the Osage, the Kansa, and the Quapaw. The five tribes had split into separate groups a few hundred years before 1800 and sometimes remained on less than friendly terms (see Smith, 1973). The name Omaha, meaning "against the current," comes from one of these separations. It differentiated the Omaha from the Quapaw, whose name means "with the current." The two tribes parted along a river, one going upstream, one going downstream. The Omaha's word for themselves is *uki'te*; it means "tribe," when used as a noun, and "to fight," as in war, when used as a verb: "The word *uki'te*, as 'tribe,' explains the common obligation felt by the Omaha to defend, as a unit, the community, the tribe" (Fletcher and LaFlesche, 1911:36).

The Omaha migrated to present-day northeastern Nebraska during the late 1700s. They settled on a stream flowing into the Missouri that they called Village or Omaha Creek, where they built their Large Village. Late in the eighteenth century they numbered 3,000 to 3,500, and they were one of the most powerful prairie tribes before they contracted both smallpox and cholera at Large Village, either in the winter of 1800–1801, or the summer and fall of 1802 (Smith 1973:268).

The two diseases, cholera and particularly smallpox, ravished the unfortunate Omaha in a very short time, causing widespread death and disfigurement: "It is said that when the enfeebled survivors saw the disfigured appearance of their children and companions they resolved to put an end to their existence, since both comeliness and vigor were gone" (Fletcher and LaFlesche, 1911:86). They even thought future children would inherit the smallpox and disfigurements of their parents. Deciding to destroy themselves as a people rather than

TABLE 5-1: **Omaha Indian Population History, Late 1700s to 1980**

Date	Population
Late 1700s	3,000–3,500
1802	Less than 300
1876	1,076
1882	1,100
1884	1,179
1910	1,105
1930	1,103
1960	1,100 (approximately)
1975	2,600
1980	3,090

SOURCES: Dorsey (1884:214), Fletcher and LaFlesche (1911:33), U.S. Bureau of the Census (1915:101, 1981), Ross (1970:22), Liberty (1975:225, 227).

wait for the disease to do it, the small group of surviving Omaha chose to die fighting and formed a villagewide war party to confront their traditional enemy, the Cheyenne (Fletcher and LaFlesche, 1911:87).

Marching west toward the territory of the Cheyenne, the Omaha encountered their relatives the Ponca. An argument ensued, leading first to battle, then eventual reconciliation. Continuing their death march, the Omaha fought not only the Cheyenne but also the Pawnee and the Oto. Finally, the Omaha grew weary of both battle and disease and realized they might not all be destroyed by the smallpox. The few survivors struggled back to the village site on Omaha Creek. They soon abandoned it, however, because of harassment by the Dakota Sioux and the Ponca from the north and the Oto and the Pawnee from the south and west. Unable completely to forget Large Village, they used the site as a burial ground, sometimes journeying long distances for a funeral.

One dying from smallpox during this time was the celebrated Omaha chief Washinga Sakba ("the Blackbird"). According to George Catlin (1844, 2:6), he was buried on a high bluff overlooking the Missouri River, astride his favorite white horse "with his bow in his hand, and his shield and quiver slung—with his pipe and his *medicine-bag*—with his supply of dried meat, and his tobacco-pouch replenished to last him through his journey to the 'beautiful hunting grounds of the shades of his fathers'—with his flint and steel, and his tinder, to light his pipes by the way." (Catlin [1844, 2:6] also reported having secretly exhumed the skull of Washinga Sakba, to add it, as he said, to "others which I have collected on my route.")

The Omaha eventually increased slightly in numbers, as is shown in table 5-1, partly by avoiding devastation in an 1830s smallpox pandemic which destroyed many tribes farther north. They were relatively untouched by the pandemic probably because they had submitted earlier to some smallpox vaccination by the United States government (see Trimble, 1983), although they did suffer in it. As shown in table 5-2, the pandemic killed over 300 of them. The tribe also had subsequent epidemics of cholera, measles, and tuberculosis; but

TABLE 5-2: **Mortality of Nineteenth-Century Epidemics Among the Omaha Indians**

Date	Epidemic	Mortality
1801–1802	Smallpox	75% (over 1,500)
1837	Smallpox	Over 300
1849	Cholera	Over 500
1874	Measles	76
1888	Measles	87
1889	Measles	50

NOTE: There were, in addition, unknown tuberculosis epidemics.
SOURCE: Liberty (1975:228).

their mortality is thought not to have been as great as from the earlier small-pox and cholera epidemics.

Today the Omaha have a reservation encompassing but a very small part of their traditional lands in northeast Nebraska. It does not contain the site of Large Village. In the 1980 census they numbered about 3,000, perhaps fewer than when they first encountered the white man.

Other Early Nineteenth-Century Smallpox Epidemics

In 1810–11 smallpox was present around the Great Lakes and on the northern plains. It affected some Sioux especially severely: 1810 is known as the "Winter of the Smallpox Epidemic" in one of their winter counts (Praus, 1962:10).

There was another, less severe smallpox epidemic in 1815 and 1816 along the Red River and the Rio Grande. The Comanches said they lost 4,000 in it, out of a population of 10,000. Both the Iowa and the Kiowa reportedly also suf-fered (Mooney, 1898:168; Stearn and Stearn, 1945:78). Two years later, in 1818–19, there was a localized though severe epidemic along the White River in present-day South Dakota, affecting especially the Assiniboin and the Sioux there (Stearn and Stearn, 1945:78): The year is known once more as "Smallpox Used Them up Again Winter" in a Sioux winter count (Mallery, 1893:317).

There was not another widespread American Indian smallpox epidemic un-til the mid-1830s, but there were serious outbreaks among California Indians (both northern and Mission Indians), among the Osage on the plains, and among the Coeur d'Alene in the Northwest. One hundred and eighty Kansa died from a 1827 smallpox epidemic (Unrau, 1973:318). In the early 1830s the Pawnee had an epidemic that may have killed half of their 20,000.

1836–40 Smallpox Pandemic

Between 1836 and 1840 there was another massive smallpox pandemic ranging primarily from the northern plains to the Pacific Northwest, Canada, and Alaska. It was perhaps the most severe episode of any disease among North American Indians, although it may very well only be the best documented. It is said that the smallpox was brought to the northern plains by a steamboat traveling the Missouri River, and killed 10,000 American Indians there in but a few weeks. The total numbers of American Indians thought to have died are overwhelming: 6,000 to 8,000 Blackfoot, Piegans, and Bloods; 2,000 Pawnee; virtually all of several thousand Mandan; one-half the 4,500 Arikara and Minnetaree; many Osage; one-third of 3,000 Crow; 400 Yanktonai Dakota; over one-half of 8,000 Assiniboin; and three-fifths of the north-central California Indians (probably an exaggeration). Traders carried the smallpox south, where it infected the Choctaw, killing 400 to 500 of them, including their famous chief Mosholatubbee ("he who puts out and kills"). Specific numbers are not recorded, but the pox is known also to have killed many Chickasaw in 1838, as well as infecting other southern tribes and the Kiowa, the Apache, the Gros Ventre, the Winnebago (including the well-known Wahcheehahska, "the man who puts all out of doors"), the Comanche, the Cayuse, and other New Mexico, Canada, and Alaska Indians (Schoolcraft, 1851:577, 599; Mooney, 1898:274−75; Stearn and Stearn, 1945:94).

Regarding the Assiniboin dead, settlers in the area said that "for many weeks together our workmen did nothing but collect the dead bodies and bury them in large pits; but since the ground is frozen we are obliged to throw them into the river" (quoted in Stearn and Stearn, 1945:89−90). It was probably this pandemic that killed 100 Kansa in a "very short time"; it was recorded that "the awful cries of the Indians around the dead sounded in our ears nearly every day" (Unrau, 1973:318).

In a Kiowa winter count, 1839−40 is noted as Ta'dalkop Sai ("Smallpox Winter"): "The disease is indicated in the conventional manner by means of the figure of a man covered with red spots" (Mooney, 1898:274). In one of the Sioux winter counts, 1837 is known as the "Winter of the Second Smallpox Epidemic" (Praus, 1962:15). Perhaps in part because of smallpox, many Sioux women committed suicide in the 1830s, as Pierre Antoine Tabeau reported (Abel, 1939:183). Of this pandemic among one band of Sioux, it was said: "Every other man amongst them was slain by it: and O-wapa-shaw, the greatest man of the Sioux, with half his band, died under corners of fences, in little groups, to which kindred ties held them in ghastly death, with their bodies swollen, and covered with pustules, their eyes blinded, hideously howling their death song in utter despair" (quoted in Hopkins, 1983:272).

Mandan Tragedy. Many tragic stories may be told of American Indians following the European arrival. I have told some; I will tell others. None is as tragic as what happened to the Mandan and to their second chief, Mahtotohpa, or Four Bears, after exposure to the smallpox pandemic in the late summer and early fall of 1837.

The Mandan lived in the Missouri River valley in the future Dakota Territory. They are generally considered to have been the first agricultural people to migrate to the area. Over the previous 1,000 years they had supplanted earlier groups there by northward movement up the Missouri River. In pre-European times the Mandan may have occupied as many as nine villages, but when encountered by the French explorer Pierre Gaultier de Varennes, Sieur de La Vérendrye, and his sons in 1738, they occupied six earth-lodge villages on the Missouri River bluffs. Their total population then has been estimated as high as 15,000, but this probably is somewhat of an exaggera-

TABLE 5-3: **Mandan Population History, 1738–1980**

Date	Population
1738	15,000
1750	9,000
1780	3,600
1837 (June)	1,600–2,000
1837 (October)	138
1855	252
1866	400
1877	420
1890	251
1904	250
1910	209
1929	329
1937	355
1980	1,013

SOURCES: U.S. Bureau of the Census (1915:100, 1981), Mooney (1928:13), Glassner (1974:45–46).

tion. They had been reduced to only about 1,600 to 2,000 by the 1830s, primarily as a result of smallpox and other diseases, especially cholera (see table 5-3). They then were living in only two villages on opposite sides of the Missouri River.

The artist George Catlin visited the Mandan on his 1830s tour of American Indian tribes. He painted a number of pictures of them and their two villages, and was particularly awed by Four Bears, whose portrait is figure 5-1. Catlin (1844, 1:114) described Four Bears as "the most popular man of the Mandans—a high-minded and gallant warrior, as well as a polite and polished gentleman." Nevertheless, a few years later Four Bears was dead, and the Mandan were almost removed from the face of the earth.

Steamboats had been traveling the upper Missouri River for years before 1837, dispatched by Saint Louis fur companies for trade with the Mandan and other Indians. At 3:00 P.M. on June 19, 1837, the American Fur Company steamboat *St. Peter's* arrived at the Mandan villages after stopping at Fort Clark just downstream. Some aboard the steamer had smallpox when the boat docked. It soon was spread to the Mandan, perhaps by deckhands who unloaded merchandise, perhaps by chiefs who went aboard a few days later, or perhaps by women and children who went aboard at the same time (Chardon, 1932:118–19; also Schoolcraft, 1851:577). (On its way up the Missouri, the *St. Peter's* surely had passed by the Omaha and perhaps was seen by survivors of their odyssey 35 years earlier.)

On July 14, 1837, the first casualty of the smallpox occurred among the Mandan. It was recorded in the journal of Francis A. Chardon, an employee of the American Fur Company at Fort Clark: "*Friday 14*—One of the warmest days that we have had this summer—Weather smokey—a young Mandan died today of the Small Pox—several others has caught it—the Indians all being out Makeing dried Meat has saved several of them" (Chardon, 1932:121).

Fig. 5-1. Chief Four Bears of the Mandan, by George Catlin. Courtesy of Smithsonian Institution, National Museum of American Art

Less than two weeks later Chardon recorded that the Mandan second chief, Four Bears, had caught the disease: "*Wednesday 26*—The Rees and Mandans all arrived to day well loaded with Meat, Mitchel also arrived with 150 pieces. The 4 Bears (Mandan) has caught the small pox, and got crazy and has disappeared from camp—he arrived here in the afternoon—the Indians of the

Little Village all arrived in the evening well loaded with dried Meat—the small pox has broke out among them, several has died" (Chardon, 1932:123).

On the following day Chardon recorded four more deaths at the Mandan village. On the day after that he reported an attempt by a young Mandan to kill him. On Sunday, July 30, he recorded death threats for bringing smallpox to the Indians, and even more Mandan dying. By then the Mandan village was in disarray from the disease.[1] George Catlin gives an account of the situation, as conveyed to him:

> It seems that the Mandans were surrounded by several war-parties of their more powerful enemies the Sioux, at that unlucky time, and they could not therefore disperse upon the plains, by which many of them could have been saved; and they were necessarily inclosed within the piquets of their village, where the disease in a few days became so very malignant that death ensued in a few hours after its attacks; and so slight were their hopes when they were attacked, that nearly half of them destroyed themselves with their knives, with their guns, and by dashing their brains out by leaping head-foremost from a thirty foot ledge of rocks in front of their village. The first symptom of the disease was a rapid swelling of the body, and so very virulent had it become, that very many died in two or three hours after their attack, and that in many cases without the appearance of the disease upon the skin. Utter dismay seemed to possess all classes and all ages, and they gave themselves up in despair, as entirely lost. There was but one continual crying and howling and praying to the Great Spirit for his protection during the nights and days; and there being but few living, and those in too appalling despair, nobody thought of burying the dead, whose bodies, whole families together, were left in horrid and loathsome piles in their own wigwams, with a few buffalo robes, etc. thrown over them, there to decay and be devoured by their own dogs. . . .
>
> So have perished the friendly and hospitable Mandans, from the best accounts I could get; and although it may be *possible* that some few individuals may yet be remaining, I think it is not probable; and one thing is certain, even if such be the case, that, as a nation, the Mandans are extinct, having no longer an existence. (Catlin, 1973, 2:257, 258)

The Mandan—fully 1,600 to 2,000 before the smallpox—numbered few more than 100 people after the pandemic (see table 5-3, again).

On Sunday, July 30, 1837, the beloved leader Four Bears made a speech to his people:

> My Friends one and all, Listen to what I have to say—Ever since I Can remember, I have loved the Whites, I have lived With them ever since I was a Boy, and to the best of My Knowledge, I have Never Wronged a White Man, on the Contrary, I have always Protected them from the insults of Others, Which they cannot deny, The 4 Bears never saw a White Man hungry, but what he gave him to eat, Drink, and a Buffaloe skin to sleep on, in time of Need, I was always ready to die for them, Which they cannot deny. I have

---

1. Catlin asserted the ravages of this pandemic between 1836 and 1840 among other American Indians "as it spread to other continuous tribes, to the Minatarrees, the Knisteneaux, the Black-feet, the Cheyennes and Crows; amongst whom 25,000 perished in the course of four or five months" (Catlin, 1844, 2:258).

done every thing that a red Skin could do for them, and how they have re-
paid it! With ingratitude! I have Never Called a White Man a Dog, but to
day, I do Pronounce them to be a set of Black harted Dogs, they have de-
ceived Me, them that I always considered as Brothers, has turned Out to be
My Worst enemies, I have been in Many Battles, and often Wounded, but
the Wounds of My enemies I exhalt in, but to day I am Wounded, And by
Whom, by those same White Dogs that I have always Considered, and
treated as Brothers, I do not fear *Death* my friends. You Know it, but to *die*
with my face rotten, that even the Wolves will shrink With horror at seeing
Me, and say to themselves, that is the 4 Bears the Friend of the Whites—
    Listen well what I have to say, as it will be the last time you will hear Me.
Think of your Wives, Children, Brothers, Sisters, Friends, and in fact all that
you hold dear, are all Dead, or Dying, with their faces all rotten, caused by
those dogs the whites, think of all that My friends, and rise all together and
Not leave one of them alive, The 4 Bears will act his Part—. (Chardon,
1932:124–25)

That same day Four Bears died. Catlin described the death, as told to him:

This fine fellow sat in his wigwam and watched every one of his family die
about him, his wives and his little children, after he had recovered from the
disease himself; when he walked out, around the village, and wept over the
final destruction of his tribe; his braves and warriors, whose sinewy arms
alone he could depend on for a continuance of their existence, all laid low;
when he came back to his lodge, where he covered his whole family in a pile,
with a number of robes, and wrapping another around himself, went out
upon a hill at a little distance, where he laid several days, despite all the solic-
itations of the Traders, resolved to *starve* himself to death. He remained
there until the sixth day, when he had just strength enough to creep back to
the village, when he enterd the horrid gloom of his own wigwam, and laying
his body along-side of the group of his family, drew his robe over him and
died on the ninth day of his fatal abstinence. (Catlin, 1844, 2:258)

There are Mandan today, but they are a relatively small American Indian
tribe. Many are mixed with other tribes on the Fort Berthold Reservation in
North Dakota. Four Bears's shirt is on display in the National Museum of
Natural History of the Smithsonian Institution, Washington, D.C.

Other Smallpox Epidemics, 1840–1900

From 1840 to the midcentury smallpox further destroyed American Indians,
though not as severely as in preceding decades. It was present among tribes in
the Oregon area in 1841, among tribes in central California in 1844, among the
Crow in 1845, among the Walla Walla in present-day Washington in 1846,
among the Iowa in 1848, and among the Coeur d'Alene and the Dakota Sioux
in 1850 (Stearn and Stearn, 1945:91–93).
    Smallpox continued widespread destruction for 50 years. For example, the
year 1850–51 is known as "The Big Smallpox Winter" in Sioux winter counts
(Mallery, 1893:323); in 1852 smallpox struck New Mexico Territory, killing
hundreds of Pueblo Indians; and from 1852 to 1854 it occurred among American Indian groups in the territories of Oregon, Washington, and Minnesota.
It was on the upper Missouri River again in 1856, killing perhaps one-fourth

of the Arikara and the Gros Ventre, and a few of the surviving Mandan. Smallpox attacked the Kickapoo in 1857, the Winnebago in 1860, and the Kiowa,
the Cheyenne, the Arapaho, the Sioux, the Seneca, the Cayuga, the Onon-
daga, the Jicarilla Apache, and the Ute in 1861–62. The winter of 1861–62
is also known as "Smallpox Winter" in a Kiowa winter count (Mooney,
1898 : 311). In 1864 smallpox was present among the Stockbridge, the Munsee,
the Oneida, and the Menominee; in 1865–66, among the Tonawanda of New
York; in the late 1860s, among tribes of the Arizona Territory and Montana;
in 1872–73, among the Santee Sioux; in 1873, among the Stockbridge, the
Munsee, the Oneida, and the Menominee again; in 1876, among the Apache;
in 1877, among the Pima, the Maricopa, and the Papago; in 1882, among the
Osage, the Kaw, and the Quapaw; in 1883, among the Ojibwe, the Ute, and
the Pueblo Indians; and in 1894, among the Blackfoot. In 1898 smallpox infected the Pueblo Indians again and the Navajo. In 1899–1900 it infected the
Creek and the Jicarilla Apache once more, the Sac and Fox, various Indian
tribes on the Colville Reservation in the state of Washington, the Choctaw,
the Chickasaw, the Seminole, the Mescalero Apache, the Crow, the Ojibwe
(again), the Shawnee, the Yakima, and the Yankton Sioux (Stearn and Stearn,
1945 : 95–115). (Some or all of these later two smallpox occurrences in 1898 and
1899–1900 may not have been the more serious of the three smallpox viruses,
Variola major, but the mildest one, *Variola minor*.)

Smallpox Vaccination and Health Care

Since smallpox was so destructive during the nineteenth century, there were
efforts to control it, which had started in the preceding century with the development of vaccination. In 1801, President Thomas Jefferson caused the first
American Indians to be vaccinated, rather than just innoculated; they were
members of a delegation of warriors visiting the District of Columbia (Stearn
and Stearn, 1943 : 603). Two years later, the explorers Meriwether Lewis and
William Clark were instructed by the president to vaccinate Indians whom
they encountered during their travels. Jefferson wrote them: "Carry with you
some matter of kinepox. Inform those of them with whom you may be of its
efficacy as a preservative from the smallpox; and instruct and encourage them
(i.e., the Indians) in the use of it. This may be especially done wherever you
winter" (quoted in Stearn and Stearn, 1943 : 603). Kinepox (*Variola vaccinia*)
is another name for cowpox, from which smallpox vaccine is derived. Lewis
and Clark do not seem to have done much in this regard, partly because they
lacked enough vaccine, which was still only obtainable from England (Stearn
and Stearn, 1943 : 603, 1945 : 56).[2]

In the following three decades isolated attempts were made by the United
States government to vaccinate certain groups of American Indians (for example, the Pawnee), and particularly, attempts were made by the Mexican
government, which still controlled areas of the present-day United States,

2. One is referred to Thwaites (1904–1905) for the complete journals of the Lewis and Clark
expedition.

including, for example, some Pueblo and California Indians (Stearn and Stearn, 1943:606–607).

During the presidency of Andrew Jackson the United States government enacted the following legislation on May 5, 1832: "That it shall be the duty of several Indian agents and sub-agents under the direction of the Secretary of War to take such measures as he shall deem most efficient to convene the Indian tribes in their respective towns, or in such other places and numbers and at such seasons as shall be most convenient to the Indian populations, for the purpose of arresting the progress of smallpox among the several tribes by vaccination" (quoted in Stearn and Stearn, 1945:62–63). There was a huge appropriation of $12,000 to carry out the act.

Yet despite the act it took a long time for American Indians to be vaccinated, even when they were in imminent danger of smallpox infection, for example, during the great smallpox pandemic between 1836 and 1840. This was due partially to Indian resistance. For example, among the Plains Indians, it was said that "they see white men urging the operation so earnestly they decide that it must be some new mode or trick of the pale face by which they hope to gain some new advantage over them" (quoted in Stearn and Stearn, 1943:608–609). Most of the failure to vaccinate Indians, however, probably was due to lack of interest on the part of United States officials. The Kansa Indians were not vaccinated though they lived near the Santa Fe Trail, a locale making them vulnerable to smallpox and other contagious disease carried along it by settlers: "Not surprisingly, then, their ranks were reduced with a vengeance in the middle of June 1855, and before the summer was over more than four hundred had died" (Unrau, 1973:319). Equally appalling is a concurrent comment by the U.S. Indian agent for the Kansa: "[smallpox] has continued fatally with a greater number of them, it seems, to the great satisfaction and admiration of all those [who] have any acquaintance with [them]" (quoted in Unrau, 1973:319–20).

Vaccination of American Indians did eventually succeed in reducing mortality from smallpox: Mooney (1898:176) asserted that it was the 1861–62 smallpox epidemic that spurred the U.S. government into action, particularly regarding the western tribes. As a result the epidemics of the late 1800s, though numerous, were less severe than those of the early 1800s. Stearn and Stearn (1945:102–103) state: "Although there was a comparatively large number of smallpox epidemics between 1870 and the end of the nineteenth century, the story for the most part is one of localizing the outbreaks by active precautionary measures, and reducing the mortality by active efforts at vaccination." (Remember, however, that some of the very late nineteenth-century epidemics may have been of the mild form of smallpox, *Variola minor*.)

United States government treaties sometimes provided for smallpox vaccination, as well as medicine and physicians. At least, these sometimes were provided as long as the Indians remained where the government claimed that they belonged—on their reservations (Stearn and Stearn, 1943:609). Some scholars have argued that because of vaccination late nineteenth-century American Indians felt the effects of smallpox less than adjacent populations of non-Indians (Stearn and Stearn, 1945:59).

Not only vaccination reduced mortality from smallpox; general health care was also important. Traditional Indian responses had mainly been ineffective; some even increased mortality. The Pima Indians in the late 1870s considered the disease an evil spirit to be placated by saying, "I like smallpox" (Stearn and Stearn, 1945:104). They feared it so that, when vaccinated, they placed "the bandages from the innoculated arms upon a certain mesquite tree" (Stearn and Stearn, 1945:104). A Kiowa chief in 1861–62 "offered a fine black-eared horse, hobbling and tying it to a tree in the hills, and allowing it to perish, as a sacrifice with a prayer for the protection of himself and family and friends" (Stearn and Stearn, 1945:100). A more typical American Indian response to smallpox symptoms was a session in a sweathouse followed by a plunge into cold water, a procedure that was likely to increase the seriousness of the illness. Other treatments also involved cold water: the Comanche were said to take cold baths when smallpox broke out (Berlandier, 1969:84); the Osage were said "to eat a great abundance of boiled corn and pumpkin and to bathe in the river" (quoted in Heagerty, 1928:63).[3] Some tribes, such as the Spokane, reported to have had more or less effective herbal treatments for smallpox (Heagerty, 1928:63).

With the health care sometimes provided by treaties came the elimination of various harmful American Indian practices and improved smallpox survival rates. For example, when 632 Pueblo Indians were infected with smallpox in 1898, 412 were under the care of physicians, and only 42 of them died, about 10 percent, whereas 163 of the other 220 died, or about 74 percent (Stearn and Stearn, 1945:15).

Health care and vaccination not only reduced smallpox mortality, they also prevented debilitating aftereffects. E. Wagner Stearn and Allen E. Stearn have explained that, "previously, in the absence of care, those who survived an attack of smallpox frequently were not only disfigured but suffered from such complications and after-effects as blindness, deafness, inflammation of the throat, lungs, kidneys and joints. Sometimes insanity followed an attack of the disease, and a disabled mentality due to terror was not rare even among those not actually attacked" (Stearn and Stearn, 1945:95).[4]

---

3. There is a story, with regard to cold-water smallpox treatments, of the vengeance of one American Indian tribe upon another: "In 1845, after the Crows had struck a mortal blow at the Blackfeet, smallpox attacked the former and spread rapidly from lodge to lodge. The Blackfeet, whose usual habitat was the great plain of Saskatchewan in the provinces of Alberta and Assiniboia, though they sometimes ranged into the northern part of Montana, had suffered severely from this plague in 1837–38. The Crows therefore asked their captives by what means they had escaped death. The Blackfeet, intending to revenge themselves, counselled cold baths as the only remedy to stop the progress of the disease. The sick immediately plunged into the water, and mothers went to the river to bathe their sick children. Soon cries of despair succeeded the shouts of victory, desolation and mourning replaced the barbarous joy of the Crows, for death visited every tent of the victorious camp" (Stearn and Stearn, 1945:91).

4. An absence of much disfigurement among a nonvaccinated group has been used to argue a low survival rate. Jean Berlandier (1969:84) asserted, regarding smallpox among the Comanche, "Very few of them show scars of this scourge, and since none of them has even been vaccinated, this is an indication of the small numbers who survive it."

Other Diseases

Smallpox was not the only nineteenth-century disease causing great American Indian mortality, though it surely seems the primary one. Others took their toll. An 1830s epidemic, perhaps of viral influenza (Taylor and Hoaglin, 1962), but more likely of malaria (Dobyns, 1983:23; also Cook, 1955), reduced dramatically the numbers of the lower Columbia River tribes in the Pacific Northwest. Before 1831 these Indians had already been reduced from an estimated aboriginal population of 75,000 to 100,000 to only 15,000 to 20,000, primarily by smallpox (Scott, 1928:149). Sherburne Cook (1955) estimated that the 1830s epidemic killed 75 percent of those infected in the tribes of the Oregon and Washington areas. The epidemic extended south, where it reportedly killed over 20,000 Indians in the central valley of California alone (Cook, 1955:322). This epidemic, which may have originated in China, reached Europe by way of Moscow and then was transmitted to the Indians by whites from England (see Taylor and Hoaglin, 1962).

Tuberculosis is thought to have been fairly rare among American Indians in the early 1800s, though it was distributed throughout the Old Northwest and the Missouri River valley. It had spread throughout the entire country by the end of the century, however, affecting many American Indian tribes (Hrdlička, 1909:2). Moreover, it was probably extremely devastating when it first infected a tribe. William McNeill noted that, "when tuberculosis first arrived among a tribe of Canadian Indians, the infection attacked organs of their bodies which remained unaffected among whites. Symptoms—meningitis and the like—were far more dramatic, and the progress of the disease was far more rapid, than anything associated with tuberculosis infections among previously exposed populations" (McNeill, 1976:54). McNeill (1976:54) also stated, "by the third generation, however, the tuberculosis infection tended to concentrate in the lungs, as mutual accommodation between hosts and parasites began to approximate the familiar urban pattern."

An 1833 cholera epidemic invaded Indian Territory, devastating the populations there (Marks and Beatty, 1976:204). This epidemic was said to have been brought to North America by Irish immigrants (McNeill, 1976:233).

The migration of the Mormons to the Great Basin region, beginning in 1847, brought diseases to formerly isolated American Indians in the region. Epidemics included not only smallpox (1853, 1856) but also measles (1848–49), cholera (1849), malaria (1849), tuberculosis (1850), scarlet fever (1853), whooping cough (1853), typhoid and intestinal parasites (1854), and mumps (1854) (Stoffle, Jones, and Dobyns, 1983). As a predictable result, the Indian populations of the Great Basin declined sharply in the following few years. In 1853 the Mormon leader Brigham Young observed, "The Indians in these mountains are continually on the decrease, bands that numbered 150 warriors when we first came here number not more than 35 now" (quoted in Stoffle, Jones, and Dobyns, 1983:1).

I have mentioned the Sioux and Kiowa winter counts of smallpox episodes. Some 1813–14 Sioux winter counts depict whooping cough during that year (Mallery, 1877b:15, 1886:108, 1893:276); others show an 1818–19 measles epidemic and cholera epidemics, as well as smallpox epidemics (Mallery, 1886 : 109–10, 1893 : 277). One Sioux winter count also records an 1844 measles outbreak: "Rash Breaks out on Babies Only" (Praus, 1962 : 16). Another Sioux winter count for 1845–46 records "Broke out on Face Had Sore Throats and Camped Under the Bluff Winter" and "Also Had Bellyache" (Mallery, 1893 : 322). An 1849–50 Sioux winter count designates that year as "Many Died of the Cramps," or cholera (Mallery, 1886 : 142); an 1860–61 count designates that year as "Broke out with Rash and Died with Pains in the Stomach Winter" (Mallery, 1893 : 325); and finally, an 1873–74 count records that year as "Measles and Sickness Used up the People Winter" (Mallery, 1893 : 327).

In a Kiowa winter count indicating an epidemic of cholera in 1849, the summer appeared as "Cramp [cholera] Sun Dance" because cholera had appeared immediately after the sun dance. The measles and fever that killed a large number of children during the summer and winter of 1877–78 appeared as "Measles Sun Dance" in the winter count for that year. Whooping cough and measles showed in 1882, and in 1892 measles killed over 200 Kiowa, almost all of them children (Mooney, 1898 : 219, 289–90, 341–42, 362–63). Of these Kiowa epidemics, the onset of cholera in 1849 is considered to have been the most depopulating, as hundreds died directly from the disease and many others committed suicide in despair (Mooney, 1898 : 173). In fact, Mooney (1898 : 173) asserted: "The Kiowa remember it as the most terrible experience in their history, far exceeding in fatality the smallpox of nine years before." Mooney (1898 : 289) further noted, "It was a disease before entirely unknown to them, and was particularly dreaded on account of its dreadful suddenness, men who had been in perfect health in the morning being dead a few hours later."

The Southern Cheyenne also remember an 1849 cholera epidemic as an important event in their history, more important than any other occurrence of disease. They say that it killed one-half their tribe (see Moore, n.d.).

WARFARE AND GENOCIDE

During the nineteenth century the total North American Indian population was not reduced nearly as much from warfare and genocide as from disease and other causes, though individual tribes in some regions were reduced virtually to extinction by them. Most of the "Indian wars" of the nineteenth century were west of the Mississippi River, where most of the Indians were then located. During this period the non-Indian American population was expanding into the trans-Mississippi West, which previously had been sparsely populated by them; and as a result more non-Indians came into more and more extended contacts with the western tribes. All was not peaceful for American Indians east of the Mississippi, however, particularly for those in the Southeast. "Over 1,600 Creeks were slaughtered within a few months during the Creek War of 1813–14" (Mooney, 1928 : 8). There was also the Seminole War from 1835 to 1842, as well as other, probably less important, conflicts between the Seminole and the Americans that greatly reduced the Seminole population. In the Northeast and mid-Atlantic states war did not cause much

American Indian population decline during the century, as most Indians there had already been depopulated or subjugated.

West of the Mississippi there were important, sometimes severe wars and battles involving American Indian tribes until the last decade of the century. One was the so-called Sioux Uprising of 1862 in which numerous Dakota Sioux were killed, including their leader Little Crow and 38 Sioux who were formally executed by hanging at Mankato, Minnesota, on December 26, 1862 (see Carley, 1976).[5] In the Southwest the Apache warred with Mexico and the United States, sometimes with both, for a 50-year period beginning around 1835: "Standing bounties being paid by Mexico for Apache scalps during most of that period, resulting in a total recorded loss of at least 2,000 killed" (Mooney, 1928:21).

On the Great Plains there was virtually constant war for almost 50 years. Railroads had crossed Plains Indian lands earlier, and the Santa Fe Trail had been established to the south. Both brought disruption to nearby American Indian peoples, but more important disruptions stemmed from trails established during the middle decades of the century, beginning with the Oregon Trail going west and northwest from Missouri in 1842. Following the Oregon Trail was the Mormon Trail from Iowa to Utah Territory in 1847, the Smokey Hill Trail between the Platt and Arkansas rivers to present-day Colorado in the late 1850s, and then the Boseman Trail going north from Nebraska Territory to Montana Territory. The trails were made by immigrants to the northwest territories and by gold miners travelling to the Colorado and California areas. Waves of travelers and new settlers followed these cuts across American Indian lands. Conflicts quickly arose, and they did not subside until the Wounded Knee Massacre of Sioux Indians in the winter of 1890.

There was, for example, the Sand Creek Massacre of 150 Southern Cheyenne and some Arapaho in eastern Colorado Territory on November 29, 1864. In this massacre, which is described in greater detail later in this chapter, American Indian women and children were deliberately murdered by U.S. soldiers, and their bodies mutilated. A later, smaller massacre of the Southern Cheyenne took place in April, 1875, on the Sappa River in northwestern Kansas. There the Cheyenne leader Little Bull and many of his followers were killed by U.S. troopers joined by buffalo hide hunters under Lieutenant Austin Henely. According to one authority on the Cheyenne, Peter J. Powell (1980:37), who is an adopted member of the Northern Cheyenne tribe, some of the surviving Indians "were buried alive when the fighting ended."

Another example of the nineteenth-century American Indian wars was the much-glorified Battle of Greasy Grass between General George Armstrong Custer and the U.S. Cavalry and the Sioux, the Northern Cheyenne, and other tribes, on the Little Big Horn River on June 25, 1876 (see figure 5-2). Although in this instance the Indians won, the victory was short-lived: "Five

---

5. Some have maintained that only 21 Dakota Sioux died in the battles, and some also have maintained that at least 450, maybe as many as 800, whites, including soldiers, were killed during the uprising (Carley, 1976:1).

Fig. 5-2. The Battle of Greasy Grass (or Little Big Horn River). Courtesy of Smithsonian Institution, National Anthropological
Archives.

months to the day after the great victory at the Little Big Horn, the soldiers
struck back, destroying the winter village of the Northern Cheyenne in the
Big Horn Mountains" (Powell, 1980 : 42). Surviving Cheyenne fled for refuge
to the Sioux, who were having their own conflicts with the U.S. Army, which
continued to 1890 (see Mooney, 1896; Utley, 1963, 1984).

American immigrants to the Northwest brought wars and battles to the
American Indians there. There were the Rogue River Wars in Oregon Territory and northern California in the 1850s (see Beckham, 1971), the Yakima
Wars of 1855–56 and 1858, the Round Valley Wars in California in the 1850s and
1860s (see Carranco and Beard, 1981), the Bannock Wars of 1877–78, the
Modoc War of 1872–73, the Nez Perce Wars of the late 1870s, which resulted in
the latter tribe's removal to Indian Territory for a period of time (see Tate,
1981), and the Ute War of 1879.

American Indians not only fought non-Indians during the century, they
also fought alongside them against other non-Indians and other American
Indian tribes. In 1836 the Karankawa Indians fought with Americans in the
Texas War for Independence from Mexico. The Cherokee in Indian Territory
(discussed in detail below and in Chapter 8) formally sided with the Confederacy in the U.S. Civil War. Since the Cherokee were factionalized, and individual Cherokee fought on both sides in the War, the results were disastrous. Charles C. Royce described the effects of the Civil War on the tribe:

> Raided and sacked alternately, not only by the Confederate and Union
> forces, but by the vindictive ferocity and hate of their own factional divi-

sions, their country became a blackened and desolate waste. Driven from comfortable homes, exposed to want, misery, and the elements, they perished like sheep in a snow storm. Their houses, fences, and other improvements were burned, their orchards destroyed, their flocks and herds slaughtered or driven off, their schools broken up, and their schoolhouses given to the flames, and their churches and public buildings subjected to a similar fate, and that entire portion of their country which had been occupied by their settlements was distinguishable from the virgin prairie only by the scorched and blackened chimneys and the plowed but now neglected fields. (Royce, 1888:254)

James Mooney, in discussing the Civil War among the Cherokee in Indian Territory, asserted that their population declined by 7,000 as a result of the five-year war, from 21,000 to 14,000, and that the war left "their whole country in ashes" (Mooney, 1900:149; also U.S. Bureau of the Census, 1894a:276, 281–82).

Perhaps the best-known genocide of North American Indians occurred on December 29, 1890, at Wounded Knee Creek, South Dakota. There several hundred Sioux men, women, and children were indiscriminately killed by U.S. Army troops, and their bodies left to the winter snows. Much has been written about the tragedy, and rightly so. I tell about it in detail in Chapter 6, "The Great Ghost Dances."

Actually, genocide of American Indians was probably most blatant in northern California and southern Oregon Territory around the middle of the nineteenth century. It also probably had more impact upon American Indian peoples there than other incidents did among tribes elsewhere in the United States. Much of the killing in California and Oregon resulted, directly and indirectly, from the discovery of gold in 1849 and the subsequent influx of miners and settlers. Newspaper accounts document the atrocities, as do oral histories of California Indians today. It was not uncommon for small groups or villages of Indians to be attacked by the immigrants, sometimes in the name of a particular war, and be virtually wiped out overnight (see Heizer, 1976). Sherburne Cook (1976a) cited from Anthony J. Bledsoe's *Indian Wars of the Northwest* (1885) some events between 1855 and 1865:

1855. Miners attack and burn "several" rancherias.
  Red Cap Rancheria attacked by miners.
  Volunteers attack two rancherias at Weitschpeck.
  A reservation is set up on the Klamath and all Indians of the region are
    removed to it.
1856. Hupa Indians under arms. Object to removal to reservation.
  A rancheria attacked on Redwood Creek.
  Another rancheria destroyed on Redwood Creek.
  A rancheria destroyed on Bear River.
  The winter of 1856–1857 was hard. "It meant a struggle for self preservation by the Indians, a struggle against natural forces in which the whites were not a factor." Many whole tribes had been pushed into the mountains. The Indians were "chastened" by the winter and were quiet in 1857.

1858. The "Wintoons" on the headwaters of Redwood Creek, the Mad and
   Eel rivers begin depradations.
   Three expeditions go out.
   Rancheria attacked on Grouse Creek.
   Two expeditions ambushed.
   Indians withdraw entirely from the Mad River to the headwaters of Yaeger
      Creek.
   Three rancherias destroyed on Yaeger Creek.
   Indians are driven slowly into a small area on the headwaters of the Mad
      and Yaeger. There are seventeen camps. These attacked and destroyed.
   A rancheria attacked on Redwood Creek.
1859. One hundred women and children sent to Mendocino Reservation.
   A big storm occurs in January. "The hostiles, unable to hunt on the moun-
      tains and afraid to go down on the streams, were actually starved into
      submission within four weeks."
   February: all rancherias raided; 160 Indians sent to Mendocino. Sporadic
      raiding on Eel River and in Mattole Valley, also on the Van Duzen and
      Mad rivers.
1860. Most of the Wintoons escape from the reservation. Indian Island mas-
   sacre—the Wiyot practically destroyed. A rancheria destroyed on Mad
   River.
   Four hundred and forty Indians sent to Klamath Reservation; in a few
      months all had escaped. They were now all dependent upon the whites
      for subsistence.
1861. A rancheria burned at Iaqua.
   A rancheria destroyed on Boulder Creek.
   Two rancherias destroyed on the Mad River.
   A rancheria destroyed on Larrabee Creek.
   Another rancheria destroyed on Larrabee Creek.
   September to December: fifteen engagements in Humboldt County, at
      least four rancherias destroyed.
1862. Conditions much the same. "The marching and countermarching was
   continuous throughout the year . . . The prisoners were mostly of friendly
   tribes, who willingly surrendered for the sake of temporary shelter and
   food."
   Camp near Arcata attacked.
   Camp on Little River destroyed.
   Eight hundred captured Indians removed to Smith River Reservation. In
      two months all had escaped and returned.
1863. Conditions much the same.
   Hupa destroy a friendly rancheria on Stone Lagoon.
   A rancheria destroyed on north fork of Eel.
   A battle on Redwood Creek.
   A rancheria destroyed in Hoopa Valley.
   A battle on south fork of the Trinity.
   Another battle on Willow Creek.
   Another battle, near Arcata, at Bald Mountain.
1864. Fighting on the South Salmon.
   A rancheria burned in Hoopa Valley.
   A battle in Mattole Valley.
   A battle between Mad River and Redwood Creek.

Skirmishing now incessant. The policy was to wear down the Indians by "keeping them moving, and preventing them from laying in supplies of food and ammunition." Also by preventing the women and children from resting.
A rancheria destroyed on Elk River.
A "number" of rancherias destroyed in April.
A rancheria destroyed in July on the Mattole.
1865. By January, 1865, "Trinity County was cleared of all Indians who lived in rancherias and tribal relations. . . . The hostile tribes had been killed or captured, had been flooded by storms and driven by man, had been starved and beaten into absolute and final subjection."
(Cook, 1976a : 282–84)

As Sherburne Cook (1976a : 284) concluded the quotation: "The record speaks for itself. No further comment is necessary."

Primarily because of the killings, the California Indian population—which some scholars say once had been at least 310,000, perhaps over 700,000—decreased almost by two-thirds in little more than a single decade: from 100,000 in 1849 to 35,000 in 1860 (see table 5-4).

Ishi, the Last of the Yahi Yana

One California Indian people massacred at this time were the Yana, a small tribe living in the Sacramento River valley east of present-day Redding, California, who were probably first contacted by Americans in 1821. They had four subdivisions or tribelets: the Northern, Central, and Southern Yana—all of which were about the same size—and the smaller Yahi Yana. Some think they numbered less than 2,000 in all (see Thornton, 1980); others have estimated the size of the Yana population as high as 3,000 (U.S. Bureau of the

TABLE 5-4: **California Indian Population History, Pre-European to 1980**

Date	Population
Pre-European	310,000?–705,000
1800	260,000
1834	210,000
1849	100,000
1852	85,000
1856	50,000
1860	35,000
1870	30,000
1880	20,500
1890	18,000
1900	15,000–20,000
1907	18,000
1980	198,275[a]

[a] Includes recent immigrants to California.
SOURCES: Merriam (1905 : 60), Mooney (1928 : 19), Cook (1976b : 69–71, 1978 : 91), Powers (1877 : 416), Swagerty and Thornton (1982 : 92), U.S. Bureau of the Census (1984 : 14).

Census, 1915:108). They were destroyed virtually overnight, partly because of epidemics and the hardships of forced removal, but in large part because of their genocide by settlers in north-central California during the mid-1800s.

The first recorded conflict between the Yana and Americans was "when Capt. John Frémont attacked a peaceful gathering of Indians on Bloody Island (at the mouth of Battle Creek) in the Sacramento River in 1846" (Johnson, 1978:362). During the next two decades there was a series of massacres in which dozens of Yana were killed, culminating in the 1867 massacre at Dig Creek, when at least 45 Yana were killed and "bodies lay on the ground as there were not enough Yana left to bury them" (Johnson, 1978:362).

As shown in table 5-5, Yana population was reduced from 1,900 to about 100 between 1848 and 1867. In part, this happened because of white claims that the Yana were killing the settlers on Yana land, although during this time span "the deaths of fewer than 50 settlers can be attributed to them with any degree of certainty" (Johnson, 1978:363). The larger Northern, Central, and Southern Yana groups were killed off first; by 1865 only the smaller Yahi tribelet had a significant population remaining. All but a very few Yahi were destroyed by massacres during the next several years. At this time the Yahi were located in the extreme southern portion of the traditional Yana territory, primarily along the Mill and Deer Creek tributaries of the Sacramento River and south and west of Mount Lassen.

One of the Yana massacres was at Three Knolls on Mill Creek at dawn on August 16, 1865, in retaliation for the killing of three settlers by Yahis. Writing in *Ishi, in Two Worlds* (1961), Theodora Kroeber described the attack under the leadership of two settlers, Hiram Good and Robert A. Anderson:

> Waiting only until there was light enough for his men to see where they were shooting, Anderson directed a continuous stream of gunfire down from above onto a sleeping village. As he had surmised, the Yahi ran downstream making for the open ford which brought them under Good's fire from below. The terrified Indians leapt into Mill Creek, but the rapid current was a sorry protection. They became targets there for Good's guns, and Mill Creek ran red with the blood of its people. Anderson reported that "many dead bodies floated down the rapid current." (Kroeber, 1961:81)

A few Yahi survived Three Knolls; one was a three-year-old boy who fled with his mother and sister, probably after seeing his father killed.

Another attack on a small Yahi Yana group took place in the next year, 1866, apparently in retaliation for starving Yahi having stolen food from a farmer. All of the Yahi were killed. In either 1867 or 1868 there was yet another attack by settlers on a relatively large group of Yahi Yana, probably in retaliation for a steer having been killed by them. In it 33 Yahi were murdered and scalped at a cave north of Mill Creek by four whites led by Norman Kingsley. Kingsley, "as he explained afterwards, changed guns during the slaughter, exchanging his .56-caliber Spencer rifle for a .38-caliber Smith and Wesson revolver, because the rifle 'tore them up so bad,' particularly the babies" (Kroeber, 1961:84–85).

TABLE 5-5: **Yana Population History, Precontact to 1980**

Date	Population
Precontact	2,000–3,000
1848	1,900
1867	100
1864	35
1910	39
1928	12
1973	20
1980	0?

U.S. Bureau of the Census (1915:108, 1981), Johnson (1978:362), Thornton (1980:703).

Another massacre of the rapidly dwindling Yahi Indians took place in 1870; here again, for the suspected killing of cattle. At this time there were only about 15 or 16 Yahi left; one was the young boy, now about eight years old, who had escaped the 1865 Three Knolls Massacre of his village. After the 1870 massacre the remaining Yahi made a brief, unsuccessful attempt to make peace with those who had invaded their lands, and then they retreated into secrecy. The Yahi survived by hunting, fishing, gathering, and occasionally, raiding settlers' food supplies and livestock. Their number soon grew smaller, until only five remained.

In 1908 a surveying party stumbled upon the five in a crudely constructed village. Four ran to the woods, leaving an old woman hidden under a pile of skins. The surveyors left the woman alone, but "gathered together every movable possession, even the food, and for some unfathomably callous reason took it all with them as souvenirs" (Kroeber, 1961:111–12). The old woman had escaped the Three Knolls Massacre with her son and daughter, who were two of the four Yahi who fled from the settlers. The son, now a middle-aged man, returned to carry off his mother, but probably never saw his sister again. Presumably she and the others who fled died shortly thereafter. The son cared for his mother afterward, but she died in a short time. Then, from November, 1908, until late summer, 1911, he lived by himself on former Yana tribal lands.

On August 29, 1911, a group of dogs cornered an Indian man in the corral of a slaughterhouse in Oroville, California. The noise awakened the butchers, they called the sheriff, then held the Indian man until he arrived. Theodora Kroeber describes the Yahi captive:

> The wild man was emaciated to starvation, his hair was burned off close to his head, he was naked except for a ragged scrap of ancient covered-wagon canvas which he wore around his shoulders like a poncho. He was a man of middle height, the long bones, painfully apparent, were straight, strong, and not heavy, the skin color somewhat paler in tone than the full copper characteristic of most Indians. The black eyes were wary and guarded now, but were set wide in a broad face, the mouth was generous and agreeably molded. (Kroeber, 1961:3–4)

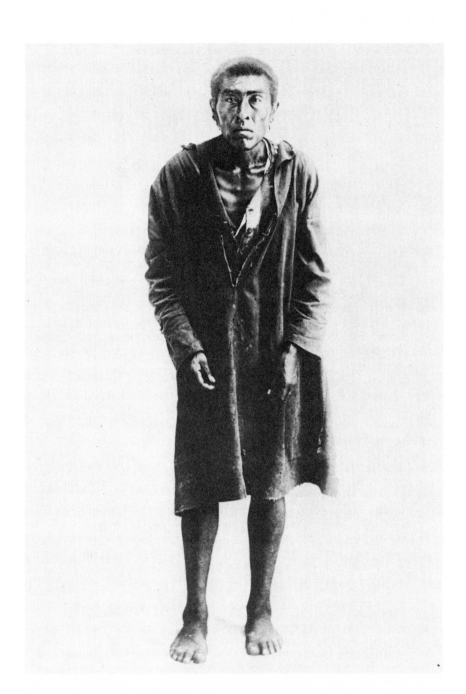

Fig. 5-3. Ishi, the Last Yahi Yana. Courtesy of Lowie Museum of Anthropology, University of California, Berkeley

Two days later, the sheriff received a telegram from the anthropologist Alfred Kroeber at the University of California, who had heard quickly of the events: "Sheriff Butte County. Newspapers report capture of wild Indian speaking language other tribes totally unable to understand. Please confirm or deny by collect telegram and if story correct hold Indian till arrival Professor State University who will take charge and be responsible for him. Matter important account aboriginal history" (quoted in Kroeber, 1961:6).

The Yahi man was taken to the Museum of the University of California under the charge of Professor Kroeber. He was given the name Ishi, which means "man" in the Yana language. (See figure 5-3.) He lived there for the next four and one-half years, dying on March 25, 1916.[6] He was the young boy who, at age three, had escaped a massacre of his people. He survived while all others died during the following decades to live his last years among the race who had destroyed his family and his people, the Yahi. He was a "wild Indian" for whom America had no place other than a university museum. He was the last full-blood Yahi. Some mixed-blood descendants may still live today, but no Yana was identified as Yana in the 1980 census.

REMOVALS AND RELOCATIONS

Removals and relocations of American Indians and the establishment of reservations, which had begun only in the seventeenth and eighteenth centuries, developed to massive proportions during the nineteenth century. They were often linked to wars between American Indians and Americans. Among the notable nineteenth-century American Indian relocations were those of the Nez Perce, the Northern Cheyenne, the Navajo, and the "Five Civilized Tribes of the Southeast," that is, the Cherokee, the Creek, the Choctaw, the Chickasaw, and the Seminole.

Most relocations occurred under the auspices of the Indian Removal Act of 1830, which provided for the exchange of American Indian lands in any state or territory of the United States but was especially instrumental in relocating tribes from the southern United States to lands in the trans-Mississippi West. In part, the act read as follows:

> *Be it enacted* . . . , That it shall and may be lawful for the President of the United States to cause so much of any territory belonging to the United States, west of the river Mississippi, not included in any state or organized territory, and to which the Indian title has been extinguished, as he may judge necessary, to be divided into a suitable number of districts, for the reception of such tribes or nations of Indians as may choose to exchange the lands where they now reside, and remove there; and to cause each of said districts to be so described by natural or artificial marks, as to be easily distinguished from every other. . . .
>
> *Sec. 2. And be it further enacted*, That it shall and may be lawful for the President to exchange any or all of such districts, so to be laid off and de-

6. The reader is referred to *Ishi, the Last Yahi: A Documentary History* (1979), edited by Robert F. Heizer and Theodora Kroeber, for a more detailed view of Ishi's life with Alfred Kroeber.

scribed, with any tribe or nation of Indians now residing within the limits of any of the states or territories, and with which the United States have existing treaties, for the whole or any part or portion of the territory claimed and occupied by such tribe or nation, within the bounds of any one or more of the states or territories, where the land claimed and occupied by the Indians, is owned by the United States, or the United States are bound to the state within which it lies to extinguish the Indian claim thereto. (Prucha, 1975: 52–53)

The Indian Removal Act was used very effectively by President Andrew Jackson to relocate southern tribes onto lands west of the Mississippi, thereby securing Indian lands east of the river for settlement by expanding non-Indian populations.

Removals and relocations always, it seems, resulted in severe disorganization for the Indians involved. Typically, they also resulted in large population losses, in some cases drastic ones. I have written elsewhere regarding the removal of the southeastern tribes:

> The Choctaws are said to have lost fifteen percent of their population, 6,000 out of 40,000; and the Chickasaw removal is said to have been ". . . a comparatively tranquil affair . . . ," though they surely suffered severe losses as well. By contrast, the Creeks and Seminoles are said to have suffered about 50 percent mortality. For the Creeks, this came primarily in the period immediately after removal: for example, "of the 10,000 or more who were resettled in 1836–37 . . . an incredible 3,500 . . . died of 'bulious fevers.'" The high Seminole mortality seems not to have resulted primarily from post-removal disease but from "the terrible war of attrition that has been required to force them to move." (Thornton, 1984a: 293)

"The Trail Where We Cried"

Exceptionally tragic was the removal of the Cherokee from the Southeast to Indian Territory during the late 1830s. It was such an ordeal that the tribe subsequently named the journey Nunna daul Tsunyi, which in Cherokee means literally, "the trail where we cried." The removal has become known in English as the Trail of Tears.

It is estimated that there were over 22,000 Cherokee during the 1600s. In the eighteenth century they suffered from the smallpox epidemics described earlier in Chapter 4. The epidemic in 1738–39 was particularly severe, reducing their size almost by half. Literally hundreds of Cherokee warriors reportedly killed themselves after seeing their disfigurement due to the disease: "Some shot themselves, others cut their throats, some stabbed themselves with knives and others with sharp-pointed canes; many threw themselves with sullen madness into the fire and there slowly expired, as if they had been utterly divested of the native power of feeling pain" (quoted in Mooney, 1900: 26). Another smallpox epidemic also depopulated them around 1760.

From the 1760s to the early 1780s the Cherokee were also in almost constant warfare with the colonists on their lands. They sided with the British in the

TABLE 5-6: **Cherokee Population History, 1650–1980**

Date	Population
1650	22,000
1808–1809	13,395
1826	17,713
1835	21,542
1851–52	15,802
1866	15,566
1875	19,717
1880	21,920
1890	28,000
1900	32,376
1910	31,489
1970	66,150
1980	232,000+

SOURCES: U.S. Bureau of the Census (1915:83, 1973a:188, 1981), Mooney (1928:8), Thornton (1984a:295, 297).

Revolutionary War, and by 1782, "they had been reduced to the lowest depth of misery, almost indeed to the verge of extinction. Over and over again their towns had been laid in ashes and their fields wasted. Their best warriors had been killed and their women and children had sickened and starved in the mountains" (Mooney, 1900:51). Then in the following year yet another small-pox epidemic devastated the tribe.

Because of these events, very early in the nineteenth century the Cherokee Indians numbered only slightly more than 13,000. Yet they increased during the next few decades so that by 1835 they numbered about what they had 200 years previously, some 22,000 (see table 5-6). Ill fate struck the Cherokee again, however.

Cherokee tribal lands had once been immense. Although their exact boundaries are not known, the lands they claimed may have extended almost from the Ohio River south to present-day Atlanta, Georgia, and west from present-day Virginia and North and South Carolina across present-day Tennessee, Kentucky, and Alabama toward the Illinois River. By the close of the Revolutionary War their lands had shrunk considerably on the north and east as populations of Americans settled those areas. By the mid-1830s, Cherokee Country, as it was called, encompassed only the area where the states of North Carolina, Tennessee, Georgia, and Alabama more or less come together.

During the period of land loss, gold was discovered on Cherokee lands, and the Cherokee were increasingly subjected to invasions of armed men from Georgia "forcibly seizing horses and cattle, taking possession of houses from which they had ejected the occupants, and assaulting the owners who dared make resistance" (Mooney, 1900:112). The Indians were all but helpless to retaliate at this point, in part because in 1828 the state of Georgia annexed Cherokee land within Georgia's chartered limits and claimed jurisdiction over it. Georgia also declared Cherokee laws "null and void" and disallowed legal testimony and suits by any Cherokee against any white man (Mooney, 1900 : III).

Subjected to continued harassment by Georgia and pressures from the U.S. government, particularly President Andrew Jackson, to cede their remaining lands and move west of the Mississippi, the Cherokee resisted as best they could. They even argued legal cases before the U.S. Supreme Court. A final case, which they won, involved a non-Cherokee missionary, Reverend Samuel A. Worcester, residing on Cherokee land with their permission. He had been arrested by the state of Georgia for helping the Cherokee, and Reverend Worcester and the Cherokee Nation contended that Georgia had no right to interfere, as the Cherokee were a sovereign nation with a definite territory. The Supreme Court agreed, but Georgia refused to release Worcester. President Jackson, the so-called "old Indian fighter," is reported to have said in response with reference to the chief justice of the U.S. Supreme Court, "John Marshall has made his decision, now let him enforce it" (Mooney, 1900 : 114).

After three years and much harassment, a treaty was signed between the Cherokee and the U.S. government, but not by the principal officers of the Cherokee Nation. The treaty was known as the Treaty of New Echota, after the new Cherokee capitol in Georgia where it was signed. The treaty signers ceded to the United States the Cherokee lands in the Southeast in exchange for lands in Indian Territory and $15 million. Leaders of the Cherokee Nation, under Chief John Ross, protested violently during the next years that the treaty should not be consummated. The protests were to no avail. The Cherokee were disarmed, then General Winfield Scott was sent to oversee their removal in 1838. James Mooney has described what happened:

> The history of this Cherokee removal of 1838, as gleaned by the author from the lips of actors in the tragedy, may well exceed in weight of grief and pathos any other passage in American history. Even the much-sung exile of the Acadians falls far behind it in its sum of death and misery. Under Scott's orders the troops were disposed at various points throughout the Cherokee country, where stockade forts were erected for gathering in and holding the Indians preparatory to removal. From these, squads of troops were sent to search out with rifle and bayonet every small cabin hidden away in the coves or by the sides of mountain streams, to seize and bring in as prisoners all the occupants, however or wherever they might be found. Families at dinner were startled by the sudden gleam of bayonets in the doorway and rose up to be driven with blows and oaths along the weary miles of trail that led to the stockade. Men were seized in their fields or going along the road, women were taken from their wheels and children from their play. In many cases, on turning for one last look as they crossed the ridge, they saw their homes in flames, fired by the lawless rabble that followed on the heels of the soldiers to loot and pillage. So keen were these outlaws on the scent that in some instances they were driving off the cattle and other stock of the Indians almost before the soldiers had fairly started their owners in the other direction. Systematic hunts were made by the same men for Indian graves, to rob them of the silver pendants and other valuables deposited with the dead. A Georgia volunteer, afterward a colonel in the Confederate service, said: "I fought through the civil war and have seen men shot to pieces and slaughtered by

thousands, but the Cherokee removal was the cruelest work I ever knew." (Mooney, 1900:124)

Almost 17,000 Cherokee were rounded up and put in stockades that were constructed on their lands for the purpose of holding them. The small groups were then aggregated at three points for removal westward: at Old Agency on the Hiwassee River, near Calhoun, Tennessee; at Ross's Landing, now Chattanooga, Tennessee; and at Gunter's Landing, now Guntersville, Alabama. About 4,000 had already left Cherokee Country to make new lives in Indian Territory, and about 1,000 escaped into the hills.

The plan was to load the Cherokee on steamboats, move them down the Tennessee and Ohio rivers to the Mississippi, and then force them to travel by land to Indian Territory. A few thousand Cherokee were so removed, but "this removal in the hottest part of the year, was attended with so great sickness and mortality that, by resolution of the Cherokee National Council, Ross and the other chiefs submitted to General Scott a proposition that the Cherokee be allowed to remove themselves in the fall, after the sickly season had ended" (Mooney, 1900:125–26).

That request was granted, and in October, 1838, the Cherokee began to remove themselves, primarily over land, in 13 recorded groups averaging about 1,000 people each (see figure 5-4). Most traveled north and west across Tennessee, Kentucky, southern Illinois, and Missouri into northeastern Indian Territory. Deaths occurred almost every day from disease, cold, hardship, and accidents. Rebecca Neugin, a Cherokee woman who made the journey as a three-year-old, remembered:

> When the soldier came to our house my father wanted to fight, but my mother told him that the soldiers would kill him if he did and we surrendered without a fight. They drove us out of our house to join other prisoners in a stockade. After they took us away, my mother begged them to let her go back and get some bedding. So they let her go back and she brought what bedding and a few cooking utensils she could carry and had to leave behind all of our other household possessions.
>
> My father had a wagon pulled by two spans of oxen to haul us in. Eight of my brothers and sisters and two or three widow women and children rode with us. My brother Dick, who was a good deal older than I was, walked along with a long whip which he popped over the backs of the oxen and drove them all the way. My father and mother walked all the way also.
>
> The people got so tired of eating salt pork on the journey that my father would walk through the woods as we traveled, hunting for turkeys and deer which he brought into camp to feed us. Camp was usually made at some place where water was to be had and when we stopped and prepared to cook our food, other emigrants who had been driven from their homes without opportunity to secure cooking utensils came to our camp to use our pots and kettles. There was much sickness among the emigrants and a great many little children died of whooping cough. (Neugin, 1978:176)

The Cherokee ordeal did not end on arrival in Indian Territory. Many survived the hardships of the journey only to be stricken with disease in the new

Fig. 5-4. The Trail of Tears, by Robert Lindneux. Courtesy of Woolaroc
Museum, Bartlesville, Oklahoma

lands or to die there of starvation (Doran, 1975–76 : 499). There are reports of
as many as one-half of the early immigrants dying before the year was out
(Foreman, 1932 : 263). James Mooney interviewed many Cherokee who made
the journey. He commented:

> It is difficult to arrive at any accurate statement of the number of Cherokee
> who died as a result of the Removal. According to the official figures those
> who removed under the direction of Ross lost over 1,600 on the journey. The
> proportionate mortality among those previously removed under military
> supervision was probably greater, as it was their suffering that led to the
> proposition of the Cherokee national officers to take charge of the emigra-
> tion. Hundreds died in the stockades and the waiting camps, chiefly by rea-
> son of the rations furnished, which were of flour and other provisions to
> which they were unaccustomed and which they did not know how to pre-
> pare properly. Hundreds of others died soon after their arrival in Indian ter-
> ritory, from sickness and exposure on the journey. (Mooney, 1900 : 127)

Mooney concluded that "over 4,000 Cherokee died as a direct result of the
removal" (1900 : 127). That total is probably far from correct: a mortality figure twice Mooney's may be more reasonable; over 8,000 Cherokee Indians
may have died as a more or less direct result of the Trail of Tears (see Thornton, 1984a). Yet the Cherokee managed to recover eventually; as enumerated
in the 1980 census, they are today the largest American Indian group in the
United States (see table 5-6, again).

Cheyenne Flight

The Cheyenne tribe is said to be "composed of those persons who are hearted alike, the ones who are the Creator's own chosen, called-out people" (Powell, 1980: vii). Anthropologists say that the Cheyenne are related to the Arapaho, the Cree, the Blackfoot, the Ottawa, the Sac and Fox, the Delaware, and the Shawnee, among others. It is generally accepted that the Cheyenne were originally in the East, but had migrated to the Minnesota River by 1675: moving farther west to the prairies, "band by band, the People slowly ventured deeper and deeper into those prairie lands, the green of the grass yellowed in summer by the brightness of Sun's rays, the moving herds of buffalo casting black shadows across the land, while overhead the endless blue sky flowed to the sacred Four Directions of the universe" (Powell, 1980:xiii).

In the last quarter of the eighteenth century the Cheyenne settled east of the Black Hills in what is now South Dakota. They may have numbered only 3,500 at this time (see table 5-7). It was "here their history as a holy people began" (Powell, 1980:xiii). Here they were given Maahotse, the four Sacred Arrows, by the Creator and told for four years how to live as a holy people: "From that time on, many Cheyennes called themselves Votostataneo, 'the particular, singled-out people,' who were the Creator's own" (Powell, 1980 : xiv). Later they met a smaller tribe with a language almost the same as theirs, and the smaller tribe joined with them, bringing their Sacred Buffalo Hat, Esevone. The Cheyenne then moved farther west to the Yellowstone River country, taking their newly acquired horses with them.

Subsequently, they split into the Northern and the Southern Cheyenne as one band went south to capture wild horses, where they became close to the Arapaho. This band moved farther south, and the split became permanent by the mid-1800s. By this time the Cheyenne had increased some in population, despite both groups' continuing battles with other Indian tribes, settlers, and the U.S. Calvary. The increase was also despite episodes of disease including the epidemic of cholera in the summer of 1849 that killed about one-half of the Southern Cheyenne, who designated 1849 as "Winter When the Big Cramps Take Place" (Powell, 1981, 1 : 95). Other tragedies would follow.

One was the 1864 massacre of the Southern Cheyenne at Sand Creek in southeastern Colorado Territory, conducted by Colorado militia led by Colonel John Chivington, a former Methodist minister. A Cheyenne village of perhaps 400 to 500 people, mostly women and children, was attacked at daylight, and there were about 150 Cheyenne casualties. Peter Powell has described some of the events:

> The slaughter along the stream bed was terrible.
> It was the slower ones, or those who hung behind, still hoping for mercy, who were shot down first. . . . Five women were among the first to be murdered. Slower than others, they had taken shelter beneath the stream bank. . . .
> One poor woman, heavy with child, fell behind the others racing up the stream bed. Soldiers killed her too. Then one of them cut her open, and pulling out her unborn baby, he threw the little one down on the earth beside her. . . .

TABLE 5-7: **Cheyenne Population History, 1780—1980**

Date	Population
1780	3,500+
1875	4,000
1880	3,767
1890	3,654
1900	3,446
1910	3,055
1930	2,695
1970	6,872
1980	9,918

SOURCES: U.S. Bureau of the Census (1915:73, 1937:37, 1973a:188, 1981), Mooney (1928:13).

Elsewhere, a little girl of about five, filled with terror, tried to escape by burrowing down into the sand along the stream bottom. In spite of that, two soldiers found her hiding there. They drew their pistols and shot her. Then they grabbed her limp arm and dragged her out of the sand, leaving her dead body lying there in the stream bed. (Powell, 1981, 1:303—304)

In 1875 the Southern Cheyenne were massacred again at Sappa River, Kansas, as described earlier in this chapter. The Southern Cheyenne surrendered to the U.S. government later that year and were relocated into what would become Oklahoma. In 1876 the Northern Cheyenne were massacred for their part in the Battle of Greasy Grass, or the Little Bighorn. Finally, part of the Northern Cheyenne also surrendered late in the winter of 1876—77. Under pressure by the U.S. government, some went south to join southern relatives, but with the promise that they could return north if they found the new lands not to their liking. They found hunger, sickness, death, and misery:

The disease that hit them hardest was measles. . . . Blotches broke out all over the faces and bodies of the little ones, with their noses pouring blood and the sores on their heads bursting open. During the first year in the South, more than fifty children died from this sickness. . . .
    Some of the finest of the young men and women died as well. The old people suffered greatly, too, with ague, the shaking sickness which left their frail bodies wracked with fits of cold, heat, and sweating. . . .
    Hunger hastened the passing of many; for once they took sick, there was not enough nourishing food to sustain them while they fought to regain their strength. (Powell, 1981, 2:1156—57)

Some Cheyenne fled in the fall of 1878, led by Little Wolf, Dull Knife (or Morning Star), Old Crow, and Wild Hog. Hundreds of soldiers pursued them as the Cheyenne "paused, fought off the soldiers, then hurried on again, always moving northward" (Powell, 1980:45). In Nebraska the bands of Dull Knife and Little Wolf split. Dull Knife's band was captured in northwestern Nebraska; Little Wolf's band journeyed farther north (see map 5-1).

After Dull Knife's capture his band was taken to Camp Robinson in a driving snowstorm. Hearing they were to be returned south again, they became

5-1. Flight of the Cheyenne

determined to die in the north, their own country. They were then locked in a barracks without food, water, or heat. Powell tells what happened next:

> It was the dead of winter, early January 1879. Determined to die together in the North country, the people waited, hungered, and froze. Then about 10:00 P.M. on the bitter cold night of 9 January 1879, the people broke through the windows of their prison barracks and fled across the hard-crusted snow, white as day in the bright moonlight. The soldiers shot down many as they fled, pursuing the last surviving party of them for days, until at last these fleeing ones were shot down together in a blood-soaked wash-out by a dry streambed. But they had died in the beloved North country. (Powell, 1980:48)

Meanwhile, Little Wolf and his followers spent that winter in Nebraska, then journeyed northward. They were captured in Montana Territory and taken home to the Yellowstone River. They eventually joined the other Northern Cheyenne on the Tongue River Reservation in Montana.

After the massacres the numbers of Cheyenne continued to decrease. In 1890 they were 3,654; in 1910 they were only 3,055; and in 1930 they were only 2,695. Most of the decrease was among the Southern Cheyenne in Oklahoma (U.S. Bureau of the Census, 1937:37; see also Campbell, 1983, for a study of Northern Cheyenne fertility in 1900). The total Cheyenne population more than doubled, however, between 1930 and 1970, and almost 10,000 people identified themselves as Cheyenne in the 1980 census.

Today the site where the Southern Cheyenne were killed at Sand Creek is marked by a small granite monument designating the "Sand Creek Battleground." Recently the Colorado Historical Society, in response to the concerns of the Cheyenne and other American Indians, agreed to provide a new marker telling the true story of what happened there. The designation "battleground" will be changed to "massacre" (see *New York Times*, 1985c).

Allotment of American Indian Lands

American Indian reservation lands were guaranteed by the U.S. government as the saying goes, "as long as the grass grows and the rivers flow." The guarantee ended quickly. Before the nineteenth century had ended, the U.S. Congress passed the General Allotment Act of 1887, which was subsequently amended, modified, and extended by the Amendment to the Dawes Act (1891), the creation of the Dawes Commission in 1893, the Curtis Act (1898), and the Burk Act (1906). Known also as the Dawes Act, the General Allotment Act authorized the president to allot American Indian tribal reservation lands in severalty, that is, to give separate possession to individual Indians at the president's discretion. The act read, in part:

> *Be it enacted.* . . . , That in all cases where any tribe or band of Indians has been, or shall hereafter be, located upon any reservation created for their use, either by treaty stipulation or by virtue of an act of Congress or executive order setting apart the same for their use, the President of the United States be, and he hereby is, authorized, whenever in his opinion any reservation or any part thereof of such Indians is advantageous for agricultural and grazing purposes, to cause said reservation, or any part thereof, to be sur-

veyed, or resurveyed if necessary, and to allot the lands in said reservation in severalty to any Indian located thereon. (Prucha, 1975: 171–72)

Also under this act, the U.S. government could retain the title to an individual's land for a 25-year period or more if the president so desired (Haas, 1957: 13). This was supposedly for the Indians' own protection against those who might swindle them out of their land. The act provided citizenship for those American Indians who would take up residence apart from their tribes, as well as to those who received individual land allotments (Haas, 1957: 13).

The General Allotment Act meant, in effect, that American Indian tribal lands could be broken up, with tribal members receiving small land parcels under their ownership rather than living on tribally owned land. This happened to many tribes, and as result, the act all but destroyed traditional land-based forms of American Indian tribal organization. The allotments produced a further deterioration of American Indian economies, societies, and cultures, even though as the anthropologist John Moore (1980) has demonstrated, the land parcels selected by individual tribal members often reflected existing kinship and residence patterns, which may have provided social stability for a time. Unallotted tribal lands were secured for settlement by non-Indians, especially homesteaders. The new lands opened for settlement were located mainly west of the Mississippi River, where they had formerly belonged to the indigenous American Indian tribes, or to tribes earlier relocated there. Of course, the opening of new lands to American settlement brought expanding populations of non-Indians west of the Mississippi.

DESTRUCTION OF WAYS OF LIFE

The destruction of American Indian ways of life continued, perhaps accelerated, during the nineteenth century, causing further reductions of Indian populations.

I have already mentioned the decimation of the buffalo (see Chapter 3). Although the buffalo had been reduced considerably by 1800, many tribes remained dependent on the surviving herds. They were all western tribes, although other American Indians farther to the east centuries previously had also been partly dependent on buffalo there. The Indians dependent, or partially so, on nineteenth-century herds were the Arapaho, the Assiniboin, the Blackfoot, the Cheyenne, the Comanche, the Crow, the Gros Ventre, the Kiowa, the Kiowa-Apache, the Sarsi, the Teton, the Santee and the Yankton Sioux, the Arikara, the Hidatsa, the Iowa, the Kansa, the Mandan, the Missouri, the Omaha, the Osage, the Oto, the Pawnee, the Ponca, the Wichita, the Plains Cree and Ojibwe, the Shoshoni, the Caddo, the Quapaw, the Kutenai, and the Flathead (McHugh, 1972: 10–11).

American Indians hunted buffalo by a wide variety of means, including rifles, bows and arrows, corrals, fire, and driving them over cliffs. The uses for the buffalo were even more varied. The tribes not only relied on the buffalo as a food source, but also used buffalo products for clothing, housing, blankets and bedding, shoes, spoons, knives and tools, bowls, saddles, musical instruments, cosmetics, jewelry and charms, armor, masks, shields, and sleds. They also used buffalo dung for fuel (McHugh, 1972:83–109). In addition, the buffalo was prominent in the symbolic and ceremonial life of Indian peoples, often having a place in their creation traditions (McHugh, 1972:110–22, 130–40). No wonder that the destruction of such an important resource led to the collapse of many American Indian societies, along with starvation and undernourishment. Perhaps indicating hard times, a Sioux winter count refers to 1865 as "Winter of Lots of Blood for Food" (Praus, 1962:20).

Other Indians also experienced starvation and undernourishment during the nineteenth century, and their populations often declined as an indirect result. How this happened may be seen in Sherburne Cook's description of undernourished northern California Indians:

> Naturally, the effect on population was largely indirect. It seldom happens that the immediate cause of death is complete lack of nourishment. . . . It is probable that seldom was food so scarce that the California Indians perished of actual starvation. However, partial starvation must have been quite common. The influence of this condition was to lower the vitality of the population in all respects. Particularly was resistance to disease so much reduced that many of the weaker members, such as children and old people, fell easy prey to whatever epidemic happened to strike them. Tuberculosis would also claim many victims in such a population. The physical weakness attending prolonged undernutrition would also contribute to mental and moral lassitude, thus preventing the group as a whole from bringing to bear its full energy in acquiring a new food supply. Moreover, the birth rate would tend to decrease, although we have no quantitative data concerning this matter. A very inadequate diet, as is well known, will prevent proper development of the fetus, make it more difficult for the mother to withstand delivery, and reduce the natural secretion of milk below the subsistence level of the newly born child. As a result of all these factors, the population would tend to decrease very rapidly.
>
> As we know, the population did decrease materially during the years of most acute hardship, owing, among other causes, to the disturbance of food supply—a major environmental factor. (Cook, 1976a:290)

Other effects of the destruction of American Indian ways of life may be seen in case histories of four other tribes: the Kalapuya of the Northwest, the Kansa Indians, the Cahuilla Indians of California, and the Indians of Texas.

The Kalapuya Economic Collapse

The Kalapuya Indians lived in Oregon's Willamette River valley. They comprised 10 groups, although some scholars indicate only eight and others as many as 16: Atfalati (Tualatin), Yamel (Yamhill), Ahantchuyuk (Pudding River Indians), Chelamela or Chemekata (Long Tom Indians), Luckiamute, Santiam, Chepenafa (Marys River Indians), Calapooia (Kalapuya), McKenzie, and Yoncalla (Ratcliff, 1973:28).

Estimates of the total Kalapuya population before European contact are speculative. They may have numbered 3,000 in 1780 (see table 5-8). Kalapuya populations were reduced initially by European diseases such as the 1780 epidemics of smallpox and venereal disease spread by sailors and traders in the area. In 1830–31 there were even greater population losses from an epidemic,

TABLE 5-8: **Kalapuya Population History, 1780–1980**

Date	Population
1780	3,000
1910	106
1970	95
1980	65

SOURCES: U.S. Bureau of the Census, (1915:85, 1973a:188, 1981), Mooney (1928:18).

perhaps of typhus (Ratcliff, 1973:27), but it may have been of influenza or malaria. Important also in the Kalapuya decline was the virtual economic collapse caused by European destruction of their way of life.

Traditional Kalapuya subsistence patterns had been based on fishing eels, salmon, trout, and steelhead; hunting elk, deer, and various small animals and insects; harvesting wild plants, nuts, berries, and especially camas; and raising tobacco. After European contact the tribe engaged in the beaver fur trade with French Canadians. After 1828, however, serious American farming and husbandry began where the Kalapuya lived, and fields of wheat and pastures for cattle, horses, and hogs soon reduced their traditional natural resources. After 1841, Euro-American settlement became even more intensive, and eventually the Kalapuya simply became unable to feed their population. Hunger and starvation resulted; the inevitable depopulation occurred. By 1844 only a few hundred Indians were left in the Willamette valley (Ratcliff, 1973:32). In 1910 there were 106 Kalapuya Indians, in 1970 there were but 95, and in the 1980 census there were only 65 people identified as Kalapuya.

Decline of the Cahuilla

The Cahuilla Indians were located in present-day southern California in an area of about 5,000 square miles along and between the San Jacinto, Santa Rosa, and San Bernardino mountain ranges, and north and northwest of the Salton Sea. Most of the land there is desert. Today the area includes the California towns of Palm Springs, Indio, Coachella, Mecca, and Banning.

A wide range has been given for the pre-European population of the Cahuilla, from 2,500 to 6,000 to 10,000 (Bean, 1978:583). In the 1850s the tribe numbered perhaps 2,000 to 3,000, by 1890 they had been reduced to between 1,100 and 1,200. In 1970 they numbered less than 1,000 (see table 5-9). The 1980 census data do not include a figure for the total Cahuilla population, though individual groups are identified.

Some Cahuilla were brought under the influence of Spanish Catholic missions in the late 1700s and early 1800s, but probably they did not suffer from this ordeal as much as did other Mission Indians. It is likely that there were epidemics of European diseases before there was much direct European contact. The most severe epidemic, however, was in 1863, when smallpox killed many Cahuilla (Bean, 1978:584). They suffered further population declines beginning 10 years later and continuing for two decades, but not from disease (Harvey, 1967:192.). Rather, the declines stemmed from the American occupation of their lands.

TABLE 5-9: **Cahuilla Population History from Aboriginal Times to 1980**

Date	Population
Aboriginal times	2,500–10,000
1850	2,000–3,000
1890	1,100–1,200
1910	755
1970	1,000
1980	?

SOURCES: U.S. Bureau of the Census (1915:97), Harvey (1967:194), Bean (1978:584).

The Cahuilla decline resulted in large part from emigration: as the Cahuilla way of life changed, many Cahuilla became attracted to other areas of California, to which they migrated. Tribal members were lost in the larger non-Indian population of California and intermarried with members of it. The anthropologist H. R. Harvey briefly summarized: "The breakdown of geographic isolation provided one of the conditions for Cahuilla population decline; and the increased number of Cahuilla reported in the urban areas of Riverside and San Bernardino by 1890 suggests that they were not dying out so much as moving out of their traditional area" (Harvey, 1967:194). Moreover, according to Harvey, most of the Cahuilla emigrants were of reproductive age; it was the aged and the very young who remained. This trend decreased the birth rate, in and of itself, and limited the number of available marriage mates, which was already limited by high maternal mortality rates and traditional exogamy.

The Cahuilla tribal population declined, as Harvey (1967:197) indicated, because, "provided with the alternative of assimilation, a situation that became possible after white contact, traditional Cahuilla society gradually lost its members and was unable to replace them."

Destitution of the Kansa

The Kansa Indians migrated from the Ohio River valley into northeast Kansas during the early seventeenth century. No one knows why they moved, or how numerous they were at that time. Early in the eighteenth century they were said to number perhaps 5,000 (Unrau, 1973:316), but late in that century they numbered only 3,000 (Mooney, 1928:13), having been reduced by disease and wars, particularly with the Pawnee (Unrau, 1973:316). By the early nineteenth century they numbered only about 1,500, though there were many of mixed Indian blood, particularly Kansa-Osage, and mixed Indian-white blood (Unrau, 1973:316–17). (See table 5-10.)

The Kansa fate, from the early nineteenth century on, was further depopulation by disease and starvation. Earlier in this chapter I have already mentioned smallpox, which killed approximately 700 Kansa from 1825 to 1855 (Unrau, 1973:322). In the following few decades the Kansa population was further reduced by over 1,000, in part because of measles and whooping cough, in large part because of malnutrition and exposure, "conditions that slowly but certainly made the afflicted individuals succumb to the ravages of

TABLE 5-10: **Kansa Population History, Early 1700s to 1980**

Date	Size
Early 1700s	5,000
Late 1700s	3,000
Early 1800s	1,500
1861	866
1870	574
1880	397
1900	217
1910	238
1980	677

SOURCES: U.S. Bureau of the Census (1915:100, 1981), Mooney (1928:13), Unrau (1973:316–21).

respiratory and digestive disorders, as well as outright starvation" (Unrau, 1973:322).

The malnutrition, exposure, and starvation resulted from the destruction of traditional Kansa ways of life. Although in exchange for land cessions the Kansa were assured the minimal necessities of life by treaties with the U.S. government (Unrau, 1973:323), they did not receive what was due them. What happened after the treaties between 1828 and 1872 is chronicled in reports by the U.S. government:

April, 1828: "Starving condition, truely deplorable"
January, 1831: "remarkable improvidence"
September, 1838: "none of the comforts of neighboring tribes"
February, 1846: "very ill with autumnal diseases"
February, 1848: "terribly destitute"
August, 1855: "have lost all confidence in each other due to destitution"
October, 1861: "many are sick and without clothes"
April, 1862: "completely destitute"
June, 1862: "many deaths for want of medicine"
January, 1866: "completely destitute"
August, 1866: "very destitute condition"
February, 1868: "completely out of blankets and food . . . have disposed of all saleable property and have exhausted their credit"
February, 1869: "We now ask, shall we starve?" (question posed by nine chiefs and ten warriors)
March, 1872: "absolutely destitute; are living on a little corn and dead animals they can find lying around"

(Quoted in Unrau, 1973:323)

So much for U.S. government treaties with American Indians! By 1900 there were only about 200 Kansa Indians, although in the 1980 census 677 individuals identified themselves as Kansa.

Lost Indians of Texas

The area that is now the state of Texas contained large numbers of a variety of American Indian tribes at the time of the first European contacts. Included

5-2. Texas Indian Tribes

were the Kiowa, the Comanche, and the Apache of the arid western plains, the Waco of the central area, the Karankawa of the Gulf Coast, and the Nacog-doche of the eastern pinewoods (see map 5-2). In fact, one authority, John C. Ewers (1973:104), has stated: "Nowhere else in the American west did tribes of so many cultures live in such close proximity in the historic period. In Texas alone, buffalo-hunting nomads of the plains met not only horticultural tribes of the plains and woodlands, but also hunter-gatherers of the south-western deserts and fishermen of the Gulf Coast."

Although we know there were many tribes with large populations, we to-day have no complete idea of the number of Texas tribes or the total Indian population; we have only clues.[7] Many tribes were gone before anything more than their names were recorded; others were surely gone before they

---

7. John Ewers (1969:99) noted: "The problem of identifying, locating and estimating the populations of the Indian tribes of Texas . . . continues to plague historians and ethnologists. More tribes have lived in Texas during historic times than in any other state of the United States."

were recorded. For example, the explorer Jean Louis Berlandier, who traveled through parts of Texas in 1828–29, when the area was part of the Mexican state of Coahuila, wrote with reference to the explorations of René-Robert Cavelier de La Salle:

> In the journal of De La Salle's expedition Mr. Joutel mentions more than 51 nations then living in Texas, none of which is known to us today. On the banks of what he calls the Princesse and Maligne rivers, by which I think he means the Rio Colorado and the Brazos, he lists the Hebahamo, Cenis, Spicheats, Kabayes, Thecamons, Theauremets, Kiaboha, Choumenes, Kouans, Arhua, Enepiahos, Ahouerhopiheim, Kioenkake, Konkone, Omeaosse, Keremen, Ahehoen, Maghai, Tecamenes, Otenmarhem, Kasayan, and Meracouman. West and northwest of these rivers lived the Kannehouan, Touhaka, Pehir, Coyabeguz, Onapien, Pichar, Tehan, Kiasses, Chanens, Tsera, Bocrettes, Tsepohoen, Fercoutcha, Panego, Petaho, Petzares, Piesacho, Peihoum, and Orcampion.
>
> These are undoubtedly names Joutel heard from the Texas tribesmen (he called them *Teas*) the expedition encountered in its quest for the Cenis villages, Still to be added to this wearisome catalogue is the great Cenis nation, with whom two of De La Salle's men took refuge at the time of his first expedition into the interior. The Assony, Pieux, Cannehatimo, Cappa, Natsoches, Nachitos, Cadodaquis, Teniguo, and Cahainihoua are still to be found in Texas.
>
> Of the 52 nations Mr. Joutel listed in 1685, scarcely three or four are known nowadays under the names the explorer gives them.[8]

Texas Indians began to decline soon after Europeans arrived in the Western Hemisphere. As early as 1528 the Karankawa experienced an epidemic, probably of cholera; subsequently there were 30 known epidemics before 1892, mostly of smallpox. Epidemic smallpox occurred in 1674–75, 1688–89, 1739, circa 1746, 1750, 1759, 1763, 1766, 1778, 1801–1802, 1816, 1839–40, 1861–62 and 1864. And "yet another smallpox epidemic was averted among the Mescalero during the winter of 1882–83 when timely vaccination enabled these Indians to escape 'without a single case of smallpox'" (Ewers, 1973 : 107). (In 1877 there was another smallpox epidemic among the Mescalero Apache of New Mexico Territory.) There were also several serious epidemics of cholera, measles, and other diseases (see table 5-11).

Although epidemics were the major cause of Texas Indian depopulation, they were not the only cause: "Intertribal warfare and wars with Spaniards, Mexicans, Texans, and citizens of the United States also took their toll. Overindulgence in liquor on the part of Indians living near white settlements also contributed to this decrease, as did veneral disease, malnutrition, and starvation" (Ewers, 1973 : 107).

We have, as I mentioned, no good figures for the total population of Texas Indians before 1690. At about that time they surely numbered at least 42,000, as indicated in table 5-12; and Ewers (1973 : 107) has asserted that they may have numbered 50,000. Certainly they had numbered far more in 1492.

---

8. John Ewers (1969 : 100) identified many tribes which Berlandier could not.

TABLE 5-II: **Epidemics Among Texas Indians, 1528–1892**

Date	Epidemic	Tribe/Area
1528	Cholera (?)	Karankawan
1674–75	Smallpox	Coahuiltecan
1688–89	Smallpox	La Salle's Fort
1691	?	Caddo
1706	Smallpox	Coahuiltecan
1718	?	Caddo
1739	Smallpox and measles	San Antonio missions
Before 1746	Smallpox and measles	Tonkawa and Atakapan
1750	Smallpox	San Xavier missions; Tonkawa and Atakapan
1751	?	San Antonio missions
1753	Malaria or dysentery	San Xavier missions; Tonkawan and Atakapan
1759	Smallpox	East Texas
1763	?	San Antonio missions
1763–64	Smallpox	San Lorenzo de la Santa Cruz Mission; Lipan Apache
1766	Smallpox or measles	Karankawan
1777–78	Cholera or plague	Caddo, Wichita, Tonkawa, or Atakapan
1778	Smallpox	Texas
1801–1802	Smallpox	Texas
1803	Measles	Caddo
1816	Smallpox	Caddo, Wichita, Comanche, Kiowa, Kiowa-Apache
1839–40	Smallpox	Kiowa, Kiowa-Apache, Comanche
1849	Cholera	Kiowa, Kiowa-Apache, Apache, Cheyenne, Comanche
1861–62	Smallpox	Kiowa, Kiowa-Apache, Comanche, Cheyenne, and Arapaho
1864	Smallpox	Wichita, Caddo
1867	Cholera	Wichita, Caddo
1877	Smallpox	Mescalero Apache
1877	Measles and fever	Kiowa, Kiowa-Apache, Cheyenne, Arapaho
1882	Whooping cough and malarial fever	Kiowa, Kiowa-Apache, Comanche, Wichita
1889–90	Influenza	Cheyenne, Arapaho
1892	Measles, influenza, and whooping cough	Comanche, Wichita, and Caddo

SOURCE: Ewers (1973:108–109).

TABLE 5-12: **Population History of Texas Indians, 1690–1890**

Tribe or Group	1690 Population	1890 Population	Reduction (%)
Karankawan	2,800	Extinct	100
Akokisa	500	Extinct	100
Bidui	500	Extinct	100
Coahuiltecan	7,500	Extinct	100
Tonkawan	1,600	56	97
Caddo (of Texas)	8,500	536	94
Wichita (of Texas)	3,200	358	89
Kichai	500	66	87
Lipan Apache	500	60	88
Mescalero Apache	700	473	32
Kiowa-Apache	300+ (1780)	326	+9
Comanche	7,000	1,598	77
Kiowa	2,000 (1780)	1,140	43
Arapaho	3,000 (1780)	} 5,630	13
Cheyenne	3,500+ (1780)		

SOURCE: Ewers (1973:106).

By 1890 many Texas tribes had become extinct or nearly so; others were but remnants of former tribes. The list includes the Texas, or Tejas, Indians who gave their name to the state.[9] The explorer Jean Berlandier (1969:149) noted: "They were one of the first native peoples in the country to welcome the missionaries. The Texas were generally friendly to the Frenchmen of De La Salle's expedition, and many deserters, including La Salle's murderers, found sanctuary with them. The Spanish founded a mission in their village to convert them and called the place San Francisco." At the time Berlandier visited in 1828–29 he found that the Texas tribe had "dwindled to a handful but which has given its name to one of the most beautiful parts of Mexico" (Berlandier, 1969:149).

Their way of life was destroyed totally.

HOPE FOR THE FUTURE? THE REPORT OF
THE DOOLITTLE COMMITTEE

At the end of its Civil War the U.S. government became alarmed at the rapid decreases in American Indian populations, perhaps in some measure because the Civil War had drastically reduced some tribes, such as the Cherokee. On March 3, 1865, a congressional resolution called for a joint special committee of Congress to investigate the depopulation, chaired by Senator James Doolittle of Wisconsin. The committee made its report on January 26, 1867. Entitled "Conditions of the Indian Tribes," the report contained a discussion of rea-

9. There is confusion about who the Texas, or Tejas, Indians were. It is discussed in Berlandier (1969:149) by John Ewers, who edited the work.

sons why the American Indian population was decreasing and suggested remedies. Its first three conclusions were:

First. The Indians everywhere, with the exception of the tribes within the Indian Territory, are rapidly decreasing in numbers from various causes: By disease; by intemperance; by wars, among themselves and with the whites; by the steady and resistless emigration of white men into the territories of the west, which, confining the Indians to still narrower limits, destroys that game which, in their normal state, constitutes their principal means of subsistence; and by the irrespressible conflict between a superior and inferior race when brought in presence of each other. . . .

Second. The committee are of opinion that in a large majority of cases Indian wars are to be traced to the aggressions of lawless white men, always to be found upon the frontier, or boundary line between savage and civilized life. . . .

From whatever cause wars may be brought on, either between different Indian tribes or between the indians and the whites, they are very destructive, no only of the lives of the warriors engaged in it, but of the women and children also, often becoming a war of extermination. Such is the rule of savage warfare, and it is difficult if not impossible to restrain white men, especially white men upon the frontiers, from adopting the same mode of warfare against the Indians. The indiscriminate slaughter of men, women, and children has frequently occurred in the history of Indian wars.

Third. Another potent cause of their decay is to be found in the loss of their hunting grounds and in the destruction of that game upon which the Indian subsists. This cause, always powerful, has of late greatly increased. Until the white settlements crossed the Mississippi, the Indians could still find hunting grounds without limit and game, especially the buffalo, in great abundance upon the western plains.

But the discovery of gold and silver in California, and in all the mountain territories, poured a flood of hardy and adventurous miners across those plains, and into all the valleys and gorges of the mountains from the east.

Two lines of railroad are rapidly crossing the plains, one by the valley of the Platte, and the other by the Smoky Hill. They will soon reach the Rocky mountains, crossing the centre of the great buffalo range in two lines from east to west. It is to be doubted if the buffalo in his migrations will many times cross a railroad where trains are passing and repassing, and with the disappearance of the buffalo from this immense region, all the powerful tribes of the plains will inevitably disappear, and remain north of the Platte or south of the Arkansas. Another route further north, from Minnesota by the Upper Missouri, and one further south, from Arkansas by the Canadian, are projected, and will soon be pressed forward. These will drive the last vestige of the buffalo from all the region east of the Rocky mountains, and put an end to the wild man's means of life.

On the other hand, the emigration from California and Oregon into the Territories from the west is filling every valley and gorge of the mountains with the most energetic and fearless men in the world. In those wild regions, where no civil law has ever been administered, and where our military forces have scarcely penetrated, these adventurers are practically without any law, except such as they impose upon themselves, viz: the law of necessity and of self-defence.

Even after territorial governments are established over them in form by Congress, the population is so sparse and the administration of the civil law so feeble that the people are practically without any law but their own will. In their eager search for gold or fertile tracts of land, the boundaries of Indian reservations are wholly disregarded; conflicts ensue; exterminating wars follow, in which the Indian is, of course, at the last, overwhelmed if not destroyed. (Prucha, 1975:102–103)

The committee report adequately assessed the reasons of American Indian depopulation and appropriately placed the blame on non-Indians. Its failing seemed to be in the solutions it recommended. One remedy offered was that the Indian Bureau should remain in the Department of the Interior rather than being transferred back to the War Department, where it had been before the Department of the Interior was established in 1849. Another recommendation was the establishment of five boards of inspection to correct or ameliorate the abuses of Indian tribes arising from the system that the U.S. government used to deal with them (Prucha, 1975:103–105).[10] Both of these recommendations were weak efforts to maintain and facilitate appropriate ways of dealing with the "Indian problem," which the committee's report stated "can never be remedied until the Indian race is civilized or shall entirely disappear" (Prucha, 1975:104).

THE NET EFFECT

The already decimated American Indian population in the United States declined even further during the nineteenth century: from about 600,000 in 1800 to a mere 250,000 between 1890 and 1900. In the last decade of the century the total population reached nadir, before beginning the slow increase that is the topic of Chapter 7, "American Indian Population Recovery: 1900 to Today." Meanwhile, the non-Indian population of the United States increased from about 5 million in 1800 to about 63 million in 1890 to over 75 million in 1900. Obviously, different demographic processes were occurring in the two distinct populations.

10. Robert M. Utley (1984:99–127) has discussed the debate over moving the Indian Bureau back to the War Department as well as the findings of the Doolittle Committee.

6. THE GREAT GHOST DANCES

They promised how we are going to live peacefully on the land we still own and how they are going to show us the new ways of living . . . , but all that was realized out of the agreements with the Great Father was, we are dying off.

—SITTING BULL (SIOUX)

Above I have heard is where they will go,
The ghosts of the people rhythmically swaying.
—WINTU EARTH LODGE CULT SONG

We shall live again; we shall live again.
—COMANCHE GHOST DANCE SONG

That part about the dead returning was what appealed to me.
—SIOUX MAN

IN RESPONSE TO SEVERE demographic losses and resulting social and cultural collapse, many western American Indian tribes, particularly the smaller ones and those that suffered larger population losses, turned not to a place in American society but away from it. They sought to reestablish former societies, cultures, even populations. To do so, they created two new religions, or revitalization movements—one around 1870, the other around 1890—which were deliberate group efforts to reaffirm or recreate established ways of the past. Prophesied in both was a return to the lifeways of the masses of American Indian dead through the performance of prescribed ceremonial dances. Hence the religious movements came to be known as Ghost Dances.[1]

Although separate movements, the 1870 and 1890 Ghost Dances were similar in basic respects. Both originated in the same area of extreme western Nevada near the Walker River Indian Reservation. The initial prophets and early disciples of both movements belonged to the same American Indian tribe: the Paviotso, or Northern Paiute. A family link even existed between them since a disciple of the 1870 dance was the father of the originator of the 1890 dance. The objectives and ceremonies were basically the same in 1870 and 1890: both Ghost Dances primarily sought a return to life of American Indian dead; both involved similar ceremonial songs and dances.

Yet despite those important similarities, each Ghost Dance was a distinct religious effort. Approximately 20 years passed between the two dances. They involved American Indians in different geographical areas with only slight

1. Parts of this first section of Chapter 6 have been published in Thornton (1981, 1982, 1986b).

6-1. Areas Influenced by the 1870 and the 1890 Ghost Dance Religions

overlap (see map 6-1). The 1870 religion spread from a late 1860s origin in western Nevada to adjacent areas of the state, then into Oregon and California, where it perhaps was the strongest and certainly was the most pervasive. In contrast, from a late 1880s origin at virtually the same location, the 1890 Ghost Dance spread only slightly into Oregon and California, though it affected tribes in Nevada. It spread primarily north, east, and south to tribes in the Idaho, Montana, Utah, Dakota, Oklahoma, New Mexico, and Arizona territories, as well as to some in other areas. As shown in map 6-1, the 1890 Ghost Dance was embraced by American Indians in much of the central portion of the western United States, as opposed to the more limited area of the 1870 religion.

THE 1870 GHOST DANCE

The originator of the 1870 Ghost Dance was the Paviotso Wodziwob. The religion began when Wodziwob fell into a trance in which it was revealed to him that spirits of Indian dead could return to earth and change it into a paradise for American Indians. There would also occur, according to his revelation, eternal life for Indians and a disappearance of all whites. Wodziwob's trance happened sometime during the late 1860s, yet the probable date of his first teaching of the new religion was 1869, or possibly 1868 (Mooney, 1896:702; DuBois, 1939:4).

In the 1870s disciples soon began to spread Wodziwob's divine prophecies. His primary disciple was a fellow Northern Paiute tribesman, Weneyuga (Frank Spencer), who became a prophet of the movement in his own right. Among the other, less important disciples was another Northern Paiute, Tavivo (or Numataivo), who was the father of Wovoka, the originator of the 1890 Ghost Dance.[2] According to scholars, Wodziwob lived until about 1918 and was arrested by the U.S. government for practicing shamanism on the Walker River Reservation only a few years before he died (Hittman, 1973:267).

As disciples and others spread the 1870 religion to more and more American Indian tribes, and the tribes adapted it to their circumstances and beliefs, new prophecies were added to Wodziwob's, as were new ways that existing prophecies might be fulfilled. A common new prophecy was the return to earth of an abundance of the animals, fish, and flora on which American Indians had depended for food (Mooney, 1896:703; Spier, 1927:47; DuBois, 1939:10). Common additions to existing prophecies involved the elimination of non-Indians (some tribes said by fire [DuBois, 1939:10], some said by merging the races [Mooney, 1896:703]); and the return of the Indian dead (some said a Supreme Ruler would bring them [Mooney, 1896:703], some said they would return from graves [DuBois, 1939:22], and some said the dead would return from the rising sun in armies [DuBois, 1939:15]). The return of the dead to life remained the central purpose of the religion (Kroeber, 1904:34).

The American Indians involved in the 1870 Ghost Dance sincerely believed that their dead would return, and that other prophesied events would occur, if they performed the ghost dance, which was derived from a Paviotso round dance used on special ceremonial occasions. In the dance men and women joined hands in a circle, then rotated the circle to the left using a shuffling sidestep. During the Ghost Dance ceremonies visions were often experienced by participants and expressed in the form of "ghost" songs. Unfortunately, none of the 1870 Ghost Dance songs were recorded or are known to exist, according to Alfred Kroeber (1925:868), although some songs did survive from the cults that later developed from the 1870 dance.

As with the prophecies, new features were added to the ceremony as the

2. The exact nature of this family link was the object of considerable scholarly debate. Although James Mooney (1896:701) attributed the origin of the 1870 movement to Tavivo (Numataivo), the father of Wovoka, the originator of the 1890 movement, he was mistaken. The anthropologist Cora DuBois (1939:3–4) correctly pointed out that the originator of the 1870 movement was Wodziwob, of whom Tavivo (Numataivo), the father of Wovoka, was a disciple.

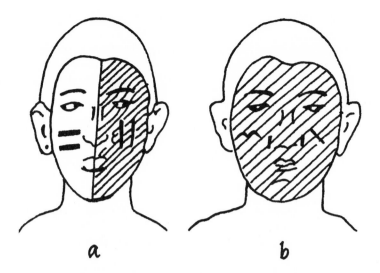

Fig. 6-1. Karok Facial Painting for the 1870 Ghost Dance: (a) for men, (b) for women. The unshaded area of the face was white; the shaded area, red; the solid area, black. Source: Dubois (1939:17).

religion spread from tribe to tribe. For example, some tribes performed the dance around a pole; some tribes had as many as 10 circles of dancers, sometimes rotating in opposite directions; and sometimes special costumes, paraphernalia, and facial painting were involved (see figure 6-1). Despite such tribal differences, two characteristics of the original Paviotso round dance seemingly were always present: a circular movement and a clasping of hands.

An 1871 Western Mono Indian (Monache) Ghost Dance ceremony in California has been described. It showed the two basic characteristics as well as some unique features:

> The dancers formed a circle, at times two or three concentric circles, depending on the number of participants, with men and women alternating. Each person clasped the hands of his neighbor, but without the fingers interlocked, and with forearms held upright so the hands were at shoulder level. The progress of movement was clockwise, with short steps to the left. The dress of the dancers differed: some wore "American" clothes, some women wore the old grass skirts or deerskin aprons, some men wore cloth or deerskin breech clouts. Everyone had his face painted. A new paint called wawun (Western Mono) of a bluish green color was brought to this dance by the Paiute. The Paiute also brought red paint but it was not new at this time. There were no special paint designs associated with the Ghost Dance cult; those persons who had totemic or moiety patterns used them, others put on any design they wished. . . .
> A group of singers sat within the circle of dancers. They wore their cus-

tomary feather headresses . . . and used the elderwood hand-clapper for accompaniment.

The whole scene was illuminated by large fires within and without the circle. (Gayton, 1930:67–68)

Once started, the 1870 religion spread quickly from western Nevada, first to adjacent bands of Paviotso Indians, then into nearer parts of the states of California and Oregon (DuBois, 1939:129; also Spier, 1927; Nash, 1937). The movement apparently did not spread far beyond this immediate area until after 1870, but from 1871 onward it spread in all four directions, particularly through Oregon and California, where the dance was performed by tribes extending south through much of the San Joaquin Valley. One dance in Tulare County, California, was said to have drawn 5,000 to 6,000 Indians from different tribes; as many as 762 danced at any one time (see *Tulares*, 1953, also 1952). Knowledge of the Ghost Dance religion even reached the Mission Indians of southern California, although it is thought that they did not actually participate because many had been converted to Catholicism (see Kroeber, 1904, 1925).

The ways that the religion reached such distant tribes varied. According to Cora DuBois (1939:135–39), information was carried by train, horseback, and buggy, either by a missionary from a practicing tribe sent to convert a tribe, or by a delegate sent by an interested tribe to inquire about the movement among a tribe already involved.

The American Indian peoples who eventually participated in the 1870 Ghost Dance or its later cults were the Achumawi, the Alsea, the Atsugewi, the Bannock, the Cahto, the Chilula, the Coos, the Costanoan, the Gosiute, the Huchnom, the Kalapuya, the Karok, the Klamath, the Konkow, the Lassik, the Miwok (Coast, Eastern, and Lake), the Modoc, the Mono (Monache), the Nisenan, the Nomlaki, the Paiute (Northern and Southern), the Patwin, the Pomo, the Santiam, the Shasta, the Shoshoni, the Siuslaw, the Tolowa, the Tututni, the Umpqua, the Ute, the Wailaki, the Wappo, the Washo, the Whilkut, the Wintu, the Yana, the Yoncalla, the Yuki, the Yokuts, and the Yurok (see Thornton, 1986b).[3]

As the 1870 Ghost Dance grew, three distinct religious cults developed among certain tribes: the Earth Lodge Cult, the Bole-Maru, and the Big Head Cult, an offshoot of the Bole-Maru.

The Earth Lodge Cult originated from the Ghost Dance among the severely depopulated Northern Yana shortly after 1870. It spread from them to the Hill Patwin, the Lake and Coast Miwok, the Cahto, the Wintu, the

---

3. The 1870 Ghost Dance is said to have spread even to the Mormons of Utah, causing excitement among them. Mooney asserted: "When the news of this (the 1870 Ghost Dance) revelation came to their ears, the Mormon priests accepted it as a prophecy of speedy fulfillment of their own traditions. . . . It is sufficiently evident that the Mormons took an active interest in the religious ferment then existing among the neighboring tribes and helped give shape to doctrine which crystalized some years later in the [1890] Ghost Dance" (Mooney, 1896:703–704). This, however, may not be true: little, if any, additional evidence exists that the Mormons really became involved in either Ghost Dance. See Mooney (1896:792–93), and Lanternari (1963:133–34) for further discussion of the Mormons and the Ghost Dance movements.

Shasta, the Achumawi, the Wappo, the Coast Yuki, the Sinkyone, the Pomo, and the Nomlaki in California, and to several of the small tribes in Oregon (Bean and Vane, 1978:670). The cult's basic tenets were that world destruction was imminent and survival could be ensured only by performing religious rituals in ceremonial earth lodges, which were especially constructed by excavating an area of earth, then constructing a wall and roof. Followers of the cult also prophesied the return of American Indian dead (DuBois, 1939:132).

The Bole-Maru name comes from the combination of Patwin and Pomo Indian words for this Ghost Dance cult, which developed among the California Hill Patwin as an offshoot from their earlier Ghost Dance (DuBois, 1939:1). Bole-Maru followers emphasized individual salvation through a Supreme Being and a ceremonial dreamer, that is, a person who could see into the future. The Bole-Maru was particularly popular among the Pomo and the nearby Maidu of California, as well as among its Patwin originators (Bean and Vane, 1978:67–71). The Big Head Cult, which used special masks, was a ceremonial variation of the early Bole-Maru. It was concentrated in northern California and Oregon (Du Bois, 1939:2, 117–27, 129). Both the Bole-Maru and the Big Head Cult prophesied the resurrection of the American Indian dead, though both likely minimized this idea in favor of other religious prophecies (DuBois, 1939:137–38).

The ceremonies of the cults also involved songs which typically were said to have been received directly from dead relatives and friends. Unlike the original 1870 Ghost Dance songs, some of the cult songs have survived, particularly those of the California Wintu. Two Wintu songs are:

> Above we shall go,
> Along the Milky Way we shall go.
> Above we shall go,
> Along the flower path we shall go.
>   (DuBois, 1939:57)

> Down west, down west,
> Is where we ghosts dance.
> Down west, down west,
> Is where weeping ghosts dance
> Is where we ghosts dance.
>   (DuBois, 1939:57)

By the mid-1870s the Ghost Dance and its three cults had diminished in importance among American Indian peoples. The religious revitalization movement can be said to have ended at that time. The Big Head Cult, however, was prevalent among some Indian peoples through the 1880s (DuBois, 1939:127), and the Bole-Maru religion continues even today (Bean and Vane, 1978:671–72).

Why did the 1870 Ghost Dance end? One reason is that some tribes were forced by fearful settlers and U.S. government agents to forsake the religion (Spier, 1927:51); although the movement was greatly needed by American Indians, it was suppressed by non-Indians. Also, some participants simply lost interest, in some cases probably because "it didn't work" (Gayton, 1930:81; Hittman, 1973:268–69).

THE 1890 GHOST DANCE

The second Ghost Dance originated with a vision by the Paviotso Wovoka (see figure 6-2), whose name means "the cutter." Yet the 1890 movement may also be traced to the 1870 Ghost Dance because of the family connection between Wovoka and Tavivo (Numataivo). Wovoka was known also as Jack Wilson. He was probably around 40 when his vision occurred, most likely in 1887 (Mooney, 1910b:180). If so, he would have been a teenager during the 1870 movement. Wovoka experienced his revelation during an eclipse of the sun at Mason Valley, Nevada, near the Walker River Reservation (Mooney, 1910b:180). The revelation directed him to:

> tell his people they must be good and love one another, have no quarreling, and live in peace with the whites; . . . that they must put away all the old practices that savored of war; that if they faithfully obeyed his instructions they would at last be reunited with their friends in this other world, where there would be no more death or sickness or old age. He was then given the dance he was commanded to bring back to his people. By performing this dance at intervals, for five consecutive days each time, they would secure this happiness to themselves and hasten the event. (Mooney, 1896:772)

Unlike the 1870 prophet Wodziwob, Wovoka actively spread his divine revelation, relying much less extensively on disciples, though they were important to the movement's ultimate growth. He lived until September 20, 1932 (Stewart, 1977), with some continued reverence. As in the 1870 dance, new prophecies, and new ways that prophecies might occur, developed in the 1890 dance as it spread among tribes. Again there was the prophecy of the restoration of game animals (Overholt, 1974), and there were variations in the ways that non-Indians would disappear (for example, some tribes said in a cyclone, some said in an earthquake, some said in a landslide [Fletcher, 1891:57]) and in how the Indian dead would return (Hill, 1944:523).

Despite the variations, the basic prophecy remained constant in the 1890 dance, just as it had earlier. James Mooney commented: "The great underlying principle of the Ghost Dance doctrine is that the time will come when the whole Indian race, living and dead, will be reunited upon a regenerated earth to live a life of aboriginal happiness, forever free from death, disease and misery" (Mooney, 1896:777).

Even the name of the ceremonial dance projected this central prophecy of the return of the dead to life. As Mooney stated, "By the Sioux, Arapaho, and most other prairie tribes it is called the 'spirit' or 'ghost' dance (Sioux, *Wana'ghi wa'chipi*; Arapaho, *Thigu'nawat*), from the fact that everything connected with it relates to the coming of the spirits of the dead from the spirit world, and by this name it has become known among the whites" (Mooney, 1896:791). Some tribes, however, named the ceremony with reference to its performance; for example, the Paiute called it the "dance in a circle," the

Fig. 6-2. Wovoka, the Northern Paiute Ghost Dance Prophet (seated).
Courtesy of Smithsonian Institution, National Anthropological
Archives

Shoshoni, "everyone dragging," the Kiowa, "dance with clasped hands," the Comanche, "with joined hands" (Mooney, 1896:791).

Although the 1890 ceremony, like that of 1870, always involved a circle dance with hands clasped, to accomplish the prophecies (see figure 6-3), specific tribal dances varied, as they had in 1870 (Grinnell, 1891:66; Mooney, 1896: chapter 11, 918; Spicer, 1962:273ff.; Dobyns and Euler, 1967:6). Again, some tribes danced around a pole or tree, which some decorated; some, particularly the Arapaho and the Sioux, wore ghost shirts[4] (see figure 6-8); and some tribes included fasting and sweat baths in their ceremonies.

Central also to the 1890 dance were hypnotic trances and songs that linked the religious prophecies with the physical activity of dancing. Dancers were often hypnotized by leaders or others who had experienced trances, or by the fasting that sometimes preceded the ceremonies, in conjunction with the rhythmic motion of the dancing and the repetitiveness of the songs. While they were hypnotized, or immediately thereafter, individuals experienced visions and sometimes expressed their individual visions in song. Mooney described this in a ceremony involving a young Indian, Paul, and the Arapaho Ghost Dance leader Sitting Bull (not the better-known Sioux chief):

> His brother had died some time before, and as Paul was anxious to see and talk with him, which the new doctrine taught was possible, he attended the next Ghost dance, and putting his hands upon the head of Sitting Bull, according to the regular formula, asked him to help him see his dead brother. . . . Sitting Bull . . . hypnotized him with the eagle feather and the motion of his hands, until he fell unconscious and did really see his brother, but awoke just as he was about to speak to him, probably because one of the dancers had accidentally brushed against him as he lay on the ground. He embodied his experience in a song which was afterward sung in the dance. (Mooney, 1896:923)

James Mooney (1896:953–1102) also reported 1890 songs, mostly from such prairie tribes as the Arapaho, the Cheyenne, the Sioux, the Kiowa, and the Caddo, but also from the Northern Paiute.

The songs which were the creations of individual participants in a dance, were highly individualistic; and a single dance might easily produce several dozen songs. Some songs with special qualities became part of a tribe's opening and closing Ghost Dance ceremonies, and in them we hear the prophecies. For example, Mooney described an Arapaho song as a call for the return of the buffalo:

> How bright is the moonlight.
> How bright is the moonlight.
> Tonight as I ride with my load of buffalo beef.
> Tonight as I ride with my load of buffalo beef.
> (Mooney, 1896:967)

---

4. James Mooney (1896:789–91, 916) related the introduction of the ghost shirts to the Mormons, for which the prophet Wovoka disclaimed any responsibility (Mooney, 1896:772), along with the ghost dresses worn by women of some tribes (see Watkins, 1944).

Fig. 6-3. 1890 Sioux Ghost Dance Ceremony. Courtesy of Smithsonian
Institution, National Anthropological Archives

Two Arapaho songs call for the return of Indian dead:

> My father did not recognize me (at first),
> My father did not recognize me (at first).
> When again he saw me,
> When again he saw me,
> He said, "You are the offspring of a crow,"
> He said, "You are the offspring of a crow."
> (Mooney, 1896:972)

> My mother gave me my *ti'qtawa* stick,
> My mother gave me my *ti'qtawa* stick.
> I fly around with it,
> I fly around with it.
> To make me see my children,
> To make me see my children.
> (Mooney, 1896:1007)

A Sioux song has a similar theme:

> Mother, come home; mother, come home.
> My little brother goes about always crying.

> My little brother goes about always crying.
> Mother, come home; mother, come home.
> (Mooney, 1896:1070)

A Sioux song has both themes:

> The whole world is coming,
> A nation is coming, a nation is coming,
> The Eagle has brought the message to the tribe.
> The father says so, the father says so.
> Over the whole earth they are coming.
> The buffalo are coming, the buffalo are coming.
> The Crow has brought the message to the tribe.
> The father says so, the father says so.
> (Mooney, 1896:1072)

Finally, two Arapaho songs, although they do not contain prophecies, vividly describe the tribe's history since the European arrival:

> My children, when at first I liked the whites,
> My children, when at first I liked the whites,
> I gave them fruits,
> I gave them fruits.
> (Mooney, 1896:961)

> Father, have pity on me,
> Father, have pity on me;
> I am crying for thirst,
> I am crying for thirst;
> All is gone—I have nothing to eat,
> All is gone—I have nothing to eat.
> (Mooney, 1896:977)

Starting from virtually the same geographic area as the 1870 movement, the 1890 religion also spread among adjacent Paviotso in Nevada, Oregon, and California. It was also practiced by the Washo, the Pit River, and the Tule River Indians in the northwest. The dance was not pervasive in that area, however, particularly not in California. Unlike the 1870 Ghost Dance, the 1890 religion spread widely to the east, northeast, and southeast. It was practiced in Idaho, Montana, Utah, Wyoming, Colorado, and the Dakotas by the Arapaho, the Arikara, the Assiniboin, the Bannock, the Cheyenne, the Gosiute, the Gros Ventre, the Hidatsa, the Mandan, the Nez Perce, the Shoshoni, the Sioux, and the Ute, eventually reaching the Dakota Sioux in Canada (see Kehoe, 1968). It also reached Nebraska, Kansas, and Oklahoma Territory, affecting the Southern Arapaho, the Caddo, the Comanche, the Delaware, the Iowa, the Kansa, the Kickapoo, the Kiowa, the Kiowa-Apache, the Oto-Missouri, the Pawnee, and the Wichita. It was also in the nearby New Mexico and Arizona territories and in southern California, practiced by the Chemehuevi, the Walapai, the Havasupai, the Taos Pueblo, and the Kichai (Mooney, 1896:pl. 85).

The Ghost Dance spread to those tribes in the same ways that it had spread in 1870. For example, delegates were sent to practicing tribes and to Wovoka himself. The agent of Wovoka's agency wrote: "His success was rapidly spreading abroad, and from that time on he has had many followers. Many Indians from distant tribes have been here and are now visiting him, and from eighty to a hundred have been to see him during the past six months. They generally pass through these headquarters and usually come with letters from their respective agents accrediting them. These visits do no good, and I would suggest caution in agents giving such letters" (U.S. Commissioner of Indian Affairs, 1891:301).

In 1890, however, the written word, including newspapers and magazines (Remington, 1890:947) and letters (Utley, 1963:67), was much more important on Indian reservations than it had been in 1870. The boarding school system established by the U.S. government for young American Indians had created a cadre who spread the written word. Mooney asserted:

> Under present conditions, when the various tribes are isolated upon widely separated reservations, the Ghost dance could never have become so widespread, and would probably have died out within a year of its inception, had it not been for the efficient aid it received from the returned pupils of various eastern government schools, who conducted the sacred correspondence for their friends at the different agencies, acted as interpreters for the delegates to the messiah, and in various ways assumed the leadership and conduct of the dance. (Mooney, 1896:820)

As was true of the 1870 religion, the 1890 Ghost Dance lasted but a few years. By the mid-1890s many American Indian tribes had ceased to perform the ceremony. Why? The reasons were the same as in 1870: suppression and "lost interest." Yet some tribes, especially those in Oklahoma Territory, incorporated the ceremony into tribal life for many years (Mooney, 1896:927).

The 1890 Sioux Ghost Dance

The death of the great Sioux Indian leader Sitting Bull and the massacre of the Sioux at Wounded Knee Creek on the Pine Ridge Reservation in South Dakota were both related to the Sioux involvement in the 1890 Ghost Dance religion.

Originally a people of the forests, the Sioux had lived across much of the upper Midwest from Lake Superior to north of the headwaters of the Mississippi River in present-day Minnesota. By the early 1700s, however, they had been driven west to the prairies by their enemies the Ojibwe. In but a short time they adapted to the prairie environment and, with the aid of the horse, became "the undisputed masters of an immense territory extending . . . from Minnesota to the Rocky Mountains and from the Yellowstone to the Platte" (Mooney, 1896:824). In this environment they soon grew dependent upon the vast herds of plains buffalo, not only for food but also for clothing, shelter, and social and cultural activities. The Sioux were living on the plains when they first came in contact with immigrant white populations.

By the year 1870, after some 20 years of war with the United States, the Sioux had "negotiated" a series of treaties with the federal government; they were left with only reservation lands, though relatively large ones. When gold was discovered in their sacred Black Hills hunting lands, however, thousands of miners and others rushed there, and the situation eventually resulted in the famous battle of Greasy Grass with General George Armstrong Custer near the Little Big Horn River in southern Montana Territory.

A new agreement was established between the Sioux and the U.S. government by which in 1876 the Sioux lost not only their sacred Black Hills but also a large portion of their other previously guaranteed lands. At this time the Sioux were relying on the federal government for food, housing, and clothing: the great buffalo herds had disappeared along with the Sioux lands. Their situation deteriorated further as more settlers moved onto former Sioux lands and population pressures increased. In 1889 another Sioux–U.S. government agreement was established, by which small reservations were made out of the former one and the Sioux lost yet another large portion of their traditional lands (see map 6-2).

Concomitantly, the Sioux were experiencing crop failures, starvation, and consequent population losses from disease both in the tribe and among their cattle: "In 1888 their cattle had been diminished by disease. In 1889, their crops were a failure. . . . Then followed epidemics of measles, grippe, and whopping cough, in rapid succession and with terribly fatal results. . . . Then came another entire failure of crops in 1890, and an unexpected reduction of rations, and the Indians were brought face to face with starvation" (Mooney, 1896: 826–27). Reliance on the U.S. government then became total dependence.

Most American Indians in the Dakotas faced difficult conditions at the time of the 1890 Ghost Dance, but it was perhaps more true of the Sioux than any other tribe that their involvement in the 1890 religion was a result of harsh experiences immediately preceding it. Having heard of the Ghost Dance through contacts with other prairie tribes, the Sioux, the Northern Cheyenne, and the Northern Arapaho sent a joint delegation late in 1889 to talk with Wovoka in Nevada (Mooney, 1896: 894). The Sioux delegates returned several months later, in March, 1890, and after deliberations with tribal leaders, they and others began to preach the doctrine of the Ghost Dance among numerous Sioux bands (Mooney, 1896: 843). As I have indicated, they called it *wanaghi wachipi*, literally the "spirit," "ghost," or "soul" dance.

The Sioux Indians were not the only ones in the Dakotas who had heard of the Ghost Dance. Settlers and U.S. Indian agents had heard of it also, and they reacted with apprehension and fear. Rumors abounded that the Sioux intended to annihilate settlers. An 1890 report of an agent at Standing Rock Reservation stated:

> I feel it my duty to report the present craze and nature of the excitement existing among the Sitting Bull faction of Indians over the expected Indian millenium, the annihilation of the white man and supremacy of the Indian, which is looked for in the near future and promised by the Indian medicine

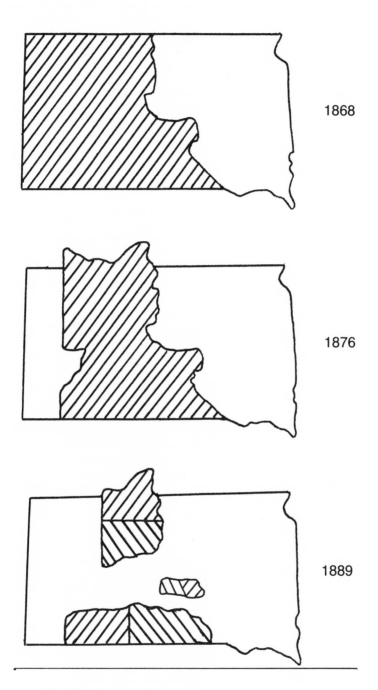

1868

1876

1889

6-2. The Sioux Reservations, 1868–89

men as not later than next spring, when the new grass begins to appear, and is known among the Sioux as the "return of the Ghosts."

They are promised by some members of the Sioux tribe, who have lately developed into medicine men, that the Great Spirit has promised them that their punishment by the dominant race has been sufficient, and that their numbers having now become so decimated will be reinforced by all Indians who are dead; that the dead are all returning to reinhabit this earth, which belongs to the Indians; that they are driving back with them, as they return, immense herds of buffalo, and elegant wild horses to have for the catching; that the Great Spirit promises them that the white man will be unable to make gunpowder in future, and all attempts at such will be a failure, and that the gunpowder now on hand will be useless as against Indians, as it will not throw a bullet with sufficient force to pass through the skin of an Indian; that the Great Spirit had deserted the Indians for a long period, but is now with them and against the whites, and will cover the earth over with thirty feet of additional soil, well sodded and timbered, under which the whites will all be smothered, and any whites who may escape these great phenomena will become small fishes in the rivers of the country, but in order to bring about this happy result the Indians must do their part and become believers and thoroughly organize. (U.S. Commissioner of Indian Affairs, 1891:125)

Settlers and agents even petitioned territorial and federal governments to undertake a military campaign against the Sioux Indians. An agent on the Pine Ridge Reservation, South Dakota, reported: "Indians are dancing in the snow and are wild and crazy. I have fully informed you that employees and Government property at this agency have no protection and are at the mercy of these dancers. Why delay by further investigation? We need protection, and we need it now. The leaders should be arrested and confined in some military post until the matter is quieted, and this should be done at once" (U.S. Commissioner of Indian Affairs, 1891:128).

On November 13, 1890, President Benjamin Harrison ordered the War Department to evaluate the situation from a military perspective (see U.S. Bureau of Indian Affairs, 1890–98). On December 4, 1890, he sent a letter to the secretary of the interior suggesting that there should be no increase in rations for uncooperative Indians, that arrests should be undertaken, and that "the amplest preparations should be made to suppress any outbreak that may result" (U.S. Bureau of Indian Affairs, 1890–98). James Mooney was sent to investigate the Ghost Dance among the Sioux and other tribes. He went first to Oklahoma Territory, then to visit the Sioux and Indians farther west, and made other trips as well. His report, "The Ghost Dance Religion and the Sioux Outbreak of 1890" (Mooney, 1896) has become the classic statement of the movement.

Several thousand U.S. troops were eventually sent to Sioux country, apparently as part of preparations to handle any outbreak. The appearance of troops created fear among the Sioux; several thousand fled their homes to take refuge in the South Dakota Bad Lands (Mooney, 1896:850–52). As a result of these circumstances, the Ghost Dance among the Sioux assumed unique characteristics.

Typical of both the 1870 and the 1890 Ghost Dances was lack of overt hostility toward non-Indians. These were peaceful movements, as viewed by American Indians, although there were sometimes dire predictions about what would happen to non-Indians. Some tribes even named the religion the Jesus Dance. But according to Mooney (1896:777), because of "chronic dissatisfaction . . . the movement assumed a hostile expression" among the Sioux.[5] Some of this hostility is thought to have resulted from direct actions by Ghost Dance disciples: "It was the Sioux disciples who introduced the most substantive alterations in the prophet's message, and in general these lay in the direction of an attitude of greater hostility toward the Whites" (Overholt, 1974:54–55).

As the movement had unique purposes for the Sioux, so did the ghost shirts assume unique features: "only among the Sioux did the disciples push the use of these shirts and relate that use to the possibility of open hostilities between whites and Indians" (Overholt, 1974:55). The disciples' teaching that a ghost shirt made one immune to soldiers' bullets was expressed in a Sioux Ghost Dance song:

> Verily, I have given you my strength,
> Says the father, says the father.
> The shirt will cause you to live,
> Says the father, says the father.   (Mooney, 1896:1073)

The Death of Sitting Bull. Sitting Bull of the Sioux (see figure 6-4) quickly became a marked man, having encouraged his people for many years to resist U.S. domination, and having fought against Custer in 1876. In 1890 he was living with his Hunkpapa band on the Standing Rock Reservation, where the agent, James McLaughlin, considered him to be "the leader and instigator of the excitement on the reservation . . . and advised his removal, and that of several other mischief makers, and their confinement in some military prison at a distance" (Mooney, 1896:848). Even Buffalo Bill Cody sought U.S. government permission to arrest Sitting Bull (see U.S. Bureau of Indian Affairs, 1890–98).

A military order for Sitting Bull's arrest came on December 12, 1890. At daybreak on December 15, 1890, the Sioux leader's house was surrounded by 43 Indian police and volunteers. He was found asleep on the floor, and when they awakened him to inform him of his arrest, he apparently did not object, but merely replied: "All right; I will dress and go with you." In the meantime, however, some 150 of his followers had surrounded his house. When Sitting Bull emerged to go with the police to the agency, he reportedly became excited by the crowd and changed his mind, refusing to go and calling for help. One follower, Catch the Bear, fired his rifle at an Indian policeman, Lieutenant Bull Head. Bull Head and another policeman, Red Tomahawk, then both shot Sitting Bull, mortally wounding him: "Thus died Tata'nka I'yota'nke, Sitting Bull, the great medicine-man of the Sioux, on the morning of December 15, 1890, aged about 56 years. . . . His influence was incompatible with

---

5. The reader should see DeMallie (1982) for an opposing view.

Fig. 6-4. Sitting Bull. Courtesy of Smithsonian Institution, National Anthropological Archives

progress, and his death marks an era in the civilization of the Sioux" (Mooney, 1896 : 860—61).

The Tragedy at Wounded Knee Creek. Following the shooting of Sitting Bull, there was a violent fight between the Indian police and Sitting Bull's followers until the police finally drove them away. Many of Sitting Bull's Hunkpapa "surrendered," but several dozen continued to perform the Ghost Dance ceremony at the Cheyenne River Reservation under the leader Big Foot. As tensions on Cheyenne River and other Dakota reservations further escalated, the Ghost Dancers soon broke away and, joined by others, fled toward the Bad Lands.

Military orders were given to intercept Big Foot. He was captured by Major Samuel M. Whitside, commander of the First Squadron of the Seventh Cavalry, on December 28, 1890, near the Bad Lands he had sought. Big Foot had asked for a parley under a white flag of truce, but was refused. When he surrendered to Major Whitside, he and his followers were taken to a location on Wounded Knee Creek in the Pine Ridge Reservation. (Mooney, 1896 : 867) Additional troops of the Seventh Cavalry, under Colonel James W. Forsythe, joined Major Whitside at Wounded Knee Creek, bringing with them four Hotchkiss machine guns. The total number of military men was now 470. There were 106 warriors with Big Foot, and numerous women and children and old men, for a total of about 350 to 375 Indians.

On December 29, 1890, the military made preparations to disarm Big Foot's warriors before taking them approximately 20 miles to the Pine Ridge agency for removal by the railroad to the Cheyenne River Reservation. Mooney (1896 : 868) described the scene: "In obedience to instructions the Indians had pitched their tipis on the open plain a short distance west of the creek and surrounded on all sides by the soldiers. In the center of the camp the Indians had hoisted a white flag as a sign of peace and a guarantee of safety." Behind the Indians on a slight rise were the four Hotchkiss guns—pointing directly toward the camp" (see map 6-3).

A little after eight o'clock in the morning the Sioux warriors were directed to deliver their arms. Only a few did, and some soldiers surrounded them while others searched the tipis. Tension was building when one warrior, Black Fox, it is said, drew a rifle from under his blanket and fired at the soldiers. They fired back, killing perhaps one-half the warriors in a single volley. Hand-to-hand combat ensued between the surviving warriors and soldiers.

The massacre had only commenced. Mooney wrote:

> At the first volley the Hotchkiss guns trained on the camp opened fire and sent a storm of shells and bullets among the women and children, who had gathered in front of the tipis to watch the unusual spectacle of military display. The guns poured in 2-pound explosive shells at the rate of nearly fifty per minute, mowing down everything alive. The terrible effect may be judged from the fact that one woman survivor, Blue Whirlwind, with whom the author conversed, received fourteen wounds, while each of her two little boys was also wounded by her side. In a few minutes 200 Indian men, women, and children, with 60 soldiers, were lying dead and wounded on the

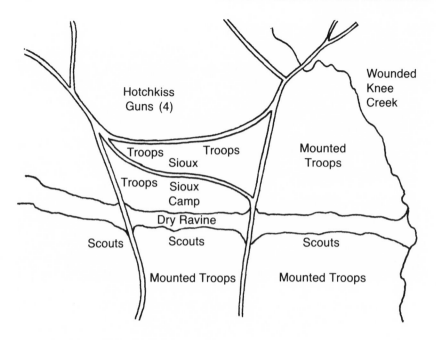

6-3. Wounded Knee, December 29, 1890

ground, the tipis had been torn down by the shells and some of them were burning above the helpless wounded, and the surviving handful of Indians were flying in wild panic to the shelter of the ravine, pursued by hundreds of maddened soldiers and followed up by a raking fire from the Hotchkiss guns, which had been moved into position to sweep the ravine. (Mooney, 1896:869)

Thirty-one soldiers were killed in the "battle" and one or two died later from wounds (Mooney, 1896:871). Reports about the total number of Indians killed at Wounded Knee differ, but it was probably around 300 (Mooney, 1896:871). Most were women and children: their bodies were found "scattered along a distance of two miles from the scene of the encounter," according to the official report of the incident by then U.S. Indian Commissioner T. J. Morgan (Mooney, 1896:870).

Shortly after the massacre, a heavy blizzard arrived. When a detachment of U.S. troops was sent to the scene on New Year's Day, 1891, they found frozen, blood-coated bodies of men, women, and children under the snow: "A number of women and children were found still alive, but all badly wounded or frozen, or both, and most of them died after being brought in. Four babies were found alive under the snow, wrapped in shawls and lying beside their dead mothers . . . . They were all badly frozen and only one lived" (Mooney, 1896:876–77). (See figures 6-5 and 6-6.) Dr. Charles A. Eastman, a Santee

Fig. 6-5. Scene of the Wounded Knee Massacre. Courtesy of Smithsonian Institution, National Anthropological Archives

Fig. 6-6. Chief Big Foot's Body at Wounded Knee. Courtesy of Smithsonian Institution, National Anthropological Archives

Fig. 6-7. Burying the Dead at Wounded Knee. Courtesy of Smithsonian Institution, National Anthropological Archives

Sioux and the physician at the Pine Ridge agency, was with the detachment. Writing in his autobiography, he described what he saw:

> Fully three miles from the scene of the massacre we found the body of a woman completely covered with a blanket of snow, and from this point on we found them scattered along as they had been relentlessly hunted down and slaughtered while fleeing for their lives. Some of our people discovered relatives or friends among the dead, and there was much wailing and mourning. When we reached the spot where the Indian camp had stood, among the fragments of burned tents and other belongings we saw the frozen bodies lying close together or piled one upon another. (Eastman, 1916:111–12)

By that time many of the bodies had been removed by other Indians. The troops then threw the remaining almost 150 dead Sioux into a large trench and buried them. The bodies were mostly naked, as the troops had stripped them of their ghost shirts: "They were only dead Indians" (Mooney, 1896:878). (See figures 6-7 and 6-8.) Later the mass grave was fenced, and the Sioux coated the fence posts with sacred red paint used in their Ghost Dance ceremonies (Mooney, 1896:779). (See figure 6-9.) Although the Ghost Dance

Fig. 6-8. A Sioux Ghost Dance Shirt Worn at the Wounded Knee Massacre.
Courtesy of Department of Anthropology, National Museum of
Natural History, Smithsonian Institution

continued among the Sioux for a period afterward, it was here at the massacre
at Wounded Knee Creek that, as the Indians say, "the dream died."

In 1903 the Sioux erected a monument over the mass grave. The inscription
reads:

> This monument is erected by surviving relatives and other Oglala and
> Cheyenne River Sioux Indians in memory of the Chief Big Foot Massacre
> December 29, 1890.
> Colonel Forsythe in command of the United States Troops.
> Big Foot was a great chief of the Sioux Indians. He often said, "I will
> stand in place till my last day comes." He did many good and brave deeds for
> the white man and the Red Man. Many innocent women and children who
> knew no wrong died here.

A Ghost Dance shirt taken after the Wounded Knee Massacre is on display
at the Smithsonian Institution's National Museum of Natural History. The la-
bel on the display says that it was obtained from the Wounded Knee "battlefield." Plans are being made to remove the shirt from display and to change
the designation "battlefield" to "massacre."[6]

6. Further detail about the Wounded Knee massacre may be found in Eastman (1945), Norbeck (1961), Utley (1963), and Hoover (1979).

Fig. 6-9. Fenced Grave at Wounded Knee. Courtesy of Smithsonian Institution, National Anthropological Archives

THE HOPE OF THE MOVEMENTS

Both Ghost Dance religions brought new hope to North American Indians at a time when they were being destroyed. Tribes saw the religious movements as a means to return to old ways, old lives, through the revitalization that they promised. Perhaps for no other group may this be seen as clearly as for the Pawnee Indians of the late 1800s.

In Pawnee society, as well as other American Indian societies, important tribal knowledge was transmitted orally or through demonstrations by the elderly to the youth of the tribe. Since some knowledge was always kept from young apprentices until the elders were ready to die, one could learn everything only if the teacher lived to an old age. And if an elder died before his time, his knowledge might be lost forever (Lesser, 1933: 110–11).

Therefore it is easy to see what sudden, large population losses could do to the Pawnee and to other American Indians. Conversely, the prospect of the dead's return could bring hope of total restoration of Indian societies by returning lost knowledge and tribal practices. As the anthropologist Alexander Lesser has expressed it,

> Indian ways were not gone, never to be recovered. Indian ways were coming back. Those who had lived before in the "golden age" were still carrying on old ceremonies, old dances, old performances, and old games in the beyond. They were coming back; they were bringing the old ways and the buffalo. Dance, dance, dance. The white man would be destroyed by a great wind. The Indian would be left with the buffalo, with his ancestors, with his old friends and his old enemies. Cast aside the white man's ways like an old garment; put on the clothes of the Indian again. Get ready for the new day and the old times.[7] (Lesser, 1933:112)

Unfortunately many scholars have incorrectly characterized the Ghost Dance movements as American Indian "mass hysteria." For example, one wrote that the 1890 dance is seen as "a hysterical reaction to the disorganization, frustration, and deprivation experienced by . . . Indians after their series of last-ditch battles" (Kehoe, 1968:302). Yet the truth was quite the contrary: the Ghost Dances were *deliberate* religious efforts by American Indians to confront their dire situations. Tribes, such as the Sioux in the 1890 dance, made careful, conscious decisions to participate, sending delegates to other practicing tribes or, in the case of the Sioux and others, to Wovoka himself. Council meetings often followed to discuss the tribe's possible participation and the implications of it. My analysis of the Ghost Dance movements from this perspective (see Thornton, 1981, 1982, 1986b) has demonstrated that the decision to participate was deliberate and closely linked to American Indian depopulation: the participating tribes generally were those who had suffered the larger depopulations, and generally they were smaller tribes in absolute numbers; the nonparticipating tribes were larger and had experienced less depopulation.[8] Participating tribes sought to recover their population losses through the central objective of the Ghost Dances: the return of the dead to life. And such a belief was not unique to American Indians. In response to severe depopulation following colonization, other native peoples of the world have turned to revitalization movements prophesying the return of the dead (Lanternari, 1963:224; Worsley, 1957:146–94).

Thomas M. Overholt commented on the 1890 Ghost Dance: "we may be tempted to write of Wovoka's millennarianism as a foredoomed and irrational response to the crises of white domination. . . . But we should be able to entertain the notion that for people who heard this message . . . calling on the supernatural for aid in throwing off this grave menace must have been, in terms of their culture, an essentially 'rational' act" (Overholt, 1974:46). It

---

7. Along this same line, Clyde A. Milner (1981) argued that nineteenth-century American Indian resistance to assimilation into the larger American society—a resistance typified by the Ghost Dances—was a result of depopulation. He even asserted, "Indians must grow and prosper in order to accept white ways" (Milner, 1981:51).

8. Although the Sioux, with their relatively large 1890 population, were an exception to the general rule, they had suffered substantial population losses immediately prior to becoming involved in the Ghost Dance religion.

made perfect sense to American Indians to perform religious ceremonies such as in the Ghost Dance to recapture the past, including the dead. The Ghost Dance was congruent with their systems of belief and knowledge; they performed it deliberately and purposefully. For example, the Sioux believed that both they and the buffalo had come into the world through a hole in the earth, and when the buffalo disappeared by the late 1800s, they assumed that the buffalo had been offended and had returned to inside the earth. If that was so, the Sioux reasoned, the buffalo could be encouraged to return to the earth's surface again by the new religion (DeMallie, 1982:391).

CONCLUSION

The Ghost Dances were, therefore, American Indian religious responses to demographic decline and attempts to recover population losses. Strange responses? Strange attempts? Perhaps so, perhaps not. The movements were analagous to Indians' and non-Indians' turning to religion and prayer in times of crisis today. Many do it, and we do not think it strange.

Moreover, the Ghost Dance religions probably made more sense to American Indians than religion today makes to many Americans. As Raymond J. DeMallie (1982:391) explained, the Ghost Dance was congruent with the Sioux knowledge system of cause and effect, since religion and science were one and the same to them. In American society today, of course, this is not the case. For us turning to religion involves turning away from scientific concepts of cause and effect.

7. AMERICAN INDIAN POPULATION RECOVERY: 1900 TO TODAY

Although I have adapted to my environment, like immigrants have done, I am still a native of the wilderness.

—RED FOX (SIOUX)

SINCE AROUND THE TURN of the twentieth century American Indians have made a remarkable population recovery as a result of their greatly improved demographic situation. Also related to the recovery have been changes in the biological nature of the Indian population and in the ways by which American Indians have been defined and counted.

TWENTIETH-CENTURY POPULATION RECOVERY

By 1980 the United States Indian population, as enumerated by U.S. censuses, had increased to 1.37 million from its 1890–1900 nadir of about 250,000. The 1980 census counted 1,366,676 American Indians and an additional 42,162 Eskimo and 14,205 Aleutian Islanders, for a grand total of 1,423,043 Native Americans (see table 7-1). After 1980 the American Indian population continued to increase: there were several hundred thousand more American Indians in the United States in 1987 than there were in 1980. Of course, the American Indian population is still far smaller than the estimated 5+ million in 1492, some 500 years ago. Moreover, as shown in table 7-1, the non-Indian population of the United States increased from about 63 million in 1890 (and from zero in 1492) to some 225 million in the 1980 census (226+ million total population minus 1+ million American Indians).[1] Of course, since 1980 the non-Indian population has also continued to increase.

Most of the American Indian population growth shown in table 7-1 took place after 1950, before which time the total United States population was growing faster than the American Indian segment. As discussed in Chapter 8, the large American Indian "increase" in the 1920s shown in table 7-1 resulted partly from changes in U.S. census procedures, as did part of the decrease between 1910 and 1920 (although that followed a depopulating 1918 influenza epidemic) and some of the increase from 1950 to 1960. Between 1950 and 1980

---

1. Part of this increase was due to immigration: according to Borrie (1970:89), between 1881 and 1940, some 28 million people immigrated to the United States from Italy (4.64 million); Austria-Hungary (4.06 million); Russia (3.30 million); Germany (2.97 million); Great Britain (2.31 million); Denmark, Norway, and Sweden (1.95 million); Ireland (1.76 million); and other areas (7.11 million). It has been estimated there were 35.5 million net migrants to the United States between 1790 and 1970, and they contributed, through natural increase, 98 million people to the 1970 United States population.

TABLE 7-1: **Census Enumerations of American Indians and the Total United States Population, 1890–1980**

	American Indian		Total United States	
Date	Size	Change from Previous Decade (%)	Size	Change from Previous Decade (%)
1890	248,253		62,947,714	
1900	237,196	−4.5	75,994,575	20.7
1910	276,927	16.8	91,972,266	21.0
1920	244,437	−11.7	105,710,620	14.9
1930	343,352	40.5	122,775,046	16.1
1940	345,252	0.6	131,669,275	7.2
1950	357,499	3.5	151,325,798	14.5
1960	523,591	46.5	179,323,175	18.5
1970	792,730	51.4	203,302,031	13.4
1980	1,366,676	72.4	226,545,805	11.4

SOURCE: U.S. Bureau of the Census (1915:10, 1973a:xi, 1982–83:6, 1984:14), Swagerty and Thornton (1982:92).

the American Indian population grew about 281 percent, while the total United States population grew only about 48 percent. In 1950 the percentage of the total United States population that was American Indian was only 0.2 percent, basically unchanged since 1890. It increased to 0.3 percent in 1960, about 0.4 percent in 1970, and 0.6 percent in 1980. In 1987 it is perhaps about 0.7 percent.

American Indian Population by State

The census data for the 50 states and the District of Columbia show that the population recovery has not been uniform. Since the turn of the century the American Indian population of some states has increased more than that of other states, as shown in table 7-2. Of importance here, in addition to a natural increase within states, has been a migration of American Indians between states. California, for example, gained many American Indians by migration; one-half of the 200,000 American Indians in California in 1980 were immigrants from other states (Heizer and Elsasser, 1980:225). Large numbers of American Indians have recently moved to California, as have large numbers of non-Indians, and these immigrants have further increased the state's Indian population through natural increases.

In 1987 there were wide variations in the numbers of American Indians from state to state just as there were wide variations in the numbers of non-Indians. Table 7-2 shows that in 1980, California had the largest American Indian population, 198,275, and Vermont had the smallest, 968. According to the 1980 census, California also had the largest total population, 23,667,837, while Alaska had the smallest total population, 401,851.[2]

2. One may wish to see Prucha (1985) for a map showing variations in the American Indian populations both between and within states.

American Indian Population by Tribal Groups

The recovery of the American Indian population has not been uniform among American Indian tribal groups. Some groups have gained population far more rapidly and to a much greater extent than others; some groups have even declined in population during the twentieth century. According to U.S. censuses, the Navajo had tremendous population growth between 1910 and 1980, from 22,455 to 158,633 (they are now far more numerous than in 1492), as did the Sioux, who increased from 22,778 to 78,588, and the Ojibwe, who increased from 20,214 to 73,491.

Other population patterns are also evident, particularly among smaller tribes. In the Northwest and northern California the populations of some smaller tribes have increased significantly (for example, that of the Tolowa, from less than 150 to about 400); others have increased very slightly (for example, the Clatsop, from 26 to 39; and the Coos Bay, from 93 to 128); and others have declined (such as the Walla Walla, from 397 to 262; the Kallapuya, from 106 to 65; and the Yana, from 39 to 0), according to census data (U.S. Bureau of the Census, 1915: 118–21, 1981). At least two American Indian tribal groups had their most drastic depopulation in the twentieth century. The largest Havasupai depopulation occurred in 1906 as a result of a two-year measles epidemic (see Alvarado, 1970). The largest San Juan Southern Paiute depopulation was a result of the 1918 influenza epidemic, which swept the entire world and killed an estimated 21 million people (see Bunte, Franklin, and Stoffle, 1983).

REASONS FOR THE POPULATION RECOVERY

Numerical population increase or decrease in a constantly defined population is the result of change in only three basic variables: births, deaths, and migrations. That is simple, but what factors cause changes in those variables, how changes occur, and the ways that the three basic variables of population change interact are very complex.

By definition, twentieth-century American Indian population recovery had to be the net result of changes in American Indian births, deaths, and migrations if the American Indian population was constantly defined during the twentieth century. American Indians increased, in part, because they had more births than deaths, and because more Indians immigrated into the United States than emigrated out. That is straightforward, yet, as we shall see, why this happened, how it happened, and the effects of the interactions among the births, deaths, and migrations is not. The Indians also increased because of changes in the way they were defined as a population, as we shall see in Chapter 8.

Demographic Transition

Before considering American Indian births and deaths and their relationship to population recovery, some further discussion of how populations grow is necessary. The primary theory of population growth assumes a *demographic*

TABLE 7-2: **American Indian Populations of the Fifty States and the District of Columbia, 1900–1980**

State	1900	1910	1920	1930	1940	1950	1960	1970	1980
Ala.	177	909	405	465	464	928	1,276	2,443	7,502
Alaska	13,152?	11,244	9,918?	10,955	11,283	14,089	14,444	16,276	21,869
Ariz.	26,480	29,201	32,989	43,726	55,076	65,761	83,387	95,812	152,498
Ark.	66	460	106	408	278	533	580	2,014	9,364
Calif.	15,377	16,371	17,360	19,212	18,675	19,947	39,014	91,018	198,275
Colo.	1,437	1,482	1,383	1,395	1,360	1,567	4,238	8,336	17,734
Conn.	153	152	159	162	201	333	923	2,222	4,431
Del.	9	5	2	5	14	?	597	656	1,307
D.C.	22	68	37	40	190	330	587	956	996
Fla.	358	74	518	587	690	1,011	2,504	6,677	19,134
Ga.	19	95	125	43	106	333	749	2,347	7,442
Hawaii	?	?	?	?	?	?	472	1,126	2,655
Idaho	4,226	3,488	3,098	3,638	3,537	3,800	5,231	6,687	10,418
Ill.	16	188	194	469	624	1,443	4,704	11,413	15,846
Ind.	243	279	125	285	223	438	948	3,887	7,682
Iowa	382	471	529	660	733	1,084	1,708	2,992	5,369
Kans.	2,130	2,444	2,276	2,454	1,165?	2,381	5,069	8,672	15,256
Ken.	102	234	57	22	44	234	391	1,531	3,518
La.	593	780	1,066	1,536	1,801	409?	3,587	5,294	11,969
Me.	798	892	839	1,012	1,251	1,522	1,879	2,195	4,057
Md.	3	55	32	50	73	314	1,538	4,239	7,823
Mass.	587	688	555	874	769	1,201	2,118	4,475	7,483
Mich.	6,354	7,519	5,614	7,080	6,282	7,000	9,701	16,854	39,734
Minn.	9,182	9,053	8,761	11,077	12,528	12,533	15,496	23,128	34,831
Miss.	2,203	1,253	1,105	1,458	2,134	2,502	3,442	4,113	6,131

Mo.	130	313	171	578	330	547	1,723	5,405	12,129
Mont.	11,343	10,745	10,956	14,798	16,841	16,606	21,181	27,130	37,598
Neb.	3,322	3,502	2,888	3,256	3,401	3,954	5,545	6,624	9,145
Nev.	5,216	5,240	4,907	4,871	4,747	5,025	6,681	7,933	13,306
N.H.	22	34	23	64	50	74	135	361	1,297
N.J.	63	168	100	213	211	621	1,699	4,706	8,176
N.Mex.	13,144	20,573	19,512	28,941	34,510	41,901	56,255	72,788	107,338
N.Y.	5,257	6,046	5,503	6,973	8,651	10,640	16,491	28,355	38,967
N.C.	5,687	7,851	11,824	16,579	22,546	3,742?	38,129	44,406	64,536
N.Dak.	6,968	6,486	6,254	8,387	10,114	10,766	11,736	14,369	20,120
Ohio	42	127	151	435	338	1,146	1,910	6,654	11,985
Okla.	64,445	74,825	57,337	92,725	63,125	53,769	64,689	98,468	169,292
Oreg.	4,951	5,090	4,590	4,776	4,594	5,820	8,026	13,510	26,591
Pa.	1,629	1,503	337	523	441	1,141	2,122	5,533	9,179
R.I.	35	234	110	318	196	385	932	1,390	2,872
S.C.	121	331	304	959	1,234	554	1,098	2,241	5,665
S.Dak.	20,225	19,137	16,384?	21,833	23,347	23,344	25,794	32,365	44,948
Tenn.	108	216	56	161	114	339	638	2,276	5,013
Tex.	470	702	2,109	1,001	1,103	2,736	5,750	17,957	39,740
Utah	2,623	3,123	2,711	2,869	3,611	4,201	6,961	11,273	19,158
Vt.	5	26	24	36	16	30	57	229	968
Va.	354	539	824	779	198	1,056	2,155	4,853	9,211
Wash.	10,039	10,997	9,061	11,253	11,394	13,816	21,076	33,386	58,186
W.Va.	12	36	7	18	25	160	181	751	1,555
Wis.	8,372	10,142	9,611	11,548	12,265	12,196	14,297	18,924	29,320
Wyo.	1,686	1,486	1,343	1,845	2,349	3,237	4,020	4,980	7,057

SOURCES: U.S. Bureau of the Census (1915:10, 112, 1937:231, 1983c:3, 1984:14), Stanley and Thomas (1978:114), Swagerty and Thornton (1982:92—93).

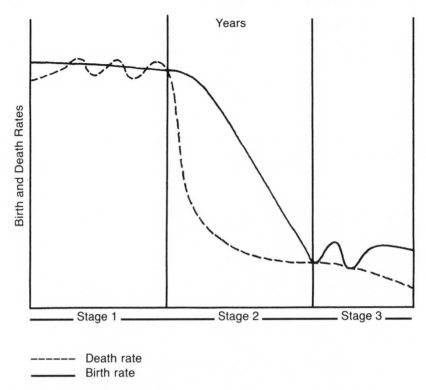

Fig. 7-1. Theory of Demographic Transition

transition[3] through three historical stages: stage one of human populations is characterized by high birth rates and high death rates; stage two, by high birth rates but declining death rates; and stage three, by low birth rates and low death rates. These stages are illustrated in figure 7-1.

Stages one and three are periods of low population growth or even occasional population decline, as the numbers of births and deaths are approximately equal: births and deaths more or less cancel out one another, making for a relatively stable population. Stage two, conversely, is a period of high growth, since the number of births greatly exceeds the number of deaths.

Generally speaking, traditional, nonindustrial societies such as historic American Indian tribes are in stage one; and so-called modern, industrial societies are in stage three. According to population theory, as traditional societies, characterized by high birth and death rates, develop industrial economies, they also foster long life expectancies. Hence, death rates decrease while birth rates remain high, and as a consequence, the society experiences a period of high, often rapid population growth, moving into stage two. Next, according to theory, birth rates decline because of changes in the desired num-

3. See Davis (1945) for a discussion of the demographic transition.

ber of children, contraceptive technologies, and so on, as societies become fully industrialized. Such societies then move into stage three, having low birth and death rates and experiencing little, if any, population growth. This stage has been termed "zero population growth."

There are problems with the demographic transition theory. An important consideration is that it is basically a description of the demographic history of certain societies, particularly those of Western Europe, the United States, and Canada. Many demographers contend that the theory does not even fit the history of those societies; they point out that "the demographic gap, or the period of rapid growth, was caused not only by a falling deathrate but by a rising birthrate as well" (Nam and Philliber, 1984 : 44). A second important problem is that while many supposedly developing societies in Asia, Africa, and South America have been in stage two for a long time, they have not experienced reduced birth rates, often despite persistent efforts to reduce them.

In general, the history of the United States American Indian population does not fit the theory of demographic transition.[4] This is true both of the total American Indian population and individual tribal populations.

The historic pattern of the total American Indian population does not fit, first, because there was an initial very sharp decline in population following European contact, although many tribes, but probably not all, had high birth and death rates before contact with Europeans. After Europeans arrived, American Indian death rates increased markedly, and American Indian birth rates surely decreased also. It was not until almost 400 years later that American Indian population growth occurred.

Second, the theory of demographic transition does not fit because, while growth was caused by decreased American Indian death rates, it was also caused by increased American Indian birth rates. The American Indian population today is characterized by high birth rates and lowered death rates. It is probable that the population will experience low birth and death rates in the not-too-distant future, but it is not possible to say when this will occur.

There have been examinations of the population histories of different American Indian tribes, particularly their twentieth-century recovery, using demographic-transition theory. Many tribes, showing individually unique patterns, seem not to fit the theory any better than the total Indian population, although some do more or less fit, such as the Navajo (see Broudy and May, 1983).

A study of the American Indian population of California indicated high

---

4. A more recent view of the historic patterns and reasons for population growth has been offered by the demographer Donald Cowgill (1949), who defined four population growth cycles: Cycle I, the so-called primitive cycle, where the birth rate stays the same while the death rate decreases and then increases; Cycle II, the so-called modern cycle where both birth and death rates decline, but the death rate declines more rapidly than the birth rate; Cycle III, the future cycle with an increasing birth rate and a constant death rate, then a decreasing birth rate; and finally, Cycle IV, an unnamed cycle in which both birth and death rates increase. To my knowledge, there have been no attempts to examine American Indian population history in relation to Cowgill's cycles.

TABLE 7-3: **Dakota Sioux Birth and Death Rates per 1,000, 1908–10 to 1926–29**

Date	Birth Rate	Death Rate
1908–10	42	28
1911–15	43	28
1916–20	43	37
1921–25	45	37
1926–29	44	36

SOURCE: Wissler (1936a:59).

birth rates and high death rates before 1800, lower birth rates and higher death rates from 1800 to 1900, and higher birth rates and lower death rates since 1900 (Cook, 1976b:103). A study of the San Juan Pueblo in New Mexico showed that, "following a decrease of one-third of the population in 1781, the San Juan Pueblo was found to have undergone three periods of growth: (1) a slow increase until 1850–60, (2) a stationary period, and (3) a rapid gain after 1905–10" (Aberle, Watkins, and Pitney, 1940:183). During this period, most population growth was caused by decreased death rates; birth rates remained fairly high (see Aberle, 1931). The population of the Havasupai, a small tribe in the Southwest, has been somewhat stable during the past 200 years, though it ranged between 300 in 1869 and 166, the nadir population in 1906. Recently, some population growth has occurred because of lower mortality through self-improved health care: the Havasupai population totaled 350 in 1970 (Alvarado, 1970:9), and 527 Havasupai were identified in the 1980 census (U.S. Bureau of the Census, 1981). The Omaha Indians had a phenomenally high nineteenth-century birth rate, supposedly to counteract tremendous mortality rates earlier. Today they continue to have high fertility despite a lowering of mortality rates (see Liberty, 1975). In studying the Gila River Pima, Cary W. Meister (1976:162) found population growth from 1700 to 1846, stability from 1846 to 1858, decline from 1858 to 1882, increase from 1882 to 1890, slight decrease from 1890 to 1895, and then increase from 1895 to 1972.

Clark Wissler (1936a) prepared twentieth-century data on population size, births, and deaths of northern Plains tribes, as shown in tables 7-3 and 7-4. With the exception of two years, 1920 and 1927, the Dakota Sioux had more births than deaths, and a slightly increasing population from 1908 to 1929 (Wissler, 1936a:58). However, as indicated in table 7-3, they also had generally increasing birth and death rates, and there was also a net migration gain of seven individuals during this period (Wissler, 1936a:22). Table 7-4 presents Wissler's data on two other United States northern Plains groups along with three Canadian groups. Here we see a pattern of population increase with fluctuating but often increasing birth rates and more or less declining death rates, with birth rates generally exceeding death rates. Wissler's findings therefore seem at variance with the demographic-transition theory.

Also at variance with the demographic transition are data on the Eskimo of Barrow, Alaska, from 1940 to 1970. They show that women beginning reproduction during periods of economic prosperity had higher fertility than did those beginning reproduction during periods of economic adversity. Fertility

TABLE 7-4: **Birth and Death Rates per 1,000 of Selected Northern Plains Populations, 1895–99 to 1925–29**

| | United States | | | | Canada | | | | | |
| | Cree | | Blackfoot | | Assiniboin | | Battleford | | British Columbia | |
Date	Births	Deaths	Births	Deaths	Births	Deaths	Births	Deaths	Births	Deaths
1895–99	46	45	43	59	47	44	..	..	30	35
1900–1904	50	49	44	67	50	45	..	..	33	45
1905–1909	53	35	39	37	41	21	48	43	37	35
1910–14	..	..	45	55	40	38	49	47	36	37
1915–19	..	..	44	46	45	35	45	47	39	33
1920–24	..	..	..	..	..	..	45	24	..	..
1925–29	..	..	..	..	..	..	43	31	..	..

SOURCE: Wissler (1936a: 60).

behavior thus rose or fell with economic conditions, not according to the tenets of demographic-transition theory (see Masnick and Katz, 1976).

Births and Deaths

In 1890, about the time of the American Indian population nadir, U.S. Indian agents reported births and deaths of American Indians on all reservations for the year ending June 30, 1890. The reports did not include the Iroquois Six Nations of New York, the Eastern Cherokee of North Carolina, the Moki (Hopi), the Pueblo in the New Mexico and Arizona territories, and the so-called Five Civilized Tribes in Indian Territory. Although the data are very incomplete, they do give some insight into American Indian births and deaths of that time. The agents reported 4,908 births and 5,208 deaths; thus there were 300 more American Indian deaths than births during the year. The American Indian population declined accordingly, assuming equal numbers of American Indian immigrants and emigrants (U.S. Bureau of the Census, 1894a:94). Since 1890–1900, generally, births have outnumbered deaths. In 1970, for example, there were 26,880 American Indian and Alaskan Native births (including the Eskimo and the Aleut), but only 5,675 deaths, for a difference of 21,205; in 1980 there were 37,346 such births, but only 6,923 deaths, for a difference of 30,423. In fact, American Indian and Alaskan Native births outnumbered deaths by 235,469 (298,546 births, 63,077 deaths) during the 1970-to-1980 intercensal period (see Passel and Berman, 1985).

Birth Rates. The recent peak of the overall birth rate for American Indians was reported in 1964, when it was 43.3 per 1,000 people. In 1971 the American Indian birth rate was still quite high, 33.0 per 1,000 people (U.S. Department of Health, Education, and Welfare, 1974:18); by 1980 it had declined to 26.7 per 1,000 (U.S. Department of Health and Human Services, 1985:15).[5] Conversely, the total United States birth rate was only 23.7 per 1,000 people in 1960, 18.4 per 1,000 people in 1970, and 15.8 per 1,000 people in 1980 (U.S. Bureau of the Census, 1982–83:xix). (In 1983 the world birth rate was 29 per 1,000 [Population Reference Bureau, 1983].)

Similarly, the 1980 age/fertility ratio—that is, the number of children ever born to 1,000 women of childbearing age (15 to 44 years old)—was 1,687 for American Indian and Alaskan Native women, but only 1,302 for the total United States population (U.S. Bureau of the Census, 1983d:24, 251–52). Thus each 1,000 Native American women of childbearing age in 1980 had 385 more children than did each 1,000 women in the total population.

Death Rates and Life Expectancy. Death rates for American Indians compared with those of the total United States population present a more complicated picture. In 1960 the American Indian death rate was 9.1 per 1,000 people; by 1971 it had decreased to 7.7 per 1,000 people; by the 1980s it had decreased further to approximately 5.0 per 1,000 people.[6] Conversely, in 1960 the total United States population death rate was 9.6 per 1,000 people, slightly higher

---

5. This rate is only for American Indians in reservation states.
6. This rate was calculated from data obtained from the U.S. Indian Health Service (1984), which includes Alaskan Natives as well as American Indians.

TABLE 7-5: **American Indian and Total United States Infant Mortality Rates per 1,000 Live Births, 1955–1980**

Year	American Indian	United States
1955	60.9	26.4
1960	45.5	26.0
1965	40.2	24.7
1970	24.3	20.0
1975	18.2	16.1
1980	13.4	12.6

SOURCE: U.S. Department of Health and Human Services (1985).

than the American Indian death rate; in 1971 it was 9.3 per 1,000 people; and in 1980 it was 8.7 per 1,000 people, which was significantly higher than the American Indian death rate (U.S. Department of Health, Education, and Welfare, 1974:18, 78–79; U.S. Bureau of the Census, 1982–83:xix). Thus during this period American Indians seemingly experienced lower overall death rates than did the total United States population. (In 1983 the world death rate was 11 per 1,000 [Population Reference Bureau, 1983].)

The death rate for American Indian infants far exceeded that of all United States infants during this period, however. In 1955, for example, the death rate for American Indian infants was 60.9 per 1,000 live births, while for the total population the death rate for infants was 26.4 per 1,000 live births. In 1970 the rates were 24.3 and 20.0, respectively; in 1980 they were 13.4 and 12.6, respectively. (See table 7-5.)

Accidents and heart disease have been overwhelmingly the leading causes of death among American Indians during the past several decades. As shown in table 7-6, the accidental death rate for American Indians and Alaskan Natives was 15.56 per 10,000 in 1955, 18.9 per 10,000 in 1967, 15.71 per 10,000 in 1971, and 9.18 per 10,000 in 1980–82; while for the total population the rates per 10,000 were 5.69 in 1955, 5.72 in 1967, and 5.38 in 1971. The death rate from heart disease among Native Americans was 13.38 per 10,000 in 1955, 14.00 per 10,000 in 1967, 14.20 per 10,000 in 1971, and 10.76 per 10,000 in 1980–82; the rates for the total U.S. population were 35.65, 36.45, and 35.84 for those years. Thus American Indians and Alaskan Natives died of accidents much more frequently, and of heart diseases less frequently, than did members of the total U.S. population. Similarly, death rates for these American Indians and Alaskan Natives from influenza, pneumonia, perinatal diseases, diseases of early infancy, cirrhosis, homicide, and suicide were higher than for the total United States population. Conversely, death rates among Native Americans from malignant neoplasms and vascular lesions were far lower than for the total United States population.

The question obviously arises: why these differences in overall Native American and total United States death rates, as well as those for specific causes? Certainly there are inaccuracies in the data, particularly for American Indians and Alaskan Natives. Important, however, are differences in the age structures of the two populations and differences in their life-styles.

TABLE 7-6: **Death Rates per 10,000 of the Ten Leading Causes of Death in the Total U.S. Population and Among the American Indians and Alaskan Natives in States Under the Indian Health Service, 1955, 1967, 1971, and 1980–82**

Cause of Death	1980–82 Indian	1971 Indian	1971 U.S.	1967 Indian	1967 U.S.	1955 Indian	1955 U.S.
Heart Diseases	10.76	14.20	35.84	14.00	36.45	13.38	35.65
Accidents	9.18	15.71	5.38	18.09	5.72	15.56	5.69
Malignant Neoplasms	5.76	6.25	16.09	7.09	15.72	5.91	14.65
Cirrhosis, etc.	2.72	4.56	1.55	3.89	1.41	1.42	1.02
Cerebrovascular Diseases (1982) and Vascular Lesions (1955–71)	2.35	4.28	10.06	4.88	10.22	4.64	10.60
Influenza and Pneumonia	1.77	3.86	2.72	5.35	2.88	8.98	2.71
Homicide	1.59	2.06	0.85	1.99	0.68	1.59	0.45
Diabetes	1.54	2.30	1.82	1.94	1.77	1.39	1.55
Suicide	1.42	1.87	1.11	1.70	1.08	.87	1.02
Perinatal (1982) and Early-Infancy (1955–71) Diseases	1.11	2.96	1.92	4.94	2.44	6.76	3.90
All Causes	50.29	77.19	92.90	86.38	93.57	92.72	93.04

SOURCES: Department of Health, Education, and Welfare (1974:79), Department of Health and Human Services (1985:21).

The American Indian population has been and is far younger than the non-Indian population. In 1970 the median age for American Indian males was 19.9 years and for American Indian females it was 20.9 years; in 1970 the median age for males of the total United States population was 26.8 years and for females of the total United States population it was 29.3 years. Similarly, in 1970 only 5.7 percent of American Indians were over 65 years of age while 9.9 percent of the total United States population was over 65 years of age (U.S. Department of Health, Education, and Welfare, 1974 : 23). In 1980 the median age for American Indians and Alaskan Natives was 23.4, and 5.2 percent of the population were 65 years or older. Meanwhile, the median age of the total United States population was 30.0 years, and 11.4 percent of the population were 65 years or older (U.S. Bureau of the Census, 1982–83 : 27, 30; 1983c : 92).

This has implications for overall death rates and specific causes of death. First, it means the overall rates for Native Americans and the total United States population should not be compared directly, since death rates typically increase with age except for a few years during childhood. Thus one may expect lower death rates for the total American Indian population than for the total United States population—all other things being equal—since the total United States population is considerably older than the non-Indian population. Since the total United States population has more aged people who die more rapidly, it only makes sense to take into account the different age structures through age-adjusted death rates. In 1967, for example, the age-adjusted death rate per 1,000 was greater for American Indians and Alaskan Natives than for the total United States population: 10.5 compared to 7.4, whereas the overall death rates were 8.6 and 9.4, respectively (Hill and Spector, 1971 : 240, 243). This basic pattern was also true in 1980 (Passel and Berman, 1985 : 8) and 1982 (U.S. Department of Health and Human Services (1985 : 23): the age-adjusted mortality rate in 1982 for American Indians and Alaskan Natives was 5.7 per 1,000, while it was 5.5 for all races, only 5.3 for the white population, and 7.0 for all others (U.S. Department of Health and Human Services, 1985 : 23). The same point is illustrated in the above reported infant death rates.

The leading causes of death for the total United States population are diseases of the older ages, that is, heart disease, malignant neoplasms, and vascular diseases. American Indians and Alaskan Natives die of these diseases less frequently than do non-Indians, although heart diseases were the leading cause of death for American Indians and Alaskan Natives in 1980–82. Such a shift in a population from deaths from infectious diseases to deaths from degenerative and man-made diseases has been termed the "epidemiologic transition" (see Omran, 1971). It is to be expected given the significant differences in the age structures of the populations.

American Indian life-styles also involve different causes of death. This is particularly true for death rates due to accidents and cirrhosis, which are both probably related to the higher incidence of alcoholism among American Indians than non-Indians.[7] Also, a study of the Mohave Indians in 1961 (see

---

7. The reader may be interested in seeing Thornton, Sandefur, and Grasmick (1982 : 39–44) for a discussion of American Indian alcoholism, particularly in urban areas.

Devereux, 1961) indicated that the higher suicide rates among American Indians compared to non-Indians may partly be the result of Indians being placed on reservations and the ensuing restrictions of life.

Important differences between the American Indian and the non-Indian population may also be seen in the life expectancies of the two groups. Table 7-7 shows that between 1969 and 1971 the life expectancy for American Indians and Alaskan Natives was 65.1 years, and 10 years later, between 1979 and 1981, it was 71.1 years [8] (but note the important differences between the life expectancies of males and females).[9] In 1970 life expectancy was around 71 years for the total United States population; it was almost 74 years for the total United States population in 1979 (U.S. Bureau of the Census, 1982–83 : 71, 72); while in 1983 the life expectancy of the total world population was 62 years (Population Reference Bureau, 1983). American Indians and Alaskan Natives have gained 20.1 years of life expectancy since 1939–41, even though in 1970 it had been "25 years since life expectancy for whites was as low as that of Indians" (U.S. Department of Health, Eduction, and Welfare, 1974 : 78). American Indians born around 1980 may expect to live about three fewer years than non-Indians.

The Indian Health Service. In large part, the recent decrease in American Indian death rates may be attributed to determined efforts by the U.S. government and its Indian Health Service. Funds were first allocated by Congress for American Indian smallpox vaccination and health care as early as 1832; however, the appropriations remained small until the middle of the twentieth century (Sorkin, 1971 : 51; also Snipp, n.d.). American Indian health care remained inadequate. For example, in the 1880s, when James Mooney was preparing to visit the Eastern Cherokee of North Carolina, he studied a recent census of them and became concerned that their death rate was higher than their birth rate. Enlisting the aid of Dr. Washington Matthews of the Army Medical Museum, he protested to the Bureau of Indian Affairs; and only then did the Bureau send a medical team to North Carolina to attempt to improve Cherokee health care (Moses, 1977 : 34).[10]

In the early twentieth century tuberculosis was an especially serious health problem; morbidity and mortality rates from it among American Indians far exceeded those among non-Indians, particularly whites but also blacks. It was most prevalent among American Indians in the north and northwestern United States and in some parts of Oklahoma, as Aleš Hrdlička (1909 : 6) discussed. In 1910, Indian Commissioner Robert Valentine noted this problem as well as other problems of Indian health in the United States, and indicated a plan to deal with them:

8. See note 6 above.

9. There are also important tribal and sex differences in life expectancy among American Indians. A study of the Navajo in the late 1970s indicated, for example, a life expectancy of 71.8 years for Navajo females, but one of only 58.8 years for Navajo males (see Carr and Lee, 1978).

10. Diane Therese Putney (1980) has discussed American Indian morbidity and U.S. government policy during the early decades of the twentieth century; Haven Emerson (1926) has discussed American Indian morbidity in the 1920s; and Clark Wissler (1936b) has discussed American Indian deaths at that time.

TABLE 7-7: **American Indian and Alaskan Native Life Expectancy at Birth, 1939—41 to 1979—81**

Date	Total	Male	Female
1939–41	51.0	51.3	51.9
1949–51	60.0	58.1	62.2
1959–61	61.7	60.0	65.7
1969–71	65.1	60.7	71.2
1979–81	71.1	67.1	75.1

SOURCE: U.S. Department of Health and Human Services (1985).

The Indian Service in its health work is not aiming merely to more effectively care for and cure those that are sick. The reduction of the death rate is not its primary interest. It is working rather to increase the vitality of the Indian race and to establish for it a new standard of physical well-being. The work is being scientifically developed along lines which have already been successfuly tried out by modern preventive medicine. The principal features of this work as it is now organized are: (1) An intensive attack upon the two diseases that most seriously menace the health of the Indians—trachoma and tuberculosis; (2) preventive work on a large scale, by means of population education along health lines and more effective sanitary inspection; (3) increased attention to the physical welfare of the children in the schools, so that the physical stamina of the coming generation may be conserved and increased. (Prucha, 1975: 212)

Further improvement was made in 1934 under the Johnson-O'Malley Act, which authorized states to contract with the federal government to pay for medical and other services provided by states. It was not until after 1955, however, that real gains in American Indian health care occurred. On July 1, 1955, the U.S. government transferred the health care of American Indians from the Bureau of Indian Affairs to the Public Health Service of the Department of Health, Education, and Welfare. A condition of this transfer was that "all facilities transferred shall be available to meet the health needs of the Indians and that such health needs shall be given priority over that of the non-Indian population" (Prucha, 1975: 237).

Since that date the Indian Health Service has done a remarkable job in many ways, in part because of increased U.S. congressional appropriations (Sorkin, 1971: 51). For example, it has reduced significantly American Indian morbidity and death rates from various causes, particularly infant and maternal death rates and deaths from tuberculosis, gastritis, influenza, and pneumonia. Serious American Indian health problems still remain, however, including injuries, alcoholism, otitis media (middle ear diseases), nutritional deficiencies, and diabetes.

A Note on the Sex Ratio. The sex ratio, expressed typically as the number of men per 100 women, also changed among American Indians during the twentieth century. At birth the sex ratio is slightly over 100, there being more male babies born than female babies. It generally decreases slowly following birth, as females tend to have lower death rates and live longer than males. Generally, too, it varies in a total population from about 95 to 105, depending on the population in question. In populations such as that of the United States, however, it is somewhat below 100. For every decade until 1970 the sex ratio for American Indians was over 100, so that, in contrast to the larger United States population, there were more male than female American Indians. In 1970, however, it was 96.2; in 1980 it was 97.5. In contrast, in 1970 the sex ratio for the total United States population was 94.8, and in 1980 it was 94.5 (U.S. Bureau of the Census, 1983c : 22, 1983d).[11]

Biological Migration

The third component of numerical population change, migration, was of little importance in either the decline of the total United States American Indian population or its twentieth-century recovery. There were American Indian migrations back and forth between the United States, Canada, and Mexico. Some Huron immigrated into the United States from Canada, as we have seen in Chapter 4. Some Dakota Sioux emigrated into Canada from the United States. Some Cherokee emigrated from the United States into Mexico. Some Kickapoo have migrated back and forth between the United States and Mexico, as we shall see in Chapter 9. And some Tuscarora have migrated back and forth between the United States and Canada. There was also an important migration of American Indians into the United States in the early part of this century. Fleeing the subjugation, forced relocation, and genocide of the Mexican government, many Yaqui Indians from northwestern Mexico came to Arizona at that time (Spicer, 1962 : 79–83, 339–42, 404). Over the decades the Yaqui tribe has gradually increased in size here: in 1981 they numbered 5,400, according to Spicer (1983 : 251).

Nevertheless, the numbers involved in these and other migrations have been small; considered together, the rates of immigration and emigration have tended to cancel out one another. Natural increases or decreases have been far more important than migrations per se in the population recovery, though, of course, migrations into or out of a tribe within the United States may have been important in a specific tribal population's recovery or decline.

There has been another type of migration coinciding with the twentieth-century recovery, and an important component of it. This may be termed "biological migration": the migration of non-Indian genes into the American Indian population, that is, the mixing of American Indians with non-Indians, particularly whites but also blacks and other groups.

During the twentieth-century population recovery of American Indians there has been an increasing amount of mixture between them and non-Indian peoples. Data documenting this may be obtained from the 1910 and 1930 U.S. censuses of American Indians (see U.S. Bureau of the Census, 1915, 1937; also Cook, 1943). The U.S. Bureau of the Census asserted (1915 : 31) "the

11. A study of the Navajo tribe indicated that this shift in sex ratio occurred after 1940 because of "(1) a decline in maternal mortality rates; (2) an increase in male mortality rates, particularly from accidents; and (3) greater out-migration of men than women" (Kunitz and Slocumb, 1976 : 33).

TABLE 7-8: **Numbers and Percentages of Full Bloods and Mixed-Bloods in the United States and Alaska, 1910**

Classification	United States		Alaska[a]	
	Number	Percent	Number	Percent
Full-Blood	150,053	56.5	21,444	84.7
Mixed-Blood	93,423	35.2	3,887	15.3
White	88,030	33.1	3,843	15.2
Negro	2,255	0.8	0	0.0
White and Negro	1,793	0.7	0	0.0
Other	80	0.0	43	0.2
Unknown	1,265	0.5	1	0.0
Not Reported	22,207	8.4	0	0.0
Total	265,683	100.0	25,331	100.0

SOURCE: U.S. Bureau of the Census (1915:31).
[a] Includes American Indians, Eskimos, and Aleuts.

Thirteenth Census [conducted in 1910] was the first at which any returns worthy of tabulation were secured as to the proportion of full-bloods and mixed-bloods in the Indian population."

In 1910 only 56.5 percent of the American Indians enumerated in the United States were full blood—150,053 out of 265,683—with the blood quantum of 8.4 percent (22,207) not reported. This is shown in table 7-8, along with racial mixture of mixed-bloods and similar data for the Alaskan Natives. In the U.S. census of 1930, however, 46.3 percent—153,933 out of 332,397—were enumerated as full bloods, and 42.4 percent (141,101) were enumerated as mixed-bloods, with the degree of Indian blood of 11.2 percent (37,363) not reported (U.S. Bureau of the Census, 1937:75). Thus, whereas American Indian population size increased by slightly over 66,000 from 1910 to 1930, the number of full-blood American Indians increased only about 4,000; most of the increase was among mixed-blood American Indians. (Data about the racial composition of the mixed-blood American Indians are not available for 1930 as for 1910.)

There were considerable intertribal differences in the percentages of full bloods in 1910 and 1930, and changes between 1910 and 1930 in the percentages of full bloods. For example, 98.6 percent of Pima Indians were full bloods in 1910, and 97.9 percent in 1930; 92.4 percent of the Arapaho were full bloods in 1910, but only 77.5 percent in 1930; 75.2 percent of the Yokuts were full bloods in 1910, but only 41.4 percent in 1930; and only 34.5 percent of the Ojibwe were full bloods in 1910, but only 18.7 percent in 1930 (U.S. Bureau of the Census, 1937:73). Tribal differences in proportions of full bloods and mixed-bloods continued in the 1980s.

It seems clear that the twentieth-century American Indian population recovery coincided with a biological mixing of the American Indian and non-Indian populations, though this varied considerably by tribe. This does not imply that the mixing caused the American Indian population to increase.

Rather, given their almost total destruction by 1890–1900, many American Indian groups intermarried with non-Indians simply to survive as a people.

The path of mixing was not one-way. Just as non-Indians have contributed to the American Indian population, so have American Indians contributed to the non-Indian population of the United States. Although the 1980 U.S. census enumerated slightly less than 1.4 million American Indians, there were then about 7 million Americans, American Indian and otherwise, with some degree of American Indian ancestry (U.S. Bureau of the Census, 1983b:2). American Indian ancestry actually ranked tenth in the total United States population, in which the nine leading ancestries were, in descending order, English (50 million), German (49 million), Irish (40 million), Afro-American (21 million), French (13 million), Italian (12 million), Scottish (10 million), Polish (8 million), and Mexican (8 million) (U.S. Bureau of the Census, 1983b:2).

BIRTHS, DEATHS, AND BIOLOGICAL MIGRATION

The changes in American Indian birth and death rates and biological migration were not separate during the twentieth-century population recovery. Quite the contrary: they interacted closely. The available data clearly show how important the interaction was.

Fecundity, Fertilty, and Vitality

The 1910 census reported special figures on American Indian fecundity, fertility, and vitality, based on data about the number of children ever born to American Indian women aged 15 to 44,[12] who had been married at least one year and had not been previously married.[13] These women thus had three characteristics: "(1) They were of childbearing age; (2) had been married long enough to have children; and (3) were living in the married state at the time of enumeration" (U.S. Bureau of the Census, 1915:157). The census obtained and reported various kinds of information from these women about them and their children. Included was information about children with differing quantums of Indian blood, since the marriages ranged from marriages between full bloods to marriages between mixed-bloods and whites (U.S. Bureau of the Census, 1915:157).

In table 7-9 are presented the data on sterility from these American Indian women. They show two significant facts. First, and perhaps most significant, the percentage of marriages between full bloods producing no children (10.7 percent) was considerably higher than the percentage of marriages between mixed-bloods producing no children (6.7 percent). Second, the percentage of childless couples decreased as the degree of white blood in a marriage increased, for example, 8.8 percent of full blood–mixed-blood marriages

12. Only women aged 15 to 44 years were included because those are typically the childbearing years.

13. Data on polygamous marriages were also collected, but are not reported here; only 401 of the 21,532 marriages analyzed were polygamous.

TABLE 7-9: **Sterility of Full-Blood and Mixed-Blood Marriages, 1910**

Marriage	Percentage with No Children
Full-Blood	10.7
Same tribe	10.4
Different tribes	16.6
Mixed-Blood	6.7
Full-blood–mixed-blood	8.8
Full-blood–white	7.7
Mixed-bloods	7.0
Mixed-blood–white	5.8

SOURCE: U.S. Bureau of the Census (1915:157).

TABLE 7-10: **Fertility of Full-Blood and Mixed-Blood Marriages, 1910**

Marriage	Percentage Bearing:		
	Two Children or Less	Three to Five Children	Six or More Children
Full-Blood	19.6	47.5	32.9
Same tribe	19.5	47.6	32.9
Different tribe	20.2	47.2	32.6
Mixed-Blood	14.2	42.4	43.4
Full-blood–mixed-blood	14.2	41.7	44.2
Full-blood–white	7.8	43.3	48.9
Mixed-blood	14.4	38.9	46.6
Mixed-blood–white	14.4	45.3	40.3

SOURCE: U.S. Bureau of the Census (1915:158).

produced no children whereas only 5.8 percent of mixed–blood-white marriages produced no children.

The fertility of women married 10 to 20 years in 1910 is shown in table 7-10.[14] The data on the number of children born to these women show the greater fertility of mixed-blood marriages in comparison with full-blood marriages. For example, a smaller proportion of mixed-blood marriages produced either two children or less (14.2 percent) or from three to five children (42.4 percent), and thus a higher proportion produced six or more children (43.4 percent) than was the case in full-blood marriages, where the percentages were 19.6, 47.5, and 32.9, respectively.

Data were collected in 1910 on the average number of children produced by the marriages, as shown in table 7-11. Here again, mixed marriages were more fertile: they averaged 5.1 children, while marriages of full bloods averaged 4.5. Marriages between full-blood Indians and whites had the highest average

14. Only women married from 10 to 20 years were included because this is typically the period of time during which childbearing is completed. There were 7,548 women in the group married for this length of time, 145 of whom were in polygamous marriages.

TABLE 7-II: **Average Number of Children Born in Full-Blood and Mixed-Blood Marriages, 1910**

Marriage	Average Number of Children
Full-Blood	4.5
Same tribe	4.5
Different tribe	4.4
Mixed-Blood	5.1
Full-blood–mixed-blood	5.1
Full-blood–white	5.4
Mixed-blood	5.3
Mixed-blood–white	4.9

SOURCE: U.S. Bureau of the Census (1915:158).

number of children, however: 5.4.[15] (This same pattern was shown by the physical anthropologist Aleš Hrdlička [1931] among Sioux on the Pine Ridge Reservation at the turn of the century.)

The Bureau of the Census also obtained data on the vitality (capacity to live and develop) of children from this group of American Indian women. The data, given in tables 7-12, 7-13, and 7-14, elaborate the differences between full-blood and mixed-blood death rates. Shown in table 7-12 are data on surviving children. Of the children of mixed-blood marriages 79 percent survived, but only 69.7 percent survived in full-blood marriages. Moreover, children with white parents had the highest survival rates: 83.0 percent and 82.9 percent. Why was this so? The Bureau of the Census concluded: "The figures bring out the fact that a larger proportion of the children having one white parent survive than of children both of whose parents are full-blood or mixed-blood Indians, but do not in themselves show whether this is due to conditions in the home or to greater virility of the offspring" (U.S. Bureau of the Census, 1915:159). We will discuss this more later.

Table 7-13 presents data on the percent of women all of whose children survived, but only for marriages in which both parents were full bloods of the same tribe, or both parents were of mixed white and Indian blood, or one parent was of mixed white and Indian blood. The data were restricted in this way in order to have a large enough number for meaningful analysis (U.S. Bureau of the Census, 1915:159). The data show generally that the greater the white blood the greater the vitality of the child. Perhaps the most important exceptions were the survival ratios of single children of full-blood and mixed-blood marriages: 88.7 and 84.3 percent, respectively. The Census Bureau asserted, however, "the number of cases of mixed-bloods is very small, and the result, therefore, cannot be considered at all definite" (U.S. Bureau of the Census, 1915:159). Similarly, in table 7-14 are the percentages of these mar-

15. Not reported is the subgroup of mixed marriages having the highest average number of children. These were marriages in which both wife and husband had some mixture of Indian, white, and black blood.

TABLE 7-12: **Average Percentage of Children Surviving in Full-Blood and Mixed-Blood Marriages, 1910**

Marriage	Percentage Children Surviving
Full-Blood	69.7
Same tribe	70.0
Different tribe	64.0
Mixed-Blood	79.0
Full-blood	69.9
Full-blood–white	82.9
Mixed-blood	77.6
Mixed-blood–white	83.0

SOURCE: U.S. Bureau of the Census (1915:158).

TABLE 7-13: **Percentage of All Children Surviving in Full-Blood and Mixed-Blood Marriages, 1910**

Children Born	Marriage		
	Full-Blood	Mixed-Blood	Mixed-Blood–White
1	88.7	84.3	91.9
2	72.8	79.5	79.2
3	62.2	62.0	71.9
4	48.6	51.8	64.4
5	35.7	42.7	51.7
6	21.5	33.3	38.5
7	10.2	23.1	30.8
8	9.7	20.0	33.8
9	10.1	11.9	11.1
10+	4.6	11.9	8.7

SOURCE: U.S. Bureau of the Census (1915:159).

TABLE 7-14: **Percentage of Full-Blood and Mixed-Blood Marriages with No Children Surviving, 1910**

Children Born	Marriage		
	Full-Blood	Mixed-Blood	Mixed-Blood–White
1	11.3	15.7	8.1
2	6.6	3.4	1.4
3	1.9	0.9	0.9
4	2.0	0.6	0.0
5	0.7	0.4	0.0
6	1.4	0.5	0.0
7	1.3	0.6	0.0
8	0.5	0.0	0.0

SOURCE: U.S. Bureau of the Census (1915:159).

riages in which all the children were deceased: with but one exception (single-child marriages), the largest percentage with no surviving children was among full-blood marriages.

Thus part of the increased mixture of American Indians with non-Indians between 1910 and 1930 was due not to intermarriage itself but to the different rates of growth of the full- and mixed-blood American Indian populations at that time. After issuing and analyzing these data, the U.S. Bureau of the Census concluded, with particular reference to the ongoing population recovery of American Indians: "The results of the studies on sterility, on fecundity, and on vitality all point toward one conclusion, and that is that the increase of the mixed-blood Indians is much greater than that of the full-blood Indians, and that unless the tendencies now at work undergo a decided change the full-bloods are destined to form a decreasing proportion of the total Indian population and ultimately to disappear altogether" (U.S. Bureau of the Census, 1915:159).

Age Structure of the American Indian Population

The 1910 census also reported data on the age distribution of American Indians, by blood. These data also show implications for the population recovery of the American Indians. Reported in table 7-15 are the percentages of the 1910 Indian population, by blood, in three age categories: under 20 years of age, 20 to 50 years of age, and 51 years of age and over. Very evident is the large percentage of mixed-blood American Indians under 20 years of age, compared with the percentage of full-blood Indians in that category. Also to be noted are the different percentages of mixed-tribal full bloods and full bloods from the same tribe. The Bureau of the Census explained: "In both cases the difference may be accounted for in part by the fact that mixed marriages had not become common until within comparatively recent years. Another reason for the predominance of the younger element among the mixed-bloods is no doubt found in the greater fertility of mixed marriages" (U.S. Bureau of the Census, 1915:58). Probably the main reason why mixed marriages had become common was that the Indian population was extremely small. American Indians often found few other possible mates in the same tribe, so that they had to intermarry with members of other tribes or the non-Indian population.

The 1930 census provided related data, but the issue was addressed using median age (the middle age of an age distribution) and degree of Indian blood quantum. The census report offers comparisons of the 1930 American Indian population with the 1920 American Indian population and also with non-Indian populations. Table 7-16 compares the median ages of the 1930 and 1920 United States American Indian populations and the median ages of these populations with non-Indian ones in those years. Thus American Indian populations in 1920 and 1930 were considerably younger than non-Indian populations, with median ages of 19.7 and 19.6, respectively, compared with, for example, ages of 25.6 and 26.9, respectively, for the white populations in those years. Furthermore, in the 1930 American Indian population, mixed-blood American Indians were considerably younger than were full-blood American Indians: the overall median age was 19.6, but the median age of

TABLE 7-15: **Blood Quantum and Age of the American Indian Population of the United States and Alaska, 1910**

Mixture	Under 20 Years (%)	20 to 50 Years (%)	51 Years and Over (%)
United States			
Full-Blood	44.7	38.9	12.0
Full-tribal	43.8	39.5	16.0
Mixed-tribal	57.4	29.9	16.3
Tribal, One Parent Unknown	54.0	30.0	12.5
Mixed-Blood	62.7	31.1	6.1
Total	51.5	36.1	12.0
Alaska			
Full-Blood	43.5	46.2	9.6
Mixed-Blood	69.6	26.1	4.0
Total	47.5	43.1	8.7

SOURCE: U.S. Bureau of the Census (1915:58).

TABLE 7-16: **Median Ages of the American Indian and Non-Indian Population of the United States, 1920 and 1930**

Population	1920	1930
Indian	19.7	19.6
White	25.6	26.9
Native	22.4	23.7
Foreign-born	40.0	43.9
Negro	22.3	23.4
Chinese	40.2	32.3
Japanese	30.2	24.5
Total	25.2	26.4

SOURCE: U.S. Bureau of the Census (1937:88).

mixed-bloods was 16.4 years, and the median age of full bloods was 22.2 years (U.S. Bureau of the Census, 1937:88). According to the 1930 census, "This indicates a rapid assimilation of the Indians into the white or Negro populations. The proportion of full blood Indians is rapidly decreasing and in every generation a smaller proportion of the children are free from race mixture. In tribes with a large admixture of non-Indian blood, the contrast is still greater. In the Chippewa tribe, for example, the median age of the 4,021 returned as full blood was 27.7 years, while that of the 17,170 mixed bloods was 16.4 years" (U.S. Bureau of the Census, 1937:88).

I do not think the differences may be attributed to a greater "virility" of mixed offspring, as the Bureau of the Census speculated in 1915. I suggest rather that they may be attributed to differences in socioeconomic conditions, particularly health care, between the two groups.[16] Nevertheless, the propor-

16. For further information see Daniel C. Swan's (1983) paper on differential fertility among the Osage in 1887.

tion of full-blood American Indians has declined markedly during this century.[17] Today surely far less than 25 percent of the American Indian population truly are full bloods (remember that the percentage was less than 50 percent in 1930). By far the majority of American Indians today have some degree of non-Indian blood.

A LOOK TO THE FUTURE

Despite warnings from the Bureau of the Census, despite a biological mixing between the American Indian and non-Indian populations, despite a lower reproductive capacity of full-blood American Indians, and despite a decline in full bloods, American Indians in the United States have not disappeared. Rather than melting into the much larger non-Indian population, American Indians are thriving today demographically.

Future Population?

Future population projections are easy to make but impossible to make accurately. They depend on assumptions about what might happen, considering past and existing population trends and birth, death, and migration rates. Since we never know what is going to happen to these trends and rates, it is impossible to predict a future population size accurately. Nonetheless, population projections are often made and used to illustrate what a future population size might be.

Analyzing changes in American Indian birth and death rates, the U.S. Department of Health, Education, and Welfare (1974) reported that, if then-current changes in birth and death rates continued, the American Indian population in the United States would increase by more than 150 percent over the next 20 years. The American Indian population has already increased by 70 percent from 1970 to 1980. If this rate of growth from 1970 to 1980 continues to the year 2000, the size of the American Indian population then will surpass 4 million (see Snipp, n.d.). But, it will likely not continue. Recently the U.S. Office of Technology Assessment (U.S. Congress, 1986) published projections of the American Indian population based on data from the Bureau of Indian Affairs. One projection is that the American Indian population will not increase to around 4 million until the year 2020. (Similarly, the total United States population for the year 2025 is projected to be over 300 million [U.S. Bureau of the Census, 1982–83:8].) It is also projected, however, that the American Indian population will increase to almost 16 million by the year 2080 (U.S. Congress, 1986:78).

Navajo Population "Explosion"

Despite the demographic devastation of American Indians following European contact, some tribes managed not only to survive but also to increase in

17. Aleš Hrdlička (1917), for example, noted (and lamented) the declining numbers of Shawnee and Kickapoo full bloods in Oklahoma around 1917; and H. J. Spinden (1928) attempted to arrive at a figure for "full-blood equivalents" in 1928: he estimated that there were 350,000 north of the Rio Grande and 26,050,000 in all of the Western Hemisphere.

size, and substantially so. Without a doubt, an excellent example of this is the Navajo Nation. At the time of the first extensive contacts with Europeans in the seventeenth century, they were considered only a moderate-sized tribe; in 1985 they had the largest formal membership of any tribe in the United States (175,893, according to information obtained from the Bureau of Indian Affairs and the Indian Health Service [U.S. Bureau of Indian Affairs, 1986b]), although the 1980 census enumerated only 158,633 Navajo, fewer than the over 232,000 self-reported Cherokee.

The Navajo are an Athapascan people; probably they migrated along the eastern foothills of the Rocky Mountains into the Southwest from ancestral origins in present-day western Canada and Alaska. They did so perhaps as early as the voyages of Leif Ericsson circa 1000 A.D., but probably the migration was as late as the voyages of Columbus, 500 years ago. The Navajo's first homeland in the Southwest covered the northeastern corner of their present reservation in the Four Corners area (which now surrounds the Hopi Reservation). The Navajo also occupy three small reservation areas in New Mexico: Ramah, Alamo, and Canoncito. On arrival in the Four Corners area, they found the remains of a vanished cliff-dwelling people whom they named the Anasazi. The Navajo called the new land Dinetah (Loh, 1971:50; also Luckert, 1975), which has been translated variously as "Land of the People," "Among the People," "Old Navajo Land," and "Home of the People." They refer to themselves as the Diné, or "people." (According to a recently published study mentioned in Chapter 1 [Williams et al., 1985], ancestors of the Navajo, the Na-Dene, were the second wave of migrants here across Beringia, perhaps about 12,000 years ago.)

The Navajo became organized as a tribe late in the seventeenth century, when they made the transition from an economy based on hunting and gathering to one based on agriculture and herding. From Pueblo neighbors they acquired improved agricultural techniques, particularly in corn planting; from Spanish invaders they acquired sheep, cattle, and horses early in the 1600s. Concomitantly, they began a gradual increase in population and expanded their territory.

In the late seventeenth century they are thought to have numbered about 8,000. They increased more or less steadily until the mid-1800s, when the tribe's population was approximately 150 percent of what it had been in 1680. This is shown in table 7-17. After the mid-1800s, however, settlers began arriving in the Southwest in increasingly large numbers, and naturally, conflicts arose.

In 1863, Colonel Christopher ("Kit") Carson (infamous among American Indians) was sent to Navajo territory to demonstrate that "wild Indians could be tamed." He pillaged the land and destroyed crops and livestock until the Navajo were brought to the brink of starvation. Carson killed a good many Navajo as well during this period of "warfare," and most Navajo consequently surrendered. They then journeyed to Fort Defiance in northeast Arizona Territory.

Over the next few years the Navajo were taken to Fort Sumner in the Bosque Redondo (*Hwelte* in Navajo, Round Grove in English), in southeast New

TABLE 7-17: **Navajo Population History, 1680–1980**

Date	Population
1680	8,000
1850s	10,000–15,000
1864	12,000
1868	10,000–11,000
1870	11,000
1890	17,000
1900	20,000
1910	22,455
1920	31,000
1930	40,000
1940	49,000
1950	65,000
1961–62	95,000
1970	96,743
1980	158,633

SOURCES: U.S. Bureau of the Census (1915:78–79, 1981), Mooney (1928:22), Johnston (1966:136–38), Goodman (1982:61).

Mexico Territory. The site was selected "for the concentration and maintenance of all captive Indians from the New Mexico territory" (Johnston, 1966:23). Their 900-mile journey there was called the "Long Walk." In all, somewhat over 8,000 Navajo were held there, suffering from syphilis and probably other diseases, starvation, cold and harsh weather, and brutality. There were even reports of murder (see Salmón, 1976).

The confinement proved a failure: in 1868 the Navajo, reduced in population by the ordeal, returned to their homelands to the north and west and settled on a reservation approximately 7,000 miles square. By the end of the nineteenth century the Navajo had recovered and had entered an era of some demographic growth, though they still remained extremely economically disadvantaged compared with U.S. society. Some have argued that their population increase was caused in part by sharply declining mortality rates (see Johansson and Preston, 1978:27).

In any case, the recovery continued into the twentieth century. By the 1930s the Navajo reservation had increased to about 25,000 square miles, and demographically the Navajo had increased because of these expanded lands, some new wealth, relatively speaking, patterns of earlier marriage, and probably an increased birth rate. In the 1930s their birth rate was between 40 and 50 per 1,000 (see Kunitz, 1974). It is likely that they also had high birth rates during the following one or two decades, but they also had lower death rates, which eventually increased because of the tribe's poverty and poor health conditions associated with it.

A study of the Ramah group of Navajo Indians (Kunitz, 1983) indicated that during the middle decades of the twentieth century they experienced both increased birth and death rates, as shown in table 7-18, with, however, a

TABLE 7-18: **Ramah Navajo Birth and Death Rates per 1,000, 1930–34 to 1940–45**

Date	Birth Rate	Death Rate
1930–34	45.3	20.5
1935–39	51.2	20.2
1940–45	51.5	23.4

SOURCE: Kunitz (1983:38).

still rapidly growing population. Whether this pattern was characteristic of all Navajo is unknown; but Stephen J. Kunitz believed "the Ramah data reflect a larger pattern of increasing mortality and fluctuating but generally high fertility" (Kunitz, 1983:39; also Carr and Lee, 1978; Broudy and May, 1983).

In more recent decades Navajo mortality rates, particularly those of infants, have dropped, due to improved medical care, and their birth rates have been lower, though they continue high (see Kunitz, 1974; Chisholm, 1983; Broudy and May, 1983). In 1978, for example, the birth rate for the Navajo was 33.1 per 1,000 while the death rate was only 6.2 per 1,000 (Broudy and May, 1983:5). Consequently, Navajo population growth has continued: according to an initial report, the U.S. Census enumerated 158,633 Navajo in 1980 (U.S. Bureau of the Census, 1981), but, as mentioned, 175,893 Navajo were formally enrolled in the tribe in 1985.

Navajo population growth has, in turn, contributed to the sharply rising power of the Navajo Nation in recent years. For one author, in fact, "population is viewed as being the key variable in explaining the rising power of the Navajo Nation in recent years as it has rapidly been extending its political and economic control over the vast stretches of Arizona, Utah and New Mexico" (Stucki, 1971:393). It is to be hoped that this growth, along with the Navajo Reservation's vast mineral resources, will enable the Navajo eventually to prosper in the future. It has even been suggested that the Navajo Reservation may become the fifty-first state of the United States.

8. POPULATION RECOVERY AND THE DEFINITION AND ENUMERATION OF AMERICAN INDIANS

> I am the last full-blood Chunut left. My children are part Spanish. I am the only one who knows the whole Chunut or Wowol language. When I am gone no one will have it. I have to be the last.
>
> —YOKUT WOMAN

THE TWENTIETH-CENTURY AMERICAN INDIAN population recovery discussed in Chapter 7 only partly resulted from demographic processes of birth, death, and migration. Even the biological mixing discussed does not explain all of the additional reasons for the recovery, although it was related to the other causes, since the mixing changed definitions of American Indians and changes in definition were important in the population recovery. Since I relied primarily on U.S. census data in depicting the recovery, the changing procedures whereby American Indians were enumerated in the censuses were also significant.

DEFINITIONS OF AMERICAN INDIANS

Defining who American Indians were was not an issue prior to the arrival of Europeans: all North Americans were American Indians (or Eskimos or Aleuts). Only after the European arrival did "American Indian" emerge as an ethnic category. Before then American Indians were merely defined vis-à-vis other American Indian tribes, whom they sometimes regarded as "non-people" or "nonhuman." In fact, in many cases the names that a tribe has for itself may be loosely translated as "people," "the people," "true people," or "real people." Questions occasionally arose relating to tribal designation; for example, when members of other tribes were adopted, or children were born of mixed tribal unions. The issues were complex, for example, in the case of a child born of a mother of a tribe tracing descent patrilineally, but fathered by a man of a tribe tracing descent matrilineally. In such a case the child really belonged in neither tribe.

General Definitions

As a group, American Indians were defined initially only from the European point of view. It surely took time for American Indians to consider themselves as a category, irrespective of tribe, vis-à-vis Europeans. Even after the first mixed European–American Indian child was born, whoever he or she may have been, whenever he or she was born (which was probably not long after the Europeans arrived), the question whether that child was American Indian probably did not arise among the Indians, though it likely did among Euro-

186

peans. Indians probably only wondered, Was the child a tribal member or European? Both or neither? Or something in between? At some point American Indians began to see themselves as American Indians as well as members of particular tribes, but even today American Indian children typically first learn to define themselves tribally—for example, as Navajo, Cherokee, or Sioux—then later as American Indians, or Native Americans.

Meanwhile, mixed offspring presented an important definitional problem for Europeans, particularly the Spanish. Tribalism did not enter into it. In the central and southern parts of the hemisphere, the Spanish *conquistadores* and those who followed them classified the offspring of Europeans and American Indians or Africans on the basis of *mestizaje* (literally, race mixture, or miscegenation): offspring of Europeans and Indians were *mestizo*, offspring of Europeans and Africans were *mulato*, offspring of Africans and Indians were *zambo* (and a non-Indian who lived like an Indian was designated *indígena*). All of these groups were eventually further classified by an elaborate, complicated scheme to denote varying degrees of color admixture (*castas de mezcla*). The Latin American historian Nicolás Sánchez-Albornoz noted:

> Every mixture possible, starting from the three pure original racial types, received its individual name. The terms *mestizo*, *mulato*, and *zambo* were of long standing, and need no further clarification. *Tercerón*, *cuarterón* (quadroon), and *quinterón* (quintroon) are self-explanatory. Peruvian Spanish of today still retains the terms *cholo* and *chino*. But who nowadays remembers the significance of such names as *castizo*, *morisco*, *lobo*, *jíbaro*, *albarazado*, *cambujo*, *barcino*, *puchuel*, *coyote*, *chamiso*, *gálfarro*, *genízaro*, *grifo*, *jarocho*, and *sambahigo*, or the more picturesque *salta atrás*, *tente en el aire*, *no te entiendo*, *ahí estés*, and so forth? (Sánchez-Albornoz, 1974 : 129–30)

To those were added *tresalbo*, *sambo prieto*, *lunarejo*, *mequimixt*, *rayado*, and other classifications (Mörner, 1967 : 59; also Wagley, 1971).

A list from eighteenth-century New Spain (which extended from present-day Mexico northward well into the present-day United States) illustrates the mixture of some of these classifications:

1. Spaniard and Indian beget mestizo
2. Mestizo and Spanish woman beget castizo
3. Castizo woman and Spaniard beget Spaniard
4. Spanish woman and Negro beget mulatto
5. Spaniard and mulatto woman beget morisco
6. Morisco woman and Spaniard beget albino
7. Spaniard and albino woman beget torna atrás
8. Indian and torna atrás woman beget lobo
9. Lobo and Indian woman beget zambaigo
10. Zambaigo and Indian woman beget cambujo
11. Cambujo and mulatto woman beget albarazado
12. Albarazado and mulatto woman beget barcino
13. Barcino and mulatto woman beget coyote
14. Coyote woman and Indian beget chamiso
15. Chamiso woman and mestizo beget coyote mestizo
16. Coyote mestizo and mulatto woman beget ahí te estás

(Mörner, 1967 : 58)

Farther north things did not become nearly so complicated for the Spanish, or the English, French, and others, although some of the Spanish names remained in use in what would become the southern United States.[1] Meanwhile, particularly in present-day Canada but also in the Pacific Northwest of the United States, French- and British-Indian mixed-bloods emerged as a group called the Métis. They did so, as they said, "Nine months after the first white man set foot in Canada" (quoted in Peterson, 1982:23).[2] Nevertheless, mixed offspring of Indians typically were called simply "half-breeds," then later "quarter-breeds" or "breeds," by Europeans. If they were of African ancestry and the darker skin predominated, they were likely to be designated "colored" or "Negro." Whether they were also American Indian would be a separate, complicated issue—an issue that is still with us.

We continue to use racial definitions of American Indian status, which tends to be defined in terms of at least one-quarter degree of Indian blood. This is the definition primarily used by the U.S. Bureau of Indian Affairs in determining individuals' eligibility for services.

Some earliest definitions of who is and is not American Indian may be found in treaties between American Indian tribes and the U.S. government. Some provided explicitly for mixed-bloods; for example, the United States government's 1830 treaty with the Sauk and Foxes, etc., the 1858 treaty with the Ponca, the 1859 treaty with the Kansa, the 1865 treaty with the Omaha (see Institute for the Development of Indian Law, n.d., a), the unratified 1865 treaty with the Blackfoot Nation of Indians, etc., the 1895 agreement with the Indians of the Fort Belknap Indian Reservation in Montana, and the 1895 agreement with the Indians of the Blackfeet Indian Reservation in Montana (see Institute for the Development of Indian Law, n.d., b).

Generally treaty benefits were extended to mixed-bloods who accepted tribal ways of life, whereas those who preferred nontribal ways were excluded. The 1858 treaty between the Ponca and the U.S. government stated:

> The Ponca being desirous of making provision for their half-breed relatives, it is agreed that those who prefer and elect to reside among them shall be permitted to do so, and be entitled to and enjoy all the rights and privileges of members of the tribe; but to those who have chosen and left the tribe to reside among the whites and follow the pursuits of civilized life . . . there shall be issued scrip for one hundred and sixty acres of land each, which shall be receivable at the United States land-offices in the same manner, and be subject to the same rules and regulations as military bounty-land warrants (Institute for the Development of Indian Law, n.d., a:67).

Mixed-bloods could also choose not to live among fellow tribesmen on reservation areas. The unratified 1865 treaty between the United States and the Blackfoot Nation of Indians, etc., stated:

1. One may see Forbes (1983) for a discussion of the terms in the United States and Bieder (1980) for a history of attitudes toward mixed-bloods.
2. The reader may wish to see *American Indian Culture and Research Journal* (1982) for historical studies of the Métis.

> The half-breeds of the tribes, parties to this treaty, and those persons citizens of the United States, who have intermarried with Indian women, of said tribes, and continue to maintain domestic relations with them, shall not be compelled to remove to said reservation but shall be allowed to remain undisturbed upon the lands herein ceded and relinquished to the United States, and shall be allowed, each to select from said ceded lands (not mineral), 160 acres of land, including as far as practicable their present homestead, the boundaries of said lands, to be made to conform to the United States surveys, and when so selected, the President of the United States shall issue to each of said persons so selecting same, a patent for said 160 acres, with such restrictions as the power of alienation of said land, by any person for whose benefit such selections are herein authorized to be made. (Institute for the Development of Indian Law, n.d., b:72)

In these instances race was not so much the issue as was acceptance of Indian ways of life, though mixed ancestry made it necessary to deal with such people separately in the first place.

The 1892 report of the U.S. Commissioner of Indian Affairs (1892:31–37) similarly addressed the question, What is an Indian? (the commissioner used the word *what* rather than *who*). As in early treaties, maintenance of a tribal identity, or in the language of the time, "tribal relations," was crucial to designation as an Indian: Indians were defined as those who lived in tribal relations with other Indians.[3]

Legal Definitions

The United States has a long history of legally defining American Indians, in large part because of the early history of considering American Indian tribes as sovereign nations. Considering the various legal definitions, the legal scholar Felix S. Cohen noted:

> The term "Indian" may be used in an ethnological or in a legal sense. If a person is three-fourths Caucasian and one-fourth Indian, that person would ordinarily not be considered an Indian for ethnological purposes. Yet legally such a person may be an Indian. Racial composition is not always dispositive in determining who are Indians for the purposes of Indian law. In dealing with Indians, the federal government is dealing with members or descendants of political entities, that is, Indian tribes, not with persons of a particu-

---

3. Interestingly, the Supreme Court of New Mexico Territory in 1869 declared the Pueblo Indians were *not* Indians in that they were "honest, industrious, and law-abiding citizens" and showed "virtue, honesty, and industry to their more civilized neighbors" (quoted in Cohen, 1942:22). The U.S. Supreme Court likewise held in 1877 that the Pueblo were not to be considered as Indians in that they were "a peaceable, industrious, intelligent, and honest and virtuous people. . . . Indians only in feature, complexion, and a few of their habits" (quoted in Cohen, 1942:22). The court, however, later decided its earlier information was incorrect and reversed itself, deciding the Pueblo really were Indians. In so doing, "the Court quoted at length from agents' reports of drunkenness, debauchery, dancing, and communal life in support of the conclusion that they were Indians, being a 'simple, uninformed and inferior people'" (Cohen, 1942:22). Thus members of Indian tribes, at least in this instance, must behave as non-Indians think they should, in order to be treated as Indian, no matter how unflattering whites make the definition.

lar race. Tribal membership as determined by the Indian tribe or community itself is often an essential element. In fact, a person of complete Indian ancestry who has never had relations with any Indian tribe may be considered a non-Indian for some legal purposes. (Cohen, 1942:19)

Given the long-standing and probably increasing importance of tribal membership or affiliation in determining who is an Indian, many statutes use tribal membership as the essential criteria, however it may be determined. One example is the Indian Self-Determination and Education Assistance Act of 1975 (Cohen, 1942:23). Similarly, Cohen (1942:20) noted: "The courts have consistently recognized that one of an Indian tribe's most basic powers is the authority to determine questions of its own membership. A tribe has power to grant, deny, revoke, and qualify membership."[4]

Membership in an American Indian tribe in the United States is generally determined by criteria specified in a written tribal constitution, typically developed after the Indian Reorganization Act of 1934 and subsequent decisions by the Indian Claims Commission.[5] This includes most of some 300 federally recognized tribes in the United States—though not all, as some tribes, for example, certain Pueblos, still operate on the basis of oral traditions and have no such written documents. There are also some 150 to 200 other American Indian groups in the United States that have the potential to be federally recognized tribes with federally approved constitutions.

Examining requirements for membership, written or not, reveals considerable diversity and complexity in tribal organizations. Membership requirements often involve blood quantum, lineage, enrollment or allotment status, and residence. Many tribes do not require a minimum blood quantum: one often has to trace only lineage to earlier tribal members at points in history. When a quantum is specified, the modal requirement is one-fourth. Although some require as much as one-half, no tribe requires more; and several tribes, particularly in California and Oklahoma, require a minimum of one-eighth or one-sixteenth. A distinction between general Indian and specific tribal blood is also often made. And typically one may not be a member of more than one tribe. Most tribes have membership committees to determine eligibility and resolve disputes. The resulting list is generally termed the tribal roll, and it includes the official members of the tribe.

Three examples from selected American Indian tribal constitutions illustrate some of the points considered. The article on citizenship of the Oklahoma *Chickasaw Nation Tribal Constitution* (1979:1) simply states:

> *Section 1.* The Chickasaw Nation shall consist of all Chickasaw Indians by blood whose names appear on the final rolls of the Chickasaw Nation approved pursuant to Section 2 of the Act of April 26, 1906 (34 Stat. 137) and their lineal descendants.

4. In many regards, the important definitions of Indian are still legal ones determined by the legislative and legal system of the United States.

5. Tribal constitutions are not new: The first one was developed by the Choctaw in 1826, and written Indian laws date from a Cherokee law of 1808 (see Hargrett, 1947; also Fay, 1970).

Section 2. The Tribal Council shall have the power to enact ordinances governing future citizenship and loss of citizenship in the Chickasaw Nation.

However, the article on membership of the *Revised Constitution of the Apache Tribe of the Mescalero Reservation* (1965 : 2 – 3) states:

Section 1. the membership of the Mescalero Apache Tribe shall consist of the following persons:
(a) Any person whose name appeared on the Census Roll of the Mescalero Apache Agency of January 1, 1936.
(b) All persons born to resident members after the census of January 1, 1936, and prior to the effective date of this constitution.
(c) Any child born to a non-resident member, prior to the effective date of this constitution, provided that such child shall have resided on the Mescalero Reservation for not less than one (1) year immediately preceding the date of enrollment.
(d) Any person of one-fourth degree or more Mescalero Apache blood, born after the effective date of this constitution, either one or both of whose parents is (are) enrolled in the membership of the Mescalero Apache Tribe.
Sec. 2. No person, being enrolled or recognized as a member of another tribe, shall be eligible for enrollment in the Mescalero Apache Tribe.
Sec. 3. The tribal council shall have the power to adopt ordinances, consistent with this constitution, governing future membership, loss of membership and the adoption of members into the Mescalero Apache Tribe, which ordinances shall be subject to review by the Secretary of the Interior.
Sec. 4. The tribal council shall have the power to prescribe rules to govern the compilation and maintenance of a membership roll, and to make corrections in the basic roll, subject to the approval of the Secretary of the Interior.
Sec. 5. The constitution of the Mescalero Apache Tribe, and ordinances enacted pursuant thereto, shall govern tribal membership and enrollment. No decree of any non-tribal court purporting to determine membership in the tribe, determine paternity, or determine the degree of Indian blood, shall be recognized for membership purposes. The tribal council shall have sole authority and original jurisdiction to determine eligibility for enrollment, except where the membership of an individual is dependent upon an issue of paternity, in which case the trial court, or the tribal council sitting as an appellate court, shall have authority and exclusive jurisdiction.

Finally, the article on membership of the *Amended Constitution and Bylaws of the Duckwater Shoshone Tribe of the Duckwater Reservation, Nevada* (1966 : 1 – 2) states:

Section 1. The membership of the Duckwater Shoshone Tribe shall consist of the following:
(a) All persons of at least one-half (1/2) degree Shoshone Indian blood who have been designated by the Secretary of the Interior as eligible for residence on lands acquired heretofore or hereafter for the benefit of the Duckwater Shoshone Tribe.
(b) All children of at least one-half (1/2) degree Shoshone Indian blood born to any member of the tribe.

Sec. 2 The initial enrollment as well as the continued enrollment of persons in the above categories shall be subject to the following provisions:
1.   They are not enrolled with any other Indian tribe or group.
2.   They do not hold an assignment of land on any other Indian reservation.
3.   They have not been allotted land on any other Indian reservation (this does not include land acquired through inheritance).
Sec. 3. The Tribal Council shall have the power to promulgate ordinances, subject to approval by the Secretary of the Interior, governing enrollment procedures, loss of membership, and the adoption of new members.
Sec. 4. Any person refused membership by the Tribal Council shall have the right of appeal to the Secretary of the Interior.

In 1986 the Bureau of Indian Affairs listed 306 American Indian tribes with which it had relations (including one tribe in Alaska and two currently unorganized tribes) (U.S. Bureau of Indian Affairs, 1986a). Some 900,000 individuals were enrolled in these tribes in the early 1980s (U.S. Bureau of Indian Affairs, 1986a, 1986b). This means that only about two-thirds of the 1.37 million American Indians enumerated in the 1980 census likely were actual members of American Indian tribes having relations with the federal government.

Definitions of Tribe

Given the importance of tribal membership in definitions of American Indians, it is necessary to note some related history.

Felix Cohen explained two definitions or uses of tribe:

> The term "tribe" is commonly used in two senses, an ethnological sense and a legal-political sense. For ethnological purposes, the term tribe depends upon a variety of technical considerations, for example, the nature of the social and political organization of its members.
>
> The term tribe has no universal legal definition. There is no single federal statute defining an Indian tribe for all purposes, although the Constitution and many federal statutes and regulations make use of the term. In most instances the question of tribal existence can be resolved by reference to a treaty, statute, executive order, or agreement recognizing the tribe in question. In other cases the definition of tribe, like many other such generic terms, will depend in part on the context and the purposes for which the term is used. (Cohen, 1942:3)

Cohen (1942:3) observed further that, "historically, the federal government has determined that certain groups of Indians will be recognized as tribes for various purposes."

Ethnological Definitions. From an ethnological perspective, I do not know when the term tribe was first applied to American Indians, or its exact meaning in the English language of that time. The usage must have been directly antecedent to the current definition, however, and descended from the Latin *tribus,* which referred to one of the three groups into which the Romans were originally divided (*tribus* was, in turn, derived from the Latin *tres,* or three). In contemporary English various definitions of *tribe* are found, for example:

1. a group of persons, families, or clans descended from a common ancestor and forming, together with their slaves, adopted strangers, etc., a commu-

nity. 2. a group of this kind having recognized ancestry; specifically, a) any of the three divisions of the ancient Romans, traditionally of Latin, Sabine, or Etruscan origin. b) any of the later political and territorial divisions of the ancient Romans, originally thirty and subsequently thirty-five in number. c) any of the phylae of Greece. d) any of the twelve divisions of the ancient Israelites. 3. any primitive or nomadic group of people of generally common ancestry, possessing common leadership. 4. any group of people having the same occupation, habits, ideas, etc.: chiefly in a derogatory sense, as, the *tribe* of daubers. 5. a subdivision of an order or suborder of animals or plants; hence, 6. any group, class, or kind of animals, plants, etc. 7. in stock breeding, the animals descended from the same female through the female line. 8. a number or company of persons or animals. 9. a family: a humorous or derogatory usage. (*Webster's New World Dictionary of the American Language*, 1960: s.v. "tribe")

In a more technical, or at least a more anthropological, sense, a tribe may be defined as a socially distinct group of people with similar ancestry, common leadership, political independence, and economic autonomy.[6] To some extent, the term *tribe*, in both today's general and technical senses, did not apply to how American Indians were organized before the European arrival. In fact, American Indians circa 1492 exhibited a variety of types of organization ranging, in what would become the United States, from small villages consisting primarily of extended families (for example, in what is now northern California) to virtual city-states (as in the Southeast) to large chiefdoms (in the mid-Atlantic region). Usage of *tribe* ignored this variation.

In 1978 the theme of the Newberry Library's First Annual Conference on Problems and Issues Concerning American Indians Today was the nature of tribalism. I was the discussant for a paper by Henry Dobyns on "Tribalism Today: An Anthropological Perspective on Reservation Enclaves and Urban Pan-Indians," of which the opening paragraph read:

> This analysis begins with the fundamental thesis that there are today no Indian "tribes" in the United States in any technical sense of the term. In other words, there no longer exist in this country any politically independent, entirely socially distinct, and economically autonomous Native American ethnic groups. All of the populations now labeled "Indian" are effectively integrated into the national society and regional subsocieties, and participate in the world market economy. (Dobyns, 1978:2)

The author then formulated the tribal concept as a more or less "ideal-type" (an analytical model divorced from reality) and compared contemporary American Indian peoples to it. He argued that Indian groups today constitute only genetically isolated enclaves, not tribes in any real sense of the word. The response from the Indians present was quick, strong, and angry. They asserted emphatically that they were still tribes.

What Dobyns had done was to define too narrowly the characteristics of a tribe, ignoring family and kinship and community. He also had failed to appreciate both the symbolic importance of membership in a tribe and the im-

6. Discussions of tribe and tribalism may be found in Dobyns (1978) and Fried (1968).

portance of tribes as social organizations—whatever their particular form—in the daily lives of contemporary Indian people. As an anthropologist, Dobyns looked at American Indians present and past and saw differences and change where American Indians saw mainly similarities and continuity.

Since 1492, the ways that American Indians have organized have undergone considerable change, to be sure. Yet the term *tribe* is still used to refer to American Indian groups, typically by both Indians and non-Indians, although other terms are also used, for example, *band, reservation, rancheria, pueblo,* and *nation.* Whether the actual organization of American Indians conforms to any technical definition is in many ways irrelevant. Indian peoples, it seems to me, are free to term themselves as they desire.

Legal Definitions. Aside from any ethnological definition of tribe, the U.S. government has a legal history of defining, and thus determining, the tribal status of American Indian groups as well as American Indian individuals:

> Congress and the Executive have often departed from ethnological principles in order to determine tribes with which the United States would carry on political relations. Congress has created "consolidated" or "confederated" tribes consisting of several ethnological tribes, sometimes speaking different languages. Examples are the Wind River Tribes (Shoshone and Arapahoe), the Cheyenne-Arapaho Tribes of Oklahoma, the Cherokee Nation of Oklahoma (in which the Cherokees, Delawares, Shawnees, and others were included), and the Confederated Salish and Kootenai Tribes of the Flathead Reservation. These and many other consolidated or confederated groups have been treated politically as single tribes. Where no formal Indian political organization existed, scattered communities were sometimes united into tribes and chiefs were appointed by United States agents for the purpose of negotiating treaties. Once recognized in this manner, the tribal existence of these groups has continued.
>
> On the other hand, Congress has sometimes divided a single tribe, from the ethnological standpoint, into a number of tribes or "bands." Examples are the Chippewas, the Sioux, and several groups which remained behind when the majority of their members were removed west during the mid-nineteenth century. These and other subdivisions of ethnological tribes are also "tribes" for federal political, legal, and administrative purposes.
>
> Although there is broad federal authority to recognize tribes, the question may arise whether that power has been exercised in a particular instance. Normally a group will be treated as a tribe or a "recognized" tribe if (a) Congress or the Executive has created a reservation for the group by treaty, agreement, statute, executive order, or valid administrative action; and (b) the United States has had some continuing political relationship with the group, such as by providing services through the Bureau of Indian Affairs. Accordingly, reservation tribes with continuing federal contact are considered tribes under virtually every statute that refers to Indian tribes.
>
> Not all tribes have been recognized in that manner, however. The United States has not established reservations for some tribes. In some cases the United States has treated with a tribe, but federal officials have failed to provide services and assistance to the same extent as with other tribes. In still other cases, Congress has terminated part, though not necessarily all, of the federal-tribal relationship. (Cohen, 1942:5–7)

(In the 1970s, for example, the Wampanoag of Massachusetts brought a law-
suit claiming ownership of several thousand acres of Cape Cod. It failed because the court held the Wampanoag were not an Indian tribe with special
rights but only an ethnic community [see *New York Times*, 1978a, 1978b].)

Indian Reorganization Act and Federal Acknowledgment Project. There are between 400 and 500 American Indian tribes or potential tribes in the United
States today. As mentioned, of those some 300 are federally recognized and
receive the services of the U.S. Bureau of Indian Affairs (American Indian
Policy Review Commission, 1977:461; U.S. Bureau of Indian Affairs, 1986a).

On March 3, 1871, legislation was enacted by the U.S. Congress effectively
destroying tribal sovereignty by ending American Indian tribal rights to ne-
gotiate treaties with the United States. The legislation stated: "Hereafter no
Indian Nation or Tribe within the Territory of the United States shall be acknowledged or recognized as an independent nation, tribe, or power with
whom the United States may contract by treaty" (Blackwell and Mehaffey,
1983:53).

Between 1871 and 1934, American Indian tribes became increasingly disor-
ganized, in part because of other legislation passed in the late 1800s calling for
the allotment of tribal lands. Then in 1934 the Indian Reorganization Act was
enacted, which acknowledged that a tribe had "rights to organize for its
common welfare," including hiring legal counsel, negotiating with government on the local, state, and federal levels, disposing of tribal lands, and
incorporating.

The Indian Reorganization Act delineated steps whereby "any Indian tribe,
or tribes, residing on the same reservation" might formally organize themselves (Cohen, 1942:13). Subsequently, states also became involved, passing
statutes such as the Oklahoma Indian Welfare Act. This trend revived American Indian self-government, since tribes that accepted the Indian Reorganization Act and established constitutions, and sometimes by-laws and corpora-
tion charters, could be eventually acknowledged as federally recognized tribes
on the basis of section 16 of the act (Porter, 1983:38–39). The U.S. government often had to make decisions, however, about which American Indian
groups were actual tribes. The most important factors considered were:

(1) That the group has had treaty relations with the United States.
(2) That the group has been denominated a tribe by act of Congress or
    Executive Order.
(3) That the group has been treated as having collective rights in tribal land
    or funds, even though not expressly designated a tribe.
(4) That the group has been treated as a tribe or band by other Indian tribes.
(5) That the group has exercised political authority over its members,
    through a tribal council or other governmental forms. (Porter, 1983:39)

Confusion resulted as decisions regarding the tribal status of various
American Indian peoples were made, since there were no clear-cut procedures
for achieving recognition. In the following decades the U.S. government

adopted policies more or less aimed at ending the special legal status of American Indian tribes, and in fact, 61 tribes were officially terminated.[7]

In 1976 the Federal Acknowledgment Project was created, in part because of President Richard M. Nixon's rejection of the idea of termination. The project specified seven mandatory criteria for federal recognition, with the "burden of proof" resting on the American Indian group in question. The criteria are:

(a) A statement of facts establishing that the petitioner has been identified from historical times until the present on a substantially continuous basis, as "American Indian," or "aboriginal." A petitioner shall not fail to satisfy any criteria herein merely because of fluctuations of tribal activity during various years. . . .

(b) Evidence that a substantial portion of the petitioning group inhabits a specific area or lives in a community viewed as American Indian and distinct from other populations in the area, and that its members are descendants of an Indian tribe which historically inhabited a specific area.

(c) A statement of facts which establishes that the petitioner has maintained tribal political influence or other authority over its members as an autonomous entity throughout history until the present.

(d) A copy of the group's present governing document, or in the absence of a written document, a statement describing in full the membership criteria and the procedures through which the group currently governs its affairs and its members.

(e) A list of all known current members of the group and a copy of each available former list of members based on the tribe's own defined criteria. The membership must consist of individuals who have established, using evidence acceptable to the Secretary, descendancy from a tribe which existed historically or from historical tribes which combined and functioned as a single autonomous entity.

(f) The membership of the petitioning group is composed principally of persons who are not members of any other North American tribe.

(g) The petitioner is not, nor are its members, the subject of congressional legislation which has expressly terminated or forbidden the federal relationship. (U.S. Bureau of Indian Affairs, 1978:3, 8–11, 17)

In the mid-1980s about 125 American Indian groups were trying to achieve federal recognition under this act.

TRIBAL MEMBERSHIP AND TRIBAL DEFINITION

Issues of tribal membership and definition often come together, one influencing the other. This, of course, may be seen in criteria "e" and "f" of the Federal Acknowledgment Project quoted above. It happens in other ways as well.

The Confederated Salish and Kootenai Tribes

Ronald Trosper examined tribal membership and definition on the Flathead Indian Reservation in northwestern Montana, where he sought to answer two

7. Termination did not mean that the tribe ceased to exist, only that the U.S. government would not recognize it or its reservation. Felix Cohen (1942:19) explained: "Express termination by Congress does not terminate the tribe's existence; it terminates only the United States' relationship with the tribe. Thus a 'terminated' tribe remains a tribe ethnologically."

basic questions: "(1) Why did the Confederated Salish and Kootenai Tribes of the Flathead Indian Reservation exist as a legally defined group in 1970? (2) Why did the Confederated Salish and Kootenai Tribes have 5,500 enrolled tribal members in 1970?" (Trosper, 1976 : 256).

The first question was important, Trosper argued, because the tribes had been disappearing as recently as 50 years ago, and in 1954 a bill had been prepared in the U.S. Congress to terminate the tribes, abolish the reservation, and end the Confederated Salish and Kootenai's status as a federally recognized tribe. The second question was important, according to Trosper, because the tribes were composed mainly of mixed-bloods:

> Thirty percent have less than one-fourth Indian blood, 40% are between one-fourth and one-half, and the remaining 30% have more than one-half Indian blood. Only 3% of the tribal membership is full-blood. . . . The requirements to enroll children have tightened since 1935. If all those with Indian blood had been included, in 1970 the tribal population would have been 7,100 rather than the enrolled 5,500. The rule since 1960 has been that only those born with a quarter or more Indian blood can become tribal members. (Trosper, 1976 : 256)

To answer both questions, Trosper studied the inhabitants of the Flathead Reservation from 1860 to 1970. He (1976 : 271) concluded: "Tribal leaders adopted the policy of entrenchment in order to protect the existence of the reservation. This policy involved adopting a definition of Indian which led to a membership of 5,500." The new definition of Indian for tribal membership emphasized blood quantum rather than community, which had been stressed previously. The different definitions are seen in the old and new tribal constitutions. Article II on membership of the old *Constitution and Bylaws of the Confederated Salish and Kootenai Tribes of the Flathead Reservation* (1935 : 1) had read, in part:

> *Section 1.* The membership of the Confederated Tribes of the Flathead Reservation shall consist as follows:
> (a) All persons of Indian blood whose names appear on the official census rolls of the Confederated Tribes as of January 1, 1935.
> (b) All children born to any member of the Confederated Salish and Kootenai Tribes of the Flathead Reservation who is a resident of the reservation at the time of the birth of said children.

In contrast, Article II of the *Amended Constitution and Bylaws of the Confederated Salish and Kootenai of the Flathead Reservation* (1960 : 1–2) reads, in part:

> *Section 1. Confirmation of Rolls*—The membership of the Confederated Tribes of the Flathead Reservation is confirmed in accordance with the per capita rolls as from time to time prepared.
> *Sec. 2. Present Membership*—Membership in the Tribes on and after the date of the adoption of this amendment shall consist of all living persons whose names appear on the per capita roll of the Confederated Salish and Kootenai Tribes of the Flathead Reservation, Montana, as prepared for the per capita distribution as shown on the per capita roll paid in February 1959 together with all children of such members, born too late to be included on such per

capita roll and prior to the effective date of this section who possess one-fourth (1/4) or more Salish or Kootenai blood or both and are born to a member of the Confederated Tribes of the Flathead Indian Reservation. Subject to review by the Secretary of the Interior, the Tribal Council shall make any necessary corrections in this 1959 membership roll so that no one eligible for membership under prior constitutional provisions shall be excluded therefrom.

Sec. 3. Future Membership—Future membership may be regulated from time to time by ordinance of the Confederated Tribes subject to review by the Secretary of the Interior. Until and unless an ordinance is adopted any person shall be enrolled as a member who shall (a) apply, or have application made on his behalf, establishing eligibility under this provision; (b) show that he is a natural child of a member of the Confederated Tribes; (c) that he possesses one-quarter (1/4) degree or more blood of the Salish or Kootenai Tribes or both, of the Flathead Indian Reservation, Montana.

Thus, the Confederated Salish and Kootenai Tribes became more exclusive in determining membership in order to protect the tribes as an entity. If they had not done so, they probably would not have survived as tribes, according to Trosper. In 1981 there were 6,210 individuals enrolled as formal members of the Confederated Salish and Kootenai Tribes (U.S. Bureau of Indian Affairs, 1986b). (In 1980, however, only 2,760 people identified as Salish or Kootenai lived on the Flathead Reservation: 2,112 were enrolled in the tribes and 303 did not report their enrollment status [U.S. Bureau of the Census, 1985:19].)

The Cherokee Nation of Oklahoma

In contrast to the survival of the Confederated Salish and Kootenai tribes is that of the Cherokee Nation of Oklahoma, many of whose ancestors were removed from southeastern homelands into Indian Territory during the late 1830s.

The Cherokee removal entailed tremendous population loss and put considerable strain on the tribal organization. The tribe was split into two geographic entities: a small group remained in the Southeast, while a much larger group joined already established early immigrants in Indian Territory. Political divisions stemmed from the geographic separation, and internal divisions arose from the forfeiture of tribal lands.

Nevertheless, both the Cherokee remaining in the Southeast and the Cherokee in Indian Territory were able to reestablish tribal life. Those in the Southeast became known as the Eastern Band of Cherokee in North Carolina, and many reside in that state on the Eastern Cherokee Reservation. The Cherokee in Indian Territory established a new tribal capital at Tahlequah and a new tribal constitution, and became known as the Cherokee Nation. As a tribe, the Cherokee Nation prospered in Indian Territory, even "adopting" some Delaware and Shawnee, yet the tribe was virtually dissolved when Oklahoma became a state in 1907; some tribal lands were then allotted to individual Cherokee, others were opened for homesteading. Moreover, the U.S. Congress granted the president of the United States the authority to appoint the principal chief of the Cherokee Nation at that time, though the Cherokee Nation of Oklahoma, as it came to be known, now elects its chief.

During the twentieth century, full-blood Cherokee lost tribal influence and retreated into isolation in the eastern Oklahoma hills. At the same time, mixed-blood Cherokee emerged as tribal leaders, eventually developing the tribe into the political and economic force in Oklahoma that it is today.

At the time of removal mixed-bloods represented less than one-quarter of the Cherokee population (McLoughlin and Conser, 1977:679). Suffering from the high population losses of the Trail of Tears and subjected to increasing intrusions of non-Indians onto their Oklahoma tribal lands, the Cherokee Nation of Oklahoma eventually became a population of predominantly assimilated mixed-bloods, while maintaining a small population of traditional full bloods. In the 1950s there were perhaps 75,000 Oklahomans with some claim of being Cherokee, but only about one-tenth of the 75,000 actually resided in Cherokee communities and participated in Cherokee communal life. The latter are often referred to as "tribal Cherokee" (see Wahrhaftig, 1968).

In developing a new tribal constitution in the 1970s, which eventually superseded the old one of 1839, the Cherokee Nation of Oklahoma, unlike the Confederated Salish and Kootenai Tribes, established no minimum blood quantum for tribal membership. Instead one must trace only descent along Cherokee lines. Article III, section 1, on membership of the *Constitution of the Cherokee Nation of Oklahoma* (1975:1) states the single membership requirement: "*Section 1.* All members of the Cherokee Nation must be citizens as proven by reference to the Dawes Commission Rolls, including the Delaware Cherokees of Article II of the Delaware Agreement dated the 8th day of May, 1867, and the Shawnee Cherokees as of Article III of the Shawnee Agreement dated the 9th day of June, 1869, and/or their descendants."

This comparatively generous definition has expanded the Cherokee Nation of Oklahoma population: in the mid-1970s there were only about 12,000 enrolled Cherokee in the Cherokee Nation of Oklahoma; in 1985 there were over 64,300 enrolled Cherokee (Cherokee Nation of Oklahoma, 1985). Also, a small group of Oklahoma Cherokee became organized as a separate band known as the United Keetoowah Band of Cherokee Indians in Oklahoma. They had about 7,500 enrolled members in 1981 (U.S. Bureau of Indian Affairs, 1986b). Only 17,638 of the Cherokees who were enrolled in 1980 lived on former Oklahoma Cherokee lands (excluding urbanized areas). There were also 18,680 people identifying themselves as Cherokee but not enrolled, and 1,925 people identifying themselves as Cherokee but not reporting their enrollment status (U.S. Bureau of the Census, 1985:99). This is a comparatively small number of the individuals nationwide identifying themselves as Cherokee: there were slightly over 232,000 self-reported Cherokee in the 1980 census (U.S. Bureau of the Census, 1981). Of course, some of those were members of the Eastern Band of Cherokee in North Carolina: there were 8,381 Eastern Cherokee enrolled in 1981, living on the reservation or not (U.S. Bureau of Indian Affairs, 1981, 1986b), although only 4,546 enrolled Cherokee lived on the Eastern Cherokee Reservation in North Carolina in 1980, along with 84 people identifying themselves as Cherokee but not enrolled, and 27 people identifying themselves as Cherokee who did not report their enrollment status (U.S. Bureau of the Census, 1985:18).

There are still full-blood and traditional Cherokee, despite the myth in Oklahoma, and elsewhere, of Cherokee assimilation. In the 1960s there were approximately 9,500 Cherokee living in over 50 Cherokee settlements in northeastern Oklahoma, and some 2,000 more Cherokee living in Indian enclaves of towns and small cities (Wahrhaftig and Thomas, 1969:42). These people spoke mainly Cherokee, were extremely traditional in outlook, and kept alive important Cherokee ceremonies. They continue in the 1980s, insulated from American society by the larger number of mixed-blood and less traditional Cherokee.

The Oklahoma Cherokee, without a reservation land base, have thus been able to survive tribally by an inclusive definition of what it is to be Cherokee. Their definition allowed relatively large numbers of people with Cherokee lineage but relatively small amounts of Cherokee blood into the tribe. This allowed the tribe to reestablish itself after virtual "dissolution" and to achieve political power in Oklahoma. The tribe, in turn, has protected a smaller group of full-blood, more traditional Cherokee from American non-Indian ways of life.

Demographic History of Two California Indian Groups

American Indians have intermarried not only with non-Indians but also with members of different tribes. Although this has not resulted in gains or losses in the total American Indian population, it has led to tribal gains and losses, and even to the continuation of some American Indian tribes as tribes. This may be seen in the history of two northern California groups, the Yuki and the Tolowa.[8]

From a pre-European population perhaps approaching 705,000, American Indians of modern-day California declined to about 260,000 at the beginning of the nineteenth century, then to only 15,000 to 20,000 at the beginning of the twentieth century (see table 5-4 in Chapter 5, again). Although population recovery has since occurred, much of it resulted from immigration of American Indians into California from other states, not from the growth of indigenous California Indian populations.

The reasons for the drastic declines among California Indians are varied. The California tribes experienced low fertility as well as mortality losses due to disease, removals and relocations, the destruction of ways of life, and wars, official and unofficial (see Merriam, 1905; Twitchell, 1925; Mooney, 1928; Cook, 1976a, 1976b, 1978). They also experienced genocide of American Indians by non-Indian Californians (see Heizer, 1974; Coffer, 1977). C. Hart Merriam summarized the devastation of native northern California peoples and the reasons for it:

> The discovery of gold, in 1848, set in motion a tremor of excitement that swept around the world like a tidal wave, gathering recruits from all nations

8. Part of the research reported here was reported previously in Thornton (1984b, 1986a).

and hurrying them by land and sea to the Golden State. During the single year 1849 no fewer than 77,000 arrived. This army of gold seekers was a heterogeneous assemblage, comprising many good and noble men, but also thousands of the rougher and more turbulent classes, not excepting the criminals. As these adventurers spread north and south over the flanks of the Sierra and penetrated the rugged mountains of the northwest, they everywhere invaded the territory of the Indians and decimated the native population. From Humboldt and Trinity counties, from the Siskiyous, and from the flanks of the Sierra, the story is the same: villages were broken up and the inhabitants scattered or massacred; men and women were debauched with whisky; men were ruthlessly killed; women were appropriated, and seeds of disease were sown which undermined the constitutions of succeeding generations. (Merriam, 1905:602)

As described in Chapter 5, the largest, most blatant, deliberate killings of North American Indians by non-Indians surely occurred in California, particularly in northern California during the mid-1800s. The documented examples of genocide there are too numerous to mention: case after case was recorded of Indian villages being massacred by larger or more powerful groups of non-Indians. In Chapter 5, I have already told what happened to the Yana, and have mentioned what happened to other tribes.

Remarkable in the history is that, although many California tribes became extinct or virtually so,[9] others managed somehow to survive, demographically and tribally. Many more or less viable California tribes continue today on present or former reservation and rancheria lands, separate from both the larger non-Indian California population and other Indian populations.

The Yuki (Ukomno'm): Demographic Decimation and Tribal Dissolution. The Yuki, the Coast Yuki, and the Huchnom were three closely related American Indian groups in the northern California area. In aboriginal times they lived on lands bordered by the Pomo and the Patwin on the south, the Nomlaki on the east, the Wailaki on the north, and the Cahto and the Sinkyone on the northwest (Heizer, 1978:14; Miller, 1978:249). For our purposes here we will concentrate on the Yuki per se and ignore the related Coast Yuki and Huchnom.

Yuki territory encompassed 400 to 900 square miles of the rugged Coast Range, including various forks of the upper Eel River (see map 8-1). The area is north and northeast of present-day Mendocino, California.

The Yuki were composed of six major subdivisions: Ta'no'm, Ukomno'm, Huititno'm, Witukomno'm, Onkolukomno'm, and Sukshaltatamno'm (Miller, 1978:249). They are typically known today collectively by the name of the largest subdivision: the Ukomno'm, the "People of the Valley," who live in the Round Valley area (Miller, 1978:249; Oandasan, 1984). All of the groups have lived in the valley, in parts, at any given time.

There was communal ownership of land among the Yuki, whose subsistence was through hunting, gathering, and fishing. Their diet included

---

9. Alfred Kroeber (1925:883) listed 63 percent of the original California Indian tribes as extinct or nearly so, that is, numbering less than 100 people, by 1910.

8-1. Yuki and Tolowa Territories

acorns, deer, and salmon, particularly, but also small game and birds, various other fish, insects, clover, berries, and other seeds and nuts.

The tribe was organized along village, or rancheria, lines. Tribelets were grouped around a larger village where a dance house and the chief's residence were located. These tribelets, in turn, "composed each of the tribal subdivisions, where members felt a sense of affinity through dialect similarity" (Miller, 1978:250). Village populations ranged from a single family to as many as 150 individuals. Structurally, the villages were composed of circular houses

TABLE 8-1: **Yuki Population History, Pre-European to 1980**

Date	Population
Pre-European	6,000–12,000 + a
1858	2,300 +
1864	600
1870	238
1880	168
1910	95
1973	32 +
1980	96

SOURCES: Miller (1975:6, 1978:250), U.S. Bureau of the Census (1981).
a Estimates of this population have ranged as high as 20,000 (see Miller, 1975, 1978, 1979).

made of bark and poles with a fire pit in the center. In summer, however, brush huts were also utilized for shelter.

The Yuki were matrilineal but patriarchal (Oandasan, 1984). Polygamy was possible, though very rare in practice. There was no particular Yuki post-marital residence rule: newly married couples might live with either the wife's relatives or the husband's.

There is very little concensus on the size of the aboriginal Yuki population. Estimates range from 2,000 to over 10 times that number (Miller, 1975:6, 1979:9–10; Thornton, 1980:703). As indicated in table 8-1, a figure somewhere between 6,000 and 12,000 appears reasonable, though perhaps conservative. Some 500 village sites are known in Yuki territory, of which 225 are in Round Valley, including 32 historic sites. The large number of villages indicates an extremely dense population.

The first intensive contact between Yuki and Americans apparently did not occur until the early 1850s: the first recorded party of Americans ventured into Round Valley in 1854. It is speculated, however, that the initial Yuki-American contact probably occurred earlier, perhaps in 1828 with the Jedediah Smith expedition. Change came swiftly, once contact had occurred. By 1846 the Nome Cult Indian Farm had been established in Round Valley for the Yuki; in 1858 it became a reservation for not only the Yuki but also other California Indians such as the Wailaki, the Maidu, the Nomlaki, the Achumawi, the Atsugewi, the Pomo, the Lassik, the Modoc and the Yana (Miller, 1978:249). Even before the mid-1860s Yuki population had declined to 600: from perhaps over 12,000 to 600 in 10 years! (See table 8-1, again.) Thereafter the population decline was gradual, until there were only about 100 Yuki at the turn of the century. Only a few dozen Yuki live today, according to scholars, although that is probably an underestimate (96 people were identified as Yuki in the 1980 census [U.S. Bureau of the Census, 1981]).

A small part of the tremendous Yuki population decline was due to introduced disease, starvation, slavery, and the relocation of individuals. The Yuki suffered from these, but probably the primary reason for the massive decline between the mid-1850s and the mid-1860s was genocide. Yuki massacres by local whites have been documented over and over again (see Miller, 1975, 1978,

1979; Heizer, 1978). Virginia P. Miller, perhaps the leading contemporary scholar on the Yuki, has commented:

> The Yuki had been victims of one of the most organized and intense geno-
> cidal campaigns in the history of the state. . . .
>   A most illuminating statement on the number of Yuki murdered came
> from Dryden Laycock, one of the first settlers in Round Valley. Laycock
> claimed that beginning in 1856, the first year whites moved into the valley,
> and continuing through February of 1860, parties of Round Valley settlers
> would frequently go out "two or three times a week" and kill "on an average,
> fifty or sixty Indians on a trip." Taking the lower of Laycock's figures, even if
> only two such trips were made each week and only fifty Indians killed on
> each trip, then the settlers would have killed 5,200 Indians in *one* year. And
> Laycock claimed that settlers' raids went on for five years, although not nec-
> essarily at a sustained pace. (Miller, 1975:10–11)

It is easy to see how a large aboriginal Yuki population of many thousands was reduced to a few hundred in a single decade.

Following the establishment of the Nome Cult Indian Farm, and later Round Valley Reservation, and coinciding with the massacres, the Yuki ceased to exist as a distinct and separate American Indian tribe. In 1936, fol-lowing the guidelines of the U.S. Indian Reorganization Act of 1934, the Yuki joined other tribes to form the Covelo Indian Community of Confederated Tribes of the Round Valley Indian Reservation. As a result, by 1962, Yuki "tribal identities had given way to a sense of primary affiliation with a ma-triarchal, extended family kin group," according to Miller (1978:250). They were a tribe no longer. In 1975 the total number of adults, including Yuki and others eligible to vote in the Covelo Indian Community, was only 100 (see *Amended Constitution and Bylaws of the Covelo Indian Community, Round Valley Reservation, California*, 1975).

The Tolowa (Hush): Demographic Survival and Tribal Reemergence. The Tolowa, or Hush (Huss), Indians were the southernmost of a group of five tribes in southwestern Oregon and northwestern California all of whom had similar cultures (see map 8-1, again). The others were the adjacent Chetco on the north, the Lower Rogue River Indians north of the Chetco; the Upper Co-quille, still farther north and on the east; and the Galice Creek Indians on the east, who were surrounded by the Takelma. Located south and southeast of the Tolowa were, respectively, the distinctive Yurok and Karok Indians.

Tolowa territory encompassed over 600 square miles in the extreme north-west of California, extending slightly across the Oregon border and more or less coinciding with present-day Del Norte County, California. The lands are varied geographically, including ocean coastline, a narrow, dense strip of red-wood forest, fir and oak forests, Lake Earl, the Smith River, and the Smith tributaries. Given the wide geographical variation, Tolowa foods were also varied. Staples included elk and deer, rabbit and quail, salmon and smelt, clams, mussels, eels, sea lions, kelp, acorns, and other seeds, berries, and roots.

The Tolowa did not have a name for themselves as a group besides "Hush," their word for a person or people (Baumhoff, 1955–61:225; Gould, 1978:136;

Bommelyn, 1983;). The name "Tolowa" came from Yurok neighbors, and apparently referred to only one of three tribal bands, the other two being the Hennaggi and the Tataten (Powers, 1877:65). Tolowa may be translated as "those people who live at Lake Earl" (Bommelyn, 1983).

The Tolowa did, however, have a strong sense of village, or rancheria, allegiance. Their villages, which constituted the basic units of Tolowa society, were named for the locations. Structurally, they were composed of family houses of redwood planks, varying only somewhat from those of southern Yurok, Karok, and Hupa neighbors. The family occupants were patrilineal kin groups with exclusive rights to the food resources of a particular area (Drucker, 1937:226–27). During most of the year individuals lived in villages along the coast, though they all but abandoned them during some summer months, when they traveled to the beaches for smelt or inland for acorns.

Each village was autonomous. Formal ties between villages occurred through bonds of blood kinship or marriage, and affinal ties often extended to other tribes as well. In fact, Tolowa men frequently took brides from the Yurok, the Karok, or the Chetco; obtaining a bride from a distant village or tribe was typically a sign of great prestige. The Tolowa were also polygynous. Wealthy men in particular had several wives, whom they obtained by paying bride prices.

Tolowa villages were formed through a patrilocal residence pattern following exogamous marriage with a bride from another village or tribal group. Both patrilocal residence patterns and the practice of exogamy appear to have been extremely important in traditional Tolowa society: "patrilocal residence seems to have been the important factor in regulating marriage. There was no definite rule against marriage within the town, and such marriages did occur (though there was a definite feeling that a man of standing would seek a wife from afar); but co-residence plus a traceable degree of kinship was a bar" (Drucker, 1937:247).

In Tolowa villages there were no such formal positions as chief, nor even councils. The villages were governed by headmen whose status was determined by their individual wealth in chipped obsidian, redheaded woodpecker scalps, and dentalia. Village lineage was traced from these headmen, although lineage could be fluid, coming into existence or disappearing as kinship group fortunes rose or fell.

There is considerable range in the scholarly estimates of pre-European Tolowa population size, but the tribe probably numbered somewhere around 2,400 (Thornton, 1980:703). At the time of the first recorded European contact the Tolowa were spread among eight different villages (Gould, 1978:128). Fourteen prehistoric and historic village sites were identified by T. T. Waterman (1925:531); and Philip Drucker (1937:226–27) listed 23 Tolowa settlements of various dates.

Direct formal contact between the Tolowa and Americans probably occurred first in 1828 during the explorations of Jedediah Smith (Dale, 1941:256–65). Yet, archaeological and oral evidence indicates that there may have been indirect contacts through Juan Francisco Bodega y Quadra in 1775 and George Vancouver in 1793, both of whom visited Trinidad Bay. Probably as a result of indirect contact, an epidemic (some say of cholera) spread to the Tolowa; it had been brought to the California area by European explorers. The epidemic probably caused the Tolowa to abandon a large village on Point Saint George (Gould, 1978:135; also Gould, 1966a). Smallpox may have reached the Tolowa even earlier, moving up from the south.

Whenever the initial European or American contacts were made, or whatever their nature, by the 1850s non-Indian settlements in Tolowa territory had become intensive as a result of gold mining operations and the founding of Crescent City on the California coast. By that time the Tolowa population had begun to decline markedly: as shown in table 8-2, Tolowa population was estimated at only 316 in the 1850s; it continued to decline until the early 1900s.

Diseases—measles, diphtheria, and cholera—and pseudomilitary engagements and genocide are typically given as the reasons for the decline in Tolowa numbers. Genocide seems particularly important, as it was among the Yuki. Baumhoff listed three instances:

> The first killing took place at Burnt Ranch, three miles south of the mouth of Smith River, at the rancheria called Yahnk-tah-kut, a name perpetuated by the district schoolhouse name. Here a large number of Indians were caught during a ceremonial dance and ruthlessly slaughtered. The Indians say this was the first killing.
> The second killing was at the rancheria of A-choo-lik on the big lagoon known as Lake Earl about three miles north of Crescent City. The Indians were engaged in gambling at the time.
> The third killing was at the large village of Hah-wun-kwut at the mouth of Smith River. (Baumhoff, 1955–61:226)

The Tolowa themselves date the first of these massacres in 1853, and they say that between 450 and 600 Tolowa people were killed then (Bommelyn, 1983; also Heth, 1976). They date the second massacre in 1854, when they assert some 150 Tolowa were killed (Bommelyn, 1983). They describe the third killing as a pitched battle between settlers and themselves. Stephen Dow Beckham (1971:134), citing Ida Pfeiffer (1856), dated this incident in 1853 and said that some 70 Tolowa were killed, a figure cited by the Tolowa themselves (Bommelyn, 1983).

The Tolowa were subjected to two tribal relocations approximately in this period. The first occurred between 1852 and 1855 when they were taken to what they now call "Klamath Concentration Camp" on the Klamath River in California, just south of their territory. The second occurred in 1860 when they were removed to the Siletz Reservation in western Oregon as a result of the so-called Rogue River Indian War between settlers and Indian groups in Oregon and northern California (Bommelyn, 1983).

The killings at the Tolowa villages are described also in modern-day Tolowa tribal oral traditions. According to one recognized authority on Tolowa history, the massacre of Yontocket village was a reprisal by settlers for an alleged Tolowa theft and coincided with an annual Tolowa ceremony. It is described more fully by the Tolowa man:

TABLE 8-2: **Tolowa Population History, Pre-European to 1983**

Date	Population
Pre-European	2,400+
1850s	316
1870	200
1910	121–150
1950	154
1981	396
1983	400–450

SOURCES: U.S. Bureau of the Census (1915:79, 1981), Kroeber (1925:883), Tax (1960), Baumhoff (1963:231), Cook (1976b:55–56), Heth (1976), Thornton (1981:703), Bommelyn (1983).

Every year we go to the center of our world. In our religion, this is where life began for our people and we dance there for ten nights. We start at about 10 o'clock in the night and then we dance all night—take breaks but we dance until the sun comes up over the hill. And we stop and rest all day. And they were in about the third night of the dancing and all of a sudden they were just surrounded and slaughtered. It was just like that. I mean, we weren't there for war. We were just . . . thanking . . . the Creator for what he had given us. You know, we had already gathered our acorns and dried our fish and gathered our deermeat and all the nuts and the food that we were going to need to live for the winter. And then we have a big feast and come together . . . and that's when it happened. And three survivors survived out of that to tell about it. (Heth, 1976:8)

How some Tolowa survived the sudden, deadly attacks also is told in contemporary tribal oral traditions. The same Tolowa man stated: "When they slaughtered at Yontocket, Echulet and Jordan Creek they didn't leave many of us. And the only ones of us that survived are the ones that ran way back into the mountains" (Heth, 1976:7). This particular man traced his ancestry to a great-great grandfather and his brother, who were apparently two of only three survivors of the Yontocket massacre. According to the informant, the three found refuge in the mountains among a neighboring group of Indians. He further related:

When the slaughtering began the people went to Mill Creek. . . . And they ran to this very tall man and he spoke the language like we did but we considered it to be broken and we understood him but it wasn't quite the same. And so they invited us to stay at their lodge for one year and that's how our particular family survived the slaughter. And then they would go down and observe the flats and they would say, "Well, they're still killing the people so stay here." And so our family lived there for a year. And then we moved back into the flatlands after it calmed down a bit. (Heth, 1976:7)

Finally, the man told how survivors of Yontocket were able to regenerate a segment of the Tolowa people:

"My great-great grandfather . . . had eight wives and . . . he had two children and this started the nucleus of our tribe over. And then up further . . .

[his brother] . . . had nine children and then they multiplied out. And they intermingled with the Coos Indians, and we intermingled with the Yurok and the Karok and the Grant's Pass people. . . . And it was interesting, you know, how these . . . practically are the only ones that started over and there are only 6 Crescent City people left out of about 400, and there's only about 15 up-river people, which I'm part of, out of maybe a thousand that come from the culture from up the river which is not the same but we have our own little different dialects and what-not, and then the mouth people were the biggest left, down at the mouth, "Hao-lun-quit." And so that's how our people kind of started over again. So now there's about 450 of us, I guess, that are Tolowa, and yet we're still part Yurok and Tolowa and Karok and Siletz and Tututni. (Heth, 1976:7–8)

As the Tolowa man indicated, a few surviving Yontocket males obtained refuge among neighboring Indians after the massacre and took several wives, according to Tolowa custom. A number of children were born in a relatively short time, and since Tolowa society was patrilocal and patrilineal, the children lived as and were considered to be Tolowa, although they were only partly so genetically. Eventually, these families returned to traditional Tolowa lands and reestablished Tolowa society. Their descendents are the Tolowa people of today: "Today, as in old times, we have genetic connections with the Yurok, Karok, Chetco, Tututni and Hupa people. . . . The Tolowa proper evolve from six families. This makes most of us related in two or three ways. This is also true in our neighboring tribes. This is why marriage from other tribes was and is so prevalent. Today we have members who range from full-blood Indian to one-sixteenth Indian blood" (Bommelyn, 1983).

The Tolowa Indians have just completed an application to the U.S. government for federal recognition as an American Indian tribe. Their case will be decided by the Bureau of Indian Affairs.

Differential Survival of the Yuki and Tolowa Indians. The Yuki and Tolowa Indians underwent similar drastic depopulations during the mid-1800s for many of the same reasons, particularly genocide. Originally, the Yuki were far more numerous than the Tolowa: the Yuki population was at least 6,000 to 12,000 (and perhaps more), compared to the aboriginal Tolowa population of about 2,400. Both the Yuki and the Tolowa underwent extremely rapid depopulations in about 10 years: the Yuki declined to only 600; the Tolowa declined to only about 300. Both tribes experienced more gradual declines during the next 30 or 40 years: the Yuki declined to about 100; the Tolowa declined to about 150.

The Yuki population continued perhaps at the same size; however, it was probably actually decreasing: in 1980 their self-reported population was less than 100. Meanwhile the Tolowa reversed their depopulation and even increased to a present-day population of over 400. Equally important, the Tolowa survived as a distinct American Indian tribal group while the Yuki merged with other tribes in the Covelo Indian Community.

The nature of their demographic declines may account in part for the difference in the tribes' populations today. Certainly, the relative magnitudes of the initial population decreases are comparable: a 93 percent decrease for the Yuki from an average population of 9,000 to one of 600; an 88 percent decrease for the Tolowa from a population of some 2,400 to one of 300. However, the Yuki were originally far larger than the Tolowa: perhaps the Tolowa were not as affected by the reductions as the Yuki were because the Tolowa had been much smaller initially. The Yuki had a dense settlement pattern compared to the sparse Tolowa pattern. Massive depopulation was perhaps more destructive to Yuki than to Tolowa tribal life, probably causing major simplifications of society and culture that Dobyns has asserted are effects of depopulation: "A good deal of social science research has noted that a growing population generates increasingly complex social organization. It must be recognized that population declines resulted in simplification of aboriginal Native American social organization" (Dobyns, 1983:328).

Another factor may have been the tribes' different reservation experiences: most of the Yuki remained on a reservation, while the Tolowa did not. Historically, a reservation location has protected the integrity of American Indian populations, helping to maintain their distinctiveness from larger, non-Indian populations,[10] but other American Indian groups were present on the reservation where the Yuki were located, and this resulted in a pattern of intermarriage that lessened Yuki tribal distinctiveness. The tribe managed to maintain "Indianness" but not tribalism per se; they became, in a very real sense, intertribal. The Tolowa did not have a reservation experience forcing them into close contact with other tribes for any extended period, as they soon left reservation areas and returned to their homelands, which had been occupied by non-Indians, but not by many other American Indians. They intermarried with non-Indians and other American Indians, but the children of mixed marriages were identified as Tolowa.

A third factor accounting for the tribes' different populations probably was the presence of social customs in Tolowa society that fostered demographic and tribal survival. The Tolowa were like the Yuki in that they were not a tightly organized tribal society, but were, though perhaps to a lesser extent, a grouping of contiguous villages with a common language and culture and some interidentification. Tolowa villages were basically extended patrilineal kinship systems, however, formed by exogamous marriages including even members of neighboring tribes, with little distinction made between marriage with a Tolowa from another village and marriage with a non-Tolowa. Polygyny was also practiced by males, particularly wealthy ones; and residence patterns following marriages were with male kin, that is, patrilocal. These Tolowa marriage and kinship patterns allowed the ready incorporation of non-Tolowa women into the tribe, and consequently the propogation by a few males of considerable numbers of Tolowa children. Had these customs not been present, it is difficult to see how the Tolowa could have continued as a tribe, either demographically or culturally (see Thornton, 1984b, 1986a). Yuki society, in contrast, was matrilineal with no postmarriage residence rule; polygamy was rarely practiced. These customs did not allow rapid demo-

---

10. One may be interested in reading Barth (1969) for a detailed discussion of ethnic group boundaries and how they are maintained.

graphic recovery for the Yuki tribe, since children of mixed marriages might be identified as American Indian but not necessarily as Yuki. Tracing themselves matrilineally, only the children of Yuki mothers were counted as Yuki offspring.

A Note on the Red-Black and the Tri-Racial

Also related to definitions of American Indian individuals and tribes are American Indians with black blood, either alone or in combination with white or other ancestry. When they have intermarried, American Indians have generally done so with the white population. While the Indian status of the resulting mixed-blood children has sometimes been problematic, it has not been nearly so much so as that of children of Indian and black parents, whom Indians and non-Indians alike have tended to consider as black rather than Indian at all. Even when their Indianness has been accepted, it has not been to the degree of the Indianness of those with white-Indian ancestry, even though the amount of Indian blood may be the same or greater. In fact, people of Indian and black ancestry have often been given special names, for example, the Red-Black people of Oklahoma, setting them apart from American Indians.

As one might expect, mixing of American Indians with blacks occurred primarily in the South and mid-Atlantic region of the United States, where there were historically large American Indian and black populations. Often the mixing was between black males and Indian females, a result of the loss of American Indian males through warfare, slavery, and so on, and the importation of black male slaves. There was a surplus of American Indian women and black men, and naturally, the two groups got together, in part because both were often slaves (see Wright, 1981:248–78). Tri-racial offspring were frequently produced by the mixing with local white populations.

Little is known about the origins of most of the black-Indian and triracial groups (see Berry, 1963), each being more or less demographically unique, defined primarily in its own terms and by its local neighbors (see Price, 1953). In the mid-1940s, William Harlen Gilbert, Jr., of the U.S. Library of Congress, conducted a survey of such communities. Gilbert found that,

> In many of the eastern States of this country there are small pockets of people who are scattered here and there in different counties and who are complex mixtures in varying degrees of white, Indian, and Negro blood. These small local groups seem to develop especially where environmental circumstances such as forbidding swamps or inaccessible and barren mountain country favor their growth. Many are located along the tidewater of the Atlantic coast where swamps or islands and peninsulas have protected them and kept alive a portion of the aboriginal blood which greeted the first white settlers on these shores. Others are farther inland in the Piedmont area and are found with their backs up against the wall of the Blue Ridge or the Alleghanies. A few of these groups are to be found on the very top of the Blue Ridge and on the several ridges of the Appalachian Great Valley just beyond. (Gilbert, 1946:438)

In 1907, James Mooney surveyed these peoples in Maryland, Delaware, Virginia, and North Carolina. He found that many had a strong identity as Indians and a fear of being absorbed into the black population (see Mooney, 1907). Gilbert estimated the aggregate size of the groups to be around 50,000 in 1946. He indicated also that they were generally increasing rapidly in size,[11] "with little evidence for the supposition that they are being absorbed to any great extent into either the white or the Negro groups" (Gilbert, 1946:438).[12] Brewton Berry (1963:57) estimated the total at 100,000 in 1960.

The main groups that Gilbert found were the Brass Ankles and other groups primarily along the coast of South Carolina, totaling about 5,000 to 10,000; the Cajun and Creole in Alabama and Mississippi, each "several thousands in number"; the Croatan of Virginia and the Carolinas, over 13,000 in number; the Guinea of West Virginia and Maryland, estimated between 8,000 and 9,000; the Issue of Virginia, only about 500; the Jackson White of New York and New Jersey, perhaps 5,000 in number; the Melungeon of the southern Appalachians, representing 5,000 to 10,000 individuals; the Moor and the Nanticoke of Delaware and New Jersey, the former about 500 and the latter about 700; the Red Bone of Louisiana, well over 3,000 in number; and finally, the Wesort in the south of Maryland, perhaps 3,000 to 5,000 in number (Gilbert, 1946:439−47).

As Gilbert (1948:438) asserted, a problem exists in defining the groups: "No satisfactory name has ever been invented to designate as a whole these mixed outcasts from both the white and Negro castes of America." Some of these groups look like American Indians, but others do not; there is much individual variation in physical appearance (see Sturtevant and Stanley, 1968).[13]

Communities of such individuals continue in many areas of the United States. Problems of identity also continue, as Darrell A. Posey (1979) has discussed for the Freejack of Louisiana. Recently, some groups have become or-

11. In another paper published two years later, William Gilbert (1948:431) reported data on Croatan fertility, showing a 1933 birth rate of 35.4 per 1,000 compared with 22.3 per 1,000 for whites and 24.5 per 1,000 for blacks. He also asserted similarly high birth rates among the Houma, Wesort, Guinea, and others (Gilbert, 1948:431). Despite no data on mortality, Gilbert concluded: "This increase, if continued, means that the Indian mixed-blood groups will play an important part in the future make-up of their respective States and may also influence future State politics" (Gilbert, 1948:431).

12. Those interested may see Gilbert (1948) for a discussion of the percentage of full bloods among Indian groups in the U.S.

13. Various studies have been conducted of these communities by sociologists and other social scientists, particularly, it seems, in the 1930s, 1940s, and 1950s. Generally, the findings indicated similar geographical isolation and marginal social status. Albert B. Harper's (1937) and Guy B. Johnson's (1939) studies of the Croatan, for example, emphasized their unique status, as did Vernon J. Parenton and Roland J. Pellegrin's (1950) study of the Sabine of the Louisiana coast region, and Margaret Mary Wood's (1943) study of the Alaskan Russian Creole. Brewton Berry's (1945) study of the Mestizo of South Carolina likewise indicated that they "have been unwilling to assume the status of either Indian or black but are unable to acquire the status of white" (Thornton and Grasmick, 1980:38). Noel Gist and Anthony Dworkin (1972) concluded that these peoples' "group consciousness" of being distinct from others depends upon both the relative size of their group and their relations with surrounding peoples.

ganized, for example, the Nanticoke-Lenni Lenape, Inc., and the Ramapo Mountain Indians. Perhaps the best known of the groups is the Lumbee Indians of North Carolina, a grouping of remnant tribes some of whom were surely the Croatan Indians. In 1956, the U.S. Congress formally recognized the Lumbee as an American Indian tribe, but excluded them from federal benefits. In the 1970 census the Lumbee were enumerated at 27,520 (U.S. Bureau of the Census, 1973a:188), and some say this was probably an under-enumeration (Blu, 1980:238). The 1980 U.S. census enumerated 28,818 Lumbee and Croatan Indians, and several other identified groups might be added to that total to make a larger population (see U.S. Bureau of the Census, 1981).

UNITED STATES CENSUS ENUMERATIONS
OF AMERICAN INDIANS

Since 1790 the United States has conducted a decennial census[14] as provided for in the U.S. Constitution: "Representatives shall be apportioned among the several states according to their respective numbers, counting the whole number of persons in each state excluding Indians not taxed. The actual enumeration shall be made within three years after the first meeting of the Congress of the United States, and within every subsequent term of ten years, in such a manner as they shall direct by law" (*Constitution of the United States*, art. I, sec. 2, par. 3, as modified by the Fourteenth Amendment). It is noteworthy that "not taxed" Indians were systematically excluded from census enumerations, although the exact meaning of that phrase, and by implication, of "Indians taxed," is not clear. The terms were supposedly explained in the 1890 census *Report on Indians Taxed and Indians Not Taxed in the United States (except Alaska)*:

> Indians taxed and Indians not taxed are terms that cannot be rigidly interpreted, as Indian citizens, like white citizens, frequently have nothing to tax. Indians subject to tax and Indians not subject to tax might more clearly express the distinction. Indians taxed have so far become assimilated in the general population that they are not exempt from tax by reason of being Indians. Indians not taxed are remnants of uncivilized tribes or bodies of Indians untaxed by reason of specific treaties or laws controlling their relation to the national government, as the Six Nations of New York and the Five Civilized Tribes of Indian Territory. (U.S. Bureau of the Census, 1894a:131)

Early U.S. censuses counted only few American Indians. Not until 1850 did a U.S. census attempt to include all of the Indians of the United States, and then they were included only in a special census and only under the authority of a clause in a June 27, 1846, Indian appropriation act stating, "And it shall be the duty of the different agents and subagents to take a census and to obtain such other statistical information of the several tribes of Indians among whom they respectively reside as may be required by the Secretary of War, and in such form as he shall prescribe" (U.S. Bureau of the Census, 1894a:15).

The results of the special census were reported in the 1850 census of the

---

14. The 1790 census was not the first in the New World. There had been earlier censuses of the populations of Virginia and New France (Petersen, 1961:44).

United States, including a statement by the then commissioner of Indian affairs dated November 10, 1853: "The aggregate, according to this statement, was 400,764, but this does not profess to be accurate, for the number of Indians in the states of South Carolina, California, and Texas, the territories of Oregon, Washington, Utah, and New Mexico, and those belonging to the Blackfeet, Sioux, Kiowa, Comanche, Pawnee, 'and other tribes,' numbering, according to the table, 272,130, are confessedly 'estimates'" (U.S. Bureau of the Census, 1894a : 15).

In 1860 "civilized" American Indians first were enumerated as a group in the census, but those in Indian territory and on reservations were not enumerated, though figures for "non-civilized" Indians were reported. The total Indian population reported, including 44,021 so-called "citizen Indians," was 339,421 (U.S. Bureau of the Census, 1894a : 17–18). In 1867, 306,925 members of American Indian tribes were reported in the United States (U.S. Bureau of the Census, 1894a : 18).

In 1870 another attempt was made to enumerate American Indians for the U.S. census, but "of the total of 383,712, 261,615, or more than 68 percent, were based on 'estimates.' Included in the estimated population were 70,000 Indians of Alaska. Deducting the 70,000 for Alaska, which was only an estimate, there will be 313,172 as the estimated total Indian population in 1870" (U.S. Bureau of the Census, 1894a : 22).

A special enumeration was also conducted in the 1880 decennial census, which enumerated 66,407 "civilized" American Indians (U.S. Bureau of the Census, 1894a : 23). The commissioner of Indian affairs reported in that same year an aggregate American Indian population of 240,136 (U.S. Bureau of the Census, 1894a : 23). The information utilized by the commissioner of Indian affairs in establishing this figure, as well as other ones, was typically obtained from Indian agents and subagents "overseeing" specific tribes or reservations, although sometimes the population figures had been, in turn, obtained directly from the Indians themselves. In at least a few cases the need for population figures for this and other purposes resulted in some unique American Indian census reports. One such was the notched Kiowa and Comanche "census sticks." Another was the Big Road census, or roster, of 1883 reporting Big Road's Sioux followers, shown in figure 8-1. Big Road submitted a pictograph of the names of leaders of his sub-bands and heads of families. The Cherokee Indians in Indian Territory also conducted censuses. They were not sticks or pictographs but written numerical records (see figure 8-2).

It was not until 1890 that the U.S. Bureau of the Census formally enumerated all of the Indians in the United States under a provision of the Census Act of March 1, 1889, which stated, "The Superintendent of Census may employ special agents or other means to make an enumeration of all Indians living within the jurisdiction of the United States, with such information as to their condition as may be obtainable, classifying them as to Indians taxed and Indians not taxed" (U.S. Bureau of the Census, 1894a : 24). As enumerated by the census and shown in table 7-1 in the previous chapter, there was a total American Indian population in the United States (excluding Alaska and Hawaii) of 248,253 on June 1, 1890 (U.S. Bureau of the Census, 1894a : 24). Of

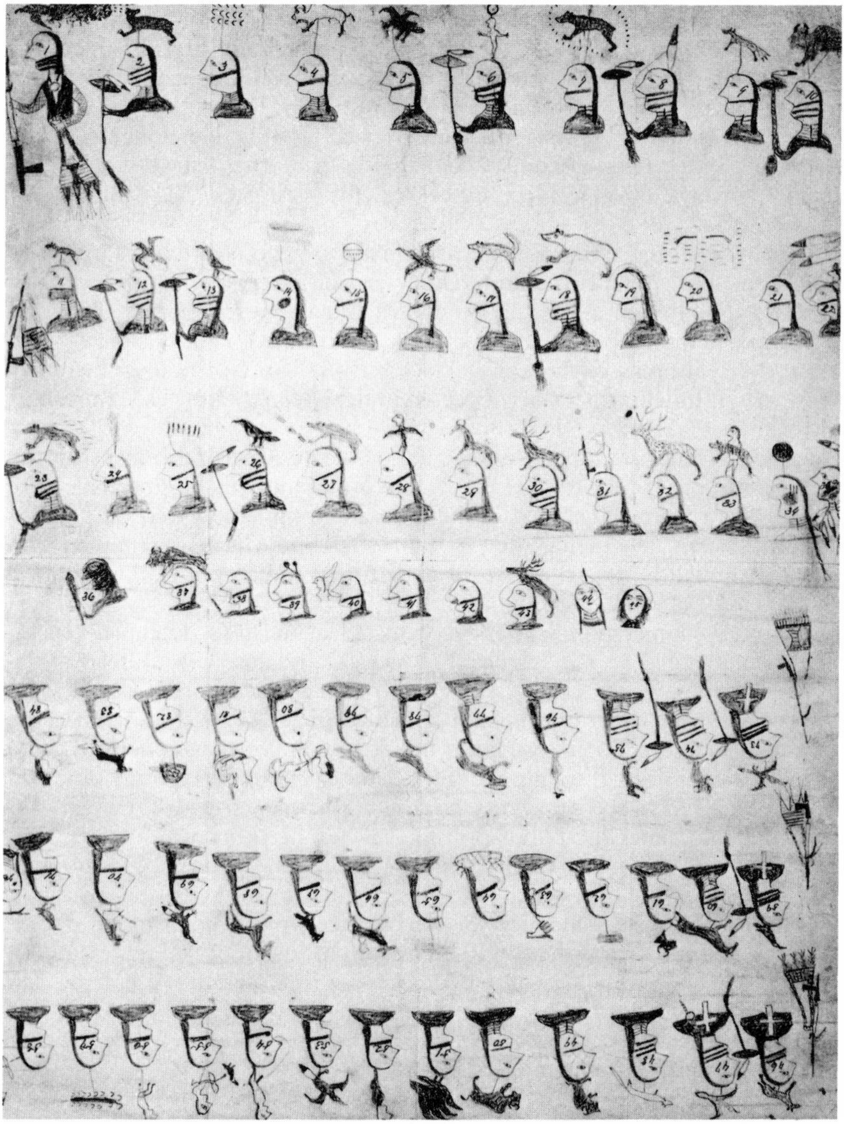

Fig. 8-1. The Big Road Census. Courtesy of Smithsonian Institution, National Antrhopological Archives

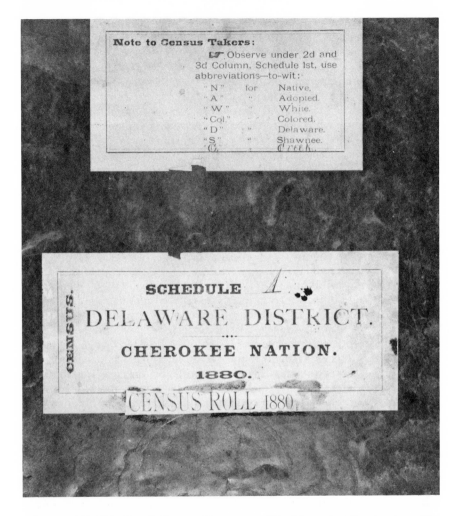

Fig. 8-1. The Big Road Census. Courtesy of Smithsonian Institution, National Anthropological Archives

the total 248,253, 58,806 were "Indians taxed" and 189,447 were "Indians not taxed." The Bureau of Indian Affairs continued to keep its own records of numbers of American Indians, and in 1890 the commissioner reported 228,000 (U.S. Bureau of the Census, 1915:10). Today the Bureau of Indian Affairs' figures continue to differ from those of the U.S. Bureau of the Census and frequently from those of the tribes themselves.

Problems of enumerating "Indians taxed and not taxed" still plagued the U.S. Census Office in 1890. It stated in its 1890 report, "Enumeration would be likely to pass by many who had been identified all their lives with the localities where found, and who lived like the adjacent whites without any inquiry as to their race, entering them as native born whites" (U.S. Bureau of the Census, 1894a : 131).

Another group presenting problems were the non-Indians with some claim to tribal status. The 1890 census report stated: "On the other hand, certain legal and proprietary claims lead persons of very slight Indian blood connections, or even pure whites by birth, to call themselves Indians by heredity or acquired right, and there are those of pure white blood who wish to be called Indians, in order to share in pecuniary advantages, who are not acknowledged by any tribes" (U.S. Bureau of the Census, 1894a : 131). The report goes further, saying, "these Indians for revenue, as they might be called, constitute a perplexing element to the courts, to the Indian Office, to the census officers, and to everyone who attempts to deal accurately with the conditions of Indians" (U.S. Bureau of the Census, 1894a : 131). (In 1888 Congress had passed an act regulating marriages between white men and Indian women, disallowing the man's rights to "any tribal property, privilege, or interest whatever" as a result of the marriage [Prucha, 1975 : 176].)

From 1890 onward all American Indians were included in the U.S. census of the United States population. Sometimes also special enumerations of American Indians were made. In 1890 there were special censuses of the Eastern Cherokee, the Six Nations of New York, the Pueblo Indians, and the Five Civilized Tribes in Indian Territory (see U.S. Bureau of the Census, 1892a, 1892b, 1893a, 1894b). Other special efforts were sometimes made as part of regular census enumerations to obtain detailed information on American Indians, tribes, ancestry, and so on; for example, in the 1890, 1910, and 1950 censuses (see table 8-3). Problematic in these censuses, however, were the different procedures whereby American Indians were enumerated.

Enumeration Procedures

In censuses before 1960 the enumeration of American Indians was made simply on the basis of enumerators' observation (U.S. Bureau of the Census, 1973a : xi). These censuses classified all individuals of obvious mixed Indian and black ancestry as Indian or black. In 1910 and 1930, however, an effort was made to enumerate all mixed-blood Indians as Indian, and in those censuses there were, as a result, significant increases in the American Indian populations reported over earlier censuses (U.S. Bureau of the Census, 1973a : xi). Then, "in 1950, persons of mixed Indian and white or Negro ancestry were included in the category 'All other races'" (U.S. Bureau of the Census, 1973a : xi). Thus the censuses of the first half of the twentieth century were not consistent in this regard.

Since 1960 self-reporting has been used to classify respondents by race. In the 1980 census, for example, respondents were asked to identify themselves as white, black or negro, Japanese, Chinese, Filipino, Korean, Vietnamese, American Indian (writing in the tribe), Asian Indian, Hawaiian, Guamanian, Samoan, Eskimo, Aleut, or "other" (writing in the identification). This approach has presented new problems to do with classifying individuals of

TABLE 8-3: **Questions Asked of American Indians in Supplemental Schedules of U.S. Census Enumerations, 1880–1970**

Question	1880	1890	1900	1910	1920	1930	1940	1950	1960	1970
Whether a chief	×	—	—	—	—	—	—	—	—	—
By what authority	×	—	—	—	—	—	—	—	—	—
Whether a war chief	×	—	—	—	—	—	—	—	—	—
Length of time on reservation	×	—	—	—	—	—	—	—	—	—
Length of time person has worn citizen's dress	×	—	—	—	—	—	—	—	—	—
No. of persons who wear citizen's dress, wholly and in part	—	×	—	—	—	—	—	—	—	—
Total population of agency, by tribe	—	×	—	—	—	—	—	—	—	—
Total population of tribe and what Indian language is spoken	—	×	—	—	—	—	—	—	—	—
Whether tribe is increasing or decreasing	—	×	—	—	—	—	—	—	—	—
No. of Negroes, mulattos, quadroons, octoroons with the tribe	—	×	—	—	—	—	—	—	—	—
No. of persons in this family	—	×	—	—	—	—	—	—	—	—
Probable wealth and wages earned	—	×	—	—	—	—	—	—	—	—
Tribe or clan (of individual)	×	×	×	×	—	—	—	×	—	—
Tribe(s) of parents	—	—	×	×	—	—	—	—	—	—
Proportions of Indian or other blood	×	×	×	×	—	—	—	×	—	—
No. of times married	—	—	×	×	—	—	—	—	—	—
Now living in polygamy (1890, no. of wives)	—	×	×	×	—	—	—	—	—	—
If living in polygamy, whether wives are sisters	—	×	×	×	—	—	—	—	—	—
Vaccinated	×	—	—	—	—	—	—	—	—	—
Personal property:										
No. and value of horses owned	×	—	—	—	—	—	—	—	—	—
No. and value of cattle, oxen, milch cows owned	×	—	—	—	—	—	—	—	—	—
No. and value of sheep owned	×	—	—	—	—	—	—	—	—	—
No. and value of swine owned	×	—	—	—	—	—	—	—	—	—
No. and value of mules and asses owned	×	—	—	—	—	—	—	—	—	—
No. and value of domestic fowls owned	×	—	—	—	—	—	—	—	—	—
Lbs. and value of wool owned	×	—	—	—	—	—	—	—	—	—
No. of dogs owned	×	—	—	—	—	—	—	—	—	—
No. and kinds of firearms owned	×	—	—	—	—	—	—	—	—	—

TABLE 8-3: (*continued*)

Question	1880	1890	1900	1910	1920	1930	1940	1950	1960	1970
Land in severalty:										
Received land allotment (give year)	—	—	—	×	—	—	—	—	—	—
No. acres held by patent	×	—	—	—	—	—	—	—	—	—
No. acres held by allotment without patent	×	—	—	—	—	—	—	—	—	—
No. acres held by tribal regulation	×	—	—	—	—	—	—	—	—	—
No. of families actually living on and cultivating lands allotted in severalty	—	×	—	—	—	—	—	—	—	—
No. of other families engaged in agriculture or other civilized pursuits	—	×	—	—	—	—	—	—	—	—
How supported (wholly or fractional):										
Self-supporting, for how many years	×	—	—	—	—	—	—	—	—	—
By family	×	—	—	—	—	—	—	—	—	—
By civilized industries	×	×	—	—	—	—	—	—	—	—
By government	×	×	—	—	—	—	—	—	—	—
By hunting	×	×	—	—	—	—	—	—	—	—
By fishing	×	×	—	—	—	—	—	—	—	—
By natural products of soil, such as roots, berries, etc.	×	×	—	—	—	—	—	—	—	—
No. of Indian children of school age	—	×	—	—	—	—	—	—	—	—
No. of Indian children for whom school accommodations are provided	—	×	—	—	—	—	—	—	—	—
No. of Indian apprentices who have been learning trades during year, and trade	—	—	—	—	—	—	—	—	—	—
No. of missionaries, by sex and denomination	—	×	—	—	—	—	—	—	—	—
No. of church members, by denomination	—	×	—	—	—	—	—	—	—	—
Ability to read English	×[a]	×[a]	—	—	—	—	—	×	—	—
Ability to write English	×[a]	×[a]	—	—	—	—	—	×	—	—
Ability to speak English	×[a]	×[a]	—	×	—	—	—	×	—	—
Ability to read or write native language	×[a]	—	—	—	—	—	—	—	—	—
Ability to read any language other than English	—	—	—	—	—	—	—	×	—	—
Ability to write any language other than English	—	—	—	—	—	—	—	×	—	—
Ability to speak any other foreign language	×[a]	—	—	—	—	—	—	×	—	—
Graduated from educational institution (name and location)	—	—	—	×	—	—	—	—	—	—

Question	1	2	3	4	5	6	7	8	9	10	11	12	13	14
In 1949, whether he attended or participated in any native Indian ceremonies[a]	—	—	—	—	—	—	—	—	—	—	—	—	—	—
Military service, with time and organization	—	—	—	—	—	—	—	—	—	—	—	X	—	—
Taxed and not taxed	—	—	—	—	—	—	—	—	—	—	—	—	—	—
No. of white persons killed by Indians, according to sex	—	X	—	X	X	—	—	X	—	—	—	—	—	—
No. and kind of crimes against Indians committed by whites	—	X	—	X	—	—	—	—	—	—	—	—	—	—
No. of whites punished for above crimes	—	X	—	—	—	—	—	—	—	—	—	—	—	—
No. of whisky sellers prosecuted, and kind and extent of punishment of each	X	—	—	—	—	—	—	—	—	—	—	—	—	—
No. of whites unlawfully on reservation	—	X	—	X	—	—	—	—	—	—	—	—	—	—
Occupation; area occupied, quality	—	X	—	X	—	—	—	—	—	—	—	—	—	—
No. of Indian criminals punished:	—	—	—	—	—	—	—	—	—	—	—	—	—	—
By courts of Indian offenses	—	X	—	—	—	—	—	—	—	—	—	—	—	—
By other methods (civil, military, or tribal authority)	—	X	—	—	—	—	—	—	—	—	—	—	—	—
No. of Indians killed by Indians of same tribe, by hostile Indians, by U.S. soldiers, by citizens	X	X	—	—	—	—	—	—	—	—	—	—	—	—
Indian deaths during year	X	X	—	—	—	—	—	—	—	—	—	—	—	—

Housing Questions

Question	1	2	3	4	5	6	7	8	9	10	11	12	13	14
House, pueblo, or lodge	X	X	—	X	X	—	—	—	—	—	—	—	—	—
Construction material, if a house	X	X	—	—	—	—	—	—	—	—	—	—	X	—
Type of floor construction	—	—	—	—	—	—	—	—	—	—	—	—	X	—
No. of houses owned by Indians	—	X	—	—	—	—	—	—	—	—	—	—	—	—
No. of houses built for Indians by government and cost of same	—	X	—	—	—	—	—	—	—	—	—	—	—	—
No. of houses occupied by Indians	—	X	—	—	—	—	—	—	—	—	—	—	—	—
If occupied by Indian, fixed or movable dwelling	—	—	X	—	—	—	—	—	—	—	—	—	—	—
No. of families in dwelling	—	X	—	—	—	—	—	—	—	—	—	—	—	—
No. of persons in dwelling	—	X	—	—	—	—	—	—	—	—	—	—	—	—
Owned or rented	—	X	—	—	—	—	—	—	—	—	—	—	—	—
If owned, whether mortgaged	—	—	—	—	—	—	—	X	—	—	—	—	—	—
Residing on own lands	—	—	—	—	X	—	—	—	—	—	—	—	—	—

[a] Asked of adults only.

SOURCE: U.S. Bureau of the Census (1973b: 27–31, 38).

mixed parentage, while maintaining some old ones. Although mostly self-reporting was used in the 1960 census, through a mailed questionnaire, respondents not identifying their race were interviewed by telephone or direct visit. Persons of mixed white and Indian ancestry were designated as Indians if they were listed on tribal or agency rolls or were considered as Indians in their community (U.S. Bureau of the Census, 1973a: xi). This change from the 1950 census, which had classified such people as "all other races," resulted in an increase in the recorded Indian populations of southern states—particularly North Carolina—containing relatively large numbers of racially mixed individuals (McKenny and Crook, 1976: 4). However, the 1960 census also classified persons of mixed American Indian and black descent as American Indian only if they were of predominately Indian ancestry or were recognized as Indians in their community; mixed-bloods of other than white or black ancestry were designated according to their father's race (U.S. Bureau of the Census, 1973a: xi).

In the 1970 census, in contrast, persons of mixed Indian, white, or black ancestry reported the race with which they identified, and persons who were in doubt about their classification were designated as belonging to the race of the father (U.S. Bureau of the Census, 1973a: xi). In the 1980 census, if they were in doubt, the race of the person's mother was used, but "if a single response could not be provided for the mother, then the first race reported by the person was used" (U.S. Bureau of the Census, 1982–83: 3). Additionally in the 1980 census, persons were designated Indian if they "did not report themselves in one of the specific race categories but entered the name of an American Indian tribe or reported entries such as Canadian Indian, French–American Indian, or Spanish–American Indian" (U.S. Bureau of the Census, 1983a: 4).

The change in enumeration procedures and the self-reporting beginning in 1960 also increased the numbers of people self-reported as American Indians. In the 1960 census questionnaire, mailed to households prior to the official census day, the respondent was asked to determine the racial category of household members so that it was not recorded by census enumerators (Rosen and Gorwitz, 1980: 21). Partially as a result, the Indian population increased between 1950 and 1960 by almost 50 percent. At issue in this Indian population increase, as well as in subsequent increases in 1970 and 1980, is how much of the increase was valid and true rather than due simply to self-reporting. The evidence is contradictory.

Census Bureau enumerators have attributed the increase between 1950 and 1960 to a failure in 1950 to identify adequately the Indians not living on reservations. This might account also for the high increase in the urban American Indian population during the decade (see Chapter 9, below), though a real increase in urban Indians also occurred (Rosen and Gorwitz, 1980: 21). Thus the increase may have been a result of improved census enumeration procedures.

Other data attest, however, that the 1960 census enumerated as American Indians people not defined as Indian for other purposes. One researcher, after comparing racial classification on death certificates with racial classification in the 1960 census, found that "more than 20 percent of the Indians who died were not identified as Indian on their death certificates; 17 percent were identified as white and the remainder were either not identified at all or were attributed to other racial groups" (Rosen and Gorwitz, 1980 : 21–22).

In 1956, Sol Tax and his associates in the anthropology department of the University of Chicago developed estimates of the number of American Indians in the United States, based on individuals listed as American Indian by the Bureau of Indian Affairs as well as individuals identified as Indians by fellow members of Indian communities (Stanley and Thomas, 1978 : 112). The total American Indian population so derived by Tax and his associates was 572,024, compared to the 1950 and 1960 census enumerations of 357,499 and 523,591, respectively. Moreover, "most of the 'extra' Indians were in Oklahoma, California, and the Dakotas. Presumably they were Indians who identified as such but might not have been living in Indian communities at that time" (Stanley and Thomas, 1978 : 112).

Similarly, indications are that American Indians were undercounted in the 1970 census. Laurence S. Rosen and Kurt Gorwitz (1980 : 22) asserted: "the 1970 census counted approximately 17,000 Indians in Michigan, but recent independent estimates fall between 28,000 . . . and 34,000. . . . The Michigan Commission on Indian Affairs believes there may even be as many as 75,000 Indians in Michigan." If such a margin of error was typical, Rosen and Gorwitz asserted, the actual American Indian population in 1970 could have been 1 million (the 1970 census enumerated 792,730 American Indians). Another study indicated that the 1970 census did not count 65 percent of Arizona's Salt River Reservation's population (see Meister, 1978); and Jeffrey S. Passel, a demographer for the U.S. Bureau of the Census, estimated that the 1970 census undercounted American Indians by about 7 percent, in part because questionnaires provided spaces to list a maximum of only seven or eight people (depending on which of two questionnaires was used) and American Indian families are often larger (Passel, 1976 : 408; Dobyns, 1984 : 28).

Yet Passel also concluded, from comparing census enumerations of American Indians with vital statistics (births and deaths), that 67,000 of the American Indian increase from 1960 to 1970 in census enumerations—the increase from 523,591 to 792,730, or 269,139—could be accounted for by individuals' changing definitions of themselves, at least as reported to the two censuses. According to Passel (1976 : 397), "many individuals who were registered as white on birth certificates and who were counted as white in the 1960 census shifted their racial self-identification from white to American Indian during the 1960s." Passel attributed this to Pan-Indianness (that is, Indian identity cutting across tribal lines) and heightened ethnic consciousness, both of which increased in the 1960s (Passel, 1976 : 404). Particularly, Passel asserted, it was the racially mixed Indians and those in mixed marriages who shifted their racial identification (Passel, 1976 : 404). Passel also did a similar study of 1970 and 1980 census data on American Indians. He found a discrepancy of 357,655 between the two censuses, which, he argued, was also a result of individuals' changing definitions of themselves as self-reported in the two censuses (see Passel and Berman, 1985).[15]

It is important to mention, too, that only recently in the United States have patterns of prejudice and discrimination toward American Indians lessened. Because of such patterns many American Indians who could pass as whites did so at the turn of the century right up to the 1960s. Recent changes in self-reporting may reflect less prejudice and discrimination toward American Indians. One does not now see signs proclaiming "No Indians or Dogs Allowed," as I did when growing up in Oklahoma!

The enumeration of American Indians is therefore a complex problem complicated by both the ways that American Indians are defined and the ways that individuals are enumerated or counted, given any particular definition (for general problems in the enumeration of Indians in past censuses, see Meister [1980], and also Jacob S. Siegel's examination [1974] of undercoverage and errors in the 1960 and 1970 censuses). Over the years the U.S. Bureau of the Census has changed or modified both its definition of American Indians and its enumeration procedures, in part as a result of the mixing of the American Indian and non-Indian populations and changing societal views of American Indians. The current self-reporting as an enumeration procedure reflecting individual self-definition will likely be continued in future censuses. It seems the most reasonable method yet devised, though it is fraught with problems.[16]

Another Census Issue

The U.S. Bureau of the Census not only counts American Indians and other groups but also obtains various kinds of information from them about, for example, their sex, age, marriages, household composition, property, and so on. Historically, the Bureau of the Census has obtained unique information such as whether an individual was a chief, wore "citizen's" clothes, or owned land in severalty. Such items on census schedules from 1880 to 1970 are shown in table 8-3.

To obtain such information, the Census Bureau typically now uses a supplementary schedule given to a sample of individuals, rather than asking everyone. In the 1970 census, for example, two samples were selected, a 20 percent sample and a 15 percent sample. The Census Bureau then multiplies the sample

15. The interested reader is referred to papers by Vine Deloria, Jr. (1984), and Duane Kendall Hale (1984) on the issue of self-identification vis-à-vis the 1980 census.

16. Censuses in other Western Hemisphere countries also are faced with questions regarding enumeration of American Indian populations. They handle the matter differently, generally having more restrictive definitions than the U.S. census. For example, Belize enumerates Amerindians (Mayans) and Caribs (mixed American Indians and blacks) and also includes a separate enumeration by language spoken; Brazil classifies people on the basis of color, including the category "parda" for people of mixed Indian descent; and Mexico uses only language, including whether the "mother tongue" is American Indian. Canada has more complicated procedures: Through 1941, Indian origin was traced through the mother (although other racial/ethnic origins were traced through the father); since then, however, "mixed Indian and white (termed half-breed in previous censuses) were classed as native Indians if they resided on a reservation; if not, origin of father was noted" (Goyer and Domschke, 1983: 369).

TABLE 8-4: **Complete and Sample Counts of 1970 Census**

Race	Complete	20% Sample	15% Sample
White	177,748,975	178,107,190	178,119,221
Negro	22,580,289	22,549,815	22,539,362
American Indian	792,730	763,594	760,572
Japanese	591,290	588,324	586,675
Chinese	435,062	431,583	433,469
Filipino	343,060	336,731	336,823
All Other	720,520	435,640	434,036
Total	203,211,926	203,212,877	203,210,158

SOURCE: U.S. Bureau of the Census (1973a:x).

size by a number, depending upon what population fraction the sample represents, to obtain a figure supposedly representing the total population.

The problem is that in the past the procedure has typically overrpresented the majority white population and underrepresented minority populations, particularly American Indians. The reason was that members of the majority white population were more likely to be included in the samples than were members of minority populations. Table 8-4 presents population estimates for various groups based on the 20 percent and 15 percent samples used in the 1970 census, along with the total census enumeration. It shows that whereas there were 792,730 American Indians enumerated in the 1970 census, the 20 percent sample generated an American Indian population of only 763,594, and the 15 percent sample, a population of only 760,572. In contrast, the white population was enumerated at 177,748,975, but the 20 percent and 15 percent samples generated white populations of 178,107,190 and 178,119,221, respectively. In the 1980 census, however, as Jeffrey Passel and Patricia A. Berman (1985) have illustrated, the 20 percent sample generated an American Indian population of 1,478,523, as opposed to a corrected enumerated population of 1,364,033 American Indians. American Indians in this instance were overrepresented by 8.4 percent (see Passel and Berman, 1985). Much information on American Indians obtained from census samples is thus misleading. The census samples of American Indians on small reservations are particularly misleading, scholars have shown: one study showed the 1970 20 percent sample underreported Indians at Arizona's Fort McDowell Reservation by 22.4 percent and overreported Indians at the Ak-Chin Indian Community, also in Arizona, by 33.8 percent (see Meister, 1978).

CONCLUSIONS AND IMPLICATIONS

In important ways, the twentieth-century American Indian population recovery has been related to changing definitions of American Indians and, according to the data presented here, changes in how American Indians were enumerated in U.S. censuses. Only in part, it seems, was the recovery a result of the fundamental demographic processes of births, deaths, and migrations discussed in Chapter 7. Even the direct implications of biological mixing, also discussed in Chapter 7, may not account for all of the recovery. Rather, biological mixing resulted in a need to change definitions of American Indians, which in turn somewhat expanded population numbers. This seems particularly true of the American Indian population growth since 1960, when self-definition has been used in census enumerations.

The various ways now used to define and enumerate American Indians in the United States, as summarized by James L. Simmons (1977:78), are (1) *legal definitions*, such as enrollment in an American Indian tribe; (2) *self-declaration*, as in recent U.S. census enumerations; (3) *community recognition*, for example, by other Indians; (4) *recognition by non-Indians*; (5) *biological definitions*, such as blood quantum; and (6) *cultural definitions*, such as acting as Indians "should."

It seems unlikely that we will achieve any single definition of American Indians in the foreseeable future: different definitions will be used for different purposes. What seems important, however, is that American Indians be allowed to do their own defining, either as individuals or as tribes. This may occur on the individual level through self-identification; it may occur on the tribal level through formal membership. One may object that self-identification allows considerable variation among individuals defined as American Indian, but American Indians have always had tremendous variation among themselves, and the variations in many ways have been increased, not reduced, by the events of history, demographic and other. Allowing self-definition and the differences it encompasses is simply to allow American Indians to be American Indians, something done all too infrequently in the short history of the United States.

9. URBANIZATION OF AMERICAN INDIANS

And when the last red man shall have perished, and the memory of my tribe shall have become a myth among the white men, these shores will swarm with the invisible dead of my tribe, and when our children's children think of themselves alone in the fields, the store, the shop, upon the highway, or in the silence of the pathless woods, they will not be alone. At night when the streets of your cities and villages are silent and you think them deserted, they will throng with the returning hosts that once filled and still love this beautiful land. The white man will never be alone.

—CHIEF SEATTLE (SUQUAMISH AND DUWAMISH)

SINCE 1950 THERE HAS BEEN a large-scale movement of North American Indians to urban areas of the United States, where the life they experience profoundly affects them as a population. In fact, American Indians are living a new chapter in their demographic history as urbanization affects their population growth, their rates of intermarriage with non-Indians, and their future identity as Indians. Ultimately, the effects of Indian urbanization may be as profound as the effects of the 400-year demographic collapse following the European arrival in the Western Hemisphere.

When one thinks of American Indian urbanization, one typically thinks only of the recent immigration to large cities. This important movement is the focus of this chapter, yet other kinds of urbanization deserve mention also.

American Indians developed urban areas of their own in the Western Hemisphere before the Europeans arrived. Urban areas and cities in Mesoamerica existed 3,000 years ago (Hardoy, 1964), apparently independent of events on the other side of the ocean, where cities were developed also. Early cities in both hemispheres were relatively modest in size by contemporary standards, although some attained populations in the hundreds of thousands. For example, the Inca capital, Cuzco, possibly had as many as 200,000 inhabitants, with thousands more in the area (Hardoy, 1964). At the time of the European arrival in the Western Hemisphere, the largest city in the world may possibly have been Tenochtitlan with 150,000 to 300,000 people.

Although North American Indians also developed urban areas and cities, they were not nearly as large as those south of the United States area. Moundville, in present-day Alabama, and Pueblo Bonito, in present-day New Mexico, had only a few thousand residents. The largest North American community, Cahokia, across the Mississippi River from present-day St. Louis, attained a population, some say, of perhaps 40,000 in about A.D. 1200 (O'Brien, 1972; Fowler, 1975), but the archaeologist James Griffin (1985) has stated that it was not nearly so large. (Griffin also says the population of Cahokia eventually dispersed to the north and west. Why we do not know.) In any event, American Indians lived in cities well before the European arrival; urbanization is not new in the Western Hemisphere, though some think that it is. Also, American Indians were involved from the beginning in the post-Columbian cities of North America. They were, for example, important residents of the California cities that grew from the early missions (Cook, 1943, 1976a, 1976b; Ronda and Axtell, 1978) and the early towns in Indian Territory (U.S. Bureau of the Census, 1907) and Arizona (Dobyns, 1976a). Their place in these towns and cities is generally overlooked.

American Indian urbanization has not taken place only within large cities such as Los Angeles, Chicago, and Minneapolis. Many urbanized Indians today live in small cities and towns in Oklahoma and other southwestern and plains states. Whether an American Indian or anyone else in the United States is urbanized depends upon the definitions of *urban* and *rural* used by the U.S. Bureau of the Census. According to the 1980 Census definition, the United States urban population comprises persons living in:

> (a) places of 2,500 or more inhabitants incorporated as cities, villages, boroughs (except in Alaska and New York), and towns (except in the New England States, New York, and Wisconsin), but excluding those persons living in the rural portions of extended cities (places with low population density in one or more large parts of their area); (b) census designated places (previously termed unincorporated) of 2,500 or more inhabitants; and (c) other territory, incorporated or unincorporated, included in urbanized areas. An urbanized area consists of a central city or a central core, together with contiguous closely settled territory, that combined have a total population of at least 50,000.
>
> In censuses prior to 1950, the urban population comprised all persons living in incorporated places of 2,500 or more inhabitants and areas (usually minor civil divisions) classified as urban under special rules relating to population size and density. To improve its measure of the urban population, the Bureau of the Census in 1950 adopted the concept of the urbanized area and delineated boundaries for unincorporated places. The 1950 definition has continued substantially unchanged, except for minor modifications in 1960, the introduction of the extended city concept in 1970, and changes in the criteria for defining urbanized areas for 1980 so as to permit such areas to be defined around smaller centers. In all definitions, the population not classified as urban constitutes the rural population. (U.S. Bureau of the Census, 1982–83 : 3)

Cities typically grow and spread into rural areas, incorporating them, and American Indians and others may become urban by having their residences engulfed by city growth. Also, urbanization includes the differential growth of urban and nonurban populations. Where no net migration from rural to urban areas is occurring, yet the natural increase in urban areas is greater than that of nonurban areas, the American Indian population is still becoming more urbanized. Rates of urbanization are determined by the differences in an urban population between two points in time, regardless of determinants of population size.

Finally, urbanization is not necessarily physical or geographic, though typically it is restricted by location. Urbanization may be viewed as a process whereby the social norms and cultural values of an urban way of life become transmitted to populations of nonurban areas. This may be through radio and television, printed matter, and other means of mass communication. One may become urban in this sense and still live in a rural area. In many important respects, American Indians in rural and reservation areas have recently become urbanized by being exposed to the norms and values of the city, and they will continue to be so exposed in the future.

PATTERNS OF GROWTH

As the United States Indian population has increased since the turn of the twentieth century, it has become redistributed from rural to urban areas. Data showing the increased urbanization during the last few decades are in table 9-1. Between 1950 and 1960, American Indians were still only 13.4 to 27.9 percent urban, respectively, but the urban Indians had increased to 44.5 percent of the total Indian population by 1970: from 1960 to 1970 the rural American Indian population grew only 16 percent, whereas the urban Indian population increased 144 percent (see Beale, 1973:944). Nevertheless, despite the widely different growth rates, less than 54 percent of United States Indians lived in urban areas, according to the 1980 census. Compared to the total United States population, American Indians were still very rural. In 1980, 73.7 percent of the total United States population lived in urban areas (U.S. Bureau of the Census, 1982–83:21).

Table 9-2 shows that urban American Indians tend to be concentrated in only a few states and urban areas. Table 9-3 shows the U.S. Standard Metropolitan Statistical Areas (SMSAs) with over 10,000 Indians in 1980. Table 9-2 shows that more of the Indians in Illinois, California, Texas, Ohio, Florida,

TABLE 9-1: **Percentage of the United States Indian Population Who Were Urban, 1890–1980**

Year	Percentage
1890	0.0
1900	0.4
1910	4.5
1920	6.1
1930	9.9
1940	7.2
1950	13.4
1960	27.9
1970	44.5
1980	49.0

SOURCES: Thornton, Sandefur, and Grasmick (1982:14), U.S. Bureau of the Census (1983d:92).

TABLE 9-2: **Urban Indian Population of States with More than 10,000 American Indians, 1970 and 1980**

State	1970		1980		% Increase
	Number	%	Number	%	
Calif.	67,202	76.1	161,192	81.3	139.9
Okla.	47,623	49.2	83,936	49.6	76.3
Ariz.	16,442	17.4	47,996	31.5	191.9
Wash.	16,102	52.2	32,843	56.4	104.0
Texas	14,567	86.1	31,811	80.8	118.4
N.Mex.	13,405	18.7	31,316	30.0	133.6
N.Y.	17,161	67.1	27,035	69.4	57.5
Mich.	10,541	65.8	25,370	63.9	140.7
Minn.	11,703	52.4	20,316	58.3	73.6
Ore.	6,976	52.8	15,439	58.1	121.3
N.C.	6,194	14.0	14,261	22.1	130.2
Fla.	4,275	66.9	13,975	73.9	226.9
Ill.	9,542	92.6	13,698	86.4	43.6
Wis.	7,439	39.6	13,625	46.5	83.2
Colo.	5,421	67.7	12,821	72.3	136.5
S.Dak.	9,115	29.4	11,816	26.3	29.6
Kans.	6,130	74.2	10,794	70.8	76.1
Utah	3,689	35.0	10,301	53.8	179.2
Ark.	4,696	29.2	9,971	45.6	112.3
Mont.	5,070	19.2	9,748	26.2	92.3
Ohio	5,079	82.2	9,219	76.9	81.5
Nev.	2,832	37.9	8,006	60.6	182.7
Mo.	3,617	74.0	7,804	64.3	115.8
La.	1,543	34.1	5,981	50.0	287.6
N.Dak.	1,810	13.3	4,120	20.5	127.6
Idaho	1,990	30.0	3,403	32.7	71.0

SOURCE: U.S. Bureau of the Census (1973a:1, 1983c:125, 128).

Colorado, Kansas, New York, Missouri, Michigan, Nevada, Minnesota, Oregon, Washington, and Utah lived in urban than in rural areas in 1980; and predictably, the states having the largest numbers of urban Indians in 1980 were California, Oklahoma, and Arizona. Table 9-3 shows that the SMSAs in 1980 with the largest number of American Indians were Los Angeles, Tulsa, Phoenix, Oklahoma City, and Albuquerque.

Relocation

One factor in urbanization of American Indians since 1950 has been the U.S. Bureau of Indian Affairs' relocation program, which has assisted Indian people in moving to selected urban areas. The program has not been responsible for all of the relatively recent American Indian migration to urban areas, or even the largest part—perhaps only 100,000 American Indians were di-

TABLE 9-3: **American Indian Population of United States Standard Metro-politan Statistical Areas with More than 10,000 American Indians, 1970 and 1980**

City (SMSA)	1970 Population	1980 Population	Percentage Increase, 1970–80
Los Angeles–Long Beach, Calif.	23,908	47,234	97.6
Tulsa, Okla.	15,183	38,463	153.0
Phoenix, Ariz.	10,127	22,788	125.0
Oklahoma City, Okla.	12,951	24,695	90.7
Albuquerque, N. Mex.	5,822	20,721	255.9
San Francisco–Oakland, Calif.	12,041	17,546	45.7
Riverside–San Bernadino–Ontario, Calif.	5,941	17,107	187.9
Minneapolis–St. Paul, Minn.	9,911	15,831	59.7
Seattle–Everette, Wash.	8,814	15,162	72.0
Tucson, Ariz.	8,704	14,880	71.0
San Diego, Calif.	6,007	14,355	139.0
New York, N.Y.	9,984	13,440	34.6
Anaheim–Santa Ana–Garden Grove, Calif.	3,664	12,782	248.9
Detroit, Mich.	5,203	12,372	137.8
Dallas–Ft. Worth, Texas	5,500	11,076	101.4
Sacramento, Calif.	3,548	10,944	208.5
Chicago, Ill.	8,203	10,415	27.0

SOURCE: U.S. Bureau of the Census (1973a : 138–41, 1983c : 201–11).

rectly moved under the program in its initial two decades (Margon, 1976)—yet it has been important.

The 1954 *Annual Report of the Commissioner of Indian Affairs* described an early year in the relocation:

During the 1954 fiscal year, 2,163 Indians were directly assisted to relocate under the Bureau's relocation program. This included 1,649 persons in over 400 family groups, and 514 unattached men and women. In addition, over 300 Indians left reservations without assistance to join relatives and friends who had been assisted to relocate. At their destination, Bureau Relocation Offices assisted this group also to adjust to the new community. The total number of relocations represented a substantial increase over relocations during the previous fiscal year.

Of the 2,163 Indians assisted to relocate, financial assistance, to cover all or part of the costs of transportation to the place of relocation and short-term temporary subsistence were provided to 1,637 Indians, in addition to relocation services. This number included 1,329 persons in over 300 family groups, and 308 unattached men and women. An additional 526 Indians, including 320 in approximately 100 family groups and 206 unattached men and women, were assisted to relocate without financial assistance, but were provided relocation services only. These services included counseling and guidance prior to relocation, and assistance in establishing residence and securing permanent employment in the new community. . . .

Approximately 54 percent of the Indians assisted to relocate came from 3 northern areas (Aberdeen, Billings, and Minneapolis), and 46 percent came from 4 southern areas (Anadarko, Gallup, Muskogee, and Phoenix). They went to 20 different States. The Los Angeles and Chicago metropolitan areas continued to be the chief centers of relocation. (Prucha, 1975:237–38)

Whether they are part of the bureau's relocation program or not, studies show that Indians still migrate to urban areas for economic reasons. Most reservations and rural areas have few job opportunities, and American Indians perceive urban areas as having good job opportunities, perhaps incorrectly (Thornton, Sandefur, and Grasmick, 1982:19).

Returnees

Not all American Indians who relocate to urban areas stay there by any means: The total return rate has been estimated between 30 and 70 percent (Margon, 1976). Studies of specific U.S. cities and tribes have been made in this regard: a study of the Fort Hall Reservation Shoshone-Bannock in Idaho found that 80 percent of those relocated to cities eventually returned to their reservation; a study of Navajo in Denver found half returned to the reservation within a three-month period; another study of the Navajo from 1952 to 1961 found that 37 percent returned; and a 1968–72 study of relocated Southern Plains Indians found that 15 percent left the city to which they had relocated during the first year (Brinker and Taylor, 1974:145).

Of the various reasons given by American Indian returnees for leaving cities, personal and economic ones seem to predominate. Table 9-4 shows the reasons given by a Navajo and a Southern Plains group: the principal reasons for the return of Navajo were personal; personal and economic reasons— probably because perceived economic opportunities did not materialize— were why most Southern Plains Indians returned.

Studies have also been completed on the characteristics of those American Indians who stay in cities, as opposed to those who return to reservations from them. One study (Sorkin, 1969) found that better-educated Indians are more likely both to move to cities and to remain there than are less-educated Indians. Another study (Martin, 1964) found that mixed-bloods are more likely to remain in cities than are those with less mixed blood. Yet another study (Chadwick and White, 1973) found that individuals with stronger self-identification as American Indians are more likely to leave cities than those who are less self-identified as American Indians. And one study (Wagner, 1976) found that Indian women with a non-Indian spouse are more likely to remain in urban areas than are those with an Indian spouse. Generally, therefore, it seems that the more Indian one is the less likely one is to remain in the city.

Finally, many American Indians exhibit a circular or cyclic pattern of move-

TABLE 9-4: **Reasons for Leaving the City Given by Two Groups of American Indian Returnees, 1952–64 and 1968–72**

	Percent of Navajo (1952–64)	Percent of Southern Plains (1968–72)
Personal	31	35
Economic	19	37
Alcoholism	18	16
Medical	23	9
Military Service	8	2

SOURCE: Brinker and Taylor (1974:141).

ment back and forth between urban and rural or reservation areas. In other words, they will move to an urban area for a period, return to a former rural or reservation area for a period, then move again to an urban area, and so on (see Hurt, 1961; Blumenfeld, 1965; Waddell, 1969; Tax, 1978). Often such movements simply follow job opportunities in the city (see Blumenfeld, 1965).

Reservations and Tribal Trust Areas

Many American Indians in the United States today continue to live not only in rural locales but on reservations and tribal trust lands. The reservations are American Indian lands established by treaties, statutes, or an order by the president or courts. In 1980 there were 278 reservations in the United States. In the vicinity of some reservations are what are called tribal trust lands associated with them. In 1980 there were 36 reservations with such trust lands, plus the Minnesota Chippewa Tribal Trust Lands, which are not associated with a specific Chippewa (Ojibwe) tribal reservation (U.S. Bureau of the Census, 1983a:4). In 1980 the U.S. census enumerated 339,836 American Indians, according to census definitions, who lived on reservations, representing 24.9 percent of the American Indian population; and 30,265 American Indians who lived on tribal trust lands, representing 2.2 percent of the American Indian population (U.S. Bureau of the Census, 1984:2). By far the largest reservation was the Navajo Reservation, where 104,978 Indians resided in 1980, along with 5,465 non-Indians; and 21,381 American Indians lived on adjacent trust lands in New Mexico, along with 3,579 non-Indians (U.S. Bureau of the Census, 1983a:13, 16, 1984:17, 20).

URBAN-RURAL DEMOGRAPHIC DIFFERENCES

We know that important demographic differences exist between American Indians living in urban areas and those living in rural areas and on reservations and tribal trust lands. The recent overall real growth of the American Indian population resulted from high birth rates and declining death rates, and the birth and death rates of urban and rural Indians are different. Generally, fertility and mortality are higher in rural areas than in urban areas, with most natural increases in populations coming among rural rather than urban residents. This has also been the case among American Indians.

Fertility

The difference in fertility rates between urban and rural American Indian populations is evident in Alan L. Sorkin's description of the 1970s United States American Indian population: "There are 5.2 children per woman for rural nonfarm and 5.4 for rural farm Indian women, compared with 3.4 and 3.6, respectively for all rural women. Among urban Indians fertility per woman is 3.8 children; for the U.S. urban population it is 3. . . . This implies that Indian women who are residing in the cities have lower birthrates than those residing on reservations" (Sorkin, 1978 : 12).

Other research on tribes shows this same urban-rural difference in fertility. For example, a 1972 study of Seminole Indians indicated that the urban women, aged 15 and over and married and/or with children, desired and had fewer children than their rural reservation counterparts (see Liberty, Hughey, and Scaglon, 1976b). The Seminole urban women had an average of only 2.54 live births, while the rural reservation women had an average of 3.22 live births. The average age of both groups was virtually the same: 30.3 years for urban women, 31.6 years for rural reservation women. The difference in fertility has been explained in terms of the urban women's greater use of birth control (see Uhlmann, 1972).

Another study by the same researchers suggested, however, that urban American Indian fertility may remain high: "A 1972 survey of fertility among 98 Omaha Indian women of child-bearing age living in rural and urban areas of Nebraska shows that the urban experience has not depressed either fertility levels or the desire for large numbers of children. Larger numbers of children were desired and produced by city women than by their reservation counterparts" (Liberty, Hughey, and Scaglon, 1976a : 59). Urban Omaha Indians had an average of 4.43 live births, and Omaha in rural areas had an average of 4.39 live births, although the average ages of both groups were approximately the same (Liberty, Hughey, and Scaglon, 1976a : 67).[1]

Whatever the differences in urban and rural fertility rates, American Indian population growth in urban areas has actually resulted primarily from migrations of young American Indian adults from rural to urban areas. This may be seen in the different age structures of urban and rural American Indian populations shown in a 1974 analysis of 1970 U.S. census data:

> There is a large difference in median age between urban and rural populations. For Indian men the urban/rural difference is 4.0 years and for women it is 4.7 years. From 1960 to 1970 the median age for rural men increased 0.3 years and for rural women 0.7 years. Yet in the urban areas the median age actually dropped. For urban men the median age in 1960 was 23.1 and in 1970, 22.0. For urban women the median age in 1960 was 23.6 and in 1970, 23.2. This drop in median age in the urban areas and the slight increase (compared to the total Indian population) in the rural areas is the result of

---

1. In part, the continued high fertility level is explained (Liberty, 1975 : 225) as resulting from a desire for large families, stemming from severe Omaha depopulations in nineteenth-century epidemics (Liberty, 1975 : 225), as I have shown in Chapter 5.

the migration of young persons from the rural to urban areas. (U.S. Department of Health, Education, and Welfare, 1974:24)

Also the same analysis showed:

Nearly a third of all adult urban Indians (35% of the men and 32% of the women) are still in their twenties. Less than a quarter of the adult rural Indians (24% of the men and 23% of the women) are this young.

55% of all adult urban Indians, but only 41% of all adult rural Indians are under 40 years of age. On the other hand, only 7% of adult urban Indians are 65 years of age or over, whereas 11% of adult rural Indians are elderly. (U.S. Department of Health, Education, and Welfare, 1974:15)

Similarly, in 1970, 50 percent of rural United States American Indians (not just adult Indians, but *all* Indians) were under the age of 18, but only 40 percent of all urban Indians were under this age. (The percentage of American Indians under 18 in urban areas was only some 6 percent higher than for the total United States population [U.S. Department of Health, Education, and Welfare, 1974:19].)

Calvin L. Beale has indicated the implications of this age differential for the future growth of American Indians in urban areas: "The current Indian rural population is extremely young in age composition—closely resembling the age structure of populations of less developed countries. Fertility is high. . . . Therefore, this population would either grow rapidly in the absence of outmigration, or give off large numbers of urban migrants (relative to the base population) in the absence of growth. The recent pattern appears to show partial population retention sufficient to result in significant growth, plus enough outmigration to create an urban population that will comprise a majority of all Indian people" (Beale, 1973:944−45).

Mortality

The scant research on how urbanization affects American Indian mortality suggests that urbanization results in better health care, lower incidence of most diseases, and a consequent decrease in mortality (Thornton, Sandefur, and Grasmick, 1982:25). We know also that mortality rates are generally higher for reservation than for nonreservation American Indians (see Kenen and Hammerslough, 1985), although the use of alcohol—an important contributor to American Indian mortality—may be higher in urban than nonurban areas (see Beltrame and McQueen, 1979). Information on accidents—another leading cause of death among American Indians—is contradictory: one study found accident rates lower in rural than in urban areas (see Wagner and Rabeau, 1964); another found the opposite (see Hackenberg and Gallagher, 1972).

The Homeless Kickapoo

In contrast to the Navajo with their large reservation, and the general movement of American Indians to cities, are a small, homeless group of Kickapoo

Indians who seek only to live on the fringes of an urban area. Although some say *Kickapoo* means "he moves about, standing here now, now there," others say that is not so (Callender, Pope, and Pope, 1978:656). Whether or not that is the meaning of the tribal name, it certainly fits the Kickapoo's history, which is a history of the all-too-frequent homelessness of American Indians as they sought peace and isolation, and experienced internal divisions, after the changes that Euro-American contact brought.

The first mention of the Kickapoo people was recorded in 1640 in a set of documents called the *Jesuit Relations* (Thwaites, 1896–1901), in which the tribe is referred to by their Huron name, Ontarahronon. In 1640 they were living on the present-day Michigan-Ohio border. Twenty-five years later they had been driven west to the southern Wisconsin area by the then powerful Iroquois. In the early 1700s some Kickapoo returned to the southern Michigan area for a while, then moved back to the Wisconsin area a few years later. It was not long before they moved again, south into what is now central Illinois and east into present-day Indiana. One band settled in each place—the Prairie Band in Illinois, the Vermillion Band in Indiana (Callender, Pope, and Pope, 1978:662).

Soon both Kickapoo bands, or parts of them, were on the move again. In 1763 some Kickapoo moved into present-day western Missouri, from which some of them later moved south to the Red River. Those in the Missouri area were eventually joined by others from the Prairie Band, some of whom moved again to join the Kickapoo in the south. In 1832, by the Treaty of Castor Hill, the Kickapoo accepted a reservation in present-day Kansas, and the last groups living in Illinois and Missouri moved onto it. A short while later, however, some of them moved south to join others on the Sabine River in Texas. The group in Texas was not stable either; portions ranged at different times through modern-day Oklahoma and western Arkansas. In 1839 most of the Texas Kickapoo settled in what is now Oklahoma, though some moved into Mexico. Shortly thereafter part of the Oklahoma group moved south to the Sabine River in Texas, from which some returned to Oklahoma lands in the mid-1800s. At the same time others on Oklahoma lands moved to Mexico, where they were joined later by Kickapoo from Kansas. Some of those in Mexico returned to present-day Oklahoma in the 1870s.

At that point there were about 1,150 Kickapoo. Roughly one-third were in Kansas, one-third in the Oklahoma area, and one-third in Mexico. By the turn of the century the Mexico group had grown to represent about half the tribe, but in the 1950s each of the three groups were roughly equal in size again (see table 9-5). They were settled at the village of Nacimiento in Coahuila, Mexico; in extreme northeastern Kansas; and along the Canadian River in central Oklahoma. In the 1980 U.S. census (1981) 2,355 people were identified as Kickapoo. In the 1980s much movement continued back and forth between the Oklahoma and Mexican Kickapoo, while the Kansas group remained virtually isolated (Callender, Pope, and Pope, 1978:662–67).

In the 1980s a subgroup of approximately 600 Oklahoma Kickapoo lived in Texas. These generally more traditionally oriented Kickapoo journeyed during winter months to Nacimiento in Mexico for religious ceremonies. Many

TABLE 9-5: **Kickapoo Population History, Late 1700s to 1980**

Location	Population
Late 1700s	
United States	2,700
1832	
United States	2,000
1875	
United States	806
Kansas	380
Oklahoma	426
Mexico	350
1905	
United States	432
Kansas	185
Oklahoma	247
Mexico	400
1950s	
United States	722
Kansas	343
Oklahoma	379
Mexico	387
1970	
United States	1,249
1980	
United States	2,355

SOURCES: U.S. Bureau of the Census (1915:74, 1973a:188, 1981), Latorre and Latorre (1976:28), Callender, Pope, and Pope (1978:666–67).

were not U.S. citizens. Their homes in Texas were tiny cane huts with cardboard roofs and dirt floors on land along the Rio Grande, some of which were underneath the International Bridge connecting Eagle Pass, Texas, with Piedras Negras, Mexico. When in the late 1970s many of these huts burned down, most of the Kickapoo moved to nearby Shelby Park, owned by the city of Eagle Pass. There they had no electricity and shared a single faucet and two restrooms provided by the city. They bathed in the river. They were some 600 squatters on urban American land that American Indians once had owned.

In 1983, Congress passed legislation to enable these Kickapoo to gain U.S. citizenship. In 1985, after years spent obtaining funds, and several acts of Congress, these homeless Kickapoo purchased 125 acres along the Rio Grande, just outside Eagle Pass. There they are to build a new settlement, a permanent home, to be called Nuevo Nacimiento (see *Minneapolis Star and Tribune*, 1985a; also *San Antonio Light*, 1981). In 1985, 143 of these Kickapoo became U.S. citizens (see *Minneapolis Star and Tribune*, 1985b).

URBANIZATION AND DEMOGRAPHIC SURVIVAL

Recent American Indian urbanization has brought new, serious threats to the demographic survival of American Indians in the United States. It has done so by influencing their rate of natural increase, rate of intermarriage with non-Indians, and tribalism.

Natural Increase

Although the pattern is unclear, it is to be expected in future decades that the American Indian population will cease to increase so rapidly, as it becomes more urbanized, and as the implications of urbanization are extended to rural and reservation populations. Its growth will become similar to total United States population growth.

Birth rates for American Indians surely will drop in the future and probably will level off at some point. The same may be predicted for American Indian death rates, though they are now fairly low, and a leveling off will likely come much sooner than that of American Indian birth rates. Thus, we can expect the American Indian population to continue to grow somewhat, as the total United States population will grow somewhat, but the percentage of the total United States population represented by American Indian population will very likely become more or less constant as the growth rates of both populations converge. American Indians then will represent a small, stable subpopulation of the United States. Their relative position will not change as it has done during the past several decades.

Intermarriage

Of perhaps greater importance to the demographic future of American Indians is the extraordinarily high rate of intermarriage with non-Indians, a high rate that becomes even higher with urbanization.

In 1970 over 33 percent of all United States Indians were married to non-Indians. This was a very high intermarriage rate, as in the total United States population only about one percent were married to someone of another race. The high rate has continued for many years (U.S. Department of Health, Education, and Welfare, 1974:35). There were, however, sharp differences between rural and urban American Indian populations regarding intermarriage.

Among urban American Indians in 1970, 51 percent of all married males had a non-Indian spouse, and 55 percent of all married females had a non-Indian spouse. In the same year, among rural Indians only 20 percent of all married males, and only 23 percent of all married females, had a non-Indian spouse (U.S. Department of Health, Education, and Welfare, 1974:35). These patterns varied somewhat by age, as shown in the intramarriage rates in table 9-6, but not greatly.

In 1980 over 50 percent of *all* American Indians—not just urban American Indians—were married to non-Indians, while only about one percent of whites and two percent of blacks were married to someone of another race (Sandefur and McKinnell, 1985; U.S. Congress, 1986:74). For example, the U.S. Bureau of the Census reported: "In 1980, 119,448 out of 258,154 married American Indian, Eskimo and Aleut couples were married within the same racial group; 130,256 Indian individuals were married to either whites, blacks, Filipinos, Japanese, or Chinese; and 8,450 Indians were married to individuals of other races" (U.S. Congress, 1986:74). Thus the rate of intermarriage in-

TABLE 9-6: **Intramarriage Rates of Married American Indians by Age Groups, 1970**

Age Groups	Urban	Rural	Total
16 to 24 Years			
Male	48	76	60
Female	47	76	59
24 to 44 Years			
Male	49	80	65
Female	45	76	61
45 Years and Over			
Male	48	81	67
Female	44	77	63
Total			
Male	49	80	65
Female	45	77	62

SOURCE: U.S. Department of Health, Education, and Welfare (1974:36).

creased about 20 percent from 1970 to 1980. As in 1970, a far greater proportion of those who were intermarried in 1980 lived in urban areas.

Also, around 1970, "barely three-fifths of all births registered as Indian list both parents as Indians. More than one-fourth of the remaining Indian births had only an Indian mother, and 15% had only an Indian father. . . . The number of Indian children born to two Indian parents declined from 66% in 1965 to 59% in 1968" (U.S. Department of Health, Education, and Welfare, 1974:37).

If these trends continue—and I suspect they will—we can expect even more blending of the American Indian and non-Indian populations, as discussed in Chapter 7. A point will be reached—perhaps not too far in the future—when it no longer will make sense to define American Indians in genetic terms, only as tribal members or as people of Indian ancestry or ethnicity. In this regard, and taking into account intermarriage rates, it has been projected that the percentage of persons in the American Indian population with one-half or more Indian blood quantums will decline from about 87 percent in 1980 to only about eight percent by the year 2080. Similarly, the percentage of persons with less than one-fourth Indian blood quantums will increase from about four percent in 1980 to almost 59 percent in 2080 (U.S. Congress, 1986:78).

Tribalism

Urbanization also affects the American Indian tribalism that is an important element in the definition and enumeration of American Indians, as well as in the lives that American Indians lead. The 1970 U.S. census yielded important differences between urban and reservation Indians in reporting tribal affiliations (see U.S. Bureau of the Census, 1973a:189, and Tax, 1978:130). Overall, some 21.2 percent of the American Indians enumerated reported no tribal affiliation; they merely reported themselves as American Indian. Among

TABLE 9-7: **Percentage of American Indians with an American Indian Language as Their Mother Tongue, 1970**

All Indians	32
On Reservations	58
By States and City (SMSA)	
South Dakota	29
California	20
Los Angeles	24
San Francisco–Oakland	26
Washington	13
Seattle	14
Oklahoma	30
Oklahoma City	24
Tulsa	19
Arizona	76
Phoenix	34
Tucson	68
New Mexico	70
Albuquerque	39

SOURCES: U.S. Bureau of the Census (1973a:192), U.S. Department of Health, Education, and Welfare (1974:48).

American Indians in urban areas this percentage was 29.1 percent; for American Indians on reservations it was only 11.8 percent. Thus urbanization may lessen the importance of tribe to American Indians. The census data indicate that about 23 percent of the American Indians reported no tribal affiliation in 1980 (U.S. Bureau of the Census, 1981), but comparable data for urban-reservation differences are not available.

Along similar lines, information was obtained in the 1970 census about the percentage of American Indians having an Indian language as the first language that they had learned. This information may also be used as an indicator of tribalism. The 1970 data are in table 9-7: overall, 32 percent of American Indians had an Indian language as their first language, while 58 percent of those living on a reservation had an American Indian language as their mother tongue. Data for selected states and cities presented in table 9-7 show how this measure of ethnicity varied with urbanization. Except for those in California and Washington state, American Indians living in cities had a lower percentage of mother-tongue speakers than was characteristic of the overall population of American Indians in their state. Perhaps California is an exception because about one-half of the Indians there immigrated to the state, predominantly to urban areas. The migrants tended to come from the Southwest, Oklahoma, and the Dakotas (and probably from rural and reservation areas of those states) where there were larger statewide percentages of mother-tongue speakers than there were for California as a whole. They therefore increased the numbers of Indian mother-tongue speakers in California cities. The same could probably be said for Washington.

The differences in tribal identification and first language spoken both suggest that urbanization lessens traditional American Indian tribalism. This, in turn, threatens the survival of American Indians as a distinct segment of the United States population to the extent their distinctiveness is tribally determined, as increasingly it seems to be.

A LOOK TO THE FUTURE

The three effects of American Indian urbanization—less natural increase, more intermarriage, and reduced tribal importance—singularly and together will influence the future of American Indians. Each alone suggests a future significant decline in American Indian population size, or at least in the rate of population growth. Considered together and interacting with one another, the causes suggest that the decline may be drastic. In other words, the seriousness of the separate effects is compounded when the three interact with one another. Intermarriage is likely to reduce tribalism, and probably, vice versa. Less natural increase in population will reduce the relative number of American Indians, or at least their relative rate of increase. Intermarriage will further reduce the relative numbers of American Indians by reducing the American Indian blood quantum of future generations. This may likely increase intermarriage rates, since there will be fewer potential American Indian mates. It may be that the demographic effects of less natural increase, more intermarriage, and less tribalism will ultimately eliminate American Indians as a distinct population, whereas 400 hundred years of population decimation after European contact did not. American Indians as Indians may eventually end, in the words of T. S. Eliot, "not with a bang but a whimper."

Optimism exists, however. American Indian tribes have persevered up to now, and tribalism is important to the future of American Indians, as we have seen. Research shows that American Indians make considerable efforts to reaffirm tribalism in urban areas by living in Indian neighborhoods,[2] by maintaining contacts with reservation areas and extended families, and by creating urban American Indian centers (see Hodge, 1967; Dowling, 1968; Tax, 1978; Red Horse et al., 1978; Paredes, 1980). Frequent results are a new tribalism for urban American Indians and, sometimes, "bicultural" individuals, that is, American Indians who live successfully in Indian and non-Indian worlds. A key to future survival, demographic or otherwise, involves American Indians learning to maintain themselves as distinct tribal people while living lives in urban areas and interacting with non-Indians. In this regard the anthropologist Sol Tax has written: "The lesson is an old one. There are no 'Indians,' but rather different communities of Indians. And that goes for so-called urban Indians, as well. Indian people from time immemorial have explored and found ways to live in new environments without losing their identities or values. They 'accepted the horse' fully, but nobody supposes they should have become horses. They are, presumably, fully capable of learning to live with us without becoming like us" (Tax, 1978:134–35).

---

2. Interestingly, American Indians tend to be less residentially segregated in American cities than either blacks or Mexican Americans (Bohland, 1982).

APPENDIX
THE NATIVE AMERICAN POPULATION
HISTORY OF ALASKA, CANADA,
AND GREENLAND

OUR EXAMINATION OF THE POPULATION decline and recovery of the American Indians of the conterminous United States has necessarily excluded the Native Americans of Alaska, Canada, and Greenland, although they are occasionally mentioned in the discussion. The Native Americans of Alaska are generally distinct from those in the United States, and the Native Americans of the United States and Canada had different histories, as did the Greenland Eskimo—though massive depopulations occurred in Canada also.[1]

ALASKA

James Mooney estimated the aboriginal population of the Alaska area at 72,600 people, including 40,000 Eskimo, 16,000 Aleuts, 6,600 Athapascans, and 10,000 members of Tlingit tribes (Mooney, 1928:30–33). This may be a very low estimate, as were most of Mooney's.[2]

Whatever the aboriginal population, sharp reductions occurred after the Russians discovered Alaska in 1732. The first permanent Russian settlement was in 1745, and the aboriginal Aleut decline began shortly thereafter. Mooney explained that, "Through the cruelties of the soldiers and irresponsible Russian traders it was estimated that within about 20 years of the Russian advent, the Aleuts had been reduced at least one-half, and when the Russian government interfered for the protection of the natives about 1795–1800 it was said, although probably with exaggeration, that the Aleuts had then been reduced to one-tenth of the original number" (Mooney, 1928:30). A smallpox epidemic followed circa 1835 among the Aleuts, further reducing their population from 6,991 to 4,007 in only four years (see Sarafan, 1977). The pox spread to them from British Columbia.

About the Eskimo and the interior Indians, Mooney asserted: "The Eskimo tribes, farther to the north, were not greatly disturbed until about 1848 when the whalers began to frequent the arctic coasts, introducing whiskey and disease, and destroying the native food supply. . . . The interior (Athapascan) tribes have probably suffered less in proportion, but have been reduced by epidemics of smallpox and fever, usually entering from the coast" (Mooney,

1. Hodge (1913), Trigger (1978), Helm (1981), and Damas (1984) contain detailed discussions of the native populations of these areas.
2. Robert M. Bone (1973) has estimated that the total aboriginal Eskimo population—not only in Alaska but elsewhere as well—ranged from 50,000 to 80,000.

1928:30). The first reported smallpox epidemic in southern Alaska was in 1775; another occurred in 1785 (Hopkins, 1983:246).

Mooney (1928:32) estimated the 72,600 total Alaskan Native American population had been reduced to 28,310 by the end of the nineteenth century. The U.S. census figures for about the same time are: 1880, 32,996; 1890, 25,354; 1900, 29,536; and 1910, 25,331. A U.S. Bureau of the Census report stated, however, "the figure for 1890 is probably incomplete, owing to the unexplored condition of the country at the time, so that the increase between 1890 and 1900 may be only apparent" (U.S. Bureau of the Census, 1915:10); also, "the figure for 1880, though based in part on an estimate, is believed to be approximately correct" (U.S. Bureau of the Census, 1915:10). Thus sometime around 1900 the native population of Alaska reached its nadir and began to increase.

By 1920 the Alaskan native population had increased to 26,558, by 1930 it was 29,983 (U.S. Bureau of the Census, 1937:2), and it has continued to increase since then. In 1980 the total Native American population of Alaska was 64,103, according to the U.S. Bureau of the Census. It comprised 21,869 American Indians, 34,144 Eskimos, and 8,090 Aleuts (U.S. Bureau of the Census 1983c:3, 1984:14). In part, the increases were due to gradually rising birth rates up to 1962, probably because of a decline in breastfeeding. Since then birth rates have declined, probably primarily because of government-sponsored family planning programs (see Blackwood, 1981).

CANADA

James Mooney estimated the aboriginal population of Canada at only 221,000.[3] I indicated in Chapter 2 that there may have been a 2+ million aboriginal population north of the United States.[4] By the last half of the nineteenth century the Canadian Native American population had dropped sharply, whatever its aboriginal size. A report in 1853 gave Canada's aboriginal population as 125,000 (see Lefroy, 1853:197); the U.S. Bureau of the Census listed it at 122,585 in 1890 (U.S. Bureau of the Census, 1894a:675). By the beginning of the twentieth century it had dropped further to only 101,000, according to Mooney (1928:33), but by 1911 it had risen to 108,261, also according to

3. Mooney's estimate included 54,200 Native Americans in eastern Canada, 50,950 in central Canada, and 85,800 in British Columbia. The difference between his actual estimate and this figure stems from his "allowing for overlappings between the United States and Canada" (Mooney, 1928:33).

4. Recently estimates have been made of aboriginal populations of Chipewyan peoples, the Kutchin, the Micmac, the Huron, and the Beothuk Indians of Newfoundland: H. Paul Thompson (1966) estimated Chipewyan Indians at 6,426, as opposed to Mooney's 3,500; Shepard Krech (1978) estimated the Kutchin population at 5,400, as opposed to Mooney's published total of 4,600 for the Kutchin and surrounding Athapascans (Mooney estimated that there were 2,700 Kutchin per se, in his manuscript notes at the Smithsonian Institution); Virginia P. Miller (1976) estimated the aboriginal Micmac population at from 35,000 to 70,000, a figure far, far higher than others have suggested; John A. Dickinson (1980) estimated the aboriginal Huron population at 30,000; and Ingeborg Marshall (1977) estimated the Beothuk population at only 352 in 1768, and perhaps 2,000 in the pre-European contact period. Another relevant paper on the demographic history of Canadian Indians is Eric Abella Roth's (1981) demographic reconstruction of a Kutchin Athapascan community.

Mooney (1913:390). Thus its nadir was around the turn of this century, close to that of the United States American Indian population.

Mooney considered that the initial disturbance of the native population of eastern Canada dated from 1600, although he admitted that Europeans had been fishing actively off the East Coast there a century earlier. According to him, the initial American Indian depopulation resulted from Iroquois use of newly acquired guns against surrounding tribes. Smallpox followed, possibly between 1616 and 1620, but particularly between 1636 and 1639 among, for example, the Huron, the Neutral, and the Algonquin, and also in 1670 among, for example, the Montagnais and, again, the Algonquin.[5] Canadian Indians reportedly observed of smallpox at about this time: "'This disease,' said many, 'has not been engendered here; it comes from without; never have we seen demons so cruel. The other maladies lasted two or three moons; this has been persecuting us more than a year. Ours are content with one or two in a family; this, in many, has left no more than that number and in many none at all'" (quoted in Heagerty, 1928:58).

Further smallpox epidemics occurred in Quebec at the beginning and the middle of the eighteenth century, and among the Ottawa at the end of that century (Mooney, 1928:23–24; Hopkins, 1983:245). The epidemic in the mid-1700s was so severe that many Indians referred to 1755 as the "Year of the Great Smallpox Epidemic" (Hopkins, 1983:245). Other important causes of American Indian depopulation included tuberculosis, recurrent patterns of famine and starvation, and alcoholism (Rogers and Leacock, 1981:172–73).

Mooney asserted that depopulation began in central Canada shortly after 1670, the year when the Hudson Bay Company was chartered. Severe depopulations occurred in the eighteenth century because of intertribal warfare and a smallpox epidemic of 1781–82. However, later smallpox epidemics of 1837–38 and 1870–71 were particularly deadly (Mooney, 1928:25). The 1870–71 epidemic "killed one hundred and twenty victims in a few weeks" (Hopkins, 1983:282) at St. Alberta, Canada, and all told, it killed over 3,000 Cree and Blackfoot in a year.

Other diseases also took their toll. Arthur J. Ray (1976) noted the effects of influenza, scarlet fever, and measles, as well as smallpox, on American Indians of western interior Canada between 1830 and 1850. Shepard Krech (1983) has examined the effects of disease between 1800 and 1850 on the Dene of the Arctic-drainage lowlands. He asserted that the Chipewyan, the Beaver, and the Slavey Indians were most often affected, but that the eastern Kutchin and the Hare also were. He stated that there was also "a raging disease in 1805–6; contagious distemper in 1825–26; influenza in 1834 and 1837–38; influenza in 1843; and some sickness in 1854" (Krech, 1983:129).

To the effects of these epidemics must be added depopulation by female infanticide among the Mackenzie District Dene during the first half of the nineteenth century (see Helm, 1980) and the effects of starvation and of hostilities between Indians and non-Indians (see Krech, 1981).

5. See Heagerty (1928:17–65) for a history of smallpox among Canadian Indians.

The destruction of Canadian Eskimo populations began later, after 1800, through disease, "dissipation," and starvation. Mooney (1928:25) asserted: "In the lower Mackenzie region an epidemic of scarlatina in 1865 is estimated to have killed about one-fourth of the population." The British Columbia native population had begun to decline, again according to Mooney, after 1780:

> The first great disturbing influence was the great smallpox epidemic of 1781–2, which swept over the whole country from Lake Superior to the Pacific. . . . The coast trade, inaugurated about 1785, marks the beginning of a steady decline, which proceeded rapidly to almost complete extinction of the coast tribes after the advent of the miners about 1858, and the consequent wholesale demoralization of the natives. The interior tribes have suffered much less in proportion from this cause, but these, however, have been greatly reduced by repeated visitations of smallpox and other epidemics which swept the Fraser River country and northward along the coast in 1862. In 1852–3 the Nootka tribes of Vancouver Island also lost heavily by this disease. (Mooney, 1928:27)

Since the beginning of the twentieth century, however, the populations of the native peoples of Canada have increased. In 1970 the official register of the Canadian Department of Indian Affairs and Northern Development listed 250,781 American Indians (Piché and George, 1973:367–68). By 1981 the Native American population had increased to almost half a million: 368,000 American Indians, 25,000 Inuit (Eskimo), and 98,000 Métis, or mixed-bloods (Romaniuc, 1984:20). In 1982 there were 578 organized bands living on 2,252 reservations (reserves).

Canadian Indian death rates were reduced quite significantly during the twentieth century, especially following World War II; and the reduction in mortality continued between 1960 and 1970. At the same time birth rates generally remained high and even increased, probably because of a change from breastfeeding to bottlefeeding, although the rates have dropped since the early 1960s (see Romaniuk and Piché, 1972; Piché and George, 1973; Romaniuk, 1981; Romaniuc, 1984). Victor Piché and M. V. George (1973:381) found that Canadian Indian "crude death rates have decreased from 10.9 in 1960 to 7.5 in 1970. . . . The birth rate has also dropped from 46.5 to 37.2, although part of this decline may be due to underregistration."

The birth rate had declined even further, to only about 28 per 1,000 by the late 1970s (Romaniuc, 1984:18). Although this rate is still about double that of the total Canadian population, and Canadian Indians will continue to increase in numbers for some time, it has been asserted that eventually "this fertility decline will profoundly alter the dynamics of growth of the Indian people as a distinct ethno-cultural entity" (Romaniuc, 1984:20).[6]

6. There have been important recent legal developments in Canada regarding Native Americans. Legislation has reversed a 114-year-old law taking Indian status away from Indian women marrying non-Indians (no similar law existed for Indian men), and another law taking Indian status from Indians leaving the reservation for work, to join the armed forces, to attend non-Indian schools, or become clerics. Those who had lost such status, even by voting as recently as 1962, were designated "nonstatus" or "enfranchised" and had lost certain Indian legal rights. In

A NOTE ON GREENLAND

The initial colonization of Greenland was about A.D. 1000 by Scandinavians, and by the first decades of the fifteenth century European colonization of Greenland seemingly had ended. Greenland then remained all but forgotten by Europeans until Danish colonization began in the eighteenth century.

The native population of the island—all Eskimo—was estimated at 10,000 in the eighteenth century, and by about 1900, Greenland Eskimo had apparently increased slightly to 11,000. By 1950 they had increased further to 16,000, and in 1970 they numbered some 28,000 (Bone, 1973:554). These figures, are, however, misleading. There is evidence that the Eskimo decreased significantly during the eighteenth century, and only increased afterward (Mooney, 1928:23). The nineteenth-century increase from 10,000 to 11,000 "is largely, if not entirely, to be accounted for by the increase of the mixed-blood stock from European intermarriage" (Mooney, 1928:22), as was surely true also of the increase from 11,000 to 28,000 between 1900 and 1970. Since the Danish government keeps population statistics on Greenland not by race but by place of birth—that is, according to whether one was born in Greenland or not—it is difficult to define properly the twentieth-century Eskimo population. In 1981 the total population of Greenland was 51,435, of whom 9,279 had been born outside Greenland (H. Kleivan, 1984:716).

1981 there were approximately 75,000 nonstatus and 293,000 status American Indians in Canada, most of whom lived on reserves (Romaniuc, 1984:20); and many Canadian Indians are now applying to regain their Indian status (see *New York Times*, 1985a). The government of Canada has also agreed in principle to create by 1987 a separate territory for the Eskimo, out of the Northwest Territories. It is to be called Nunavut ("our land" in the Inuktitut language of the Eskimo), and some say that it could eventually become a separate province (see *New York Times*, 1985b).

REFERENCES

Abel, Annie H., editor
1939   *Tabeau's Narrative of Loisel's Expedition to the Upper Missouri*. Norman: University of Oklahoma Press.
Aberle, S. B. D.
1931   "Frequency of Pregnancies and Birth Interval Among Pueblo Indians." *American Journal of Physical Anthropology* 16 : 63–80.
Aberle, S. D., J. H. Watkins, and E. H. Pitney
1940   "The Vital History of San Juan Pueblo." *Human Biology* 12 : 141–87.
Aikens, C. Melvin
1983   "The Far West." Pp. 149–201 in Jessie D. Jennings, ed., *Ancient North Americans*. New York: W. H. Freeman and Co.
Allaire, Louis
1980   "On the Historicity of Carib Migrations in the Lesser Antilles." *American Antiquity* 45 : 238–45.
Allison, Marvin J.
1979   "Paleopathology in Peru." *Natural History* 88 : 74–82.
Allison, Marvin J., Daniel Mendoza, and Alejandro Pezzie
1973   "Documentation of a Case of Tuberculosis in Pre-Columbian America." *American Review of Respiratory Disease* 107 : 985–91.
Alvarado, Anita L.
1970   "Cultural Determinants of Population Stability in the Havasupai Indians." *American Journal of Physical Anthropology* 33 : 9–14.
Amended Constitution and Bylaws of the Confederated Salish and Kootenai Tribes of the Flathead Reservation
1960   Article II.
Amended Constitution and Bylaws of the Covelo Indian Community, Round Valley Reservation
1975   Article III.
Amended Constitution and Bylaws of the Duckwater Shoshone Tribe of the Duckwater Reservation
1966   Article II.
American Indian Culture and Research Journal.
1982   Special Métis Issue 6.
American Indian Policy Review Commission Task Force Ten
1976   *Report on Terminated and Nonfederally Recognized Tribes*. Washington, D.C.: U.S. Government Printing Office.
Anonymous
1978   "Emigration Detachments." Special Issue of *Journal of Cherokee Studies* 3 : 17.
Ascher, Robert
1959   "A Prehistoric Population Estimate Using Midden Analysis and Two Population Models." *Southwestern Journal of Anthropology* 15 : 168–78.
Aschmann, Homer
1959   *The Central Desert of Baja California: Demography and Ecology*. Ibero-Americana 42. Berkeley: University of California Press.

Ashburn, Percy M.
1947   *The Ranks of Death*. Edited by Frank D. Ashburn. New York: Coward
        McCann.
Aten, Lawrence E.
1983   *Indians of the Upper Texas Coast*. New York: Academic Press.
Axtell, James
1981   *The European and the Indian: Essays in the Ethnohistory of Colonial North
        America*. New York: Oxford University Press.

Bada, Jeffrey L., and Patricia M. Masters
1982   "Evidence for a 50,000-Year Antiquity of Man in the Americas Derived
        from Amino-Acid Racemization of Human Skeletons." Pp. 171–79 in
        Jonathan E. Ericson, R. E. Taylor, and Rainer Berger, eds., *Peopling of
        the New World*. Los Altos, Calif.: Ballena Press.
Barth, Frederick
1969   "Introduction." Pp. 9–38 in Frederick Barth, ed., *Ethnic Groups and
        Boundaries: The Social Organization of Culture Difference*. London:
        George Allen & Unwin.
Baumhoff, Martin A.
1955–61 "California Athabascan Groups." *University of California Publications,
        Anthropological Records* 16:157–238.
1963   "Ecological Determinants of Aboriginal California Populations." *Uni-
        versity of California Publications in American Archaeology and Ethnology*
        49:155–236.
Bauxar, J. Joseph
1978   "History of the Illinois Area." Pp. 594–601 in Bruce G. Trigger, ed.,
        Northeast, vol. 15 of *Handbook of the North American Indians*. Washington,
        D.C.: Smithsonian Institution.
Beale, Calvin L.
1973   "Migration Patterns of Minorities in the United States." *American Jour-
        nal of Agricultural Economics* 55:938–46.
Bean, Lowell John
1978   "Cahuilla." Pp. 575–87 in Robert F. Heizer, ed., *California*, vol. 8 of
        Handbook of North American Indians. Washington, D.C.: Smithsonian
        Institution.
Bean, Lowell John, and Sylvia Brakke Vane
1978   "Cults and Their Transformations." Pp. 662–72 in Robert F. Heizer, ed.,
        California, vol. 8 of *Handbook of North American Indians*. Washington,
        D.C.: Smithsonian Institution.
Beckham, Stephen Dow
1971   *Requiem for a People: The Rogue Indians and the Frontiersman*. Norman:
        University of Oklahoma Press.
Beltrame, Thomas, and David U. McQueen
1979   "Urban and Rural Indian Drinking Patterns: The Special Case of the
        Lumbee." *International Journal of Addiction* 14:533–48.
Berlandier, Jean Louis
1969   *The Indians of Texas in 1830*. Edited and introduced by John C. Ewers.
        Washington, D.C.: Smithsonian Institution Press.
Berry, Brewton
1945   "The Mestizos of South Carolina." *American Journal of Sociology* 51:34–41.
1963   *Almost White: A Study of Certain Racial Hybrids in the Eastern United
        States*. New York: Macmillan Company.

Beverley, Robert
1705   *The History and Present State of Virginia*. Edited by Lewis B. Wright. Chapel Hill: University of North Carolina Press, 1947.
Bieder, Robert E.
1980   "Scientific Attitudes Toward Indian Mixed-Bloods in Early Nineteenth Century America." *Journal of Ethnic Studies* 8:17–30.
Bishoff, James L., and Robert J. Rosenbauer
1981   "Uranium Series Dating of Human Skeletal Remains from the Del Mar and Sunnyvale Sites." *Science* 213:1003–1005.
Black, Lydia T.
1983   "Some Problems in Interpretation of Aleut Prehistory." *Arctic Anthropology* 20:49–78.
Blackwell, Charles W., and J. Patrick Mehaffey
1983   "American Indians, Trust and Recognition." Pp. 50–73 in Frank W. Porter, III, ed., *Nonrecognized American Indian Tribes: An Historical and Legal Perspective*. Occasional Papers Series, no. 7. Chicago: The Newberry Library.
Blackwood, Larry
1981   "Alaska Native Fertility Trends, 1950–1978." *Demography* 18:173–79.
Blasingham, Emily J.
1956   "The Depopulation of the Illinois Indians." *Ethnohistory* 3:pt. 1, 193–224; pt. 2, 361–412.
Bledsoe, Anthony J.
1885   *Indian Wars of the Northwest*. San Francisco: Bacon and Company.
Blu, Karen I.
1980   *The Lumbee Problem: The Making of an American Indian People*. New York: Cambridge University Press.
Blue, Brantly
1974   "Foreword." Pp. iii–v in *The Indian Removals*. New York: AMS Press.
Blumenfeld, Ruth
1965   "Mohawks: Round Trip to the High Steel." *Transaction* 3:19–22.
Bohland, James R.
1982   "Indian Residential Segregation in the Urban Southwest: 1970 and 1980." *Social Science Quarterly* 63:749–61.
Bommelyn, Loren (Tolowa)
1983   Personal communication.
Bone, Robert M.
1973   "The Number of Eskimos: An Arctic Enigma." *Polar Record* 16:553–57.
Borah, Woodrow
1964   "America as Model: The Demographic Impact of European Expansion upon the Non-European World." Pp. 79–87 in *Acts y Memorias*, vol. 3 of *XXXV Congreso Internacional de Americanistas, México, 1962*. México, D.F.: Editorial Libros de México.
1976   "The Historical Demography of Aboriginal and Colonial America: An Attempt at Perspective." Pp. 13–34 in William M. Denevan, ed., *The Native Population of the Americas in 1492*. Madison: University of Wisconsin Press.
Borrie, W. D.
1970   *The Growth and Control of World Population*. London: Weidenfeld and Nicolson.
Boserup, Ester
1966   *The Conditions of Agricultural Growth*. Chicago: Aldine.

Bowman, J. N.
1965   "The Names of the California Missions." *The Americas* 21:363–74.
Brasser, T. J.
1978   "Early Indian-European Contacts." Pp. 78–88 in Bruce G. Trigger, ed., *Northeast*, vol. 15 of *Handbook of North American Indians*. Washington, D.C.: Smithsonian Institution.
Braudel, Fernand
1979   *The Structures of Everyday Life*. Vol. 1, *Civilization and Capitalism, 15th-18th Century*. Translated and Revised by Siân Reynolds. New York: Harper and Row.
Brauer, Gunter
1984   "A Craniological Approach to the Origin of Anatomically Modern *Homo sapiens* in Africa and Implications for the Appearance of Modern Humans." Pp. 327–410 in Fred H. Smith and Frank Spencer, eds., *The Origin of Modern Humans*. New York: Alan R. Liss, Inc.
Brinker, Paul A., and Benjamin J. Taylor
1974   "Southern Plains Indian Relocation Returnees." *Human Organization* 33:139–46.
Broek, Jan O. M.
1967   "Discussion" (of Dodge). Pp. 237–41 in Sol Tax, ed., *Indian Tribes of Aboriginal America: Selected Papers of the XXIXth International Congress of Americanists*. New York: Cooper Square Publishers, Inc.
Brose, David S., and N'omi Greber, editors
1979   *Hopewell Archaeology*. Kent, Ohio: Kent State University Press.
Broudy, David W., and Phillip A. May
1983   "Demographic and Epidemiologic Transition Among the Navajo Indians." *Social Biology* 30:1–16.
Bryan, Alan
1969   "Early Man in America and the Late Pleistocene Chronology of Western Canada and Alaska." *Current Anthropology* 10:339–65.
Buikstra, Jane E., editor
1981   "Prehistoric Tuberculosis in the Americas." *Scientific Papers*, no. 5. Evanston, Ill.: Northwestern University Archeological Program.
Buikstra, Jane. E., and Lyle W. Konigsberg
1985   "Paleodemography: Critiques and Controversies." *American Anthropologist* 87:316–33.
Bunte, Pamela A., Robert Franklin, and Richard Stoffle
1983   "Epidemics and Territorial Rearrangements: The San Juan Southern Paiutes and the 1918 Influenza Epidemic." Paper presented at the 1983 Native American Historical Epidemiology Conference, The Newberry Library, Chicago.
Bunzel, Ruth L.
1932   "Zuñi Origin Myths." *Forty-Seventh Annual Report of the Bureau of American Ethnology . . . 1929–30*. Washington, D.C.: U.S. Government Printing Office.
Butlin, Noel
1983   *Our Original Aggression: Aboriginal Populations of Southeastern Australia, 1788–1850*. Sydney: George Allen & Unwin.

Callender, Charles
1978   "Illinois." Pp. 673–80 in Bruce G. Trigger, ed., *Northeast*, vol. 15 of

Handbook of North American Indians. Washington, D.C.: Smithsonian Institution.

Callender, Charles, Richard K. Pope, and Susan M. Pope
1978   "Kickapoo." Pp. 656–72 in Bruce G. Trigger, ed., *Northeast*, vol. 15 of *Handbook of North American Indians.* Washington, D.C.: Smithsonian Institution.

Campbell, Gregory R.
1983   "Child Spacing Among the Northern Cheyenne: An Ethnohistoric and Demographic Analysis." Paper presented at the meetings of the American Society for Ethnohistory, Albuquerque.

Carley, Kenneth
1976   *The Sioux Uprising of 1862.* St. Paul: Minnesota Historical Society.

Carneiro, Robert L.
1967   "On the Relationship Between Size of Population and Complexity of Social Organization." *Southwestern Journal of Anthropology* 23 : 234–43.

Carr, Barbara A., and Eun Sul Lee
1978   "Navajo Tribal Mortality: A Life Table Analysis of the Leading Cause of Death." *Social Biology* 25 : 279–87.

Carranco, Lynwood, and Estle Beard
1981   *Genocide and Vendetta: The Round Valley Wars of Northern California.* Norman: University of Oklahoma Press.

Casteel, Richard W.
1980   "A Sample of Northern North American Hunter-Gatherers and the Malthusian Thesis: An Explicitly Quantified Approach." Pp. 301–19 in David L. Browman, ed., *Early Native Americans.* The Hague: Mouton Publishers.

Castillo, Edward D.
1978   "The Impact of Euro-American Exploration and Settlement." Pp. 99–127 in Robert F. Heizer, ed., *California*, vol. 8 of *Handbook of North American Indians.* Washington, D.C.: Smithsonian Institution.

Catlin, George
1844   *Letters and Notes on the Manners, Customs and Conditions of the North American Indians.* 2 vols. Reprint. New York: Dover Publications, Inc., 1973.

Chadwick, Bruce A., and Lynn C. White
1973   "Correlates of Length of Urban Residence Among the Spokane Indians." *Human Organization* 32 : 9–16.

Chardon, Francis A.
1932   *Journal at Fort Clark, 1834–39.* Pierre, S. Dak.: State of South Dakota.

Chavers, Dean
1971–72 "The Lumbee Story, Part I—Origin of the Tribe." *Indian Voice* 1 : 11–12, 24.

Cherokee Nation of Oklahoma
1985   Personal Communication from the Cherokee Registration Committee, Tahlequah, April 22.

Chickasaw Nation Tribal Constitution
1979   Article II.

Chisholm, James S.
1983   *Navajo Infancy: An Ethnological Study of Child Development.* New York: Aldine Publishing Co.

Churcher, C. S., and W.A. Kenyon
1960   "The Tabor Hill Ossuaries: A Study in Iroquois Demography." *Human Biology* 32:249–73.
Clark, Colin
1977   *Population Growth and Land Use.* 2d ed. London: Macmillan Press.
Cockburn, Aidan
1961   "The Origin of the Treponematoses." *Bulletin of the World Health Organization* 24:221–28.
Coffer, William E.
1977   "Genocide of the California Indians." *The Indian Historian* 10:8–15.
Cohen, Felix S.
1942   *Handbook of Federal Indian Law.* Reprint. New York: AMS Press, 1982.
Colton, Harold S.
1936   "The Rise and Fall of the Prehistoric Population of Northern Arizona." *Science* 84:337–43.
Constitution and Bylaws of the Confederated Salish and Kootenai Tribes of the Flathead Reservation
1935   Article II.
Constitution of the Cherokee Nation of Oklahoma
1975   Article III.
Constitution of the United States
1787   Article I, Section 2, Part 3.
Cook, Noble David
1981   *Demographic Collapse: Indian Peru, 1520–1620.* Cambridge, England: Cambridge University Press.
Cook, Sherburne F.
1935   "Diseases of the Indians of Lower California in the Eighteenth Century." *California and Western Medicine* 43:432–34.
1940   *Population Trends Among the California Mission Indians.* Ibero-Americana 17. Berkeley: University of Calfornia Press.
1943   "Migration and Urbanization of the Indians in California." *Human Biology* 15:33–45.
1945   "Demographic Consequences of European Contact with Primitive Peoples." *Annals of the American Academy of Political and Social Science*: 237:107–11.
1955   "The Epidemic of 1830–1833 in California and Oregon." *University of California Publications in American Archaeology and Ethnology* 43:303–26.
1973a   "Interracial Warfare and Population Decline Among the New England Indians." *Ethnohistory* 20:1–24.
1973b   "The Significance of Disease in the Extinction of the New England Indians." *Human Biology* 45:485–508.
1976a   *The Conflict Between the California Indian and White Civilization.* Berkeley: University of California Press.
1976b   *The Population of the California Indians, 1769–1970.* Berkeley: University of California Press.
1976c   *The Indian Population of New England in the Seventeenth Century.* University of California Publications in Anthropology, vol. 12.
1978   "Historical Demography." Pp. 91–98 in Robert F. Heizer, ed., *California*, vol. 3 of *Handbook of North American Indians.* Washington, D.C.: Smithsonian Institution.

Cook, Sherburne F., and Woodrow Borah
1948   *The Population of Central Mexico in the Sixteenth Century.* Ibero-Americana 31. Berkeley: University of California Press.
1971–79 *Essays in Population History.* 3 vols. Berkeley: University of California Press.
Cordell, Linda S.
1979   "Pre-history: Eastern Anasazi." Pp. 130–51 in Alfonso Ortiz, ed., *Southwest,* vol. 9 of *Handbook of North American Indians.* Washington, D.C.: Smithsonian Institution.
Cowgill, Donald Olen
1949   "The Theory of Population Growth Cycles." *American Journal of Sociology* 55:163–70.
Crosby, Alfred W., Jr.
1972   *The Columbian Exchange: Biological and Cultural Consequences of 1492.* Westport, Conn.: Greenwood Press.
1976   "Virgin Soil Epidemics as a Factor in the Aboriginal Depopulation in America." *William and Mary Quarterly* 33:289–99.
Culbert, T. Patrick
1983   "Mesoamerica." Pp. 495–555 in Jessie D. Jennings, ed., *Ancient North Americans.* New York: W. H. Freeman and Co.
Cushing, Frank Hamilton
1883   "Zuñi Fetiches." Pp. 3–45 in *Second Annual Report of the Bureau of [American] Ethnology . . . 1880–81.* Washington, D.C.: U.S. Government Printing Office.

Dale, Harrison Clifford, editor
1941   *The Achley-Smith Explorations and the Discovery of a Central Route to the Pacific 1822–1829.* Rev. ed. Glendale, Calif.: The Arthur H. Clark Co.
Damas, David, editor
1984   *Arctic.* Vol. 5, *Handbook of North American Indians,* ed. William C. Sturtevant. Washington, D.C.: Smithsonian Institution.
Davis, Kingsley
1945   "The World Demographic Transition." *Annals of the American Academy of Political and Social Sciences* 237:1–11.
1955   "The Origin and Growth of Urbanization in the World." *American Journal of Sociology* 60:429–37.
Davis, Kingsley, and Judith Blake
1956   "Social Structure and Fertility: An Analytic Framework." *Economic Development and Cultural Change* 4:211–35.
Deloria, Vine, Jr.
1984   "The Popularity of Being Indian: A New Trend in Contemporary American Society." *Centerboard* 2:6–12.
DeMallie, Raymond J.
1982   "The Lakota Ghost Dance: An Ethnohistorical Account." *Pacific Historical Review* 51:385–405.
Denevan, William M.
1970   "Aboriginal Drained-Field Cultivation in the Americas." *Science* 169:647–54.
1976   "Epilogue." Pp. 289–92 in William M. Denevan, ed., *The Native Population of the Americas in 1492.* Madison: University of Wisconsin Press.

Devereux, George
1961   *Mohave Ethnopsychiatry and Suicide: The Psychiatric Knowledge and the Psychic Disturbances of an Indian Tribe*. Bureau of American Ethnology Bulletin no. 175. Washington, D.C.: U.S. Government Printing Office.
Dickinson, John A.
1980   "The Pre-Contact Huron Population: A Re-Appraisal." *Ontario History* 72:173–79.
Di Peso, Charles C.
1979   "Pre-history: O'otam." Pp. 91–99 in Alfonso Ortiz, ed., *Southwest*, vol. 9 of *Handbook of North American Indians*. Washington, D.C.: Smithsonian Institution.
Dobyns, Henry F.
1966   "Estimating Aboriginal American Population: An Appraisal of Techniques with a New Hemisphere Estimate." *Current Anthropology* 7: 395–416.
1976a   *Spanish Colonial Tucson: A Demographic History*. Tucson: University of Arizona Press.
1976b   *Native American Historical Demography: A Critical Bibliography*. Bloomington: Indiana University Press.
1978   "Tribalism Today: An Anthropological Perspective on Reservation Enclaves and Urban Pan-Indians." Paper presented at the First Annual Conference on Problems and Issues Concerning American Indians Today, The Newberry Library, Chicago.
1983   *Their Number Become Thinned*. With the assistance of William R. Swagerty. Knoxville: University of Tennessee Press.
1984   "Native American Population Collapse and Recovery." Pp. 17–35 in William R. Swagerty, ed., *Scholars and the Indian Experience*. Bloomington: Indiana University Press.
Dobyns, Henry F., and R. C. Euler
1967   *The Ghost Dance of 1889 Among the Pai Indians of Northwestern Arizona*. Prescott, Ariz.: Prescott College Press.
1980   *Indians of the Southwest: A Critical Bibliography*. Bloomington: Indiana University Press.
Dodge, Stanley D.
1967   "Notes on the Theory of Population Distribution in Relation to the Aboriginal Population of North America." Pp. 234–37 in Sol Tax, ed., *Indian Tribes of Aboriginal America: Selected Papers of the XXIXth International Congress of Americanists*. New York: Cooper Square Publishers, Inc.
Doran, Michael F.
1975–76 "Population Statistics of Nineteenth Century Indian Territory." *Chronicles of Oklahoma* 53:492–515.
Dorsey, J. Owen
1884   "Omaha Sociology." *Third Annual Report of the Bureau of Ethnology . . . 1881–82*. Washington, D.C.: U.S. Government Printing Office.
Dowling, John M.
1968   "A 'Rural' Indian Community in an Urban Setting." *Human Organization* 27:236–39.
Driver, Harold E.
1961   *Indians of North America*. Chicago: University of Chicago Press.

1968   "On the Population Nadir of Indians in the United States." *Current Anthropology* 9:330.
1969   *Indians of North America.* 2d ed., rev. Chicago: University of Chicago Press.
Drucker, Philip
1937   "The Tolowa and Their Southwest Oregon Kin." *University of California Publications in American Archaeology and Ethnology* 36:221–300.
DuBois, Cora
1932   "Tolowa Notes." *American Anthropologist* 34:248–62.
1939   *The 1870 Ghost Dance.* Anthropological Records, no. 3. Berkeley: University of California Press.
Duffy, John
1951   "Smallpox and the Indians in the American Colonies." *Bulletin of the History of Medicine* 25:324–41.
1953   *Epidemics in Colonial America.* Baton Rouge: Louisiana State University Press.
Dumond, Don E.
1980   "The Archaeology of Alaska and the Peopling of America." *Science* 209:984–91.
1983   "Alaska and the Northwest Coast." Pp. 69–113 in Jesse D. Jennings, ed., *Ancient North Americans.* New York: W. H. Freeman and Co.
Durand, John D.
1977   "Historical Estimates of World Population: An Evaluation." *Population and Development Review* 3:253–96.

Eastern Band of Cherokee
1985   Personal communication with Douglas H. Ubelaker.
Eastman, Charles A. (Ohiyesa)
1916   *From the Deep Woods to Civilization.* Boston: Little, Brown and Co.
Eastman, Elaine Goodale
1945   "The Ghost Dance War and Wounded Knee Massacre of 1890–91." *Nebraska History* 26:26–42.
Emerson, Haven
1926   "Morbidity of the American Indians." *Science* 63:229–31.
Ericson, Jonathan E., R. E. Taylor, and Rainer Berger, editors
1982   *Peopling of the New World.* Los Altos, Calif.: Ballena Press.
Etling, James J., and William Starna
1984   "A Possible Case of Pre-Columbian Treponematosis from New York State." *American Journal of Physical Anthropology* 65:267–73.
Ewers, John C.
1969   "Introduction." Pp. 1–25 in Jean Louis Berlandier, *The Indians of Texas in 1830.* Washington, D.C.: Smithsonian Institution.
1970   "Contraceptive Charms Among the Plains Indians." *Plains Anthropology* 15:216–18.
1973   "The Influence of Epidemics on the Indian Populations and Cultures of Texas." *Plains Anthropologist* 18:104–15.

Fay, George E.
1970   *Charters, Constitutions and By-Laws of the Indian Tribes of North America.* 13 pts. Occasional Publications in Anthropology, Ethnology Series, no.

8. Greeley, Colo.: Museum of Anthropology, University of Northern Colorado.

Feest, Christian F.

1973   "Seventeenth Century Virginia Algonquin Population Estimates." *Archaeological Society of Virginia* 28 : 66–79.

1975   "Virginia Algonquins." Pp. 253–71 in Bruce G. Trigger, ed., *Northeast*, vol. 15 of *Handbook of North American Indians*. Washington, D.C.: Smithsonian Institution.

Ferrell, Robert E., et al.

1981   "The St. Lawrence Island Eskimos: Genetic Variation and Genetic Distance." *American Journal of Physical Anthropology* 55 : 351–58.

Fitting, James E.

1978   "Regional Cultural Development, 300 B.C. to A.D. 1000." Pp. 44–57 in Bruce G. Trigger, ed., *Northeast*, vol. 15 of *Handbook of North American Indians*. Washington, D.C.: Smithsonian Institution.

Fladmark, K. R.

1979   "Routes: Alternate Migration Corridors for Early Man in North America." *American Antiquity* 44 : 55–69.

1986   "The First Americans: Getting One's Berings." *Natural History* 95 : 8–10, 14, 16–19.

Fletcher, Alice C.

1891   "The Indian Messiah." *Journal of American Folk-Lore* 4 : 57–60.

Fletcher, Alice C., and Francis LaFlesche

1911   *The Omaha Tribe. Twenty-seventh Annual Report of the Bureau of American Ethnology . . . 1905–06*. Washington, D.C.: U.S. Government Printing Office.

Forbes, Jack D.

1983   "Mustees, Half-Breeds and Zambos in Anglo North America: Aspects of Black-Indian Relations." *American Indian Quarterly* 7 : 57–83.

Foreman, Grant

1932   *Indian Removal*. Norman: University of Oklahoma Press.

Fowler, Melvin T.

1975   "A Pre-Columbian Urban Center on the Mississippi." *Scientific American* 233 : 92–101.

Fried, Merton H.

1968   "On the Concepts of 'Tribe' and 'Tribal Society.'" Pp. 3–20 in June Helm, ed., *Essays on the Problem of Tribe*. Seattle: University of Washington Press.

Funk, Robert C.

1983   "The Northeastern United States." Pp. 303–71 in Jessie D. Jennings, ed., *Ancient North Americans*. New York: W. H. Freeman and Co.

Gad, Finn

1984   "History of Colonial Greenland." Pp. 556–76 in David Damas, ed., *Arctic*, vol. 5 of *Handbook of North American Indians*. Washington, D.C.: Smithsonian Institution.

Gayton, A. H.

1930   "The Ghost Dance of 1870 in South-Central California." *University of California Publications in American Archaeology and Ethnology* 28 : 57–82.

Gilbert, William H., Jr.

1946   "Memorandum Concerning the Characteristics of the Larger Mixed-

Blood Racial Islands of the Eastern United States." *Social Forces* 24:438–47.

1948 "Surviving Indian Groups of the Eastern United States." *Annual Report of the Smithsonian Institution*: 407–38.

Gist, Noel P., and Anthony G. Dworkin, editors
1972 *The Blending of Races: Marginality and Identity in World Perspective*. New York: Wiley-Interscience.

Glassner, Martin Ira
1974 "Population Figures for Mandan Indians." *The Indian Historian* 7:41–46.

Glassow, Michael A.
1967 "Considerations in Estimating Prehistoric California Coastal Populations." *American Antiquity* 32:354–59.

Goldstein, Marcus S.
1953 "Some Vital Statistics Based on Skeletal Material." *Human Biology* 25:3–12.

Goodman, James M.
1982 *The Navajo Atlas*. Norman: University of Oklahoma Press.

Gould, Richard
1966a *Archaeology of the Point St. George Site, and Tolowa Prehistory*. University of California Publications in Anthropology, no. 4.
1966b "Indian and White Versions of 'The Burnt Ranch Massacre.'" *Journal of the Folklore Institute* 3:31–42.
1978 "Tolowa." Pp. 128–36 in Robert F. Heizer, ed., *California*, vol. 8 of *Handbook of North American Indians*. Washington, D.C.: Smithsonian Institution.

Goyer, Doreen S., and Elaine Domschke
1983 *The Handbook of National Population Censuses: Latin America and the Caribbean, North America, and Oceania*. Westport, Conn.: Greenwood Press.

Greene, Evarts B., and Virginia D. Harrington
1932 *American Population Before the Federal Census of 1790*. New York: Columbia University Press.

Griffin, James B.
1979 "The Origin and Dispersion of American Indians in North America." Pp. 43–55 in William S. Laughlin and Albert B. Harper, eds., *The First Americans: Origins, Affinities and Adaptations*. New York: Gustav Fischer.
1983 "The Midlands." Pp. 243–301 in Jesse D. Jennings, ed., *Ancient North Americans*. New York: W. H. Freeman and Co.
1985 Personal communication.

Grinde, Donald A., Jr.
1984 "Yamasee Family Ecology and Demographic Change in the Colonial Southeast." Paper presented at the meetings of the American Indian Historians Association, The Newberry Library, Chicago.

Grinnell, George Bird
1891 "Account of the Northern Cheyennes Concerning the Messiah Superstition." *Journal of American Folk-Lore* 4:61–68.

Grumet, Robert Steven
1983 "'How Strangely They Have Decreast by the Hand of God': An Historic Epidemiology of the Upper Delawaran People." Paper presented at the 1983 Native American Historic Epidemiology Conference, The Newberry Library, Chicago.

Gumerman, George J., and Emil W. Haury
1979   "Pre-history: Hohokam." Pp. 75–90 in Alfonso Ortiz, ed., *Southwest*,
        vol. 9 of *Handbook of North American Indians*. Washington, D.C.: Smith-
        sonian Institution.
Gunther, Erna
1972   *Indian Life on the Northwest Coast of North America*. Chicago: University
        of Chicago Press.

Haas, Theodore H.
1957   "The Legal Aspects of Indian Affairs from 1857 to 1957." *Annals of the
        American Academy of Political and Social Science* 311:12–22.
Hackenberg, Robert A., and Mary M. Gallagher
1972   "The Costs of Cultural Change: Accidental Injury and Modernization
        Among the Papago Indians." *Human Organization* 31:211–26.
Hackett, C. J.
1963   "On the Origin of the Human Treponematoses." *Bulletin of the World
        Health Organization* 29:7–41.
Hale, Duane Kendall
1984   "A Review of Full-Blood Membership and Cultural Continuity in Okla-
        homa Tribes." *Centerboard* 2:46–51.
Hamor, Ralphe
1615   *A True Discourse of the Present Estate of Virginia*. Amsterdam: Da Capo
        Press and Theatrum Orbis Terrarum Ltd., 1971.
Hardoy, Jorge E.
1964   *Pre-Columbian Cities*. New York: Walker.
Hargrett, Lester
1947   *A Bibliography of the Constitutions and Laws of the American Indians*.
        Cambridge, Mass.: Harvard University Press.
Hariot, Thomas
1588   *A Briefe and True Report of the New Found Land of Virginia*. Amsterdam:
        De Capo Press and Theatrum Orbis Terrarum Ltd., 1971.
Harper, Albert B.
1979   "Life Expectancy and Population Adaptation: The Aleut Centenarian
        Approach." Pp. 309–30 in William S. Laughlin and Albert B. Harper,
        eds., *The First Americans: Origins, Affinities, and Adaptations*. New York:
        Gustav Fischer.
Harper, Roland M.
1937   "A Statistical Study of the Croatans." *Rural Sociology* 2:444–56.
Harvey, M. R.
1967   "Population of the Cahuilla Indians: Decline and Its Causes." *Eugenics
        Quarterly* 14:185–98.
Haynes, C. Vance
1982   "Were Clovis Progenitors in Beringia?" Pp. 383–98 in David M. Hopkins
        et al., eds., *Paleoecology of Beringia*. New York: Academic Press.
Heagerty, John J.
1928   *Four Centuries of Medical History in Canada*. Vol. 1. Bristol, England:
        John Wright and Sons.
Heidenreich, Conrad
1971   *Huronia: A History and Geography of the Huron Indians, 1600–1650*. On-
        tario: McClelland and Stewart Limited.
1978   "Huron." Pp. 368–88 in Bruce G. Trigger, ed., *Northeast*, vol. 15 of

Handbook of North American Indians. Washington, D.C.: Smithsonian Institution.

Heizer, Robert F., editor
1974   *The Destruction of California Indians*. Salt Lake City and Santa Barbara: Peregrine Smith, Inc.
1978   *California*. Vol. 8, *Handbook of North American Indians*, ed. William C. Sturtevant. Washington, D.C.: Smithsonian Institution.

Heizer, Robert F., and Martin A. Baumhoff
1956   "California Settlement Patterns." Pp. 32–44 in Gordon R. Willey, ed., *Prehistoric Settlement Patterns in the New World*. Viking Fund Publications in Anthropology, no. 23. New York: Viking Press.

Heizer, Robert F., and Albert B. Elsasser
1980   *The Natural World of the California Indians*. Berkeley: University of California Press.

Heizer, Robert F., and Theodora Kroeber, editors
1979   *Ishi, the Last Yahi: A Documentary History*. Berkeley: University of California Press.

Helm, June
1980   "Female Infanticide, European Disease, and Population Levels Among the Mackenzie Dene." *American Ethnologist* 7 : 259–85.

Helm, June, editor
1981   *Subarctic*. Vol. 6, *Handbook of North American Indians*, ed. William C. Sturtevant. Washington, D.C.: Smithsonian Institution.

Heth, Charlotte
1976   Unpublished recording of Yurok and Tolowa Indians. Department of Music and American Indian Studies Center, University of California, Los Angeles.

Hill, Charles A., Jr., and Mozart I. Spector
1971   "Natality and Mortality of American Indians Compared with U.S. Whites and Nonwhites." *HSMHA Health Reports* 86 : 229–46.

Hill, W. W.
1944   "The Navajo Indians and the Ghost Dance of 1890." *American Anthropologist* 46 : 523–27.

Hittman, Michael
1973   "The 1870 Ghost Dance at the Walker River Reservation: A Reconstruction." *Ethnohistory* 20 : 247–78.

Hodge, Frederick W.
1913   *Handbook of Indians of Canada*. Ottawa: C. H. Parmelee.

Hodge, William
1967   "Navajo Urban Silversmiths." *Anthropological Quarterly* 40 : 185–200.

Holder, Preston
1970   *The Hoe and the Horse on the Plains*. Lincoln: University of Nebraska Press.

The Holy Bible
1953   Revised Standard Version. New York: Thomas Nelson and Sons.

Hooton, Earnest A.
1930   *The Indians of Pecos Pueblo: A Study of Their Skeletal Remains*. New Haven: Yale University Press.

Hoover, Herbert T.
1979   *The Sioux: A Critical Bibliography*. Bloomington: Indiana University Press.

Hopkins, David M.
1979 "Landscape and Climate of Beringia During Late Pleistocene and Holocene Time." Pp. 15–41 in William S. Laughlin and Albert B. Harper, eds., *The First Americans: Origins, Affinities, and Adaptations*. New York: Gustav Fischer.
Hopkins, David M., editor
1967 *The Bering Land Bridge*. Stanford: Stanford University Press.
Hopkins, David M., et al., editors
1982 *Paleoecology of Beringia*. New York: Academic Press.
Hopkins, Donald R.
1983 *Princes and Peasants: Smallpox in History*. Chicago: University of Chicago Press.
Hornaday, William T.
1889 *The Extermination of the American Bison*. Washington, D.C.: U.S. Government Printing Office.
Howells, W. W.
1973 "Cranial Variation in Man." *Peabody Museum Paper* 67:1–259.
Howells, W. W., and I. Schwidetzky
1981 "Oceania." *Rassengeschichte der Menschheit* 8:115–66.
Hrdlička, Aleš
1909 *Tuberculosis Among Certain Indian Tribes of the United States*. Bureau of American Ethnology Bulletin no. 42. Washington, D.C.: U.S. Government Printing Office.
1917 "The Vanishing Indian." *Science* 46:266–67.
1931 "Fecundity in the Sioux Women." *American Journal of Physical Anthropology* 16:81–90.
Hudson, E. H.
1965a "Treponematosis and Man's Social Evolution." *American Anthropologist* 67:885–901.
1965b "Treponematosis in Perspective." *Bulletin of the World Health Organization* 32:735–48.
Hume, Ivor Nöel
1963 *Here Lies Virginia. An Archaeologist's View of Colonial Life and History*. New York: Alfred A. Knopf.
1982 *Martin's Hundred*. New York: Alfred A. Knopf.
Hurt, Wesley R.
1961 "The Urbanization of the Yankton Indians." *Human Organization* 20:226–31.

Institute for the Development of Indian Law
N.d., a *Treaties and Agreements of the Indian Tribes of the Northern Plains*. The American Indian Treaties Series. Washington, D.C.: Institute for the Development of Indian Law.
N.d., b *Treaties and Agreements of the Indian Tribes of the Pacific Northwest*. The American Indian Treaties Series. Washington, D.C.: Institute for the Development of Indian Law.

Jacobs, Wilbur R.
1972 *Dispossessing the American Indian: Indians and Whites on the Colonial Frontier*. New York: Charles Scribner's Sons.

Jantz, Richard L.
1972   "Cranial Variation and Microevolution in Arikara Skeletal Populations."
         Plains Anthropologist 17 : 20–35.
1973   "Microevolutionary Change in Arikara Crania: A Multivariate Analysis."
         American Journal of Physical Anthropology 38 : 15–26.
Jarcho, Saul
1964   "Some Observations on Disease in Prehistoric North America." *Bulletin*
         of the History of Medicine 38 : 1–19.
Jennings, Francis
1975   *The Invasion of America: Indians, Colonialism and the Cant of Conquest.*
         Chapel Hill: University of North Carolina Press, for the Institute of
         Early American History and Culture.
Jennings, Jesse D.
1978   "Origins." Pp. 1–41 in Jesse D. Jennings, ed., *Ancient Native Americans.*
         San Francisco: W. H. Freeman and Co.
1983   "Origins." Pp. 25–68 in Jesse D. Jennings, ed., *Ancient North Americans.*
         New York: W. H. Freeman and Co.
Jett, Stephen C.
1983   "Precolumbian Transoceanic Contacts." Pp. 557–613 in Jesse D. Jennings,
         ed., *Ancient North Americans.* New York: W. H. Freeman and Co.
Johansson, S. Ryan
1982   "The Demographic History of the Native Peoples of North America: A
         Selective Bibliography." *Yearbook of Physical Anthropology* 25 : 133–52.
Johansson, S. Ryan, and S. Horrowitz
1986   "Estimating Mortality in Skeletal Populations: The Influence of the
         Growth Rate on the Interpretation of Levels and Trends During the
         Transition to Agriculture." *American Journal of Physical Anthropology*
         71 : 233–50.
Johansson, S. Ryan, and S. H. Preston
1978   "Tribal Demography: The Hopi and Navajo Population as Seen Through
         Manuscripts From the 1900 U.S. Census." *Social Science History* 3 : 1–33.
Johnson, Guy B.
1939   "Personality in a White-Indian-Negro Community." *American Socio-*
         logical Review 4 : 516–23.
Johnson, Jerald Jay
1978   "Yana." Pp. 361–69 in Robert F. Heizer, ed., *California*, vol. 8 of *Hand-*
         book of North American Indians. Washington, D.C.: Smithsonian
         Institution.
Johnston, Denis Foster
1966   *An Analysis of Sources of Information on the Population of the Navajo.* Bu-
         reau of American Ethnology Bulletin no. 197. Washington, D.C.: U.S.
         Government Printing Office.
Joralemon, Donald
1982   "New World Depopulation and the Case of Disease." *Journal of Anthro-*
         pological Research 38 : 108–27.
Juricek, John T.
1969   "The Westo Indians." *Ethnohistory* 11 : 134–73.

Kehoe, Alice B.
1968   "The Ghost Dance Religion in Saskatchewan, Canada." *Plains Anthro-*
         pologist 13 : 296–304.

Kenen, Regina, and Charles R. Hammerslough
1985   "A Comparison of Reservation/Non-Reservation American Indian Mortality, 1970–78." Paper presented at the meetings of the American Sociological Association, Washington, D.C.
Kessell, John L.
1979   *Kiva, Cross and Crown: The Pecos Indians and New Mexico, 1540 to 1840.* Washington, D.C.: U.S. Government Printing Office.
Kleivan, Helge
1984   "Contemporary Greenlanders." Pp. 700–17 in David Damas, ed., *Arctic,* vol. 5 of *Handbook of North American Indians.* Washington, D.C.: Smithsonian Institution.
Kleivan, Inge
1984   "History of Norse Greenland." Pp. 549–55 in David Damas, ed., *Arctic,* vol. 5 of *Handbook of North American Indians.* Washington, D.C.: Smithsonian Institution.
Krech, Shepard, III
1978   "On the Aboriginal Population of the Kutchin." *Arctic Anthropology* 15:89–104.
1983   "The Influence of Disease and the Fur Trade on Arctic Drainage Lowlands Dene, 1800–1850." *Journal of Anthropological Research* 39:123–46.
Kroeber, Alfred L.
1904   "A Ghost-dance in California." *Journal of American Folk-Lore* 17:32–35.
1925   *Handbook of the Indians of California.* Washington, D.C.: U.S. Government Printing Office.
1939   "Cultural and Natural Areas of Native North America." *University of California Publications in American Archaeology and Ethnology* 38:1–242.
Kroeber, Theodora
1961   *Ishi in Two Worlds.* Berkeley: University of California Press.
Krzywicki, Ludwik
1934   *Primitive Society and Its Vital Statistics.* London: MacMillan and Company.
Kunitz, Stephen J.
1974   "Navajo and Hopi Fertility, 1971–72." *Human Biology* 46:435–51.
1983   *Disease Change and the Role of Medicine: The Navajo Experience.* Berkeley: University of California Press.
Kunitz, Stephen J., and John C. Slocumb
1976   "The Changing Sex Ratio of the Navajo Tribe." *Social Biology* 23:33–44.

Lallo, John W., and Jerome C. Rose
1979   "Patterns of Stress, Disease and Mortality in Two Prehistoric Populations From North America." *Journal of Human Evolution* 8:323–35.
Langer, William L.
1963   "Europe's Initial Population Explosion." *The American Historical Review* 69:1–17.
Lanternari, Vittorio
1963   *The Religions of the Oppressed.* New York: Alfred A. Knopf.
Latorre, Felipe A., and Delores L. Latorre
1976   *The Mexican Kickapoo Indians.* Austin: University of Texas Press.
Laughlin, William S., Jørgen B. Jørgensen, and Bruno Frølich
1979   "Aleuts and Eskimos: Survivors of the Bering Land Bridge Coast." Pp. 91–144 in William S. Laughlin and Albert B. Harper, eds., *The First Americans: Origins, Affinities and Adaptations.* New York: Gustav Fischer.

Laughlin, William S., and Susan I. Wolf
1979   "The First Americans: Origins, Affinities, and Adaptations." Pp. 1–11 in
        William S. Laughlin and Albert B. Harper, eds., *The First Americans:
        Origins, Affinities, and Adaptations*. New York: Gustav Fischer.
Leechman, Douglas
1946   "Prehistoric Migration Routes Through the Yukon." *Canadian Histori-
        cal Review* 27:383–90.
Lefroy, Captain J. H.
1853   "Native Indian Population of British America." *The Canadian Journal*
        1:193–98.
Lehmer, Donald J., and David T. Jones
1968   *Arikara Archeology: The Bad River Phase*. Smithsonian Institution, River
        Basin Surveys, Publications in Salvage Archeology, no. 7.
Lesser, Alexander
1933   "Cultural Significance of the Ghost Dance." *American Anthropologist*
        35:108–15.
Liberty, Margot
1975   "Population Trends Among Present-Day Omaha Indians." *Plains An-
        thropologist* 20:225–30.
Liberty, Margot, David V. Hughey, and Richard Scaglion
1976a   "Rural and Urban Omaha Indian Fertility." *Human Biology* 48:59–71.
1976b   "Rural and Urban Seminole Indian Fertility." *Human Biology* 48:741–55.
Lipe, William D.
1983   "The Southwest." Pp. 421–93 in Jesse D. Jennings, ed., *Ancient North
        Americans*. New York: W. H. Freeman and Co.
Locay, Luis
1983   *Aboriginal Population Density of North American Indians*. Ph.D. diss.,
        University of Chicago.
Loh, Jules
1971   *Lords of the Earth: A History of the Navajo Indians*. New York: Cromwell-
        Collier Press.
Luckert, Karl W.
1975   *The Navajo Hunter Tradition*. Tucson: University of Arizona Press.

McEvedy, Colin, and Richard Jones
1978   *Atlas of World Population History*. New York: Facts on File.
McFalls, Joseph A., Jr., and Marguerite Harvey McFalls
1984   *Disease and Fertility*. Orlando, Fla.: Academic Press.
McHugh, Tom
1972   *The Time of the Buffalo*. With the assistance of Victoria Hobson. New
        York: Alfred A. Knopf.
McKenny, Nampeo D. R., and Karen A. Crook
1976   "Census Data and Native Americans." Paper presented at the meetings of
        the Association of American Geographers, New York City.
McLoughlin, William G., and Walter H. Conser, Jr.
1977   "The Cherokees in Transition: A Statistical Analysis of the Federal
        Cherokee Census of 1835." *The Journal of American History* 64:678–703.
McNeill, William H.
1976   *Plagues and Peoples*. Garden City, N.Y.: Anchor Doubleday.
1979   "Historical Patterns of Migration." *Current Anthropology* 20:95–98.

Mallery, Garrick
1877a "The Former and Present Number of Our Indians." *Proceedings of American Association for Advancement of Science* 26 : 340–66.
1877b *A Calendar of the Dakota Nation.* Washington, D.C.: U.S. Government Printing Office.
1886 "Pictographs of the North American Indians. A Preliminary Paper." Pp. 3–246 in *Fourth Annual Report of the Bureau of Ethnology to the Secretary of the Smithsonian Institution, 1882–1883.* Washington, D.C.: U.S. Government Printing Office.
1893 "Picture-Writing of the American Indians." Pp. 3–807 in *Tenth Annual Report of the Bureau of Ethnology to the Secretary of the Smithsonian Institution, 1888–89.* Washington, D.C.: U.S. Government Printing Office.

Malthus, T. R.
1798 *An Essay on Population.* Vol. 1. Reprint. London: J. M. Dent & Sons, 1914.

Margon, Arthur
1976 "Indians and Immigrants: A Comparison of Groups New to the City." *Journal of Ethnic Studies* 4 : 17–28.

Marks, Geoffrey, and William K. Beatty
1976 *Epidemics.* New York: Charles Scribner's Sons.

Marshall, Ingeborg
1977 "An Unpublished Map Made by John Cartwright Between 1768 and 1773 Showing Beothuck Indian Settlements and Artifacts and Allowing a New Population Estimate." *Ethnohistory* 24 : 223–49.

Martin, Calvin
1976 "Wildlife Diseases as a Factor in the Depopulation of the North American Indians." *Western Historical Quarterly* 7 : 47–62.

Martin, Harry W.
1964 "Correlates of Adjustment Among American Indians in an Urban Environment." *Human Organization* 23 : 290–95.

Martin, Paul S.
1973 "The Discovery of America." *Science* 179 : 969–74.
1979 "Pre-History: Mogollon." Pp. 61–74 in Alfonso Ortiz, ed., *Southwest,* vol. 9 of *Handbook of North American Indians.* Washington, D.C.: Smithsonian Institution.
1982 "The Pattern and Meaning of Holarctic Mammoth Extinction." Pp. 399–408 in David M. Hopkins et al., eds., *Paleoecology of Beringia.* New York: Academic Press.

Masnick, George S., and Solomon H. Katz
1976 "Adaptive Childbearing in a North Slope Eskimo Community." *Human Biology* 48 : 37–58.

Matson, G. Albin, et al.
1967 "Distribution of Hereditary Blood Groups Among Indians in South America: IV in Chile." *American Journal of Physical Anthropology* 27 : 157–93.

Means, Philip A.
1931 *Ancient Civilizations of the Andes.* New York: Charles Scribner's Sons.

Meigs, Peveril, III
1935 *The Dominican Mission Frontier of Lower California.* University of California Publications in Geography, no. 7. Berkeley: University of California Press.

Meister, Cary W.
1976 "Demographic Consequences of Euro-American Contact on Selected American Indian Populations and Their Relationship to the Demographic Transition." *Ethnohistory* 23:161–72.
1978 "Misleading Nature of Data Obtained from the Bureau of the Census Subject Report on 1970 American Indian Population." *The Indian Historian* 7:12–19.
1980 "Methods for Evaluating the Accuracy of Ethnohistorical Demographic Data on North American Indians: A Brief Assessment." *Ethnohistory* 27:153–68.
Merriam, C. Hart
1905 "The Indian Population of California." *American Anthropologist* 7:594–606.
Miller, Virginia P.
1975 "Whatever Happened to the Yuki." *The Indian Historian* 8:6–12.
1976 "Aboriginal Micmac Population: A Review of the Evidence." *Ethnohistory* 23:117–27.
1978 "Yuki, Huchnom, and Coast Yuki." Pp. 249–55 in Robert F. Heizer, ed., *California*, vol. 8 of *Handbook of North American Indians*. Washington, D.C.: Smithsonian Institution.
1979 *Ukomno'm: The Yuki Indians of Northern California*. Los Altos, Calif.: Ballena Press.
Milner, Clyde A., II
1981 "Off the White Road: Seven Nebraska Indian Societies in the 1870s—A Statistical Analysis of Assimilation, Population, and Prosperity." *Western Historical Quarterly* 22:37–52.
Minneapolis Star and Tribune
1985a January 20.
1985b November 22.
Mobley, Charles M.
1980 "Demographic Structure of Pecos Indians: A Model Based on Life Tables." *American Antiquity* 45:518–30.
Momaday, N. Scott
1969 *The Way to Rainy Mountain*. Albuquerque: University of New Mexico Press.
Momeni, Jamshid A.
1984 *Demography of Racial and Ethnic Minorities in the United States: An Annotated Bibliography With a Review Essay*. Westport, Conn.: Greenwood Press.
Mook, Maurice A.
1944 "The Aboriginal Population of Tidewater Virginia." *American Anthropologist* 46:193–208.
Mooney, James
1889 "Indian Tribes of the District of Columbia." *The American Anthropologist* 2:259–66.
1891 *Myths of the Cherokee and Sacred Formulas of the Cherokee*. Reprint. Nashville: Charles and Randy Elder, Booksellers, 1982.
1896 "The Ghost-Dance Religion and the Sioux Outbreak of 1890." Pp. 641–1136 in *Fourteenth Annual Report of the United States Bureau of Ethnology . . . 1892–93*, pt. 2. Washington, D.C.: U.S. Government Printing Office.

1898   "Calendar History of the Kiowa Indians." Pps. 129–445 in *Seventeenth Annual Report of the Bureau of American Ethnology . . . 1895–1896*, pt. 1. Washington, D.C.: U.S. Government Printing Office.

1900   *Historical Sketch of the Cherokee*. Reprint. Chicago: Aldine Publishing Company, 1975.

1907   "The Powhatan Confederacy, Past and Present." *American Anthropologist* 9:129–52.

1910a   "Population." Pp. 286–87 in Frederick W. Hodge, ed., *Handbook of American Indians North of Mexico*. Vol. 2. Smithsonian Institution, Bureau of American Ethnology Bulletin no. 30. Washington, D.C.: U.S. Government Printing Office.

1910b   "The Indian Ghost Dance." *Collections of the Nebraska State Historical Society* 16:168–86.

1911   "Passing of the Delaware Nation." Pp. 329–340 in B.F. Shambaugh, ed., *Proceedings of the Mississippi Valley Historical Association*. Cedar Rapids, Iowa: Torch Press.

1913   "Population." Pp. 389–90 in Frederick W. Hodge, ed., *Handbook of Indians of Canada*. Ottawa: C. H. Parmelee.

1928   "The Aboriginal Population of America North of Mexico." Pp. 1–40 in John R. Swanton, ed., *Smithsonian Miscellaneous Collections*, vol. 80.

Moore, John H.

1980   "Aboriginal Indian Residence Patterns Preserved in Censuses and Allotments." *Science* 207:201–203.

N.d.   "Structured Dispersion: A Cheyenne Response to Epidemic Disease." Paper, Department of Anthropology, University of Oklahoma.

Morison, Samuel Eliot

1965   *The Oxford History of the American People*. New York: Oxford University Press.

1971   *The European Discovery of America: The Northern Voyages, A.D. 500–1600*. New York: Oxford University Press.

1974   *The European Discovery of America: The Southern Voyages, A.D. 1492–1616*. New York: Oxford University Press.

Morissonneau, Christian

1978   "Huron of Lorette." Pp. 389–93 in Bruce G. Trigger, ed., *Northeast*, vol. 15 of *Handbook of North American Indians*. Washington, D.C.: Smithsonian Institution.

Morlan, Richard E., and Jacques Cinq-Mars

1982   "Ancient Beringians: Human Occupation in the Late Pleistocene of Alaska and the Yukon Territory." Pp. 353–81 in David M. Hopkins et al., eds., *Paleoecology of Beringia*. New York: Academic Press.

Mörner, Magnus

1967   *Race Mixture in the History of Latin America*. Boston: Little, Brown and Company.

Morse, Dan

1961   "Prehistoric Tuberculosis in America." *American Review of Respiratory Disease* 83:489–504.

Moses, Lester George

1977   *James Mooney, U.S. Ethnologist: A Biography*. Ph.D. diss., University of New Mexico.

Muller, Jon

1983   "The Southeast." Pp. 373–419 in Jessie D. Jennings, ed., *Ancient North Americans*. New York: W. H. Freeman and Co.

Müller-Beck, Hansjürgen
1983   "Late Pleistocene Man in Northern Alaska and the Mammoth-Steppe
        Biome." Pp. 329–52 in David M. Hopkins et al., eds., *Paleoecology of
        Beringia*. New York: Academic Press.
Murdock, George P.
1949   *Social Structure*. New York: Macmillan.

Nam, Charles B.
1979   "The Progress of Demography as a Scientific Discipline." *Demography*
        16:485–92.
Nam, Charles B., and Susan Gustavus Philliber
1984   *Population: A Basic Orientation*. 2d ed. Englewood Cliffs, N.J.: Prentice-
        Hall, Inc.
Nasatir, A. P., editor
1952   *Before Lewis and Clark: Documents Illustrating the History of the Missouri,
        1785–1804*. 2 vols. St. Louis: St. Louis Historical Documents Foundation.
Nash, Philleo
1937   "The Place of Religious Revivalism in the Formation of the Intercultural
        Community on Klamath Reservation." Pp. 377–442 in Fred R. Eggan,
        ed., *Social Anthropology of the North American Tribes*, 2d ed. Chicago:
        University of Chicago Press, 1955.
Neel, James V.
1971   "Genetic Aspects of the Ecology of Disease in the American Indian." Pp.
        561–90 in Francisco M. Salzano, ed., *The Ongoing Evolution of Latin
        Populations*. Springfield, Ill: Charles C. Thomas.
Neugin, Rebecca
1978   "Memories of the Trail." Special Issue of *Journal of Cherokee Studies* 3:176.
Newcomb, W. W., Jr.
1961   *The Indians of Texas*. Austin: University of Texas Press.
1983   "Karankawa." Pp. 359–67 in Alfonso Ortiz, ed., *Southwest*, vol. 10 of
        Handbook of North American Indians. Washington, D.C.: Smithsonian
        Institution.
Newman, Marshall T.
1976   "Aboriginal New World Epidemiology and Medical Care, and the Im-
        pact of the Old World Disease Imports." *American Journal of Physical An-
        thropology* 45:667–72.
New York Times
1978a   January 5.
1978b   January 7.
1981   September 6.
1985a   August 18.
1985b   August 18.
1985c   September 22.
Norbeck, Edward
1961   *Religion in Primitive Societies*. New York: Harper and Row.

Oandasan, William (Yuki)
1984   Personal communication.
O'Brien, Patricia J.
1972   "Urbanism, Cahokia and Middle Mississippian." *Archaeology* 25:188–97.

O'Donnell, James M., III
1973   *Southern Indians in the American Revolution*. Knoxville: University of Tennessee Press.
Officer, James E.
1971   "The American Indian and Federal Policy." Pp. 8–65 in Jack O. Waddell and O. Michael Watson, eds., *The American Indian in Urban Society*. Boston: Little, Brown.
Olsen, Fred
1974   *On the Trail of the Arawaks*. Norman: University of Oklahoma Press.
Omran, Abdel R.
1971   "The Epidemiologic Transition: A Theory of the Epidemiology of Population Change." *Milbank Memorial Fund Quarterly* 49:509–38.
Opler, Morris E.
1983   "Mescalero Apache." Pp. 419–39 in Alfonso Ortiz, ed., *Southwest*, vol. 10 of *Handbook of North American Indians*. Washington, D.C.: Smithsonian Institution.
Ortiz, Alfonso, editor
1979   *Southwest*. Vol. 9, *Handbook of North American Indians*, ed. William C. Sturtevant. Washington, D.C.: Smithsonian Institution.
1983   *Southwest*. Vol. 10, *Handbook of North American Indians*, ed. William C. Sturtevant. Washington, D.C.: Smithsonian Institution.
Otterbein, Keith F.
1979   "Huron vs. Iroquois: A Case Study in Inter-Tribal Warfare." *Ethnohistory* 26:141–52.
Overholt, Thomas W.
1974   "The Ghost Dance of 1890 and the Nature of the Prophetic Process." *Ethnohistory* 21:37–63.
Owen, Roger C.
1984   "The Americas: The Case Against an Ice-Age Human Population." Pp. 517–63 in Fred H. Smith and Frank Spencer, eds., *The Origin of Modern Humans*. New York: Alan R. Liss, Inc.

Palkovich, Ann M.
1981   "Demography and Disease Patterns in a Prehistoric Plains Group: A Study of the Mobridge Site (39WWl)." *Plains Anthropologist* 26:71–84.
Paredes, J. Anthony
1980   "Chippewa Townspeople." Pp. 324–96 in J. Anthony Paredes, ed., *Anishinabe: Six Studies of Modern Chippewa*. Tallahassee: University Press of Florida.
Paredes, J. Anthony, and Kenneth J. Plante
1982   "A Reexamination of Creek Indian Population Trends: 1738–1832." *American Indian Culture and Research Journal* 6:3–28.
Parenton, Vernon J., and Roland J. Pellegrin
1950   "The 'Sabines': A Study of Racial Hybrids in a Louisiana Coastal Parish." *Social Forces* 29:148–54.
Parkman, Francis
1867   *The Jesuits in North America in the Seventeenth Century*. Boston: New Library, 1909.
Passel, Jeffrey S.
1976   "Provisional Evaluation of the 1970 Census Count of American Indians." *Demography* 13:397–409.

Passel, Jeffrey S., and Patricia A. Berman
1985   "An Assessment of the Quality of 1980 Census Data for American In-
        dians." Paper presented at the meetings of the American Statistical Asso-
        ciation, Las Vegas.
Petersen, William
1975   "A Demographer's view of Prehistoric Demography." *Current Anthro-
        pology* 16:227–45.
1961   *Population.* New York: Macmillan Co.
Peterson, Jacqueline
1982   "Ethnogenesis: Settlement and Growth of a New People." *American In-
        dian Culture and Research Journal* 6:23–64.
Pfeiffer, Ida
1856   *A Lady's Second Journal Around the World.* New York: Harper and Bros.
Phillips, George Harwood
1974   "Indians and the Breakdown of the Spanish Mission System in Califor-
        nia." *Ethnohistory* 21:291–302.
Piché, Victor, and M. V. George
1973   "Estimates of Vital Rates for the Canadian Indians, 1960–1970." *Demog-
        raphy* 10:367–82.
Plog, Fred
1979   "Prehistory: Western Anasazi." Pp. 108–30 in Alfonso Ortz, ed., *South-
        west,* vol. 9 of *Handbook of North American Indians.* Washington, D.C.:
        Smithsonian Institution.
Population Reference Bureau, Inc.
1983   *World Population Data Sheet.* Washington, D.C.
Porter, Frank W., III
1983   "An Historical Perspective on Nonrecognized American Indian Tribes."
        Pp. 2–49 in Frank W. Porter, III, ed., *Nonrecognized American Indian
        Tribes: An Historical and Legal Perspective.* Occasional Papers Series,
        no. 7. Chicago: The Newberry Library.
Posey, Darrell A.
1979   "Origin, Development and Maintenance of a Louisiana Mixed-Blood
        Community: The Ethnohistory of the Freejacks of the First Ward Settle-
        ment." *Ethnohistory* 26:177–82.
Powell, Peter J.
1980   *The Cheyennes: A Critical Bibliography.* Bloomington: Indiana University
        Press.
1981   *People of the Sacred Mountain.* 2 vols. New York: Harper and Row.
Powers, Stephen
1877   *Tribes of California.* Contributions to North American Ethnology, vol. 3.
        Reprint. Washington, D.C.: U.S. Government Printing Office, 1976.
Praus, Alexis
1962   *The Sioux, 1798–1922: A Dakota Winter Count.* Bloomfield Hills, Mich.:
        Cranbrook Institute of Science.
Price, Edward T.
1953   "A Geographic Analysis of White-Indian-Negro Racial Mixtures in the
        Eastern United States." *Annals of the Association of American Geographers*
        43:138–55.
Prucha, Francis Paul
1975   *Documents of United States Indian Policy.* Lincoln: University of Nebraska
        Press.

1985   *Map of American Indians in the United States, 1980.*
Putney, Diane Therese
1980   *Fighting the Scourge: American Indian Morbidity and Federal Policy, 1897–1928.* Ph.D. diss., Marquette University.

Quinn, David Beers
1955   *The Roanoke Voyages, 1584–1590.* 2 vols. London: Cambridge University Press for the Hakluyt Society.
1974   *England and the Discovery of America, 1481–1620.* New York: Alfred A. Knopf.
1977   *North America from Earliest Discovery to First Settlements: The Norse Voyages to 1612.* New York: Harper and Row.
1985   *Set Fair for Roanoke.* Chapel Hill: University of North Carolina Press.
Quinn, David Beers, editor
1971   *North American Discovery, Circa 1000–1612.* Columbia: University of South Carolina Press.

Ratcliff, James L.
1973   "What Happened to the Kalapuya? A Study of the Depletion of Their Economic Base." *The Indian Historian* 6:27–33.
Ray, Arthur J.
1976   "Diffusion of Diseases in the Western Interior of Canada, 1830–1850. *Geographical Review* 66:139–57.
Red Horse, John G., et al.
1978   "Family Behavior of Urban American Indians." *Social Casework* 59:67–72.
Remington, Frederic
1890   "The Art of War and Newspaper Men." *Harper's Weekly* 34:947.
Revised Constitution of the Apache Tribe of the Mescalero Reservation.
1965   Article IV.
Rightmire, G. Philip
1984   "*Homo sapiens* in Sub-Saharan Africa." Pp. 295–325 in Fred H. Smith and Frank Spencer, eds., *The Origin of Modern Humans.* New York: Alan R. Liss, Inc.
Riley, Carroll L., et al.
1971   *Man Across the Sea: Problems of Pre-Columbian Contacts.* Austin: University of Texas Press.
Rivet, Paul
1924   "Langues américaines." Pp. 597–712 in Antoine Meillet and Marcel Cohen, eds., *Les Langues du monde*, vol. 16. Paris: Société de Linguistique de Paris.
Rivet, Paul, G. Stresser-Péan, and Č. Loukotka
1952   "Langues de l'Amérique." Pp. 941–1160 in Antoine Meillet and Marcel Cohen, eds., *Les Langues du monde*. Paris: Centre national de la recherche scientifique.
Roe, Frank Gilbert
1970   *The North American Buffalo: A Critical Study of the Species in its Wild State.* 2d ed. Toronto: University of Toronto Press.
Rogers, Edward S., and Eleanor Leacock
1981   "Montagnais and Naskapi." Pp. 169–89 in June Helm, ed., *Subarctic*, vol. 6 of *Handbook of North American Indians*. Washington, D.C.: Smithsonian Institution.

Romaniuc, A.
1984   *Fertility in Canada: From Baby-boom to Baby-bust*. Ottawa: Statistics Canada.

Romaniuk, A.
1981   "Increase in Natural Fertility During the Early Stages of Modernization: Canadian Indians Case Study." *Demography* 18:157–72.

Romaniuk, A., and V. Piché
1972   "Natility Estimates for the Canadian Indians by Stable Population Models, 1900–1969." *Canadian Review of Sociology and Anthropology* 9:1–20.

Ronda, James P., and James Axtell
1978   *Indian Missions: A Critical Bibliography*. Bloomington: Indiana University Press.

Rosen, Laurence S., and Kurt Gorwitz
1980   "New Attention to American Indians." *American Demographics* 2:18–25.

Rosenblat, Ángel
1945   *La población indígena de América desde 1492 hasta la actualidad*. Buenos Aires: Institución Cultural Española.
1967   *La población de América en 1492: Viejos y nuevos cálculos*. México, D.F.: El Colegio de México.
1976   "The Population of Hispaniola at the Time of Columbus." Pp. 43–66 in William M. Denevan, ed., *The Native Population of the Americas in 1492*. Madison: University of Wisconsin Press.

Rosenstiel, Annette
1983   *Red and White: Indian Views of the White Man, 1492–1982*. New York: Universe Books.

Ross, Ronald David
1970   "The Omaha People." *The Indian Historian* 3:19–22.

Roth, Eric Abella
1981   "Demography and Computer Simulation in Historic Village Population Reconstruction." *Journal of Anthropological Research* 3:279–301.

Rouse, Irving
1974   "On the Meaning of the Term 'Arawak.'" Pp. viii–xvi in Fred Olsen, *On the Trail of the Arawak*. Norman: University of Oklahoma Press.

Rowe, Frederich W.
1977   *Extinction, The Beothuks of Newfoundland*. Toronto: McGraw-Hill Ryerson Limited.

Royce, Charles C.
1888   *The Cherokee Nation of Indians*. Reprint. Chicago: Aldine Publishing Company, 1975.

Ruff, Christopher B.
1981   "Reassessment of Demographic Estimates for Pecos Pueblo." *American Journal of Physical Anthropology* 54:147–51.

Russell, Frank
1906   "The Pima Indians." Pp. 3–389 in *Twenty-sixth Annual Report of the Bureau of American Ethnology . . . 1904–05*. Washington, D.C.: U.S. Government Printing Office.

Rutman, Darrett B., and Anita H. Rutman
1976   "Of Agues and Fevers: Malaria in the Early Chesapeake." *William and Mary Quarterly* 33:31–60.

Salisbury, Neal
1982   *Manitou and Providence: Indians, Europeans, and the Making of New England, 1500–1643*. New York: Oxford University Press.
Salmón, Roberto Mario
1976   "The Disease Complaint at Bosque Redondo (1864–68)." *The Indian Historian* 9:1–7.
San Antonio Light
1981   September 27.
Sánchez-Albornoz, Nicolás
1974   *The Population of Latin America: A History*. Translated by W. A. R. Richardson. Berkeley: University of California Press.
Sandefur, Gary D., and Trudy McKinnell
1985   "Intermarriage Among Blacks, Whites and American Indians." Paper presented at the meetings of the American Sociological Association, Washington, D.C.
Sando, Joe S.
1979   "The Pueblo Revolt." Pp. 194–97 in Alfonso Ortiz, ed., *Southwest*, vol. 9 of *Handbook of North American Indians*. Washington, D.C.: Smithsonian Institution.
Sapper, Karl
1924   "Die Zahl und die Volksdichte der Indianischen Bevölkerung in Amerika vor der Conquista und in der Gegenwart." Pp. 95–104 in *Proceedings of the Twentyfirst International Congress of Americanists, First Part, The Hague*. Leiden: E. J. Brill.
1948   "Beitraege zur Frage der Volkszahl und Volksdichte der vorkolumbischen Indianerbevoelkerung." Pp. 456–78 in *Reseña y trabajos científicos del XXVI Congreso Internacional de Americanistas, Sevilla (1935)*. Madrid: S. Aguirre.
Sarafan, Winston L.
1977   "Smallpox Strikes the Aleuts." *Alaska Journal* 7:46–49.
Sauer, Carl Ortwin
1968   *Northern Mists*. Berkeley: University of California Press.
1971   *Sixteenth Century North America: The Land and the People as Seen by the Europeans*. Berkeley: University of California Press.
Schoolcraft, Henry R.
1851   *Personal Memoirs of a Residence of Thirty Years With the Indian Tribes of the American Frontiers: With Brief Notices of Passing Events, Facts, and Opinions, A.D. 1812 to A.D. 1842*. Philadelphia: Lippincott, Grambo & Co.
Schroeder, Albert H.
1979   "Pre-history: Hakataya." Pp. 100–107 in Alfonso Ortiz, ed., *Southwest*, vol. 9 of *Handbook of North American Indians*. Washington, D.C.: Smithsonian Institution.
Scott, Leslie M.
1928   "Indian Diseases as Aids to Pacific Northwest Settlement." *Oregon Historical Quarterly* 29:144–61.
Secoy, Frank G.
1953   *Changing Military Patterns on the Great Plains (17th Century Through Early 19th Century)*. Seattle: University of Washington Press.
Seton, Ernest Thompson
1909   *Life Histories of Northern Animals*. Vol. 1. New York: Charles Scribner and Sons.

1929   *Lives of Game Animals*. Vol. 3, Pt. 2. Garden City, N.Y.: Doubleday, De-
        son and Company.

Sheehan, Bernard
1980   *Savagism and Civility: Indians and Englishmen in Colonial Virginia*. Cam-
        bridge: Cambridge University Press.

Siegel, Jacob S.
1974   "Estimates of Coverage of the Population by Sex, Race, and Age in the
        1970 Census." *Demography* 11:1–23.

Simmons, James L.
1977   "One Little, Two Little, Three Little Indians: Counting American In-
        dians in Urban Society." *Human Organization* 36:76–79.

Simmons, Marc
1966   "New Mexico's Smallpox Epidemic of 1780–81." *New Mexico Historical
        Review* 41:319–26.

Smith, C. T.
1970   "Depopulation of the Central Andes in the 16th Century." *Current An-
        thropology* 11:453–64.

Smith, Fred
1976   "The Skeletal Remains of the Earliest Americans: A Survey." *Tennessee
        Anthropologist* 1:116–47.

Smith, G. Hubert
1973   "Notes on Omaha Ethnohistory, 1763–1820." *Plains Anthropologist*
        18:257–70.

Snipp, C. Matthew
N.d.   *The First of This Land: Native Americans in the Late Twentieth Century*
        (tentative title). New York: Basic Books, forthcoming.

Snow, Dean R.
1979   *Native American Prehistory: A Critical Bibliography*. Bloomington: In-
        diana University Press.
1980   *The Archaeology of New England*. New York: Academic Press.
1984   "Native American Prehistory." Pp. 1–16 in William R. Swagerty, ed.,
        Scholars and the Indian Experience. Bloomington: Indiana University
        Press.

Sorkin, Alan L.
1969   "Some Aspects of American Indian Migration." *Social Forces* 48:243–50.
1971   *American Indians and Federal Aid*. Washington, D.C.: The Brookings
        Institution.
1978   *The Urban American Indian*. Lexington, Mass.: Lexington Books.

Spicer, Edward H.
1962   *Cycles of Conquest: The Impact of Spain, Mexico, and the United States
        on the Indians of the Southwest, 1533–1960*. Tucson: University of Arizona
        Press.
1983   "Yaqui." Pp. 250–63 in Alfonso Ortiz, ed., *Southwest*, vol. 10 of *Hand-
        book of North American Indians*. Washington, D.C.: Smithsonian In-
        stitution.

Spier, Leslie
1927   "The Ghost Dance of 1870 Among the Klamath of Oregon." *University of
        Washington Publications in Anthropology* 2:39–56.

Spinden, H. J.
1928   "The Population of Ancient America." *The Geographical Review* 28:
        641–61.

Stanley, Sam, and Robert K. Thomas
1978   "Current Demographic and Social Trends Among North American Indians." *Annals of the American Academy of Political and Social Science* 436:111–20.
Starna, William A.
1980   "Mohawk Iroquois Populations: A Revision." *Ethnohistory* 27:371–82.
Stearn, E. Wagner, and Allen E. Stearn
1943   "Smallpox Immunization of the Amerindian." *Bulletin of the History of Medicine* 13:601–13.
1945   *The Effect of Smallpox on the Destiny of the Amerindian.* Boston: Bruce Humphries, Inc.
Steward, Julian H.
1945   "The Changing American Indian." Pp. 282–305 in Ralph Linton, ed., *The Science of Man in the World Crises.* New York: Columbia University Press.
1949   "The Native Population of South America." Pp. 655–68 in Julian H. Steward, ed., *The Comparative Ethnology of South American Indians*, vol. 5 of *Handbook of South American Indians.* Bureau of American Ethnology Bulletin no. 143. Washington, D.C.: U.S. Government Printing Office.
Stewart, Omer C.
1977   "Contemporary Document on Wovoka (Jack Wilson), Prophet of the Ghost Dance in 1890." *Ethnohistory* 24:219–22.
Stewart, T. Dale
1973   *The People of America.* New York: Charles Scribner's Sons.
1979   "Patterning of Skeletal Pathologies and Epidemiology." Pp. 257–74 in William S. Laughlin and Albert B. Harper, eds., *The First Americans: Origins, Affinities, and Adaptations.* New York: Gustav Fischer.
1981   "The Evolutionary Status of the First Americans." *American Journal of Physical Anthropology* 56:461–66.
Stoffle, Richard W., Kristine L. Jones, and Henry F. Dobyns
1983   "Direct European Immigrant Transmission of Old World Pathogens to Great Basin Native Americans During the Nineteenth Century." Paper presented at the 1983 Native American Historical Demography Conference, The Newberry Library, Chicago.
Storey, Rebecca
1985   "An Estimate of Mortality in a Pre-Columbian Urban Population." *American Anthropologist* 87:519–35.
Stucki, Larry R.
1971   "The Case Against Population Control: The Probable Creation of the First American Indian State." *Human Organization* 30:393–99.
Sturtevant, William C.
1985   Personal communication.
Sturtevant, William C., general editor
1978–   *Handbook of North American Indians.* 20 vols. Washington, D.C.: Smithsonian Institution.
Sturtevant, William C., and Samuel Stanley
1968   "Indian Communities in the Eastern United States." *The Indian Historian* 1:15–19.
Swagerty, William R., and Russell Thornton
1982   "Preliminary 1980 Census Counts for American Indians, Eskimos and Aleuts." *American Indian Culture and Research Journal* 6:92–93.

Swan, Daniel C.
1983   "Differential Fertility and Osage Ethnic Identity: An Ethnohistoric Re-
         construction." Paper presented at the meetings of the American Society
         for Ethnohistory, Albuquerque.
Swanton, John R.
1928   "Social Organization and Social Usages of the Indians of the Creek Con-
         federacy." *Forty-second Annual Report of the Bureau of American Ethnology
         . . . 1924–25.* Washington, D.C.: U.S. Government Printing Office.
Swedlund, Alan C., and George J. Armelagos
1976   *Demographic Anthropology.* Dubuque, Iowa: Wm. C. Brown Company,
         Publishers.
Szathmary, Emöke J. E.
1979   "Blood Groups of Siberians, Eskimos, Subarctic and Northwest Coast
         Indians: The Problem of Origins and Genetic Relationships." Pp. 185–
         209 in William S. Laughlin and Albert B. Harper, eds., *The First Ameri-
         cans: Origins, Affinities, and Adaptations.* New York: Gustav Fischer.
Szathmary, Emöke J. E., and Nancy S. Ossenberg
1978   "Are the Biological Differences Between North American Indians and
         Eskimos Truly Profound?" *Current Anthropology* 19:673–85.

Tate, D. David
1981   "The Nez Perces in Eastern Indian Territory: The Quapaw Agency Ex-
         perience." Pp. 8–23 in Robert E. Smith, ed., *Oklahoma's Forgotten In-
         dians.* Oklahoma City: Oklahoma Historical Society.
Tax, Sol
1960   *Map of the North American Indians: 1950 Distribution of Descendants of the
         Aboriginal Population of Alaska, Canada and the United States.* Chicago:
         Department of Anthropology, University of Chicago.
1978   "The Impact of Urbanization on American Indians." *Annals of the
         American Academy of Political and Social Science* 436:121–36.
Taylor, Herbert C., Jr.
1963   "Aboriginal Populations of the Lower Northwest Coast." *Pacific North-
         west Quarterly* 54:158–65.
Taylor, Herbert C., Jr., and Lester L. Hoaglin, Jr.
1962   "The 'Intermittent Fever' Epidemic of the 1830s on the Lower Columbia
         River." *Ethnohistory* 9:160–78.
Thompson, H. Paul
1966   "Estimating Aboriginal American Population: A Technique Using An-
         thropological and Biological Data." *Current Anthropology* 7:417–24.
Thornton, Russell
1978   "Implications of Catlin's American Indian Population Estimates for Re-
         vision of Mooney's Estimate." *American Journal of Physical Anthropology*
         49:11–14.
1979   "American Indian Historical Demography: A Review Essay with Sug-
         gestions for Future Research." *American Indian Culture and Research
         Journal* 3:69–74.
1980   "Recent Estimates of the Prehistoric California Indian Population."
         Current Anthropology 21:702–704.
1981   "Demographic Antecedents of a Revitalization Movement: Population
         Change, Population Size and the 1890 Ghost Dance." *American Socio-
         logical Review* 46:88–96.

1982   "Demographic Antecedents of Tribal Participation in the 1870 Ghost Dance Movement." *American Indian Culture and Research Journal* 6:79–91.

1983   "Where the Problem Is: Native American Historic Epidemiology." Keynote address, 1983 Native American Historic Epidemiology Conference, The Newberry Library, Chicago.

1984a   "Cherokee Population Losses During the 'Trail of Tears': A New Perspective and a New Estimate." *Ethnohistory* 31:289–300.

1984b   "Social Organization and the Demographic Survival of the Tolowa." *Ethnohistory* 31:187–96.

1984c   "But How Thick Were They? Review Essay of *Their Number Become Thinned*," by Henry F. Dobyns. *Contemporary Sociology* 13:145–50.

1986a   "History, Structure and Survival: A Comparison of the Yuki (Unkomno'n) and Tolowa (Hush) Indians of Northern California." *Ethnology* 25:119–30.

1986b   *We Shall Live Again: The 1870 and 1890 Ghost Dance Movements as Demographic Revitalization.* New York: Cambridge University Press.

Thornton, Russell, and Mary K. Grasmick
1980   *Sociology of American Indians: A Critical Bibliography.* Bloomington: Indiana University Press.

Thornton, Russell, and Joan Marsh-Thornton
1981   "Estimating Prehistoric American Indian Population Size for United States Area: Implications of the Nineteenth Century Population Decline and Nadir." *American Journal of Physical Anthropology* 55:47–53.

Thornton, Russell, Gary D. Sandefur, and Harold G. Grasmick
1982   *The Urbanization of American Indians: A Critical Bibliography.* Bloomington: Indiana University Press.

Thwaites, Reuben Gold, editor
1896–   *The Jesuit Relations and Allied Documents.* 73 vols.
1901   Cleveland: Burrows Brothers Company.
1904–   *Original Journals of the Lewis and Clark Expedition, 1804–1806.* 7
1905   vols. and atlas. New York: Antiquarian Press Ltd., 1959.

Tooker, Elizabeth
1978   "Wyandot." Pp. 398–406 in Bruce G. Trigger, ed., *Northeast*, vol. 15 of *Handbook of North American Indians*. Washington, D.C.: Smithsonian Institution.

Trigger, Bruce G., editor
1978   *Northeast.* Vol. 15, *Handbook of North American Indians*, ed. William C. Sturtevant. Washington, D.C.: Smithsonian Institution.

Trimble, Michael K.
1983   "Patterns of Death: A Critical Re-Examination of the 1837–38 Missouri River Native American Smallpox Epidemic." Paper presented at the 1983 Native American Historic Epidemiology Conference, The Newberry Library, Chicago.

Trinkaus, Erik
1984   "Western Asia." Pp. 251–93 in Fred H. Smith and Frank Spencer, eds., *The Origin of Modern Humans*. New York: Alan R. Liss, Inc.

Trosper, Ronald L.
1976   "Native American Boundary Maintenance: The Flathead Indian Reservation, Montana, 1860–1970." *Ethnicity* 3:256–74.

Los Tulares
1952   December, no. 13.
1953   December, no. 14.
Turner, Randolph
1973   "A New Population Estimate for the Powhatan Chiefdom of the Coastal Plain of Virginia." *Archaeological Society of Virginia* 28:57–65.
Twitchell, Edward W.
1925   "The California Pandemic of 1833." *California and Western Medicine* 23:592–93.

Ubelaker, Douglas H.
1974   "Reconstruction of Demographic Profiles from Ossuary Skeletal Samples: A Case Study from the Tidewater Potomac." *Smithsonian Contributions to Anthropology*, no. 18. Washington, D.C.: Smithsonian Institution Press.
1976a   "Prehistoric New World Population Size: Historical Review and Current Appraisal of North American Estimates." *American Journal of Physical Anthropology* 45:661–66.
1976b   "The Sources and Methodology for Mooney's Estimates of North American Indian Populations." Pp. 243–88 in William M. Denevan, ed., *The Native Population of the Americas in 1492*. Madison: University of Wisconsin Press.
N.d.   Untitled paper to be published in *Environment, Origins, and Population*. Vol. 3, *Handbook of North American Indians*, ed. William C. Sturtevant. Washington, D.C.: Smithsonian Institution.
Ubelaker, Douglas H., and Richard L. Jantz
1986   "Biological History of the Aboriginal Population of North America." *Rassengeschichte der Menschheit* 11:7–79.
Uhlmann, Julie M.
1972   "The Impact of Modernization on Papago Indian Fertility." *Human Organization* 31:149–62.
U.S. Bureau of the Census
1892a   *Indians. The Six Nations of New York. Extra Census Bulletin*. Washington, D.C.: U.S. Census Printing Office.
1892b   *Indians. Eastern Band of Cherokees. Extra Census Bulletin*. Washington, D.C.: U.S. Census Printing Office.
1893a   *Report on the Conditions of 15 Pueblos of New Mexico in 1890. Extra Census Bulletin*. Washington, D.C.: U.S. Census Printing Office.
1893b   *Moqui Pueblo Indians of Arizona and Pueblo Indians of New Mexico. Extra Census Bulletin*. Washington, D.C.: U.S. Census Printing Office.
1894a   *Report on Indians Taxed and Indians Not Taxed in the United States (except Alaska) at the Eleventh Census: 1890*. Washington, D.C.: U.S. Government Printing Office.
1894b   *The Five Civilized Tribes in Indian Territory. Extra Census Bulletin*. Washington, D.C.: U.S. Government Printing Office.
1896   *Abstract of the Eleventh Census: 1890*. Washington, D.C.: U.S. Government Printing Office.
1907   *Population of Oklahoma and Indian Territory: 1907*. Bulletin 89. Washington, D.C.: U.S. Government Printing Office.
1915   *Indian Population of the United States and Alaska, 1910*. Washington, D.C.: U.S. Government Printing Office.

1937   *The Indian Population of the United States and Alaska*. Washington, D.C.: U.S. Government Printing Office.

1953   *Census of Population 1950, Vol. II: Characteristics of the Population: U.S. Summary*. Washington, D.C.: U.S. Government Printing Office.

1972   *Census of Population: 1970*. Washington, D.C.: U.S. Government Printing Office.

1973a   *1970 Census of the Population. Subject Report. American Indians*. Final Report PC (2)-1F. Washington, D.C.: U.S. Government Printing Office.

1973b   *Population and Housing Inquiries in U.S. Decennial Censuses, 1790–1970*. U.S. Department of Commerce Working Paper 39. Washington, D.C.: U.S. Government Printing Office.

1981   Unpublished American Indian population data from 1980 census.

1982–83 *Statistical Abstract of the United States, 1982–83*. Washington, D.C.: U.S. Government Printing Office.

1983a   *American Indian Areas and Alaska Native Villages: 1980*. Washington, D.C.: U.S. Government Printing Office.

1983b   *Ancestry of the Population by State: 1980*. Supplementary Report PC80-SI-10. Washington, D.C.: U.S. Government Printing Office.

1983c   *General Population Characteristics: United States Summary*. PC80-1-B1, pt. 1. Washington, D.C.: U.S. Government Printing Office.

1983d   *General Social and Economic Characteristics: United States Summary*. PC80-1-C1. Washington, D.C.: U.S. Government Printing Office.

1984   *1980 Census of Population, Supplementary Report. American Indian Areas and Alaska Native Villages: 1980*. PC80-S1-13. Washington, D.C.: U.S. Government Printing Office.

1985   *1980 Census of Population, Vol. II: Subject Reports. American Indians, Eskimos and Aleuts on Identified Reservations and in the Historic Areas of Oklahoma (excluding Urbanized Areas)*. PC80-2-1D. Washington, D.C.: U.S. Government Printing Office.

U.S. Bureau of Indian Affairs.

1890–98 *Special Case 188, The Ghost Dance*.

1978   Guidelines for Preparing a Petition for Federal Acknowledgement as an Indian tribe. Washington, D.C.: photocopy.

1981   Personal communication with Douglas H. Ubelaker.

1986a   *Tribal Leaders List*. Washington, D.C.: Mimeographed.

1986b   Unpublished date provided by Edgar Lister of the Indian Health Service.

U.S. Commissioner of Indian Affairs

1891   *Annual Report of the Commissioner of Indian Affairs to the Secretary of the Interior for the Year 1891*. Washington, D.C.: U.S. Government Printing Office.

1892   *Annual Report of the Commissioner of Indian Affairs to the Secretary of the Interior for the Year 1892*. Washington, D.C.: U.S. Government Printing Office.

U.S. Congress (Office of Technology Assessment).

1986   *Indian Health Care*. OTA-H-290. Washington, D.C.: U.S. Government Printing Office.

U.S. Department of Health, Education, and Welfare

1974   *A study of Selected Socio-Economic Characteristics of Ethnic Minorities Based on the 1970 Census*. Vol. 3, *American Indians*. Washington, D.C.: Department of Health, Education, and Welfare.

U.S. Department of Health and Human Services
1985   *Indian Health Service: Chart Series Book, April 1985.* Washington, D.C.:
        Indian Health Service.
U.S. Department of the Interior
1902   *The American Bison in the United States and Canada.* Senate Document,
        no. 445. Washington, D.C.: U.S. Government Printing Office.
U.S. Indian Health Service
1984   Unpublished American Indian and Alaskan Native vital events data.
Unrau, William E.
1973   "The Depopulation of the Dheghia-Siouan Kansa Prior to Removal."
        New Mexico Historical Review 48: 313–28.
1979   *The Emigrant Indians of Kansas: A Critical Bibliography.* Bloomington:
        Indiana University Press.
Upham, Steadman
1986   "Smallpox and Climate in the American Southwest." *American Anthro-
        pologist* 88: 115–28.
Utley, Robert M.
1963   *The Last Days of the Sioux Nation.* New Haven: Yale University Press.
1984   *The Indian Frontier of the American West, 1846–1890.* Albuquerque, Uni-
        versity of New Mexico Press.

Vaughn, Alden T.
1978   "'Expulsion of the Savages': English Policy and the Virginia Massacre of
        1622." *William and Mary Quarterly* 25: 57–84.
Vogel, Virgil J.
1970   *American Indian Medicine.* Norman: University of Oklahoma Press.

Waddell, Jack O.
1969   *Papago Indians at Work.* Anthropological Papers of the University of Ari-
        zona, no. 12. Tucson: University of Arizona Press.
Wagley, Charles
1971   "The Formation of the American Population." Pp. 19–39 in Francisco
        M. Salzano, ed., *The Ongoing Evolution of Latin Populations.* Springfield,
        Ill.: Charles C. Thomas.
Wagner, Carruth J., and Erwin S. Rabeau
1964   "Indian Poverty and Indian Health." *United States Department of Health,
        Education, and Welfare Indicators,* March: xxiv–xliv.
Wagner, Jean K.
1976   "The Role of Acculturation of Selected Urban American Indian
        Women." *Anthropologica* 18: 215–29.
Wahrhaftig, Albert L.
1968   "The Tribal Cherokee Population of Eastern Oklahoma." *Current An-
        thropology* 9: 510–18.
Wahrhaftig, Albert L., and Robert K. Thomas
1969   "Renaissance and Repression: The Oklahoma Cherokee." *Transaction*
        6: 42–48.
Walker, Ernest P.
1983   *Walker's Mammals of the World.* Vol. 2. 4th ed. Baltimore: The Johns
        Hopkins University Press.
Walter, Paul A. F.
1952   *Race and Cultural Relations.* New York: McGraw-Hill.

Ward, R.H., and K. M. Weiss
1976   "The Demographic Evolution of Human Populations." Pp. 1–23 in
            R. H. Ward and K. M. Weiss, eds., *The Demographic Evolution of Human
            Populations.* London: Academic Press.
Waterman, T. T.
1925   "Village Sites in Tolowa and Neighboring Areas of Northwestern Cali-
            fornia." *American Anthropologist* 27: 528–43.
Watkins, Frances E.
1944   "Kiowa Woman's Ghost Dance Dress." *The Master Key*: 118–19.
Webster's New World Dictionary of the American Language.
1960   College edition, s.v. "tribe."
Wedel, Waldo R.
1955   *Archeological Materials From the Vicinity of Mobridge, South Dakota.* Bu-
            reau of American Ethnology Bulletin no. 157. Washington, D.C.: Smith-
            sonian Institution.
1983   "The Prehistoric Plains." Pp. 203–41 in Jessie D. Jennings, ed., *Ancient
            North Americans.* New York: W. H. Freeman and Co.
Weiss, K. M., and P. E. Smouse
1976   "The Demographic Stability of Small Human Populations." Pp. 59–73
            in R. H. Ward and K. M. Weiss, eds., *The Demographic Evolution of Hu-
            man Populations.* London: Academic Press.
Wells, Robert V.
1975   *The Population of the British Colonies in America Before 1776.* Princeton:
            Princeton University Press.
Wilcox, R. R.
1960   "Evolutionary Cycle of the Treponematoses." *The British Journal of the
            Venereal Diseases* 36: 78–91.
Williams, Herbert U.
1909   "The Epidemic of the Indians of New England, 1616–1620, with Re-
            marks on Native American Infections." *Johns Hopkins Hospital Bulletin*
            20: 340–49.
Williams, Robert C., et al.
1985   "GM Allotypes in Native Americans: Evidence for Three Distinct Mi-
            grations Across the Bering Land Bridge." *American Journal of Physical
            Anthropology* 66: 1–19.
Wissler, Clark
1936a   "Changes in Population Profiles Among the Northern Plains Indians."
            Anthropological Papers of the American Museum of Natural History 26, pt.
            1: 1–67.
1936b   "Distribution of Deaths Among American Indians." *Human Biology*
            8: 223–31.
Wolpoff, Milford H., Wu Xin Zhi, and Alan G. Thorne
1984   "Modern *Homo sapiens* Origins: A General Theory of Hominid Evolu-
            tion Involving the Fossil Evidence from East Asia." Pp. 411–84 in Fred
            H. Smith and Frank Spencer, eds., *The Origin of Modern Humans.* New
            York: Alan R. Liss, Inc.
Wood, Corinne Shear
1975   "New Evidence for a Late Introduction of Malaria Into the New World."
            Current Anthropology 16: 93–104.
Wood, Margaret Mary
1943   "The Russian Creoles of Alaska as a Marginal Group." *Social Forces*
            22: 204–208.

Wood, William
1634   *New Englands Prospect*. Amsterdam: Da Capo Press and Theatrum Ltd., 1968.
Woodbury, Richard B.
1979   "Zuni Prehistory and History to 1850." Pp. 467–73 in Alfonso Ortiz, ed., *Southwest*, vol. 9 of *Handbook of North American Indians*. Washington, D.C.: Smithsonian Institution.
Worsley, Peter
1957   *The Trumpet Shall Sound*. London: MacGibbon and Kee.
Wright, J. Leitch, Jr.
1971   *Anglo-Spanish Rivalry in North America*. Athens, Ga.: University of Georgia Press.
1981   *The Only Land They Knew: The Tragic Story of the American Indians in the Old South*. New York: Free Press.

Yi, Seonbok, and Geoffrey Clark
1985   "The 'Dyuktai Culture' and New World Origins." *Current Anthropology* 26:1–20.

INDEX

283